The TOTAL TRAVELER BY SHIP

by Ethel Blum

1985–1986 Edition

A complete guide to sea travel...

To

MILTON
the man in my life who makes per
person double occupancy worthwhile.
He showed me the world
and now has a hard time keeping me at home.

and to

ROGER
a young man of the sea . . .
the life he leads is for the likes of me

Published by Travel Publications, Inc.
One Lincoln Road, Suite 214
Miami, Florida 33139

Library of Congress Cataloging in Publication Date

Distributed by:

Hippocrene Books
171 Madison Avenue
New York, NY 10016
(212) 685-4371

ISBN 0-87052-024-5

CONTENTS

History of Cruising • In the Good Old Days • Ships of the Future

Consulting a Travel Agent • Reading a Cruise Brochure • Tonnage • Ship Registry • Stabilizers • Space and Service Ratios • Cabins • Ambience • Price • Long or Short Itineraries • Ports of Embarkation • Safety at Sea

Which Cabin? • Traveling Alone • Paying for the Cruise • Before you Embark • *Mal de Mer,* or Will I get Seasick? • Dining at Sea • Drinking at Sea • Activities • What to Wear When • Cruising with Children • Sanitation at Sea • Tipping • Toward the Journey's End • Embarkation • Making the Most of Your Cruise

Recent Changes • U.S. Customs Regulations • Canadian Customs • Hints and Tips

Baltimore • Boston • Charleston • Los Angeles • Miami • New York • Port Everglades (Fort Lauderdale) • San Francisco • San Juan

Acknowledgments

NO ONE PERSON can research and keep up with the many facets of cruising. My thanks to the cruise industry at large, and to cruise line marketing departments which entrusted advance marketing and pricing plans to me so this edition would be up-to-date at press time. Special thanks to the 20 professional travel reporters, 18 travel agents and 20 travelers addicted to cruising who participated in our rating survey. They shall remain anonymous for obvious reasons and I shall guard their identity so they can continue to observe and report their findings without special attention. Their honest evaluations make TOTAL TRAVELER ratings a lot more than one woman's opinion. Their cooperation provided an impartial cross-section and objective comparison of vessels. Also, thanks to Roger Blum, who contributed research on ship genealogy. Roger is a young man whose love of the sea should take him to the highest crest. A very special thanks to my husband, Milton, whose patience and understanding have made this and my other works possible.

Ethel Blum

ABOUT THE TOTAL TRAVELER BY SHIP

The first edition of THE TOTAL TRAVELER BY SHIP was published in 1975. In 225 pages, it covered everything a passenger needed to know about ships at that point in the evolving history of cruising. As the industry grew, so did THE TOTAL TRAVELER BY SHIP. A conservative estimate has it that a minimum of 15 million travelers crossed gangplanks during those 10 years. A new generation of ships was born during the 1970s and a new generation is being berthed to meet the demands of the 1980s and '90s. This 10th Anniversary edition of THE TOTAL TRAVELER BY SHIP tells the complete story. In more than 400 pages, it covers everything you need to know about ship travel—cruise, freighter, cargoliner • **HOW TO MAKE THE MOST OF YOUR HOLIDAY AT SEA** from how to select your ship, your cabin and your dining room table • dining and drinking • tipping and entertainment • gambling at sea • **GENEALOGY OF SHIPS** • **BARGAIN CRUISE OPPORTUNITIES** • air-sea packages and how to take advantage of them • **PORTS OF CALL** • what to do, see and buy in ports throughout the Bahamas, Caribbean, West Indies, Canada, Alaska, Mediterranean, Greek Islands, North Cape, Baltic, China and the Pacific • And, **MORE, MUCH MORE,** ports of debarkation, does the ship tender or dock • **WHEN IS A CRUISE A BARGAIN** • what to expect from a cruise experience • and, **FOR THE FIRST TIME,** ships are **RATED BY PRICE CATEGORY** with Golden Anchor Awards to outstanding vessels.

ABOUT THE AUTHOR

Ethel Blum speaks for THE TOTAL TRAVELER in a syndicated weekly travel column carried in 45 newspapers and in a daily syndicated radio show. Her articles appear regularly in major publications in the United States and abroad. She has been the recipient of national and regional awards for journalism and photography during her career spanning some 20 years as a travel writer and broadcaster. Ethel Blum has a reputation for accurate reporting and is a committed advocate of travelers' rights. She is the "official" First Lady of the Port of Miami, a singular honor bestowed on her by the shipping community in recognition of her faith in, devotion to, and sincere promotion of travel by ship. Ethel also has been recognized by her peers. She was 1983 President of the prestigious Society of American Travel Writers (SATW).

A Note to the Reader

EVERY EFFORT has been made to verify accuracy of rates, itineraries, and ship specifics. Cruise prices, package rates, and shore excursion charges are subject to change. Itineraries may change with little or no notice. Fuel surcharges may be assessed, mixed drinks may go up, and even flags on the mast are subject to change if the ship is sold or marketed differently.

In this highly competitive and volatile marketplace, it is impossible to avoid errors in spite of careful research. It also is impossible for the author to sail on every ship and inspect every galley and stateroom every month. She does look under the bunks when she sails from port to port on a couple of dozen ships each year. Twenty travel writers and other industry professionals send their personal evaluations of cruise experiences to Ethel Blum and their overall evaluations are included in THE TOTAL TRAVELER BY SHIP. Readers who find food or service better or worse than expected on board ships profiled in THE TOTAL TRAVELER BY SHIP are encouraged to write to Ethel Blum in care of Travel Publications, Inc., One Lincoln Road, #214, Miami, Florida, 33139. Your comments will not be ignored. She'll pass your words along to the steamship companies concerned and alert them that future editions may earn them a "Rusty Anchor."

No cruise ship advertising was accepted for this book, but we have accepted a limited number of "commercial messages" from destinations. The advertising in no way influenced the editorial content of this book. The colorful displays serve as an additional source of information for the sea traveler, and help defray the high cost of publishing this book.

TTT
(Total Traveler Tip)

Tips for the total traveler by ship are highlighted throughout this book by the abbreviation **TTT**. This is the author's way of pointing out particularly useful information in the form of advice that will save time or money, provide you with a shortcut, or otherwise help make your cruise easier, more memorable and enjoyable. Look for the **TTT**. You'll probably profit from the hint that follows it.

A Word in Advance

SHIPBOARD TRAVEL always bring scenes of romance to our happy daydreams—visions of champagne, caviar, and delightful ship-mates bent on sharing romantic encounters on board floating luxury resorts. Romance has been implied and over-rated in cruise brochures. To add to our fantasies, we now have the landlubber's Saturday-night favorite "The Love Boat," a TV production that bears a closer resemblance to life in a floating soap opera than to lifestyle aboard any of today's cruise ships.

The fantasy begins with the opening scene. The one that shows the captain, doctor, cruise director, purser, and bartender eagerly anticipating arrival of boarding passengers. The passengers. Young, well dressed, exciting, looking for romance on the high seas.

That's the fantasy of cruising, circa 1985. Real life passengers are often closer to the fifty age mark, casually dressed, and in search of relaxation rather than romance. What they find aboard the ship of their dreams seldom comes close to the story line of "The Love Boat." But they disembark happy and about 75 percent return for another holiday at sea.

But romantic fantasies surround life aboard these floating resorts. Cruise companies keep it alive by embellishing reality in descriptive brochures. Even back in the "good old days" of 1818, a 424-ton vessel with two decks and three masts, the James Monroe, advertised "extensive and commodious" accommodations. She was grandly decorated with Egyptian porphyry, carved arches, black cloth-covered chairs, and shiny mahogany tables. But her staterooms were described as "sleeping closets" by the passengers. They were seven feet square, though paneled in satinwood. Over the entrance to each cabin was an arch supported by pillars of pure white Carrara marble. Commodious? Hardly! In those days, passengers were regarded as cargo, assigned to quarters that should have been holding salt or cotton. The emigrant was thankful for passage and could be counted on to sweep the decks, cater to the crew, and of course, pay for passage.

Because of severely overcrowded conditions caused by greedy owners eager to earn a fast dollar on each voyage, the U.S. Congress passed a law aimed at curing the situation, but it wasn't until eighteen years later, when a second statute was passed, that each passenger was guaranteed 14 clear feet of deck space.

As scheduled voyages increased, competition for passengers reached a heady level and appointments and fittings on rival ships became as much a matter of public romance as speed records. The Liverpool is an example of a famous ship of the last century that fell into this category. Her single feature touted to attract passengers was a bathing room where they could shower with salt water hauled aboard by the crew. Fastidious passengers determined to bathe, or the equivalent, had to be brave. Bathtubs on ships were not even in the blueprint stage, and running water did not exist. On other ships, arrangements had to be made with a crew member to haul a bucket of sea water aboard and douse the passenger in semi-private somewhere on the ship, but the Liverpool had a special room for this "luxury'.

With competition on the upswing, ship owners changed their view of passengers, who were no longer regarded as the cash equivalent of cargo. Service improved, and the privileged on three-class vessels began to dine gluttonously, sleep fitfully, and devise activities to break the boredom of long weeks at sea. Four times during every 24 hours, ladies and gentleman of quality sat down to a table of largess sufficient to nourish an emigrant for a week. They called it the "Groaning Board" for obvious reasons.

Many sea styles have carried over into twentieth-century cruising. For instance, there's a logical explanation of why passengers are not encouraged to socialize with crew members other than officers. It all started long ago. As ships became vehicles of mass transport, moral fortitude sank. The number of young emigrant girls en route to America who embarked as virgins and disembarked as outcasts moved the priests of Galway to protest publicly against the lack of adequate shipboard chaperonage. When the taxpayers of New York City got fed up with supporting illegitimate children born of transatlantic dalliances, they took their case to Congress. The result was an act providing that if any member of an American crew seduced a passenger 'under promise of marriage, or by threats, or by the exercise of his authority, or by solicitation, or the making of gifts or presents," he had either to marry the girl or pay a fine of $1,000 or spend a year in jail.

Those emigrant girls were filled with dreams as they embarked for new lives in the land of milk and honey, but these are not the dreams that sent a couple of million passengers up the gangplanks of U.S.-

based ships last year. Those millions and the three million or so who boarded ships beyond our shores were more than likely induced to spend their vacations at sea by promises of a lifestyle that would not remind them of home — a lifestyle more closely resembling an image of the good old days of semi-luxury and service. What they got was sometimes not what they expected.

Remember the bartender always visible on "The Love Boat"? On a real ship, let an officer catch him in a passenger's cabin, or the passenger in his cabin, and the bartender will find himself unemployed and disembarked at the next port of call. As for the doctor, his encounters with passengers are usually limited to dispensing sea-sickness remedies, curing indigestion, and dispensing aspirin. The cruise director is involved with the nitty-gritty of daily activities and has little time for personal dalliance of any kind. And then there is the purser, who heads a staff of mostly young and energetic men and women charged with running the hotel side of the ship. Most are unmarried, and I must admit, some pursers do make the most of shipboard encounters. I know of one case where the purser engaged in what he thought was an arrangement for the duration of the voyage. She thought differently. He now works on shore, the father of two.

I am reminded of a woman who lived quietly in St. Petersburg, Florida. A gentle lady in her seventies, she attracted the attention of a young reporter on a local newspaper. It seems she collected metal cans that could be recycled. She sold them and was saving her money to make her lifelong dream come true. She lived in a wooden house heated by a cast iron stove but her most precious possessions were packed in a closet. They were reminders of better days — a photograph of a lovely young woman in white gloves and a yellow evening gown taken in the glittering ballroom of a great ocean going ship. She talked of those days and of the nights waltzed away with her husband as they traveled to distant countries. Now widowed and existing on very limited means, she collected beer cans as a "means to an end." Before sunup every day, the woman who once drank champagne with ship captains, wheeled her bicycle through the back alleys of St. Petersburg to collect what others threw away. But the aging widow didn't consider herself strange because she scrounged in trash cans to realize her dream.

"Little by little," she said, "I saved money from the cans because I had a dream. Just once before I die, just one more time, I wanted to dance again on one of those big ships that sails across the ocean."

The lady from St. Petersburg took her cruise a couple of years ago. She emerged from her dreams into the real world for that one last cruise. It is for her and for the rest of you who dream of ships that I write **THE TOTAL TRAVELER**. Every aspect of your dreams will not come true on board ship these days, but you will experience is a late 20th century facsimile. If you know what to expect, know how to take advantage of all the alternatives and select your ship carefully and wisely, your dreams can be realized, at least for the most part.

Cruising aboard a first class ship to interesting ports can be one of the supreme pleasures of life. It is civilized, unhurried, and economical in spite of inflation, especially when you consider services rendered and included in the basic cruise fare. Cruising also is a unique form of travel. Some people take to the seas for special purposes like bridge tournaments, romance, gourmandizing, entertainment, or just plain rest. Movement from port to port has been stripped of the urgency that goes along with merely being transported to a specific destination.

Romance? Romance at sea is listening to music, attending floor shows, and dressing formally without worrying about an escort if you travel alone. The romance of cruising lies in eliminating the necessities of going anywhere with someone and — more important — never having to eat alone. There's no chance of being seated at the most undesirable table in the dining room just because you're traveling solo, and no reason to hesitate about starting a conversation with a fellow passenger of either sex.

On a North Sea cruise a couple of years ago, the passenger manifest was made up of people of many nationalities. When the Americans on board discovered I was a travel reporter, they fell upon me with their complaints, as though I could wave a magic wand at the captain and compel him to come up with caviar and lobster. That specific cruise is a good example of the importance of selecting your ship wisely. The series of North Sea voyages was designed primarily for the lower-middle-class European market, and each cruise was priced far below those of competing vessels. The comparatively inexpensive package was developed to introduce a rebuilt vessel into the marketplace, and the galley was not overly generous with food (not that anyone left the dining room hungry). But Americans who boarded with visions of grandeur at bargain prices complained constantly. Europeans ate everything served and were content with their bargain holiday. On the other hand, had the American travelers (or their travel agents) known what to expect, they could have enjoyed the voyage knowing they were saving money or they might have opted for a higher priced vessel offering better quality food and more luxuries.

Somehow food seems to be the one shipboard delight that causes the most preoccupation and the most complaints. We should levy some of the blame for the emphasis on food on cruise companies that tend to overshadow quality with picture displays of quantity. Some ships have hired catering professionals who use some precooked convenience foods, and in those cases word spreads quickly within the travel industry and among passengers. Food catering by an outside company does not necessarily mean inferior food. In some cases, it does just the opposite. The cruise sticks to the cruise business and has turned over food preparation and service to professionals in that field. The cruise company budgets a specific amount of money per passenger, set the standards and keeps a close watch on the on menus and food quality.

Another worry that tugs at confidence in sea travel is the question of solvency of cruise companies. With so many cruise lines with so many ships, how safe is the money passengers are required to pay in advance. It seems that Uncle Sam's enforcement folks have considered the risk, and there is a strict bonding system under which ships operate from U.S. ports. The law does not cover Americans boarding ships in foreign ports, but it does offer more consumer protection if you sail from the United States than is available to sea travelers in any other part of the world. The source of this protection is Section 3 of U.S. Public Law 89–777, enacted in 1966 to prevent cruise company failures that could cost the traveler money and leave him stranded.

The shipping industry has faced an amazing situation during the past decade. There has been tremendous expansion of cruise fleets, caused by steady introduction of new or reconditioned vessels. This, coupled with public acceptance and satisfaction, has accounted for more ships cruising to more places than at any time in the previous history of sea travel.

The contemporary cruise passenger represents a cross section of America, perhaps slightly on the upbeat side. Among passengers are couples and singles, secretaries, company presidents, blue-collar workers, shop owners, housewives, movie stars, doctors, lawyers, and merchant chiefs. Dull and uninteresting people tend to stay at home.

It is estimated that about 250 passenger-carrying ships operate around the world. About 90 berth in, or regularly sail out of, North American ports. THE TOTAL TRAVELER BY SHIP profiles in detail 135 ships and covers about 40 others with information useful to passengers. These ships sail the Caribbean, Atlantic, Canadian, Alaskan, Mediterranean, Greek islands, South American, North Cape and Pacific routes. It is estimated that the ships discussed in this edition of THE TOTAL TRAVELER BY SHIP will board more than four million passengers within the next year. The average passenger will spend seven days at sea and will pay $1250 for the cruise. Per day rates will run from from $50 (on a freighter) to $3,500 (on a super-deluxe liner), and the passenger will spend an additional $225 during the week between shore excursions, tips and the bar. There will be a choice of about 2,000 departures.

A survey of last year's passengers indicates that 90 percent plan to vacation at sea again. And a survey of Americans returning from Europe by air indicates that 95 percent have never cruised and 80 percent are considering spending their next holiday at sea.

THE TOTAL TRAVELER BY SHIP is dedicated to confessed cruise-aholics like me and to the millions who will join our ranks in the coming years. Research for the book took more than twenty-five years. I traveled some 4.25 million air and sea miles to islands and foreign countries, inspected thousands of staterooms and kitchens, interviewed dozens of cruise ship owners and thousands of passengers. The book covers everything a traveler should know about ships (cruise ships, transit vessels, and freighters) from the first inclination toward ship travel to planning the next holiday. The information is factual. It is intended as guidance in selecting and enjoying your cruise by presenting all the options.

Everyone has a favorite ship. I keep mine a secret. When you finish THE TOTAL TRAVELER BY SHIP, you'll have a few clues as to which ship is 'mine." For the first time, the THE TOTAL TRAVELER BY SHIP rates ships and ratings are not mine alone. (See Ship Ratings) My personal evaluations were fed into the computer along with the others. I waited 10 years before publishing ratings because I am convinced there is a ship for every traveler and every traveler has a ship waiting at a port with facilities almost tailor-made to meet his demands.

Judging cruise ships is very much like judging a beauty contest. Broad beams, narrow beams, tall or short—to each his own. As long as the passenger knows all about the ship he selects, the rates, itineraries, service and atmosphere, he is qualified to judge for himself.

Ralph Waldo Emerson wrote, "Sea life is an acquired taste, like that for tomatoes and olives." I like to add, "caviar."

There are many reasons for ship travel; for me, the sea is enough.

Bon voyage!

An Overview
of Cruising

I LIKE TO THINK cruise passengers owe Cleopatra a vote of thanks for setting the mood and lifestyle on cruise ships. When she took that historic cruise up the Nile, her vessel was more than point-to-point transportation It was the setting for a romantic escapade, and it must have served its purpose. Cleopatra ended up with a couple of husbands and a lover.

Current nostalgic leanings may not extend quite that far back in time, but many a traveler has been converted to cruise addiction for reasons similar to Cleopatra's.

The late Somerset Maugham was a devoted cruiser who termed shipboard life an "experience above all else." Millions of Americans turning to cruise holidays are discovering that both Maugham and Cleopatra had the right ideas on holiday spirit.

Cruising took the lead some 14 years ago as the fastest growing segment of the multi-billion-dollar travel industry, It continues to maintain a healthy lead mid-way through the decade of the 1980's and promises to hold the position through the end of the century at least. While sagging economies dented occupancy at many travel destinations, cruise ships continue to register increased numbers of passengers in spite of increased capacity on the sea lanes.

Taking a cruise in 1985 or 1986 doesn't come with a money-back guarantee that passengers will be pampered in the style of Cleopatra or that experiences will live up to Somerset Maugham's fancy, but they are assured of a holiday at sea—a total experience stretching from sunup to sundown and beyond.

Passenger shipping wasn't always the pampered traveler's favorite. There have been periods of ups and downs, and many a down turned glamorous ocean queens into rusty maidens waiting in drydock for the fickle traveler to turn again in their direction.

In 1845, a German ship owner placed an ad in a Hamburg paper proposing to equip one of his large sailing vessels for a cruise around the world. "The fare for the whole voyage is so low that it only represents a very slight addition to ordinary living costs incurred on shore. In return, the passenger will have many opportunities of acquiring a first hand knowledge of the wonders of the world," he wrote. The ship owner was about a century ahead of his time. The same ad in any newspaper travel section today would bring sufficient responses to fill a dozen sailing vessels. But in those days passenger ships were for transportation between ports. They provided the only way for emigrants to move to new countries promising greater opportunity, and the only way for merchants to hawk their wares in countries separated by oceans. Passenger use of ships on a round-trip basis offering sightseeing and service began to attract attention when, some 45 years later, another imaginative German suggested switching the *Auguste Victoria* from her Hamburg-New York run to a Mediterranean cruise.

At the beginning of the 1870s, Rotterdam was a very busy port without a very promising future. Trade with the United States was expanding and the newly opened Suez Canal provided a steamer route to the East Indies; both factors favored introduction of larger ships. The size of vessels entering Rotterdam, however, was seriously limited by the Voorne Canal. A maximum length of about 270 feet was imposed by the locks at Hellevoet, although larger ships could pass at high water with the gates open. A more serious handicap was the draught limit of about 17 feet, making it necessary for larger ships to part-load or unload at Flushing or elsewhere. So ship owners moved their ships and cargo to the rival port of Amsterdam.

At about that time, the private firm of Plate, Reuchlin and Company was founded by two young partners with sufficient capital to build only two ships — not four as originally hoped. Equally disappointing was the late delivery of the two ships, the first of which, the *Rotterdam,* did not sail on her maiden voyage to New York until October 15, 1872. During her trial trip, the builder announced that it was his firm's custom to interpret orders generously and the owners would find they had obtained a vessel somewhat longer than specified! When entering the lock at Hellevoetsluis, the ship's carpenter stood at the bow and the boatswain at the stern, hatchets in hand, ready to cut away ornamental scroll work. But to the great relief of all on board, the lock gates barely closed with a fender at the bows and the counter of the stern just touching the outer lock gate.

The *Rotterdam* was an iron ship of nearly 1,700 tons gross, brig-rigged, with a single screw driven by a 1,300-horsepower compound engine giving her a service speed of 10.5 knots. She could carry eight first-class passengers, 380 steerage passengers and 1,500 tons of cargo. She could make the voyage to New York in about 15 days and with her sister ship, the *Maas,* (later *Maasdam*), a monthly service was maintained.

Results of the first voyage were encouraging, and expansion was decided upon; but as Plate, Reuchlin and Company had insufficient capital, the firm was consolidated with a much older man, W. Van der Hoeven, as managing director. This was the Nederlandsch-Amerikaansche Stoomvaart-Maatschappij (Netherlands-American Steam Navigation Company), or NASM for short founded in April 1873. From about 1896, this famous concern became the Holland America Line.

Two new and larger ships, fittingly named after two great benefactors of the company, were ordered: the *P. Caland* and the *W. A. Scholten.* Over 2,500 tons gross, they could carry 50 cabin and 600 steerage passengers, as well as 2,400 tons of cargo. Barkentine-rigged, they were the only clipper-bowed ships built for the line. Unfortunately, the promising state of affairs was not destined to last, for in the autumn of 1874, when the new ships were due to come into service, a severe depression in the United States set in. Freight rates and the number of steerage passengers fell alarmingly. In 1875, very heavy weather crippled the *W.A. Scholten.*

Ninteenth-century ships carried mail and emigrants and were a great source of national pride. Speed was of utmost importance because ships linked the continents. One of the first transatlantic races was in 1847 between the newly commissioned U.S. flag carrier, the *Washington,* and Cunard's *Britain.* Although the pride of the American fleet lost the race, she was feted on her arrival in England because she was the first ship to offer an alternative to first class or steerage travel. She provided respectable second class passage, thereby opening sea lanes to another level of travelers. The Washington offered amenities passengers had come to expect, and her salons were decorated in marble and gilt.

The *Washington* was part of a five-ship fleet owned by an American, Edward Collins. Two of his ships, the *Atlantic* and the *Pacific,* were of 2,856 tons, larger than any other except Cunard's *Britain.* Both ships were launched in 1849 and introduced charismatic appeal previously lacking at sea. The *Atlantic* was rounded at the stern, which gave her a tub-like appearance, but Collins made up for her looks with steam heat on board, bathrooms, and a barber shop that because of the luxurious amenities it offered, was considered almost a miracle by ocean voyagers.

Collins was successful in luring passengers from Cunard. He broke speed records, and his name and his ships made headlines; but his ledgers were written mostly in red ink. His extravagances in food and service were not open to curbs or compromise. Speed demanded extra coal and larger crews, and Collin's menus made Cunard's look like boarding school fare; but the outlay was crippling. Collin's captains were paid $6,000 a year; Cunard's, $2,500. Cunard survived the century; Collins did not.

During the same period of maritime history, another American was rocking the sea lanes. Cornelius Vanderbilt had worked almost all his life. Now, at fifty-nine, he wanted to take his first real vacation with family and friends. His family included eleven children, a wife, and a number of servants. This Horatio Alger of American financing was already pulling in a couple of million dollars a year. Vanderbilt planned his dream holiday — a grand tour of the capitals of Europe by sea and land. His plans and his voyage would influence shipping for the next 150 years. He arranged the first publicized pleasure cruise in luxurious accommodations.

Other people had yachts, but Vanderbilt would have nothing less than his own ocean liner. The result was the 2,500-ton *North Star,* which cost $500,000 and was ultimately launched in 1853. The rosewood furniture in the main salon was Louis XV, updated with Victorian plush velvet upholstery. There were family quarters consisting of ten staterooms enameled in white, each with a plate-glass door and berths fitted in silk. The crew was made up of young men from prominent families who simply wanted to be part of the entourage. The steward of the famed Racquet Club was enticed aboard to serve as purser, and the ship had her own clergyman and physician. Vanderbilt's welcome when the *North Star* arrived in London was somewhat less cordial. Seems the American merchant seaman's yacht was more splendid than the Queen's.

Toward the end of the last century, ocean transport was showing a pattern and a temper. The passenger market was still made up mostly of people who traveled out of necessity, so speed was important. But a new breed of traveler was emerging; a traveler who thought a round trip to Europe might be good for one's physical condition. A sea cure, some felt, was just the thing for damaged emotions. A young woman who had fallen in love with a ne'er-do-well, or had been left waiting on the church steps, was bundled off to Liverpool so she could avail herself of the one sure cure for lovesickness — an ocean voyage.

Probably the most notable ship at the end of the century was the first *Oceanic.* She was the forerunner and archetype of six sister ships that flew the red swallowtail burgee with the five-pointed star of the White Star Line. Her greatest innovation was not her size, but the placement of her grand ballroom. It was high and amidships, ending the tradition in force since the Middle Ages of confining privileged travelers to quarters in the rump of the stern. The lounge extended the full width of the ship, was lighted by huge chandeliers (candle-lit), and had fireplaces at both ends of the room. Cabins were larger and there was a bell in every cabin that commanded the instant attention of stewards. There were taps for water and steam heat.

Top of the luxury line at that time was the *City of Rome,* the biggest and most beautifully appointed. She made her maiden voyage to New York in 1881, with a figurehead of the Emperor Hadrian, three times larger than life, leaning out over the waves. On her stern, embossed in gold, glittered the arms and crest of the Eternal City. Her hull was jet black, her superstructure the color of cream. Her music room was paneled in ebony and gold. Luxury had been carried just about as far as human invention and imagination could take it; but, again, the financial burden of limited capacity and high operating costs was too much for her owners. The *City of Rome* ended up on the auction block.

Holland America also was adding tonnage during this decade and was expanding as quickly as Dutch and other European harbors were deepened to accommodate its ships. In April 1898, the base color of their funnels was changed from black to yellow to avoid confusion with funnels of an American company operating at that time. The Spanish-American War had just broken out and a resemblance to American ships might have been risky.

Late the same year, the new *Statendam* was setting passenger-freight records, and the company commissioned construction of three twin-screw 12,500-ton vessels—the *Potsdam, Ryndam,* and *Noordam.*

American authorities were feeling the lack of suitable merchant ships during the Spanish-American War, so the government began buying interests in foreign shipping companies under the title of International Mercantile Marine Company (IMM), a combine that embraced the Atlantic Transport, National, American, Red Star, Leyland, White Star and Dominion lines into a fleet totaling one million gross tons. Holland America Line was an unwilling participant in IMM.

Another type of ocean traveler was developing almost unnoticed while shipping companies were busy wooing the elite, real or pretended. Young Americans were going to sea. Of modest means, they simply wanted to see the Louvre and the Prado, sign their names in visitors' books in famous castles, shout *prosit* in Munich beer halls, and meet the famous women of Paris. This astounded Europeans and made for excited parlor conversation about uninhibited American men and women traveling alone and in large, unchaperoned groups.

A good part of this movement was introduced by Thomas Cook, the man responsible for mass travel in the Western world. In a period of less than four decades, the domestic trips that Cook first organized in the English Midlands had grown into grand tours. With fresh tourist money pouring in, what at first seemed like a boon to some areas soon turned into a nightmare as they were overrun with hordes of people. Thomas Cook, undaunted by the criticism and ignoring complaints of rudeness or lack of "refinement," continued to group thirty or forty people who found it convenient and beneficial to travel on the same train or ship and to sojourn in the same city.

When large numbers of genteel young people reported they had survived the rigors of steerage class and had seen Europe for less than the cost of first class passage on one of the luxury liners, an endless army of students began to travel the Atlantic on their own.

Another milestone in ship travel came with the advent of the turbine engine, which brought a different dimension to transatlantic voyages. Sea lanes once considered romantic avenues of freedom, golden tracks of commerce, adventure, and history, now became highways for hundreds of thousands of people who insisted on being pampered, beguiled, entertained day and night, and delivered precisely on schedule. The broad Atlantic had been narrowed and regulated. Instead of challenging the whims of the sea gods, the traveler merely tested the limits of his self indulgence. Among a plethora of offerings, voyagers could pick and choose the most convenient time, the right ship, the best accommodations, and even the type of companions most likely to prove congenial.

German ship interests also were becoming involved in passenger traffic, but they were largely concerned with transporting endless streams of America-bound emigrants from *Mittel-Europa*. Their ships were sound but hardly spectacular. The *Deutschland* docked in New York in 1847, part of a fleet belonging to Hamburg Amerikanische Packetfahrt Actien Gesellschaft (Hamburg-Amerika Lines in later years). In 1856, the same company introduced the first German transatlantic steamship. Several other German companies competed for the emigrant traveler, and they rode the Atlantic to the Teutonic merriment of lager beer, cheese, and pretzels while the band played merrily for the seasick passengers.

In 1900, the rival Red Star Line of Antwerp put the 12,000-ton *Vaderland* into service, the first of a very successful series of four-masted, twofunneled ships.

In 1904, Holland America Line ordered a larger and improved version with only one funnel. The 17,000-ton *Nieuw Amsterdam* was named after the first settlement in New York. She sailed on her maiden voyage in April 1906 and subsequently became one of the best-known ships in the world. At the time, she was the largest ship under the Dutch flag. Her graceful lines belied her huge capacity of 417 first-class, 391 second-class, and 2,300 third-class passengers and more than 14,000 tons of cargo. Although she was not fast, her comfort, cuisine, and standards set levels still anticipated by passengers today. The *Nieuw Amsterdam* was the last of the company's ships to carry sails for emergency use, but they were never used.

The immediate success of the *Nieuw Amsterdam* led to ordering a much larger ship, the fourth *Rotterdam* (24,000 tons), for many years the largest vessel in the Dutch merchant marine and the seventh largest in the world at that time. Her two pole masts, two funnels, and long superstructure made her typical of the graceful liners of the Edwardian period. Completed in 1908, she was the first large Atlantic liner to be built with a glassed-in promenade deck. Carrying 520 first-class and 555 second class passengers and 2,500 emigrants, the *Rotterdam* was driven by two fine quadruple-expansion engines, each exceeding 7,000 horsepower, giving her a speed of 17 knots. In 1909, the Dutch government awarded the Rotterdam-New York mail contract to the Holland America Line and, in the following year, a call at Plymouth was included in the schedule.

Because the *Rotterdam, Nieuw Amsterdam, Potsdam, Ryndam, Noordam,* and *Statendam* were more than capable of maintaining weekly Rotterdam-New York service, the *Statendam* was sold to the Allan Line and renamed the *Scotian,* which, as the Canadian Pacific Marglen, was finally scrapped in 1927. Before being sold at the end of 1910, the *Statendam* sailed on the second Holland America cruise, which included the Holy Land. The company's first cruise was to Copenhagen by the *Rotterdam 2* in June 1895.

One of the largest and most lavish ships of the time was operated by Hamburg-Amerika, the 24,000-horsepower *Kaiser Friedrich.* At the turn of the century, German sea power claimed Atlantic speed records, and German vessels paraded their finery in the sea lanes as though on military parade on the *Unter den Linden.*

Albert Ballin was a frequently heard name in shipping circles at that time. He was Chairman of Cunard's greatest competitor, Hamburg Amerika Line. Ballin paid careful attention to every detail of passenger comfort and quickly developed an enthusiastic and loyal following for Hamburg Amerika vessels. He was the first in the industry to employ interior decorators, chefs de cuisine and other specialists. He built large steamers in direct competition to North German Lloyd,

Cunard's other major competitor. His *Columbia* and *Augusta Victoria* were considered among the finest of their day. By 1900 Hamburg Amerika Line was a recognized leader in the industry. The 16,500-ton *Atlantic* set transatlantic speed records, but she was too expensive to operate, and Ballin decided to build large, very comfortable, passenger-oriented slower vessels. His *Imperator* was launched in 1912 and considered by some as a 52,226-ton monster; but passengers loved her, so the 56,000-ton *Vaterland* and *Bismarck* were inaugurated in 1914.

That was the year of World War I. By the time it was over, German passenger shipping companies were just about out of business. Ballin committed suicide in 1918, but his company regrouped and built new, smaller liners. The first was called the *Albert Ballin* and made her maiden Atlantic voyage in 1923. Other ships came on line soon thereafter, and by the end of the decade, Hamburg Amerika was again one of the world's largest shipping companies. It eventually merged with North German Lloyd, and is known today as Hapag-Lloyd.

North German Lloyd is another story. When Cunard introduced the *Mauretania*, North German Lloyd dominated the North Atlantic. Founded in 1857, the company was prosperous almost from its inception. By 1887, its ships were plying Caribbean and South American routes to Brazil and Argentina. But it wasn't always smooth sailing for North German Lloyd. In fact, the company came in for more than its share of disasters. The *Deutschland* ran aground in 1875 and was a total loss. A few years later the *Condor, Hansa* and *Mosel* were wrecked, and before the end of the century, the *Eider* and *Elbe* were also lost. But it's most disastrous day occurred in 1900 at a New York pier. Fire broke out and seriously damaged the *Bremen, Main* and *Saale*. The company's flagship, *Kaiser Wilhelm der Grosse* was also dockside at the time, but was towed clear of the raging fires.

New leadership at the beginning of the twentieth century changed the direction of the company. More economically feasible, medium-sized vessels were ordered. The 24,000-ton *George Washington* was probably the most notable. But, like other companies, North German Lloyd found itself virtually out of business at the end of World War I. They regrouped and re-emerged as an industry leader with the introduction of the 32,500-ton *Columbus* on transatlantic service. She was followed by the *Europa* and the *Bremen,* two super-ships. But, with the advent of World War II, NGL vessels were again caught in a world war. The *Bremen* was destroyed, and at the end of the war the *Europa* was ceded to France and became the *Liberte* in 1945.

One notable change in cruise styles was tried again and again but was ultimately destined to fail—the introduction of meal options. The traveler could now buy his steamer ticket with or without meals. If he chose the latter, he dined in a lavishly decorated room, presided over by Escoffier trained chefs and waiters schooled at the Paris Ritz. There were no fixed meal hours and no prix fixe, an arrangement that pleased the affluent traveler.

At the beginning of the century, sea traffic was a great source of revenue for the British, Germans, French and Scandinavians. Americans were again eyeing the sea lanes for profitable ventures. Men like J.P. Morgan, already railroad-rich, decided to enter the field; but, once more, Americans just couldn't make money at sea.

Cunard had meanwhile been named sponsor of a royal succession of liners and again emerged as a leader. The first vessels of its 20th century fleet were the *Caronia* and *Carmania,* big-funneled ships with black hulls and cluttered high, white superstructures. The ships were known as the "pretty sisters," but their real distinction was not in their looks but in their character, their ambience. They offered total British atmosphere — the afghan throw, high tea, and well-mannered service. Therein began a period when ships developed an affectionate following of contented passengers who would remain faithful for generations.

Cabins and accommodations were spacious in first class, smaller in second, and crowded but profitable in steerage. Twentieth-century technology took over on the bridge of new vessels but brought with it unusual problems. Most notorious were the loud-speaking telephones and public address system.

Other notable vessels that contributed to today's cruise ship style were the Scottish *Lusitania* and the English *Mauretania.* They introduced elevators, marble statues, trees, and such amenities as private bathrooms, genuine antique furniture, and original decorative oil paintings. Ships became seagoing museums showing unrelated art works from every period.

It was at about this time that hotelism crept into shipping. The idea was to give passengers the feeling that they were not at sea but on terra firma.

Etiquette on board ships was clearly spelled out. A gentleman just didn't hop up on a bar stool next to a lady and offer to buy her a drink. For one thing, a lady didn't sit at the bar, and for another, there was a "proper" route for introductions. A friend in common back home or, better still, a tip to one of the pursers brought a "proper" introduction, but it was "always done with diplomacy and tact, "according to society wags of the time.

The captain, already king of the ship, was also, under English maritime law, a magistrate at sea. He could, if he wanted to, perform marriages on board that were as binding as those performed on shore. He could require a woman of suspicious repute to sequester herself, and he could put even his company's president in irons, if he so desired. Listings in Who's Who determined priority for invitations to the captain's table.

The *Mauretania* rapidly gained the affection of her passengers because of her homey character. She wasn't a beauty, but she cut through the waters with grace and charm. The famous and the infamous sailed on her, and Franklin Delano Roosevelt, in a letter describing his trip, said, "If there ever was a ship which possessed a thing called 0soul,' the *Mauretania* does . . . every ship has a soul, but the *Mauretania* had one you could talk to. At times she would be wayward and contrary as a thoroughbred. As the captain once said to me, she had the manners and deportment of a great lady and behaved herself as such."

The *Mauretania* burned 1,000 tons of coal a day; her furnaces were attended by a Black Squad of 324 firemen and trimmers.

Competition between liners of different countries in attracting passengers to sail the Atlantic knew no bounds. No other shipping route in the world spawned such extravagances and follies. Ships were fitted with Byzantine chapels and Pompeian swimming pools, with dining rooms in the style of the Palace of Versailles and lounges decorated like Turkish baths and Eastern harem-rooms.

A trio of liners ranging from 45,000 to 50,000 tons proved to be the ships that broke the economic back of sea travel. They were the *Olympic, Titanic,* and *Brittanic* (also called *Gigantic*), and the era of truly great passenger liners was born. Later decades produced replicas of these superships, but only a handful ever surpassed them in tonnage.

The French also were in the passenger shipping business and were loath to have their national pride tarnished by imitations of their ships' amenities aboard British, German, and American competitors' vessels. For years, the French had maintained a standard of comfort and modest luxury on their ships that appealed to the cultured, affluent traveler. But by 1912 they, too, entered the competition by building the *France,* which promised to outdo the tapestried ambience, haute cuisine, and decor of any ship afloat. At 24,000 tons, the *France* was smaller than her rivals, but the design afforded more deck and lounge space. Her low funnels were placed far astern, and her lounge was de luxe *grande.* There were royal suites of rooms large enough to accommodate six passengers. As to cuisine, the France was tops. Records indicate that provisions for every voyage included 18 barrels of *pate de foie* gras.

Ship travel was reaching new heights of popularity, and the decade before 1914 was one of great expansion for shipping lines. In 1911,

Holland America ordered construction of the 32,000-ton *Statendam.* This ship would have put Holland America in league with the shipping giants of the time, but the war intervened and the great ship was destined to become a U-boat victim without ever flying the Dutch flag.

After the outbreak of war in 1914, the *Rotterdam, Nieuw Amsterdam, Potsdam, Noordam,* and *Ryndam* continued to maintain New York service. With other vessels, they formed the principal link between neutral Europe and America. Passage on these ships was in enormous demand. In November 1914, the *Noordam* was mined in the North Sea but reached port, where she was under repair for some months. As the war progressed, the demand for passage fell off and emigration ceased; thus, in 1915, the *Potsdam* was sold to the Swedish America Line, and became their *Stockholm.* In the spring of 1916, the *Ryndam* was mined off the English coast. The *Tubantia,* a 14,000-ton passenger liner of another Dutch line, the Royal Holland Lloyd, was torpedoed and sunk by a U-boat. The *Rotterdam* was taken out of service and laid up. The *Noordam* was again mined and put out of action in August 1917, and the *Ryndam* was chartered by America as a troopship, leaving only the *Nieuw Amsterdam* valiantly maintaining the run to New York. American passengers in the early days of the war were so grateful for the service provided under very difficult conditions that they presented to Captain Baron of the *Nieuw Amsterdam* a memorial tablet that was mounted in the ship.

This story would be incomplete without further description of the 32,000-ton *Statendam,* ordered in 1911 and never put in the company's service. Launched on July 9, 1914, she was taken over, after a delay in her completion, by the British Government and left the docks in 1917 as the *Justicia.* Interesting features of this ship were the glassed-in promenade deck and the triple-screw machinery layout. Since she was to be a troopship on war service, her third class accommodations were fitted out to carry 286 noncommissioned officers and 4,031 men. On July 19, 1918, she was hit by a torpedo off North Ireland and taken in tow by escorting ships. During the next twenty hours she was hit by four more torpedoes and finally sank. After World War I, sophisticated travelers who had been everywhere at least twice were joined by new travelers who had never been anywhere outside their own home city. This was the self-confident American, part of the "uncultured masses" who wanted to see more of the world. Irvin S. Cobb described this traveler as the one "who would swap an Old Master for one peep at a set of sanitary bath fixtures." He also advised that the best way to travel the Atlantic was to go over on an English ship, if the traveler was looking for "exclusability," and to come back on a German ship, if he wanted "sociableness."

The last of the four-funneled ships, the *Aquitania,* introduced innovations that became traditional over the years. The crew was trained in a sort of father-to-son heritage of stewardship that marked whole families in Liverpool and Southhampton. Service was on a par with British tact, grace, and professionalism, which positively dizzied American travelers, although some travelers considered the attention excessive to the point of being downright 'rude."

At the end of World War I, the Allies shuffled the German merchant fleet into oblivion. Ships worn and weary were repaired and reconverted, refurbished, and sent out again, but business just wasn't there. The German and British ocean giants had been built just in time to be converted from floating pleasure palaces into barracks or hospitals.

The *Nieuw Amsterdam* was still in the company's New York passenger service in 1918 and the *Rotterdam* rejoined her in February 1919, the *Noordam* in March, and the *Ryndam* in the autumn of that year, after her release from American troop service. Two new 15,000-ton turbine ships, the *Volendam* and *Veendam,* were ordered from Harland and Wolff and completed in 1922–23. When they came into service, the *Noordam* was chartered to the Swedish-America Line as the *Kungsholm.*

A new *Statendam,* similar to her previous namesake but somewhat smaller and with cruiser, instead of counter, stern, was also ordered. She was launched in 1924, but American immigration restrictions of that year changed the whole pattern of North Atlantic passenger services, and work was suspended until 1927, when the ship was towed to Holland for completion. She sailed on her maiden voyage in April 1929, reaching New York on the 300th anniversary of the arrival of the first Dutch ships carrying the founders of the settlement that has since become New York City. Before 1914, publicity material had depicted a very large, three-funneled Holland America liner named *Statendam.* Now at last for ship lovers a long-standing mystery was solved. The ship had accommodations for 510 first class, 344 second class, 374 tourist, and 426 third class passengers. Single-reduction geared turbines of 20,000 horsepower driving twin screws gave her a speed of 18 knots. In her day, this fine ship was known as the "Queen of the Spotless Fleet." Accommodations on other passenger ships were also altered as a result of immigration restrictions: The *Rotterdam* carried 539 first class passengers and 643 tourist passengers; the *Nieuw Amsterdam,* 300 cabin passengers and 860 tourist passengers.

When hostilities ceased, other ships were once again converted. Their engines were changed from coal-burners to oil-guzzlers, and their appointments were hauled out of storage. The *Olympic,* one of the first, had an enormous passenger capacity, but she hit the sea lanes just as the United States restricted immigration and liquor sales. One by one, the ships started depending heavily on their liquor stores and a great advantage was handed to foreign-flag carriers. American-flag ships were "dry" by Act of Congress, so Prohibition sent American travelers on board foreign-flag ships and inaugurated the golden age of ocean travel. Ships became more and more like hotels, and because family travel was encouraged, day-long children's activities were organized and around-the-clock merriment was in order for the adults.

The waterways out of New York were soon jumping to the beat of Dixieland bands. Embarkations resembled class reunions, as passengers in formal ties posed squinting for the inevitable sailing-day photograph. The person center-front always had his head stuck through a life preserver on which the ship's name was printed.

With the advent of Prohibition, economically hard-pressed steamship companies came up with a new marketing idea. Instead of letting their fleets gather rust in shipyards, why not send them on short voyages to Nassau, Palm Beach, Havana, Miami?

Thus the birth of the "booze cruise," the low-cost junket into society playgrounds; the weekend at sea where the secretary could rub elbows with her boss for $49.50. Bathing-suit-clad beauties were substituted for ships in advertising, and the swinging sets of the 1930s set sail.

No one can truly say which ship offered the first pleasure cruise for paying passengers. The only thing certain about cruises, as compared to ocean voyages, is that they did not happen until the rigors of sea travel had been modified to the point where passengers could endure and enjoy the travel experience.

Short cruises by big ships during Depression years were a sad and almost futile attempt to keep these liners alive. When business on the Atlantic picked up, the ocean traveler demanded new ships. By then, big ships gathering rust in shipyards had to be replaced by smaller vessels built to follow the sea lanes of the Caribbean, Mediterranean, and North Sea.

The unquestioned authority on what to wear on ships was Emily Post, who wrote it all down in 1925. "On deluxe ships," she said, "nearly everyone dresses for dinner; some actually in ball dress, which is in the worst possible taste, and, like overdressing in public places, indicates that they have no other place to show their finery. People of position never put on formal evening dress on a steamer, not even in the a la carte restaurant. In the dining saloon, they wear afternoon dresses, without hats for dinner. In the restaurant, they wear semi-dinner dresses. Some smart men on ordinary steamers put on a dark sack suit for dinner after country clothes all day, but in the deluxe restaurant, they wear tuxedo coats. No gentleman wears a tailcoat on shipboard under any circumstances whatsoever."

The art of mass travel, that phenomenon begun with a few 19th century lovers of Old Masters, had moved into the tourism industry. Anyone who could scrape together $80 or $90 for a round trip ocean ticket and another $200 for a long summer in Europe could join the scene. This led to phenomenal success in third-class travel, now called tourist class, and to the eventual abolishment of this level of travel. Eventually, the one class liner, a floating symbol of democracy, took over the sea lanes. It was as American as apple pie, and it changed the entire character of ocean travel.

Americans whose parents had stood at the steerage rail were taking to the ships. The big three in the late 1920s were the *Berengaria,* the *Aquitania,* and the *Mauretania.* In popularity they were followed by the *Conte di Savoia,* with its Italian dash, and the *Ile de France.* The Germans, back in passenger shipping, had two new vessels, the *Bremen* and the *Europa.* The *Bremen,* a passenger ship with the cut and capabilities of a destroyer, was launched in 1929 to the strains of *Deutschland uber Alles.* Her hull was constructed on an oval plan, and her lines gave her an air of graceful staunchness. The two massive funnels were stocky and short (and eventually were replaced by taller ones), and a streamlined profile emanated from her rounded bridge. She was 102 feet wide, which gave her the broadest beam on the Atlantic. Her interior was the first to be designed along 'functional" lines eliminating the grandeur that added weight and personnel. She set transatlantic speed records and traveled at an average of 28 knots.

In the annals of vanished Atlantic liners, the *Normandie* figures as a ship without equal. She was a lively and beloved legend. She was launched early in 1935, a year before the *Queen Mary.* A compact and graceful 80,000 tons with a clipper-type bow, she was requisitioned during the war and converted into a troopship, the *U.S.S. LaFayette.*

The first of the great British ships was the *Queen Mary.* Her power was estimated to be equal to the muscle-power of seven million galley slaves rowing in unison.

For the record, the largest passenger liner ever built was the *Queen Elizabeth,* whose construction began in the summer of 1935. Much the same type of ship as her sister the *Mary,* the *Elizabeth* had one less funnel, a few more cabins, and more decorative art. Where the *Norman-*

die had a full-sized tennis court, the *Elizabeth* had a big, partially enclosed deck for the use of tourist class passengers. With her fast elevators and increased deck space, she was finally ready to sail after five years under construction. But instead of having streamers fluttering from her decks, she found herself painted battleship gray and sitting in New York Harbor. One year after she was launched, the Elizabeth was carrying troops across the Atlantic.

Another new silhouette appeared on the Great Circle, the *America.* The U.S. standard-bearer was launched in 1939 but during the war sailed as the *West Point* for 500,000 miles.

It didn't take long after the end of World War II for shipping companies to convert liners which had served the Allies into ocean going passenger vessels. A 12 year high in transatlantic traffic was inaugurated by Norwegian America Line's *Stavangerfjord* in August 1945. Other liners fresh from refittings quickly took to the same sea lanes. Demand was heavy. Displaced persons, immigrants, the military and a new breed of American tourist quickly occupied available berths. New passenger ships sailed side-by-side with older favorites like the *Queens Elizabeth* and *Mary,* the *Liberte, Nieuw Amsterdam* and the *Ile De France.* New and luxurius amentities were introduced. Cabins were being built with private facilities and the *Kungsholm* was built with all outside cabins. Outside swimming pools became design standards once American Exoport put them on the *Excalibur, Exeter* and *Exochorda.*

Business was brisk on the Atlantic and new tonnage was ordered to accommodate the growing mass market. The industry was unprepared and overstocked in 1958 when a Pan American jet cut transatlantic travel time from six days to a little over six hours. Within a year, airlines were carrying 1.5 million across the Atlantic and ships were sailing with empty berths.

Maritime history comes up with a single grande dame in every decade, and the *United States,* a mechanically and structurally advanced vessel, ruled the 1950s. The *United States* was built in secrecy in a special shipyard. Her defense features were those of full-scale warships, and her capacity was great enough to transport 14,000 troops. She was of aluminum construction and held together by 1.2 million rivets. At 53,000 tons, she was only two-thirds as large as either of Cunard's Queens, yet she could carry as many passengers. With a length of 940 feet and a beam of 132 feet, she could still glide through the Panama Canal if she had to. Nothing on the *United States* was inflammable, and she became the first big ship to be completely fireproof. She also was the first to be fully air conditioned. The least decorated of all ships in her class, she was graceful, had the lines of a clipper, and was fast.

During the 1950s, the aging *Ile de France* was joined by the *Liberte* and the *Flandre,* the first transatlantic vessels to come out of a French shipyard after World War II. Holland America Lines welcomed her *Nieuw Amsterdam* in New York in 1940 as she sought safe haven during the war. Used as a troopship for six years, she finally headed home for Holland on the seventh anniversary of her launching. A beautiful gray ship, she was an immediate favorite with sea travelers. She retained three classes, old manners and comforts, and satisfied the postwar hunger of thousands of travelers who wanted something close to what they had once enjoyed. Her owners were responsible for a major change in the class system when they launched their sister ships, *Maasdam* and *Ryndam.* These ships each accommodated 800 tourist class passengers and 40 first class passengers.

In a single stroke, travelers in first class became almost underprivileged. Their cabins were larger, certainly, but their dining room was not much bigger than that in a modest private house, and their deck space was limited to the size of a dog-run. Their less affluent shipmates drank at 10 cents per, danced into the late hours, and had the run of the rest of the ship. The reversal of privileges of first and tourist classes was so successful that almost every company followed suit. By the time the one class *Statendam* was joined by the huge *Rotterdam,* tourist and first classes had melded into a one class system.

One bright morning in the 1960s, a go-go ocean liner pulled out of her Manhattan berth and moved down the Hudson River. Termed the "pearl of the American Merchant Marine," the *Independence* looked more like a painted billboard advertising a product than a ship. She offered cut-rate 'experimental" cruising where passengers could cruise and pay for their meals in any one of four restaurants.

This option was not popular. Cruise passengers wanted, and still want, a sea experience that includes more food than they can possibly consume. While European countries were raking in money on passenger shipping efforts, American vessels with outstanding qualities — the *United States, Constitution, Independence, Argentina, Brasil,* and *Santa Rosa,* were in serious financial trouble.

The last great liner built in our era was the 66,000-ton *France,* the longest ocean liner ever constructed. She promised to return ocean travel to the luxuries of old. Her handsome and proud design included two great funnels with swept-back wings. Inside, she was overly ornate, with gilt and glitter mixed with ironwork, carved gold-edged windows, and ceramic wall-plates. A single error in construction planning made it impossible for her to transit the Panama Canal. She is a couple of inches too wide.

Her vastness, however, was enough to lure passengers, and she quickly became the most successful Atlantic carrier of the decade. Italy countered with her own glamour vessels, the *Leonardo da Vinci,* followed by the *Michelangelo* and the *Raffaello.*

The 1960s and 1970s witnessed construction of compact smaller ships, with only the *Queen Elizabeth 2* remaining as the last of the big liners built in this decade. With about two-thirds of the tonnage of the *Mary* and the old *Elizabeth,* her length is less than theirs, her height a little more. She is computerized with the precision of a Rolls-Royce and designed and decorated in a mood of controlled elegance. She was conceived as more of a cruise ship than a transatlantic liner, because that's the way the dollar crumbles. Yet she fills up on around-the-world voyages because there are passengers with money willing to pay for the upper-priced cabins that sell first on what may be Cunard's last *Queen.* She still travels transatlantic with two classes of passengers, and she is probably the most beautifully and efficiently designed passenger ship of all time.

A few words are in order about the importance of passenger vessels in time of war. This was obvious in the Faulklands/Malvinas dispute between Britain and Argentina. When Britain urgently needed to transport troops to a combat zone some 8,000 miles away, the government ordered takeover of the *Queen Elizabeth 2, Canberra* and *Uganda* for military duty. All three ships are registered in the U.K. Under laws of the country (and other agreements) they were requisitioned and saw some battle.

And, it could happen in other countries. All it would take in the United States, for example, would be a presidential declaration of a national emergency. The Merchant Marine Act of 1936 authorizes the Maritime Administration to requisition or buy any ship owned by U.S. citizens, companies or under construction in U.S. shipyards. In actuality, only the *Independence* and *Constitution* could carry enough troops to justify requisition. The other U.S. flags that could be put back into service and used to transport troops are the *Santa Rosa, Monterey* and *United States.*

Old ships, like great generals, never die . . . They just change names and sail on to different waters with new owners, flags, crews, and passengers. It's like a game of musical names on the bows of some vessels. Old names stubbornly cling and refuse to be completely obliterated. It is possible to see traces of former names beneath freshly painted bows.

The *Emerald Seas* is a vessel with a long list of former names. She was built as a troop transport in 1944 and named the *General W.P. Richardson;* in 1949, she changed hands and became the *La Guardia* until 1956, when her new owners christened her the *Leilani.* Fate and economics added another new owner in 1961, and she became the *President Roosevelt;* then the *Atlantis* in 1970. Her current name-change came with ownership by Eastern Steamship in 1972.

Chandris is a good place to search for old favorites that continue to sail. The *Lurline,* built in 1932, flies the Greek flag now as the *Ellinis.* The *President Hoover* was built in 1939 as the *Panama,* sailed as the *James Parker* and then as the *Panama* again; sailed briefly as the *Regina;* and is now cruising the Mediterranean as the *Regina Prima.* The once-beautiful *America* (my all-time favorite), of 1940 vintage, became the *Australis* and now sails as the *Italis,* but just ain't what she used to be.

And the *Bremerhaven,* commissioned in glory in 1960, is now Sun Line's *Stella Maris.* They also own the former *Santa Paula,* built in 1958. She now sails as the *Stella Polaris.*

The second *Kungsholm,* built in 1953, became the *Europa.* She sailed the North Atlantic for Hapag-Lloyd muntil the new *Europa* was built. She is now sailing under the Costa banner as the *Columbus* and plies the waters between Europe and South America.

Watch out for a ship named the *Elizabeth A.* She cruises the Mediterranean and flies a Cypriot flag. Her former name was the *Yarmouth,* and she was built in 1927.

The Polish liner *Stefan Batory,* which has been offering super trans-atlantic bargains, was the *Maasdam,* built in 1952.

Norwegian Caribbean Line's first *Sunward* was purchased by an American and is now being operated as a floating Holiday Inn in Saudi Arabia. She joins Zim's former *Bilou,* which had the Hebrew writing scraped off and now flies the Saudi flag as the *Saudi Moon,* transporting pilgrims to Mecca. The Italian Line's *Raffaello* and *Michelangelo* have joined the floating hotel fleet at the Iranian port of Banda Abbas.

If you happen to be in the Mediterranean, you'll spot some freshly painted ships built by the Zim Israel Navigation Company (Zim Line) when the Israelis thought passengers cruising would bring hard currency to their fledgling country. Ulysses Line's *Ithaca* (rebuilt in 1973) was the Lion, built in Germany in 1956. She sailed from 1966 until 1972 as the *Amelia de Mello,* but the Hebrew writing is still visible on the ironwork. She now sails as the *Dolphin* from Miami. The *Veracruz,* which sails from New York and Tampa was the *Theodor Herzl,* built as part of the Zim fleet in 1957. She has sailed as the *Carnival* and as the *Freeport.*

Costa Line, one of the largest privately owned passenger-shipping companies in the world, has a few oldies hanging around its docks too. The *Carla C* was built in 1952 as the *Flandre;* the *Flavia* is of 1947 vintage and was built as the *Media;* the *Andrea C* was built in 1948 as the *Ocean Virtue;* and a rusty anchor should be showing on the *Franca C,* which was built in 1914 as the *Medina* and later sailed as the *Rome.*

At last count about 50 ships built before 1950 are still in service today, albeit under different names for the most part and under different flags. Most of the ships mentioned have been updated, some beyond recognition. In some, engines have been changed, profiles have been extended, furnishings have been replaced and interiors have even been completely gutted and rebuilt. (See "Ship Profiles" chapter). Still others retain the same outward appearance with internal face-lifts the only evidence of the passage of time. Other less fortunate glamorous ladies of the sea have ended up as rusty wrecks or as somebody's Toyota. Still others are serving as hotels. The magnificent *Queen Elizabeth* was retired in 1968 and sold to a Hong Kong shipping magnet. She was renamed *Seawise University* only to be destroyed by fire in the Hong Kong harbor in 1972. Her sister, the *Queen Mary* is a hotel and sightseeing attraction in Long Beach, California. Holland America's *Nieuw Amsterdam* was scrapped in 1974 and the *Homerica* (built as the *Mariposa* in 1931) was destroyed in 1974. The *Oranje* launched in 1939 for world service sailed as the *Angelina Lauro* for 15 years before she was destroyed by fire dockside in St, Thomas. The number of cruise passengers has increased more than five fold since 1969. At the Port of Miami alone the number increased from 569,000 in 1969 to 1,466,581 in 1980 and to 2.1 million in 1984. In one year, passenger loads increased by a whopping 35.8 percent! Although normal year-to-year increases in the cruise industry seem to average out at close to 15 percent, the next five years will see a major phenomenon developing. The number of cruise ship beds is slated to increase by closer to 26 percent. This represents a growth trend greater than that achieved by the airline industry during the period after introduction of wide bodied jets.

There's no doubt in anyone's mind that transatlantic liner service has continued to decline dramatically since after World War II. This is the basis of many a misunderstanding. When a famous old liner gives up the ghost, it seems to make more of an impact on the public psyche than the building of twelve new ships designed specifically for cruising during the 1980s.

The last couple of years saw some liners meet with terrible happenings; others changed flags, owners and routes; still others are awaiting their fates in far flung shipyards.

Holland America's "baby" of the fleet, the *M.S. Prinsendam,* made headlines when a fire broke out on board as she was cruising Alaskan waters before heading for Singapore in October, 1980. She had a full complement of passengers on board and happily, swift action by the crew prevented any loss of life. Holland America has not replaced the vessel per se, but has built two new ships, the *Nieuw Amsterdam* and *Noordam,* which were introduced in 1983 and 1984. An interesting side note: after passengers and crew were safely ashore, the company sent tow barges to bring the *Prinsendam* to port for an appraisal of her damages. In calm seas and for no apparent reason, the 9,000-ton lady just rolled over and sank.

The *S.S. Galileo Galilei* and the *S.S. Guglielmo Marconi* have had a less than smooth cruising history although they have never been touched by disasters at sea; only disasters as far as determination of management. Both ships were built in 1963, are 27,900 tons and are again in or nearing passenger service. The *Galileo Galilei* was purchased by Chandris Cruises and is sailing on short cruises out of the Port of Miami on charter to Fantasy Cruises. The *Marconi* now belongs to Costa Cruises and is currently undergoing complete renovations before inaugurating service probably out of a Florida port in mid–1985.

Costa's *Angelina Laura* and *Leonardo da Vinci* both burned while in different ports. The *Angelina* had a fire while in port in St. Thomas and the *Leonardo* suffered the same fate in a Mediterranean port. They have been scrapped. No loss of life or injuries were incurred.

Over on the coast of China, a ship called the *Aquamarine* was making waves carrying passengers on 14-day cruises between Hong Kong and Kobe (Japan) via three or four stops in People's Republic of China ports. Financial and operational difficulties forced cancellation. The company then leased the *T.S. Melody,* but withdrew the ship two weeks before the first scheduled sailing. The route is now being operated by the *Pearl Of Scandinavia* (ex *Finnstar*). See "Ship Profiles'.

Word of mouth is keeping cruise ships alive and prospering; that, and the value passengers receive. As ships change, so do passengers. They grow younger every year.

Nothing really comes close to the feeling that accompanies the whistle as the crew gets ready to pull up the lines. It's a feeling that comes with the popping of champagne corks when visitors have disembarked. The ship puts out to sea and there's hardly a dry eye on shore. On board? The party is just beginning.

The Good Old Days—Then and Now

Everything seems to look better in retrospect, but when it comes to cruising, the good old days are now—and the future is very bright. On board conveniences are getting better and better, and passengers have reached new heights in importance.

Take the early 1800s, for example. Accommodations on ocean-going vessels placed the passenger behind cargo in importance. In the old days passenger cabins were in the least desirable locations, and the motion of the ocean far forward or aft must have sent passengers in those pre-stabilizer and pre-private bathroom days to the rails in droves. But, as competition increased, the pendulum started to swing in favor of the passenger. By the latter half of the 1800s, iced drinks, private bathrooms and good food were no longer considered outlandish requirements.

And, a new word was added to to the vocabulary: POSH. It began as P.O.S.H. stamped on tickets of Indian Ocean travelers and indicated cabin location—"Port Out; Starboard Home", the most desirable on each leg of the voyage. But "posh" took on another meaning on board ships as amenities increased and lines competed for paying passengers.

The media reporting on these trends toward opulence was hard-pressed to find words to express the lengths to which ship owners were going to impress passengers. No expense was spared as ships competed in decor, amenities and entertainment. What resulted was 0the ultimate' in social scenes.

It became a matter of one-upsmanship as jewels and ball gowns, tuxedos and white ties became the 'normal' way to dress on transatlantic crossings. One journalist's description of a Captain's Dinner caught my attention. He wrote: 'Hundreds of multi-coloured fairy lamps shed their soft gradients on forms of beautiful women gloriously gowned and handsome men in immaculate evening dress who danced the hours away to music provided by jolly orchestras."

Life aboard those liners was a kaleidoscope with little relationship to life on shore. Like today's ships, romance and adventure were foremost in the minds of passengers boarding superliners at the close of the century and into the 1900s.

In that kind of setting, pity the poor Captain who had to select the creme de la creme of the passenger manifest to share his prestigious table during the voyage. With a veritable Who's Who in royalty, politics, the arts and letters, a seat at the Captain's table was an important, sought-after honor. No wonder ship masters have abandoned the practice of sharing their tables with a select few for the entire voyage. On most vessels, VIP dinner guests are invited to the Captain's table for one meal only.

The staff on superships of those times faced a mammoth task just keeping up with this social whirl and passenger efforts to outshine each other. There seemed to be a total disregard for money, and transatlantic crossings developed definite snob appeal. As life aboard ship became more glamorous, it became more sought after. The middle class wanted a piece of the life seemingly reserved for the upper-crust with lots of money. Some saved for years for a singular experience, and life in the first-class section became a high point in the American Dream.

Demand by the growing American middle class influenced changes aboard ships, and by the mid–1920s, a new look was developing in shipboard life. New vessels were built to accommodate more passengers, but their interiors were just as opulent in appeal to the tinsel-seeking crowds. Social barriers were bending as ships divided passengers by the price of their tickets into first class and tourist class. Steerage became third class and was used by immigrants and students, for the most part. The good life was in first, the fun times in tourist class. It was permissible for first-class passengers to mix and participate in tourist class activities, but the doors opened only on the first-class side. It took a steward to unlock them on the tourist-class side. It is said, many a first-class steward retired with money reaped on gratuities required to open that door.

At about this time, shipboard life was showing the first signs of shedding some of the fictional Hollywood image, and passengers continued to climb the gangplanks for the same reasons. They came for those special experiences, the camaraderie of loosened inhibitions, and, of course, the promise (implied or real) of a romantic interlude.

SHIPS OF TODAY

Cruise companies began building ships specifically for cruising purposes in the early 1970s. While ship owners kept a careful eye on profitable ventures, they expended huge amounts of money to improve amenities. In the process, cruising was democratized and first class was eliminated and there was no need to duplicate public space for two classes. Swimming pools became larger, theaters and lounges, supper clubs and ballrooms were built to accommodate at least half of the ship0s capacity. Ships were from 17,000 to 25,000 tons; staterooms became compact and standardized; and cargo was eliminated as public rooms took on the same atmosphere as shoreside resorts. In the mid-

1970's, the industry experienced an unprecedented rebirth and demand far outstripped supply and ship owners realized they had underbuilt the size of their fleets. They searched shipyards for overlooked tonnage and some oldies came back to the sea lanes. Other owners began thinking new tonnage which would take three or four years to complete and still others decided to to simply expand capacity by stretching their fairly new ships. Royal Caribbean's *Song of Norway* was the first to be cut in two and have a new identically matched mid-section installed. The expansion was so successful, the company immediately had the same operation performed on the *Nordic Prince*. Royal Viking Line had all three of its ships stretched by the same method and it's hard to to find the seams binding the new and old sections.

All of the new ships, and many of the older refurbished vessels, have the same basic amenities considered luxuries not too many years ago. Stabilizers, air conditioning, private facilities, swimming pools, and exercise rooms or spas are standard on almost every ship. On board sanitation systems, garbage compactors, satellite navigation and television in cabins are almost common on the new generation of ships.

Fuel prices and shortages during the latter half of 1970 became an important consideration and influenced the size and shape of ships built and under construction in the decade of the '80s. Except for Sitmar Cruises' new *Fairsky,* ships built during the '70s and '80s were and continue to be built with diesel engines instead of steam turbines for propulsion. Marine engineers are quick to point out advantages and some disadvantages in both types of engines but there is total agreement that diesel powered engines use a lot less fuel than a steam turbine ship. A great disadvantage to diesel powered ships is vibration caused by pistons moving up and down. While advances have been made to minimize vibration, it has not yet been eliminated on any of the new and very large ships. Greatest advantage to diesel engines is economy of movement which helps keep cruise prices within affordable ranges. The operations officer of one of the largest cruise companies with both new and older ships in its fleet confided that it costs less to operate its new 36,000-ton, 1,400 passenger ship than it does to run one of their 25,000 ton vessels with 1,000 passengers on board.

SHIPS OF THE FUTURE

A dozen or so years ago, even a shipaholic like me was skeptical about the future of cruising, let alone demand for THE TOTAL TRAVELER BY SHIP. But, when the book approached "best-selling" status, my faith in the traveler's return to the leisurely form of travel offered by ships was restored and encouraged. Just a few short years ago, I didn't think THE TOTAL TRAVELER BY SHIP would ever include a chapter covering ships of the future and that the future was immediate and not on the horizon.

In the early 1970s, passenger shipping tonnage inventoried in the millions and was gathering rust, abandoned in shipyards around the world. Glamour queens of the sea had been deserted by fickle jet setters who have a way of setting travel trends, and perhaps dictating where we go and how we get there. They opted for wide-bodied jets to transport them across oceans and to romantic islands at speed rivaling that of sound.

But trends are cyclical and as the world indulges in nostalgic thoughts and desires, a yearning for the good-old-days of relaxation and slower paces is emerging. Today's travelers in all economic and social strata are no longer obsessed with speed. They want a measure of service and luxuries not accustomed to in daily life and they want to experience it all while they float to strange sounding places with names they can hardly pronounce. It's a trend that is breathing new life into an industry that looked for a while like it was fading away and becoming obsolete.

With more travelers and vacationers seeing the world than ever before in recorded history, aircraft are taking off on transatlantic and transpacific flights to tropical islands and foreign countries with few empty seats, in spite of ever-increasing fares. Ships were pulling in their lanes with hardly an empty berth on board until 1980. Ship owners were riding high and without hesitation committed themselves to additional tonnage. They backed up their bullish outlook with investments of more than a billion dollars for construction of new ships.

In January, 1982, the first of this new generation of ships inaugurated service. Carnival Cruise Line's *M. S. Tropicale* cost in the neighborhood of $110 million, and that's some neighborhood. Home Line's *Atlantic* was completed the same year at about the same cost. She's a 33,800 ton ship that accommodates over 1,000 passengers. In December 1982, Royal Caribbean Cruise Line introduced its new *Song of America,* a $140 million, 37,584 ton ship that accommodates 1414 passengers. Holland America Cruises' *Nieuw Amsterdam* began service in mid-1983 and and her almost identical sister-ship the *Noordam* was completed a year later. Each ship accommodates 1,214 passengers, is 33,930 tons and cost around $150 million. In April 1984 Sea Goddess Cruises introduced the first of its luxury 4,000 ton ships, the *Sea Goddess I.* Sitmar Cruises also introduced the new *Fairsky,* the only newly built passenger ship with turbo engines. The 46,314 ton *Fairsky* is the largest ship built exclusively for cruising but records don't hold up very long in the cruise industry. The year was topped off with style in late November when Princess Cruises christened the new *Love Boat, Royal Princess,* and inaugurated sailings. The 45,000 ton vessel cost nearly $200 million to build and will accommodate 1,200 passengers, all in outside cabins. Construction by a half dozen other companies is either nearing completion or progressing from drawing boards to shipyards. Modifications of existing tonnage have been ordered and capacity in most fleets is being increased.

Although 1985 and 1986 may not turn out to be banner profit years for owners, they anticipate a turn around by mid–1986 when they expect demand will again outstrip supply and they are banking on this future development.

Ships launched in the 1980s have a different look from those built before the turn of the decade. The economics of operating passenger ships, inflation and the uncertainty of fuel supply and costs are having marked effects on construction and reconstruction plans. With the price of building new ships soaring above the $150 million mark in 1985, owners and operators are diligently searching shipyards for vessels in good repair and with engines that can be converted to meet requirements for profitable operations through the end of the century. Some are being found in Arabian ports where they were hastily purchased and docked for use as hotels until construction on land could catch up with needs. Other ships will be coming out of forced shipyard retirement to be upgraded to modern standards. In some cases, they will be stripped down to their hulls and engines, then completely rebuilt to conform with needs of the industry.

As new tonnage comes on line, some companies are selling off older vessels. Interesting to note, what is considered tonnage needing to be replaced in some company fleets is considered desirable by others who quickly buy up the older vessels. In some cases, a complete refurbishing job is done; in others, merely some cosmetic work. In either instance, flags on the mast are changed. A new name goes on the bow and she is sold to another segment of the cruising public. The ship takes on a new personality, although it is hard to erase every aspect of her past.

Most companies bent on increasing the size of their fleets are making financial commitments for construction of new ships, an illustration of optimistic views of the economic future of the cruise industry. These new vessels will be the fleets of the future. In general, they will be over 30,000 tons, with some reaching over 45,000 tons, as compared with the 17,500-ton generation of vessels, built during the early 1970's. They will be heavier and broader beamed, have such fuel conserving devices as bulbous bows and be more maneuverable, thereby requiring fewer tugs in ports. Cabins will be larger than on the ships of the 1970s, but the greatest difference will be in public facilities. They will be huge! Newer designs and construction concepts allow for what might seem oversized public space by today's compact standards. The economics of cruising is forcing sizes and passengers manifests into higher numbers ranges.

This trend offers great advantages for cruise lines and even greater advantages for passengers. In some respects, ships of the late 1980's and maybe the 1990's will bear a greater resemblance to ships of the good old days. Engines will be piston-operated instead of steam driven and will be engineered to cut down on vibration and noise generally associated with piston driven engines.

Another trend developing is conversion of North Sea ferries to Caribbean, Mexico and Alaska cruise ships. These ferries are hardly the type on which passengers book deck space for short transfers between nearby ports. Some ferries are as big as apartment houses to which their designs also bear striking resemblances. Other companies have added length by stretching ship midsections in procedures identical to the method used on freighters.

Cruise companies think big but cruise aficionados think even bigger. A company in San Diego, California, with the name of Titanic Steamship Line, Inc. announced grandiose plans for construction of three 46,000 ton superliners. They said the ships would be registered in Great Britain and sail with all-English crews. First of these ships would cost $400 million and accommodate about 50 people on superlative voyages around the world. Without tongue in cheek, they named her the *Titanic.* Even before the second Titanic met her first wave, plans ran aground and the Federal Maritime Commission ordered the company to cease communication, written or verbal, with the media concerning the *Titanic.*

While this $400 million per ship venture is probably permanently shelved, estimated cost of new construction is reaching upwards of $180 million and it is not surprising to find renderings of dream ships that may soon reach that $400 or so million lofty height.

Carnival Cruise Line

Even before the $110 million new *M. S. Tropicale* was delivered to Carnival Cruise Lines, owner and operator of the *Carnivale, Festivale* and *Mardi Gras,* the company committed about one-half a billion dollars to construction of three more vessels in the growing fleet. Similar to the *Tropicale* in concept, the *Holiday, Jubilee* and *Celebration* will be operated by huge horse-power diesel engines. They will be 40 feet longer than the *Tropicale* and be over 40,000 tons. They'll each have one additional deck, 710 cabins, feature two full decks of public space, two dining rooms, and be capable of world-wide service. Passenger capacity will be fixed at around 1,250 with some very plush suites with private balconies. As in the *Tropicale,* all cabins will be equipped with closed-circuit television and stereo. They are being built in a European ship-yard, and the first, the *Holiday,* is slated for service in June 1985. Construction of another vessel will begin in 1985. She'll be an almost exact sister to the *Holiday* and will be completed and ready for service in 1987, the same year the *Celebration* is introduced. The *Jubilee* will be introduced in 1986. The company anticipates a 10 vessel fleet by the turn of the decade.

Home Lines

Home Lines will take delivery of its new 35,000 ton passenger ship in Spring of 1986. In keeping with traditions of the sea, the new vessel will be christened the *m.v. Homeric.* It will be 686 feet long, have a beam of 95 feet and will accommodate 1,260 passengers. Estimated cost is around $150 million. The ship is under construction at the Joseph L. Meyer Shipyard in West Germany. She will sail alongside her not quite sister ship, the *Atlantic,* from New York to Bermuda in summer months and from Florida to the Caribbean during the winter.

Norwegian Caribbean Cruise Lines

Norwegian Caribbean Lines has a way of coming up with shockers. The company took the industry by surprise when it purchased Royal Viking Line, thereby increasing its five passenger fleet to eight, although RVL will continue to operate at the luxury end of the market while the other vessels will remain in the moderate price category. Now Norwegian Caribbean is talking about building the biggest passenger ship ever, a behemoth weighing in at 210,000 tons, or three times the size of the *Norway.* If built, it will cost about $450 million, have 2,000 staterooms and accommodate 4,000 passengers in state of the art luxury. It's name — the *Phoenix* but it will rise not out of ashes but from the dreams of its architect and designer Tage Wandborg. At press time, the venture is still being studied as to feasibility and possible profitability. If all proves positive, the Phoenix could be ready for her maiden voyage in 1988 and will undoubtedly change the way we cruise. The *Phoenix* would be a self contained resort with four 500-seat tenders moored inside its own marina in the stern. It would be floating city with its own on-board transportation system of monorails and moving sidewalks. *Phoenix* design calls for it to have its own sandy shores along a huge S-shaped central lagoon, four tennis courts, a fleet of helicopters, bowling alleys and fully enclosed lifeboats with full kitchens on board. She would be able to cruise anywhere but could not maneuver the Panama Canal. All of the conveniences planned are already available on smaller ships and one of the problems facing the architect is figuring out a way for the *Phoenix* to get into ports, including her home port of Miami. At that size, she would have to anchor at sea and tender even embarking passengers.

Royal Caribbean Cruise Lines

Royal Caribbean Cruise Lines wasn't talking at press time, but it's more than a rumor the company is negotiating with shipyards to build from one to three additional ships. Plans call for vessels to be in the image and style of the *Song of America* but larger. If negotiations are completed, the first of the additions to the RCCL fleet should be introduced in 1988.

Sitmar Cruises

Sitmar Cruises is in the drawing plan stage prior to construction of two new ships that will probably be ready for service in 1988 and 1989. Ships will be a departure from traditional Sitmar vessels and according to President John Bland "will be totally contemporary and set new styles in the way ships are built and designed." In all probabilities, the new ship will continue to be turbo operated, be in the 45,000 ton range and include amenities heretofore not seen at sea.

United Sates Lines

When it comes to ships of the future a vessel launched at Newport News almost 35 years ago may grab the headlines. The *S.S. United States* entered service in 1952 and during her 17 years in service, she set speed records that have never been broken. She had an insatiable appetite for fuel and when transatlantic traffic ceased to a near halt in 1969, she was laid up and protected by a special Act of Congress which directed the Maritime Administration to buy the ship for the U.S. Reserve Fleet and to resell her only to U.S. buyers for use in U.S. waters under continued U.S. registry.

In 1978, the *United States* was purchased by Richard Hadley, a Seattle financier, and his associates. They paid about $45 million for her, but her future was uncertain until recently. The company is now in the first stages of modernizing the ship which they say will enter service in late 1986. Hadley and his associates feel that national pride in the Stars and Stripes on the mast will bring passengers on board.

The *S.S. United States* was built by the Newport News Shipbuilding And Dry Dock Company and was christened in June 1951. She cost a whopping $79.5 million (a lot of money in 1951). More aluminum was used in her construction than in any other structure on land or sea. She measures 990 feet (five city blocks) in length and 101.6 feet across the beam, but her gross tonnage is only 53,329 because the use of aluminum resulted in light displacement. She could travel the seas at more than 38 knots, but all that will change if Hadley's plans are realized. United States Cruises (Hadley's company) plans to run her on one engine in order to reduce her speed. Passenger capacity will be reduced from 2,000 to about 1,500.

Reconstruction is scheduled in two phases. In November 1984, the ship was stripped of its old decor and a new deck was being added. After that work is completed, she will be towed to Hamburg, Germany where her interior will be stripped and rebuilt. Whereas the old *United States* was almost stark , the new "Big U" will have a softer look with woods and other contemporary materials. Cabins will be redesigned so the three former categories of accommodations are merged into one. An interesting feature will be seven restaurants each featuring a different cuisine. Passengers will be allowed to eat when they like and in whichever restaurant appeals to them. The ship will also have a full-size tennis court and other amenities only a vessel this size allows. The new *United States* will sail from U.S. ports on seven and 14 day cruises with rates averaging out at $250 a day. Total cost to ready her for service is estimated at about $100 million, almost the cost of new ship.

When the *United States* re-enters service, she will fly the U.S. flag. Recent legislation assured the owners of the right to sail her between the U.S. mainland and Hawaii. The same act, introduced by Senator Daniel Inouye (D. from Hawaii) cleared the way for purchase and operation of other vessels, particularly the *S. S. Independence, Monterey* and *Mariposa.*

How to Choose
Your Cruise

After a couple of hundred cruises, there's little doubt in my mind that a more pleasant way to spend a vacation has yet to be invented. But I would be less than honest if I didn't confess that no two cruise experiences are identical; no two ships the same. And, not every voyage rates a perfect 10 on the enjoyment scale. In all fairness, however, I can honestly say I have enjoyed every cruise experience albeit in different ways.

Travelers should understand that a cruise is an experience and no two experiences of any kind are exactly alike. It's those differences that balance the pleasure scales. While there are no exact clones when it comes to ships, they have much in common. They transport, feed and entertain passengers in holiday ambience in as painless as environment as 20th century technology allows. It's the obvious and the sometimes subtle differences that influence the cruise experience from start to finish.

All ships develop loyal followings, and there's no chance you'll find a devotee sailing on any vessel other than the one to which he or she has become faithful. On a Holland America cruise I met one passenger on her 100th voyage on the same ship, the *Rotterdam*. In her mind no ship afloat compared with her 'home at sea". On a *Mardi Gras* cruise I met a gentleman who sailed the ship every month for five years. The line named a suite in his honor.

Not even twin ships are identical, and only the truly experienced observer detects differences which do not show up on deck plans. Often, in spite of similar construction, ship decor differs. In spite of similar menus, cuisine differs. The human element involved in service also varies, even on ships operated by the same company.

The experienced cruise passenger has learned to discriminate in selection of ships. The land-lover, newly turned on to sea travel, has a greater tendency to be concerned with where the ship is going. Veterans of the sea are more apt to turn their attention to the amenities offered before selecting a vessel. And, cruise line concerns about filling their ships have resulted in innovative expansion of itineraries, amenities and facilities.

Cruise companies are constantly researching and planning new itineraries, a delicate and complex process that often involves financial risks. Science may have produced a heavily automated ship, but to discover new itineraries, cruise areas, or ports to satisfy passengers' sightseeing and shopping requirements is an art. In the competitive marketplace, cruise lines must continue to deliver more and different offerings to an ever increasing and diverse segment of the travel market.

The future of the cruise industry depends on attracting first-time passengers. Ship owners believe, and have been proven right, that once a traveler has tasted the salt of the sea, he comes back again and again. It's even more addictive than sand in his shoes for he has discovered that few land-packages can equal value received at sea.

Offerings are diversified and and a quick glance at what's available is likely to convince even the most skeptical that cruising is for everyone, providing he and she board a ship with personalities that most closely matches their own.

The Caribbean cruise is the most difficult to classify because it attracts a greater cross-section of Americans. But there is no such difficulty in making up a profile of three-month around-the-world cruise passengers. Cruise rates alone determine who they are. High-priced cruises also mean older passenger with time on their hands and money to spare. There is greater informality on short cruises than on long cruises catering to the well-to-do.

Food remains a major preoccupation on all cruise ships. If there is any doubt, watch the action on deck, in the dining room, and at buffets. Amazingly, if you consider the range of activities and distractions, food is the subject that continues to surface in any conversation on shipboard, or on land, when you mention a cruise.

Service is the next priority in selecting a ship. It is ironic that many American passengers, who may never have had the services of a maid in their homes, become quite emotional on the subject, especially if it involves foreigners. I have heard complaints about the most trivial shortcoming in service that somehow is magnified on board ship. The same passenger may endure the rudeness of a New York waiter, but once he boards a cruise ship, he expects the kind of service promised in brochures.

A vessel's physical appearance is important, but ambience is even more so to most passengers. "Ambience" defies precise definition. Unlike seeing a jet airliner, once you've seen one steamship, you haven't seen them all. The room where you sleep for a week or two is more important than the seat you'll snooze in for a couple of hours.

There are new ships and old ships, big ones and little ones, and like people, each has a unique personality. Even ships that look alike can be quite different, depending on the character of the crew and staff.

Let's take the age of a ship for starters. If the lady is an old and famous luxury liner that has been refurbished, air-conditioned, and brought up to today's luxury standards, passengers generally have nothing to worry about. A ship that was patronized by millionaires a couple of decades ago, when she was in world service, is likely still to be exceptional. For some, the newest luxury motel will never come close to the Waldorf Astoria.

But not all old ships measure up. If it's a refurbished ship no one has ever heard of, watch out — especially if the vessel originally operated in European waters and the ship happens to measure under 10,000 tons. These ships were built for the European market of a decade ago; a market looking for economy and bargain holidays and not inclined to lodge a single complaint if the mattress was hard and lumpy.

Passengers need not be leery of any ship, large or small, that was built or torn down and completely rebuilt during the past fifteen years. Ships in this category were designed for the American-style cruise trade, and they all measure up.

While there may be some differences in riding qualities between a big ship (over 25,000 tons) and a smaller one, the degree of difference may not be large enough to notice. A small, newer ship may have modern engineering features to make her sail more smoothly than a large, older vessel. Most ships of any size can give you a pretty good bouncing around in rough weather, but since cruises are usually planned for calm waters, rough sailings are not a common problem. As a captain friend said "It's not the roll of the ship but the motion of the ocean." One important difference between small and large ships is that the big ones may not be able to tie up at piers at all ports. This necessitates going ashore by tender, which means descending steps (gangplank) and boarding a smaller boat for a short ride to the dock.

Another difference between older and newer ships is in accommodations. On old ships, cabins range from very small to comfortably large, and sometimes no two will be alike. There will be inside cabins and outside cabins, singles, doubles, twins, studios, and double-decker bunk rooms, some accommodating as many as four passengers. Some old ships still have cabins without private facilities (bathrooms).

New ships, particularly those built specifically for cruise service, are constructed so that nearly all rooms are identical, except for a few suites or deluxe cabins. Unlike traditional vessels, they were planned for so-called one-class service. Usually, cabins are not very large and often have showers and no bathtubs, but they are functionally designed to make the most of available space. On a few ships, all staterooms have windows or portholes. Cruise rates are based on a combination of the ship's equipment, cabin size, services offered, and other real and imagined factors considered desirable.

Ships, like people, have personalities, and finding the ship with a profile to match your own is like shopping for a special piece of jewelry. As you depend on the reliability of the jeweler, you will find your travel agent can be of enormous help; but take your time and let your fingers do the walking through dozens of brochures until you come up with the "right" ship.

Relying on a travel agent is good advice, but ask the agent whether he has sailed the ship. If the answer is "no", don't take his word as gospel, but talk to someone who has sailed her, particularly if that someone has tastes similar to yours.

Even if your wallet is fat, you should look for a ship that offers the most for your time and money. As a guide to determining whether you can go the financial short or long route, moderately priced cruises average around $165 a day per person, double occupancy (which means two people share a cabin and each pays that $165 a day). This is true for short as well as long cruises, but it does not mean that you can't sail for less or for more. If you book far in advance, you can probably reserve a minimum-rate cabin for somewhere around $110 on the same per-person double-occupancy basis. (See Air-Sea Chapter)

Experts predict that more than 75 percent of next year's cruise passengers will be sailing for the first time. Here's a recommended step-by-step method of selecting a ship and reading the cruise brochure:

ITINERARIES

More and more cruises are bringing the arts, music, sports and the pursuit of fitness to life at sea. No matter what the interest may be, you'll find it on board a ship offering lectures and enrichment in that field. Cruise the Mediterranean and your fellow passengers are most likely lovers of history and antiquity. Shore excursions will allow for stops at ancient walled cities, homes of great artists, museums housing treasures we learned about in school. In selecting a Mediterranean cruise, one needs only to focus on a favorite period in history and select an itinerary that covers that region.

Archaeology buffs are delighted with Eastern Mediterranean cruises to Egypt, Israel, Greece and Turkey. It's a chance to see monuments of the ancient world blended into modern societies. A typical itinerary could include a couple of Greek islands, Haifa for a day in Jerusalem, Alexandria for a tour to the pyramids. Closer to home are cruises to the Western Caribbean and a chance to visit Mayan ruins in the Yucatan.

For a close-up of American life along the Mississippi, there are steamboat cruises and for a glimpse of Asia's carefully guarded past there are voyages through China and Japan, Hong Kong and Singapore, India and Sri Lanka and down through the South Pacific and New Zealand.

Sun and fun attract passengers to ships cruising Caribbean, Atlantic and Mexican waters and adventure seekers are taking to ships cruising Amazon and uncharted seas. There are companies devoted to sending their vessels to hard to reach places of the world and one company (Salen Lindblad Cruises) even retraces three Northwest Passage from Newfoundland across the northern ice cap to Yokohama, Japan.

THE LONG AND THE SHORT

There's a wide gulf between a weekend cruise from Miami to Nassau or an overnight cruise to nowhere and a North Cape cruise, between a 10-day Caribbean trip and a world cruise. Obviously, in each case passengers and their interests are different.

The weekend trip to Nassau attracts those who want to be entertained aboard ship, to sun themselves on beaches, and to gamble in the Nassau casinos. The contrasting North Cape passenger is generally the type of tourist who prefers the wonders of sea travel over fast indoor entertainment; in other words, he is a sophisticated traveler more at home in the ozone-filled air of a quiet fjord than in the noise of a smoke-filled nightclub.

Filling all of those new ships depends on attracting first timers and converting them to repeat passengers. So, ships are redesigning on board facilities, activities and entertainment to to attract contemporary travelers seeking floating life styles in tune with the good life ashore. The result is all-encompassing choices of itineraries from A to Z, focus on special interests from computers to archaeology, music and fitness.

Cruises last from an overnight or day trip to nowhere to around the world voyages lasting 95 days. Quick to capitalize on a growing international desire for short, different and easy to book quickie get-a-ways, several ships are now positioned as year around "weekenders." They also sail on Monday to Friday schedules but it is the Friday afternoon sailing returning early Monday morning that attracts the working crowd anxious to leave it all behind for three nights. From Florida, Carnival Cruise Lines, Eastern Cruise Lines, Dolphin Cruises, Chandris-Fantasy Cruises and Norwegian Caribbean Lines offer voyages to the Bahamas. Some include a stop at a Bahamas Out Island as well as Nassau. The Monday sailing also includes a visit to Freeport in addition to Nassau. Sailing out if the Port of Los Angeles on a similar schedule is Western Cruise Line's *Azur Seas* which cruises to one port in Mexico..

Wherever you find yourself in your travels if there's an ocean nearby, there are bound to be short cruises. Inland American waters are being navigated in New England on American Cruise Lines. There are riverboats on the Ohio River and KD German Rhine Line offers two and three day cruises up the Mosel River and the Rhine. There are dozens of short cruises from Piraeus (Athens) to the Greek Islands and there's even a 23 hour cruise (*Prince of Fundy*) from Portland, Maine.

Best opportunity to test the waters on superliners which concentrate on longer voyages is when one of these companies finds itself with a day or two between voyages or is sending its ship to a new position for seasonal sailings. The latter is called a positioning voyage. Rather than leave the ship sitting idle at the dock or crossing the Atlantic without passengers, the company runs a "sale" either to fill the ship or introduce it to potential customers.

Few people are aware they can book the *QE 2* for a short cruise. Last year the ship had a couple of cruises to nowhere out of New York between transatlantic crossings. The consensus of opinion on board was that going nowhere can be a marvelous experience. There are no ports of call, but there are lots of activities, entertainment and superb food and service.

By far the most popular cruise length is the one weeker. During a seven night period, the ship visits three to five foreign ports of call aboard contemporary cruise vessels in every price range sailing from East and West Coast ports. During summer months, a half dozen very good ships sail from Vancouver in British Columbia for Alaskan waters. Next in popularity are 10 to 14-day voyages from these same ports and from more exotic embarkation points like Hong Kong, Singapore and Kobe, Japan.

In 1985 six vessels are circumnavigating the globe in dream itineraries lasting from 79 to 99 days. In all, about 4,500 passengers paid as much as $900 a day and there are very few empty berths. Around the world voyages are so popular, reservation books open on 1986 voyages before the 1985 journeys began. Holland America's *Rotterdam* completed is completing her 26th world cruise. Royal Viking Sky is taking her longest voyage—99 days while the *Queen Elizabeth 2* and *Sagafjord* are on partial global voyages where passengers may connect with the other vessel to continue around the world. P&O's *Sea Princess* is making her third voyage and Costa sent the *Danae* on a historic world cruise.

TTT: If you live in a port city, and there's a three or-four-day cruise going to a foreign island, it might be a good way to get your sea legs, but don't compare food, service and ambience on these ships with a vessel like the *QE 2*. They are farther apart then apples and rasberries. Short cruises are for quick getaways, for limited budgets, and for the fun of it. Selecting a ship for a short cruise follows a different set of rules. The distance covered generally does not take much longer than overnight, so the way she rides and the size of the ship are not too important.

Itineraries are more important when the cruise lasts longer than one week. Where a ship travels concerns first-time cruisers more than veterans. If you're a sailor at heart and are cruising for the love of the sea, don't select a ship that calls at a different port every day. You'll be happier on board a vessel that spends more time at sea, especially if you're looking to cultivate new friends. On the other hand, if the pulse of a ship renders you lethargic, sail a vessel that puts into port at least every other day.

SPECIAL INTEREST CRUISES

Special interests are not confined to ports of call or itineraries but have become integral segments of on board entertainment programs. Music lovers have marvelous choices at sea. Classical, jazz, big band, chamber and disco sounds ring through theaters and lounges. There are music festivals at sea with outstanding solo performances by musicians, ballerinas and lecturers.

Just about every major cruise line has given in to passenger demands for on board casino gambling and most have black jack, roulette and dozens of slot machines. Some have crap tables and other games.

Sports at sea aren't exactly news. Everyone expects the table tennis tournament and the shuffleboard play off but now ships are offering a lot more. While most ships can't build even a three par hole on the sports deck, the really big ones have a golf pro in residence and a place to practice the shots. They organize visits to championship courses on shore and returning world cruise passengers have listed the golf experiences in the Philippines and Singapore as highlights of the 9O days. Tennis players can also sharpen their skills on many ships and when it comes to diving, lessons are given in ships' swimming pools in anticipation of diving expeditions in exotic warm water ports of call.

Even an opportunity for computer literacy is offered on board the *Queen Elizabeth 2* which has installed a computer center complete with 14 IBM personal computers and expert instructors. It proved to be so popular, it is being doubled in size.

Newest rage is cruising for physical fitness which some may find as a direct contradiction to the fantasy of cruising dominated by over-indulgence in the dining room. Contemporary passengers have forced contemporary cruise ships to become floating health spas. Sophisticated equipment has been installed, professional instructors hired, jogging tracks marked, Jacuzzis built and complete spa programs advertised.

CONSULTING A TRAVEL AGENT

TTT: If you have never used a travel agent before, selecting your agent should come before final selection of the cruise ship. Look for the ASTA (American Society of Travel Agents) shield in the window or in advertising. ASTA membership is an indication that the company has been recognized by the professional organization and that the company has pledged to uphold industry standards. This does not mean the travel agent is an expert in every field. You'll know after ten minutes whether the travel agent is patient, understanding, and willing to spend time to help you. You pay no fee for the travel agent's services. He is an agent for the ship operator and is paid his commission by the cruise company or the airline. Be wary if the agent tells you "XYZ ship is the only one for you." Some cruise lines pay higher commissions and overrides, and this can influence the travel agent's recommendations. A good travel agent will offer a couple of suggestions and will take time to explain differences between ships.

Be honest. Tell him exactly how much money you want to spend, how much time you have, whether you want informal atmosphere or dress-up parties, whether there are specific ports you would like to visit.

Chances are excellent the travel agent will start loading you up with a couple of dozen brochures, all colorful, glowingly descriptive, and somewhat misleading. There's always a handsome gray-haired fellow dancing with a youngish blond, he in the white dinner jacket and she is in a ballgown dripping with jewels. There are always bikini-clad girls playing shuffleboard, and buffet tables laden with caviar and lobster. Disregard the photos of people. The good-looking man is a professional model, and his partner's jewels would be out of place on most cruise ships these days. And the food? It was a setup for the photo session.

TTT: If you don't relish the thought of going down steps into a small boat in order to get ashore, check the brochure carefully and ask your travel agent: "Does the ship tender or dock in every port?" If the answer is "tenders, in some," expect to go down the ladder. Don't be timid about tendering, and don't let it put you off the ship of your choice. It requires care but there is no danger with plenty of sailors to assist you. Sometimes tendering in a port (like St. Thomas) puts you right in the middle of town and has an advantage. You arrive mid-city and don't have to take a taxi to explore. For more tender information, look in the "Ship Profiles" chapter under the ship you are considering.

READING A CRUISE BROCHURE

All brochures are beautiful, multicolored, and enthusiastically descriptive. All brochures picture life aboard a cruise ship "Love Boat" style, but not all ships are equipped to live up to their brochures.

Selecting the right ship with the right itinerary at the right price is almost a game of elimination. If you long for a relaxed, informal lifestyle and book on a ship with brochures showing black tie-clad men, your dream cruise could turn out to be a nightmare. If you require a special diet and the ship's kitchen is not equipped to handle your needs, you could turn out to be the one passenger in a million who disembarks hungry. If you travel with the kids and the ship doesn't have a playroom or planned children's programs, you and the rest of the family could be climbing the mast by the time the cruise is over. Conversely, if you want to get away from the patter of little feet and you happen to find your way up the gangplank of a ship catering to families, you might be tempted to jump ship at the first port.

There are a few basics that should help send you up the right gangplanks. Study brochures. True, most look alike, and except for the logos and names it is hard to tell one brochure from another, but there are clues.

TTT: Seasoned travelers have learned to translate some of the key words this way:

Informal atmosphere: Not necessary to wear jackets in the dining room.

Special children rates: Lots of kids, counselors, and planned activities.

Elegant dining: More than two out of seven dress-up nights.

European crew: More expensive, higher rates.

Compact cabins: Small staterooms.

Dietary arrangements: Special menus possible.

Standard stateroom: Minimum-sized.

Gala evenings: Captain hosts a cocktail party for the entire ship, and there is a special menu for dinner that night.

Casual night: Men, leave your jackets and ties in the stateroom. Ladies, follow your inclinations, but keep it on the dressy side.

Night owls: Late-night hangout for swingers and insomniacs.

Ultimate: See "Intimate."

Intimate: See "Ultimate." Both words top the lexicon of over-used and meaningless brochure adjectives.

TONNAGE

This can be misleading because there are many ways to figure tonnage. There's a good chance that if the ship is over 20,000 tons she was built for transocean voyages and has changed itineraries to accommodate the shorter cruise market. Or, she could be one of the ships of the '80s, recently built to meet marketing and economic demands.

Tonnage was first measured in 1422, when the British stipulated that vessels carrying coal had to be measured and marked. No clear system was organized as to how this was to be carried out. Some say the term "tonnage" came into use when fees charged were based on the number of casks of wine a vessel carried. The "tun" at that time was a legal standard measurement, so a tun of wine measured no less than 252 gallons. Over the years various commissions were appointed, and they formulated rules for determining tonnage. The Moorsom System, developed in 1854, is the basis for all current tonnage laws and regulations of most maritime nations.

Tonnage laws provide for gross and net, under tonnage and over tonnage (the sea line), and to the layman it has come to mean the size of the ship. Actually, gross tonnage is the under-deck tonnage, together with the between-deck spaces and all enclosed spaces above deck, including access of hatchways.

To judge the size of a passenger ship, consider the tonnage, but look a more closely at the length, the beam, and the number of decks.

BIG OR SMALL?

Depending on preferences, there are advantages and disadvantages to both. Besides rideability, big ships have many public rooms and you'll probably have your choice of nightclubs, quiet and busy lounges, show rooms, and possibly more than one swimming pool. Because of size, there's more varied entertainment and generally a wider choice of cabin accommodations. With more minimum priced and more maximum price cabins, there is a wider choice and a better chance at hard to get minimum priced staterooms.

But there are disadvantages. The larger the ship, the more problem and the more unlikely it will be able to pull up dockside at many of the small islands and tendering will be required. And, when it returns to home port at the end of the voyage, disembarkation and customs formalities may take longer.

While small ships offer "intimacy", large ships offer the opportunity to meet more of your fellow passengers and there are "intimate" lounges hidden away for special "encounters" and quiet moods.

SPACE RATIO

It doesn't necessarily follow that passengers have more elbow room and feel less crowded on larger ships, but it usually turns out that way. If you long for quiet corners, would rather walk a mile than stand in line, and would rather switch than fight, passenger space ratio should be considered before selecting a ship. In all fairness, ship management has crowd handling down to a science on most ships, but I like to blend activities with solitude on board ships and how much space is mine is important.

So, big ship or small ship. Ships over 25,000 gross registered tons are considered big; anything under 10,000 GRT is small. As for passenger capacity if the vessel carries over 900 passengers it is big; under 500 small.

To find the amount of space per passenger, the gross registered tonnage (GRT) is divided by the number of passengers. Hence the Oceanic at 39,241 tons carries 1,000 passengers and has a space ratio of 37.73. With the industry average closer to 26. A small ship does not necessarily mean a crowded ship. the 2,500 GRT *Lindblad Explorer* carries only 92 passengers, so space ratio is a comfortable 27.17. By comparison, the plush *Sagafjord* at 25,000 tons and 425 passengers offers a spacious 58.82 ratio. For space ratio, see Ship Profiles Chapter.

RATIO OF SERVICE CREW TO PASSENGER

It stands to reason that if a ship has 500 crew member and 500 passengers, there's a good chance you'll be pampered. Should the ship have 1,000 passengers and the same crew of 500, you're going to share that attention with another passenger; and should the ship have 1,000 passengers and a crew of 300, it will cut the service even more.

The number of lounges and ballrooms will determine the amount of elbow space per passenger. If the ship carries 1,000 passengers and has one nightclub and one ballroom for entertainment, count on lots of togetherness. On the other hand, if the ship carries 1,000 and has eight lounges, three nightclubs, two ballrooms, six bars, you'll have plenty of opportunity to find a couple of intimate corners, in spite of the number of passengers. In fact, when there is a complete deck devoted to public space, chances are you will never be totally aware of the number of passengers on board.

SHIP REGISTRY

Where the ship is registered or the flag she flies has little influence on the type of vessel she really is. Most ships are registered in countries that offer the most "conveniences." Translated into layman's language, this literally means tax and other financial savings. Hence, a "flag of convenience" is defined as that of a nation with which is registered a merchant ship owned by a person of another nation, so that the owner may effect savings on such expenses as wages and taxes. This practice has become wide-spread over the years, as ship-operating conditions have changed. One thing, however, is certain. Growth of large international companies and the pressure of trade unions have combined to make flag havens welcome ports of refuge for a large number of ships.

Many rusty old tubs found it convenient after World War II to trade under a Panlibhonco (Panama, Liberia, Honduras, Costa Rica) flag, and conditions aboard these vessels varied. To the outsider it appeared that these countries were building substantial fleets, when, in fact, almost all of the ships were foreign-owned.

So you are sailing under a flag of convenience if the control and ownership of the vessel is other than in the country whose flag is flying from the mast.

In response to the many inquiries by passengers, I have checked further into ship registry and have come up with some rather startling statistics. A recent report of the United Kingdom Chamber of Shipping indicates how the flags are flying these days. Back in 1939 Britain had

16,892 ships flying the royal colors; Liberia had none; Japan had 5,427; and Panama had 722. By the end of the last decade the figures had changed dramatically. Britain had 21,782; Liberia had 18,404; Japan had 11,902; and Panama had 4,255; and in 1973 (the latest figures available at press time) Liberia had 49,824; Japan had 35,031; Panama had 9,414; and British flags remained constantly at around 20,000.

The number of ships mentioned include tankers, freighters, cargo liners, and only a small percentage may carry passengers. Also, some countries have built real fleets of merchant and fishing vessels, and it is not easy to determine under which flag the ships of multi-national companies should sail.

Another rather starting figure has surfaced. It is estimated that vessels registered in Cyprus, Honduras, Lebanon, Liberia, Panama, Singapore, and Somalia now represent 23 percent of world tonnage.

The reason for these so-called flags of convenience lies in one word: money. A number of passenger cruise ships have been withdrawn from service or sold because paying union wages has put them in a non-competitive price range. New owners quickly register the vessels in countries where taxes are either minimal or nonexistent.

Many Greek-owned vessels are flying Cypriot flags, and Liberia, until recently, has been regarded purely as a get-rich-quick flag haven. However, the Liberians are getting tougher since a Liberian was elected to the International Maritime Consultancy Organization's Safety Committee. Liberian inspectors now board ships flying their flag three or four times a year, without warning, and look for violations of a new, strict safety code. Licensing of officers has been tightened and continues to be based on United States examinations, the toughest in the world.

So, you ask, what happened to all those ships flying the Stars and Stripes? Tied up, for the most part, or sold off to foreign owners after the waiting period imposed by Congress. But there's more to it.

The real answer was presented on the Senate floor a couple of years ago during a debate designed to channel more oil-tanker trade to U.S.-flag vessels. The gist of the verbal combat indicated it costs an American shipper considerably less to operate under the Liberian flag than to use a vessel registered in the United States.

Liberia offers hard-to-match advantages to shippers. The Liberian government charges $1.20 per 100 feet of cargo space, plus a yearly tax of 10 cents per registered ton of capacity. By contract, American corporate taxes for a ship operating under the U.S. flag could run up to 50 percent of the revenue produced by the vessel.

In addition, American crews cost more. An American seaman is paid at least $20,000 a year, or about twice what his foreign counterpart earns. American-flag ships must deal with American unions and pay costs of work benefits, while Liberian registry is much more lenient and does not require a minimum-size crew, for example.

So, don't be surprised to find that the ship's flag has little influence on the personnel working on board ship. Most vessels turn out to be a tossed salad of nationalities. The engine-room crew may be recruited from one country, the catering and housekeeping from another, while the flag on the mast is of a third. Take Commodore Cruise Line's *Boheme,* for example. The ship is registered in Panama, flies that country's flag, was owned by Swedes and Germans, is operated by an American company, has a German, Spanish, and Italian deck crew and service is by Caribbean and Korean service crew. Even many lines traditionally identified with one country are usually hybrids. P & O has predominantly Genoese, not English, waiters, although the *QE 2* still claims an all-English service and deck staff. Cunard's new *Princess* and *Countess* maintain tradition with British deck crews and service staffs from a dozen Caribbean islands. Royal Caribbean Lines flies the Norwegian flag, has a deck crew from Norway and a service crew from Spain, Korea, and the Caribbean. Sitmar Cruises flies Liberian flags on its vessels, which are staffed by Italians and Portuguese. Carnival Cruise Line's ships fly Panamanian flags, but I couldn't find a single citizen of Panama on board. The deck crew is Italian; the service crew, mixed Korean and Caribbean; and the purser's office is strictly American.

SAFETY AT SEA

The flag flying from the mast has little effect on the safety of passengers and crew because every ship calling at a U.S. port and boarding paying passengers must operate under the rules and regulations of the 1960 SOLAS (Safety of Life at Sea) Law.

All passenger ships (American and foreign registry) are inspected by the U.S. Coast Guard when they call at U.S. ports to make sure they comply with SOLAS. The criteria applied are very close to U.S. safety standards, covering such things as emergency equipment, fire safety regulations, drills for the crew, and safety of the hull and ship's machinery. These standards are agreed to by all major seafaring countries (about 90 nations, including the United States) and have been in effect since 1966.

Even ships from countries not covered by the 1960 SOLAS convention are also inspected and must meet present U.S. standards for safety at sea, which are even more stringent.

Coast Guard inspections are always held during a ship's first call at a U.S. port. A thorough check of safety equipment is made at that time and the vessel is certified to embark passengers in the U.S. After that, periodic inspections are held at least once every three months, when the cruise ship comes dockside at a U.S. port. The Coast Guard has about 90 inspectors assigned to check for ship safety.

So what happens if a ship doesn't measure up? The Coast Guard can either detain the vessel until the problem is corrected, or prohibit her from boarding passengers in U.S. ports until the ship meets requirements.

Shipping companies welcome these Coast Guard inspections and cooperate. I am reminded of a Panamanian-flag ship that recently entered the cruise market. She was highly touted and advertised, but came inaugural sailing day and Coast Guard inspectors were not satisfied with the way her electrical system was put together. She didn't receive sailing papers, and passengers already boarded for this first cruise were disembarked and sent home while the cruise line imported electricians, completely rewired the vessel, and delayed her entry into the U.S. market for about three weeks until she met tough Coast Guard standards.

Since 1965, cruise ships have tightened safety standards at sea by adding automatic fire-doors, smoke detectors, and sprinkling systems. They have eliminated most combustibles used in ship construction. Also, now built into all cruise ships are water-tight compartments with water-tight doors that can be closed from the bridge to prevent the ship from sinking even if several compartments are flooded.

International convention requires that all passengers participate in lifeboat drills on cruise ships. If there is an emergency at sea, passengers will be told via a public-address system what to do. Ship personnel are assigned responsibility for specific passengers. Don't disregard the drill just because it is a nuisance to don the life jacket and report to a muster station. Although accidents at sea are rare, passengers should be familiar with boat stations and emergency procedures.

As far as ship construction is concerned, modern cruise ships are considered fireproof. All countries abiding by the present international convention are required to conduct at least yearly inspections of every ship's hull, machinery, and safety equipment, regardless of the age of the vessel. All of these inspections are in addition to U.S. Coast Guard drills.

According to Lieutenant Commander Theodore J. Polgar, of the

U.S. Coast Guard's inspection-compliance unit, passengers can feel safe on a cruise ship. He says, "You will be safer on a modern cruise ship than in some of the new high-rise buildings; both are designed to be basically fireproof, but on a complying ship there is less danger."

The only time you should check as to whether the ship meets SOLAS requirements is when the ship boards passengers outside the United States and offers air-sea packages. In this type of situation — for instance, when passengers board the ship in Barbados or Martinique or a romantic Greek port — the ship is not inspected by the U.S. Coast Guard, and it's up to travelers to ask whether the ship meets SOLAS requirements.

STABILIZERS

The most highly developed of the active stabilizers is the fin type, usually shaped like a balanced rudder. They are retractable in housings within the vessel. The fins are arranged to tilt through an angle of about 20 degrees. With the ship rolling to port, the port fin is inclined downward from the leading edge and the starboard fin upward. Each fin thus contributes a stabilizing movement. On a roll to starboard, the slope of the fin is reversed. In practice, fins are normally designed to give a roll reduction of about 90 percent, which means that if the ship is equipped with stabilizers, the seas won't seem quite as rough when the fins are in use. Stabilizers don't help when the ship hits seas that cause pitching from bow to stern. That's the motion of the ocean, and technology hasn't yet found a solution to that situation.

CABINS

Selection of your cabin by size should be the most important decision made after selection of the ship you want to sail. You should bear in mind that every penny spent over the advertised minimum rate is spent on the size, location and decor of your cabin. On one class ships, everyone eats the same food, sees the same entertainment and travels to the same ports of call. Only the cabin is different.

Size of your cabin is much more important on long cruises than on short ones because you will be spending more time in the stateroom. Cabin size becomes less important on short cruises and on a ship with an especially lively schedule of activities and entertainment. In selecting a cabin, you should also consider that the cabin is your hotel room for the duration of the voyage.

Photographers shooting pictures for brochures have a way with lenses and angles, and all cabins look huge in brochures. This is misleading. Most newer ships built specifically for cruising are like motels, built for compact efficiency. The more cabins a ship can hold, the greater the passenger capacity and the greater the possibility of financial success. Cabins are larger on older vessels. In determining the size of a cabin from a brochure, compare it on the diagram with the size of the largest suite.

How big is your cabin? That seems an easy-to-answer question, but the information is not readily available on most ships. Deck plans in brochures are color-coded by price and category, but I have found some minimum-sized cabins larger than higher-priced accommodations on some ships. Most passengers sailing newer ships are disappointed when they board and are ushered into their cabin for the first time. They find cabins small, smaller, and smallest. But take heart—even the smallest cabin has space to stow your gear, and as one travel writer put it: "Cabins somehow get larger toward the end of the cruise."

Another ship "expert" recommends a formula as a guide to cabin size. He says most shipboard berths measure 3 by 6 feet (18 square feet). Estimate the number of additional berths the cabin could accommodate. He cites an example: If the diagram shows the cabin has enough room to accommodate two more berths in addition to the berths already in the cabin, multiply 18 square feet by two, giving you 36 square feet. Add to that the two berths in the cabins (an additional 36 square feet) and you come up with 72 square feet. Measure the space off in your own bedroom and decide whether you can live in it or whether it's a sure route to claustrophobia.

TTT: If cabin space is what you're looking for, check the deck plan for the number of closets in the stateroom. A cabin with four or five closets is bound to be larger than one with two closets. Also, unless you don't mind climbing the ladder into an upper berth, be sure the cabin you select shows two larger beds in the diagram. The term generally used is "twin-bedded stateroom," and that could mean one bed on top of the other. Be sure the brochure reads "two lower beds." Another guide to judging cabin size is to check the number of chairs in the cabin. These are indicated on the plan. Some cabins are so small there's no space for even a single chair. (More on cabins in How To Choose Your Cruise Chapter)

AMBIENCE

That's the unknown quality that decides the personality of a ship. Cruise ships usually like to identify with an ethnic group as to food and service. If you are an Anglophile, look for a ship British in flavor. If Italian food is your weakness, look for a ship proud of her Italian chefs and staff. You may even want to combine your ancestry with the type of ship you select. Many passengers do. Ambience also means atmosphere aboard the ship. If you like to dress for dinner and consider a cruise a good time to air out the finery, select a ship that boasts about "formal" nights. If you're the slacks or jeans and no-tie type, look for a ship proud of its "informal casual atmosphere."

Ambience is not confined to ships but is equally applicable to hotels, resorts, restaurants, shops, and bars. Its effect is simple: It makes you feel very comfortable. And it is ambience aboard a ship that results in fierce passenger loyalties, even if the ship is not luxurious. In part, ambience explains the often puzzling passenger attachment to a certain vessel over its more opulent sister. Sometimes such attachments or loyalty extend to an entire steamship line and partially explain heavily patronized cruises sailing side by side with others that have a hard time filling the staterooms. Selecting a cruise ship involves an emotional element not required when booking an airplane seat.

PRICE

The cruise price remains the most complete, all-inclusive package offered in the travel market place. Your ticket includes transportation to the ports listed in the itinerary, room, meals (as much as you can eat and as often as eight times a day and more), shipboard activities, entertainment, use of ship facilities such as swimming pools. Your ship is a floating hotel complex. When you purchase a cruise you buy a total vacation package. Not included in some quoted rates are port taxes (which are collected when you pay for your cruise), and personal onboard expenses. A passenger on a tight budget can figure almost to the penny what his expenses will be for a given number of days on a given ship. There are no cover charges in the nightclubs, no minimums assessed for drinks. Everything in the brochure is included, except for soft drinks, alcoholic beverages, gratuities, shore excursions and gambling. On some European and Greek ships, there are charges for coffee at the bar. Even some American-based ships charge for ice cream in the ice cream parlor, but this is not usual.

TIME IN PORT

How long a ship stays in each port should be a major consideration, if visiting that island or that city influences your selection of the ship. Less than six hours in any port is almost a waste of time. To find actual time in port, add at least an hour to the scheduled arrival time, because it takes that long to clear formalities in each country; then subtract an hour from the sailing time. What you're left with is the time you'll have on shore. And if that leaves you with a feeling of having rushed around a hot and sticky island, don't cruise the ship because of the specific port; look for other reasons. Should you sail anyway, figure the visit was a teaser for your return at another time. Subtract an additional hour or two if the ship tenders. It takes at least that long for the round trip tender ride from ship to shore and back again to mother ship.

Remember that cruising is that unique form of travel where transportation is incidental and the urgency of arriving at a specific destination has been deleted as a requirement. The sojourn aboard ship is the major consideration, the ports of call an added attraction. Read the fine print on your passage contract (cruise ticket), and you'll find the captain has the right to change the itinerary at his discretion, and he does, when certain conditions prevail. There is no voting on his decisions. His vote (and the ship owners') is the only one that counts, and passengers have little to no recourse if the ship doesn't visit all of the ports listed on the brochure. Be assured, however, changes are made only when necessitated by tides or ship mechanical functions, and decisions are not made frivolously.

TTT: In times of fuel shortages and rising costs, ships have a tendency to change course mid-ocean in order to fill up the tanks and probably to conserve fuel. So, cruise lines reserve the right to change itineraries without prior notice. When international conditions swing around to that kind of situation, there's a good chance you may not reach the farthest point on a short cruise. And, the passenger has no recourse. It won't help to threaten to sue and it won't help if fellow passengers take up the cry and pass a petition demanding a refund. The "conditions" of your cruise purchase preclude this type of responsibility. Cruise lines making itinerary changes usually notify travel agents and passengers already booked, so they have the option of canceling prior to sailing time. When changes are made for mechanical reasons, there are no options open to passengers. Select your cruise for the ship and the cruising area of the world. If you happen to miss an island or two, you'll disembark having had more time at sea, and that's not all bad.

TTT: Competition is keen in the cruise industry, and operators are wooing passengers in a number of ways. Special-interest or theme cruises often are staffed with celebrities who perform, lecture, or just sign autographs. During the past year there were "cruises to lose" (weight), gourmet voyages for those interested in learning to cook or who merely enjoy eating; others for those trying to kick the smoking habit; and one that is usually repeated every year before Christmas, for shopping addicts. There have been cruises for singles, lectures on high finance on the high seas, voyages for bird watchers, jazz fiends, science-fiction fans, and those with green thumbs. There are cruises where bridge addicts can earn master points and tennis buffs can improve their game. Cruise ships have served as lecture halls, and even Art Buchwald expounded on the capital on an 'Inside Washington Cruise." There are schools at sea and cruises with a 'Musical Festival at Sea." Shakespeare and concerts were featured on several voyages. Showboats and "name" entertainers are used as lure for passengers. Country-music fans dominated special entertainment cruises. I have never selected a cruise because of a special interest on boat, but if something in particular turns you on, by all means let that influence your choice of ship. It costs no more, and you're bound to meet other people who share your passion for onions or tomatoes, jazz or classical. (More information listed under "entertainment".

PORT OF EMBARKATION

If you live in or near the port of embarkation (port from which a ship sails), by all means visit the ship before you make reservations. Most vessels will welcome you aboard and arrange for an escort to show you through the ship and let you look at the cabin you are planning to book. Other ships require that your travel agent arrange for a visitor's pass in advance. If you are not using a travel agent, you can arrange for your own visitor's pass by telephoning the cruise line office a few days in advance of your proposed visit. The port of embarkation is particularly import if you do not live in a port city and must travel to the ship by plane or by car. Most cruise companies are spending great sums of money to introduce cruising to middle America through air-sea packages that offer reduced-cost air travel to the port of embarkation. (See "Fly and Cruise" chapter.)

Cruising habits are changing, and new ports are emerging as favorites. They are conveniently located for easy outlet to the ocean and easily reached by car, train, or plane. There are guarded parking lots for storing your car while you cruise, and limousines, taxis, and buses to transport you quickly to hotels and airports. (See "Ports of Embarkation" chapter.)

Everything You
Wanted to Know
About Cruising

YOU HAVE SELECTED the ship and the itinerary; now come questions and decisions which should affect your choice.

WHICH CABIN?

Cruising in a deluxe suite with a private terrace adds another dimension to the experience but unless money means very little, be sure you understand that every dollar paid for a cabin above the "loss leader" minimum price is being paid for your cabin on one-class ships. It's the price of the cabin that determines the price of your cruise. You can sail for a lot less than average daily rates on most ships, so once basic price category is matched up with your holiday budget, travelers are well advised to spend time selecting a cabin.

First decision is inside or outside. There are advantages to both with the most obvious being a trade off—a view of the ocean vs money saved. To help with that decision take a look at activities offered on board ship. If you don't plan to spend much time in the cabin, other than sleeping and changing clothes, cabin choice will not make much difference.

You might want to request a deck plan from your travel agent or from the cruise company handling your booking before you make any final decisions. You can select a specific cabin by number and location, or you can decide on a price category and ask your travel agent to talk up for you with the cruise line and get you the best possible cabin within that price category. Savvy agents who do a lot of business with cruise lines have a way of coming up with more than you purchased and cabins are sometimes up-graded. Even if your brochure study comes up with a specific cabin that interests you, give your travel agent a choice of more than one.

The ship brochure tells a lot about the ship. It's a sales tool, but it's also a diagram and map handy when it comes to getting around the ship. The legend explains the symbols, and it's easy to find the dining room, swimming pool, purser's office, or any of the public areas on the diagram. It's more difficult when it comes to judging cabin size. Two straight lines may indicate a bed. A toilet will be shaped like a toilet, but all rooms look large and attractive.

Unfortunately, nothing could be further from the truth. Newer ships built in the 1970s and designed for short cruises offer "compact" cabins, which translates into "very small" to most of us. This in no way means they are not adequate or comfortable for a weekend, a week, or even two weeks of cruising. Cabins are designed so everything has its place, and there is a place for everything you'll need during your time on board. You won't be able to host a cocktail party for more than four, unless your guests use beds and the floor instead of chairs.

In most cases, unless you book far, far in advance, the cabin you select will have already been booked by some other wise cruiser, and you will be forced to take another cabin in the same price category. To help you make a selection, brochures indicate cabin categories (price differentials) by a color-coding system on the deck plan. Check the plan carefully for comparative sizes, facilities, location, and sleeping arrangements.

Cabin prices and categories are determined by space, location, and view. Passengers with definite tastes can choose between extremes—the highest priced suite on the least expensive ship, or the minimum-priced cabin on the most expensive ship. High livers probably won't enjoy the minimum on a ship like the *QE 2*, but that cabin or the minimum cabin on any cruise ship afloat is the best buy on the vessel.

The bad news on "minimum" is: There are very few. Sometimes less than three percent of the total number of accommodations are classified as minimum," and they sell quickly. It is interesting to note that the most expensive and the least expensive accommodations on all ships are booked first, which leaves average-priced cabins in the "usually available" category.

For a better insight on cabin prices: Highest-priced accommodations go for about two or three times the cost of the lowest, while actual physical differences are rarely in the same proportion. Middle-range staterooms are likely to differ from the best or the worst by deck and a few square feet of elbow room in the cabin. On many ships, cabins are identical, and only location by deck and view determines price differentials.

Higher-priced cabins on some ships mean tub bath and twin beds, while lowest priced will have a shower and an upper and lower bunk.

Many of the newer vessels and some older ships built for transocean voyages do not have these differences. Most cabins have lower beds and facilities (wash basin, toilet, shower and/or tub bath). A few of the older vessels still have cabins with "share facilities," which means the bathroom is between two staterooms and four persons share. Outside cabins are always priced higher than inside cabins because of portholes and windows with a view of the waters. But unless you are claustrophobic, the inside cabin may have just as much to offer as the outside. Size could be the same, and it may be located on the same deck in the same ship position, across the hall from the outside cabin. A disadvantage to some outside cabins is you may have to keep curtains drawn to protect your privacy from peeping deck-strollers.

Portholes are no longer a source of fresh air. They are sealed on all completely air-conditioned cruise ships. Many have individual temperature controls in each stateroom, called "climate controls" in the Profiles Chapter.

Another point worth noting, and one that influences the price of your cabin, is: The higher the deck, the higher the cost. Ours is not to reason why, except that uppermost decks are "status symbols."

LOCATION OF THE CABIN

How far forward or aft are you willing to book in order to save money? And how far up or down are you willing to sleep for the same reason?

A tradition of the sea is "the higher the price, the higher the deck." Before air conditioning and modern, quiet engines (diesel ships may still vibrate a bit more but are faster than turbine), upper-deck cabins were coolest, quietest, and sunniest. They still may be sunniest and most prestigious, but disadvantages make them a poor money value. Because they are farther from the ship's center of gravity, there is more motion, and, on some ships, topside may be a long way to public rooms and the dining room, which are usually close to the water line.

If you are thinking of sailing high, you should know that late-late bars are generally located topside, and swingers have been known to be noisy until dawn. Another source of noise and activity are the nursery and teen rooms. I was once berthed in a cabin directly below a teenager discotheque, and the rock and roll beat like steel hammers over my head into the wee hours.

Study deck plans carefully! Do you want to be close to the dining room, bar, nightclub, swimming pool? Will early-morning joggers pass your windows as you settle into a deep sleep? If you depend on elevators, do you want a long walk before you reach one? Cabins close to engine rooms and air-conditioning units may vibrate more than others, and if your cabin is near the galley, remember: Chefs start working when the rest of the ship goes to bed.

A vertical cutaway of the deck plan will show how close a cabin is to the various public rooms, so look closely at whether your cabin is on or off a main passageway (it's a lot quieter off).

Decks may have fancy names or be designated by alphabet letters from the water line and below, but that's where most minimum-priced cabins without windows or portholes are located.

Some people buy the highest-priced cabins and suites for the intangibles they offer (like dressing room, bidet and sitting areas), not to mention a guaranteed invitation to the captain's private VIP party. Some passengers prefer the lowest-priced cabins because they are getting the best buy on the ship; but most of us find comfort, convenience, and happiness in average-priced cabins, inside or outside, as long as they are on a middle deck. (Dead center of the ship is the point with the least motion.)

TTT FOR HONEYMOONERS: If you are planning to honeymoon on board ship (first, second, or repeat), and are looking forward to sharing the bed with your mate, be sure to check the bed arrangements on the ship of your choice. Most ships have single beds that cannot be moved together, and you'll get nowhere with the purser when you try to explain that your travel agent said the beds could be moved together. Almost all ships have a limited number of cabins with double or king-size beds. One super-nice ship has only two suites with king-size beds, and no double beds. A couple of ships have staterooms that convert to double-bedded accommodations, and some are now offering "junior double" beds and a promise of much togetherness. More and more ships are converting less desirable cabins into double-bedded cabins because of heavy demand. However, a number of the very new ships of the 1980s only have single beds which do not move. Many well planned pre-sailing arrangements made by travel agents have turned into disappointments the minute honeymooners are shown to their cabin and discover stationary single bunks. Worse still when they discover upper and lower bunks. Travel agents are not infallible and if a double, queen or king-sized bed is important to the enjoyment of your cruise, check-up it out yourself. The type of bed in each cabin is described in the brochure. If you aren't sure, telephone the cruise line and be sure your confirmation of reservations and payment shows the type of sleeping arrangements you have been promised. Whatever you do, my best advice is don't count on rearranging the furniture to accommodate your sleeping habits once you leave port. Many a romance at sea has stalled at the rail because of cabin bed-arrangements. I read someplace that 75 percent of the world's married couples sleep in the same bed at home, and if altering your sleeping habits will ruin your cruise, look for a different ship. Moving mattresses to the floor can become quite a hassle and can be embarrassing if you don't put them back on the beds before the room steward arrives in the morning. Check the "Ship Profiles" chapter for ships with double-bedded cabins.

TTT UPDATE: Some of the new $100 million-plus vessels are taking double-bed requests seriously and are designing shipboard sleeping arrangements so single beds can swing together for instant conversion into doubles. Room stewards can flip them around without any problem, but the cabin will become instantly smaller with that arrangement. These same room stewards don't want to bother, in most cases, with converting the cabins to suit your day and/or night requirements, so what you decide — single or double beds — is what you'll cruise with for the duration.

TRAVELING ALONE

Nothing gripes a single passenger more than rate quotes of "per person, double occupancy," when all he or she wants is "single occupancy." There are ways of traveling solo and still taking advantage of the per person, double rate. Most cruise companies will go to some length to team single travelers (of the same sex), but it is easier to find a roommate if you're a woman. Most shared cabins are occupied by two women rather than two men. For some reason, men are reluctant to share. Some ships are offering their least desirable or smallest cabins to singles at no price increase over the per-person, double-occupancy rate.

Cabins are not limited to sleeping arrangements for two, and on some ships three and even four can share, and often at handsome savings. Your travel agent or the cruise line will try to find roommates, and all you need to do is pay the per-person rate. If you get lucky, you may pay for one-fourth of the cabin and end up with just a single roommate.

When booking, if you are traveling alone, tell your travel agent or ship line that you will book only on the per person, double basis. Once the cruise company has accepted your money, they will try to find a roommate (of the same sex and near your age), and the two of you will meet at sailing time. Should the ship be unable to come up with a roommate, you'll have the cabin to yourself at no extra cost. Should the cruise company refuse to accept your booking for half the cabin until they can find a roommate, last minute rechecking often changes their attitude.

If you are single and want to remain that way in your cabin, expect to pay from 50 to 100 percent over the per person, double rate. For instance, if the per person, double occupancy rate is $500, the total cabin would sell for $1,000 and sailing alone will cost you from $750 to $1,000 for the cabin. What price solitude!

Cruise ships are not always completely filled and some companies are marketing aggressively to the single market by offerings to "guarantee" the per person, double rate 30 days before sailing date. Information is detailed in Ship Profiles Chapter.

TTT: Traveling alone on board ship is not the same as traveling alone on shore. There's one great difference. You may not know anyone when you board, but if you disembark in the same condition, it's because you preferred it that way. Ships have a way of blending strangers. Without even trying, you will know your fellow tablemates in the dining room, the passengers who sit near you at entertainment events, out on deck, in game rooms and at activities. If you want to meet other singles, there are single parties where cruise staff members handle introductions. One ship has even designated a smaller bar-lounge as gathering grounds for "Singles' Happy Hours" on a daily basis. Women traveling alone who are uncomfortable about frequenting a bar without male companionship have nothing to feel uncomfortable about on board ship. Fellow single travelers are in the "same boat". Singles who don't want to meet other singles and/or other people, don't vacation on cruises. My best advice is pre-request dining room seating at the largest possible table. I always select a table for eight. That way I'm fairly certain I'll find at least four compatible folks with whom to share my meals. When pre-selection is not possible, as soon as you board, run, don't walk, to the maitre d'. With your best smile showing (and perhaps a gratuity), ask for a table for eight with other singles. If you are female, make sure you will not be dining with seven others of the same sex. It is sometimes safer to request a "mixed table', meaning a few singles and a married couple or two. If you are male, don't worry. You have a good chance of being outnumbered by the opposite sex.

You need only worry about the age of your tablemates. Single travelers usually prefer late seatings. There's more time in the lounges to linger longer before dinner.

TTT: Check on Royal Cruise Line's "socializers" program if you are a single woman and want to make sure you are asked to dance a few times during the cruise. (See Royal Cruise Line profile)

PAYING FOR THE CRUISE

Deposits and cancellation penalties vary slightly from ship to ship, but the usual procedure requires a 25 percent deposit with your travel agent or cruise line at the time your reservation is confirmed. The balance is due 60 days before departure. There is no penalty if you cancel at least 30 days before sailing. At the discretion and policy of the cruise line you can be charged 25 percent of your cruise fare as a penalty if you cancel within 6 to 30 days of sailing. There could be a 50 percent penalty if you notify the company of your changed plans within five days of sailing, and if you don't show when the ship pulls up the lines, you can be charged full fare. You can also forfeit the price of the cruise if you simply miss the ship. Obviously, if you or a member of your family becomes too sick to sail, you can usually get a full rebate, but the cruise line may ask for doctor's verification of the fact.

It's easy to understand the ship's position. An empty cabin at sailing time is revenue that can never be recouped.

TTT: Travel insurance to cover last-minute cancellations or a return home before the end of the cruise because of illness in the immediate family, or because you have taken ill, is available at nominal rates through travel agencies. If your cruise is taking you halfway around the world or out of your familiar neighborhood, travel insurance is strongly recommended. Some companies now offer trip-interruption insurance which covers emergency situations requiring air transport to hospitals.

TTT: For the cabin of your choice on the ship and sailing of your choice, book as far in advance as possible. In checking with fifteen cruise lines I learned that minimum cabins are booked sometimes one year in advance, but this does not mean minimums are not available as sailing time draws near. There are usually cancellations in every price category, and cruise lines have been known to realign cabin categories. There's a good chance of getting what you want on a last-minute basis. Some cruise lines accept T.B.A. reservations at minimum or average rates. T.B.A. means "to be assigned" and guarantees that you will sail on the specific cruise in a cabin at least as good as the price you paid. Your tickets will be issued "T.B.A." with no cabin number showing. At check-in time you will be assigned a cabin, and chances are it will be better than what you paid for. Ask your travel agent whether a T.B.A. is possible on the ship of your choice. (Also known as "guaranteed rate".)

TTT: All cruise ships offer discounts of about 10 percent for group sailings. Unlike airlines, which are controlled by government regulations as to the size of a "group," each cruise line makes it own rules. Generally, the discount is available through travel agents for groups using fifteen or more cabins. The travel agent also receives "free" cabins in direct relationship to the number of cabins purchased by the group. These "free" cabins are intended for the use of "tour conductors" but are frequently turned back to the group in order to offer further price reductions to participating passengers.

BEFORE YOU EMBARK

Documentation and Inoculations

Depending on your ship's itinerary, you may need a passport or other proof of citizenship. United States and Canadian citizens traveling by ship to Caribbean islands, Bermuda, Bahamas or Mexico need only proof of citizenship in the form of a passport (either valid or recently expired), a birth certificate or certified copy, Voter's Registration Card showing your signature, or a U.S. naturalization certificate.

Aliens who have been admitted to the United States for permanent residence should bring their Alien Registration Receipt Card, Form I–151 or I–155l. In addition, some aliens may be required to have sailing permits and should check with their local Internal Revenue Office. Other noncitizens must have valid passports and necessary visas for the countries visited during the cruise. They must also have a visa that allows re-entry into the United States if it is a round trip cruise.

No documentation is required of U.S. citizens for cruises to Alaska and Canada. In some ports—Leningrad, for example—the visa requirement is waived for one-day visitors or the ship is given a "group visa" which covers all passengers eligible to go ashore. Mediterranean and North Sea cruises require passports, although most have dropped visa requirements for cruise passengers.

For Mexico, ports in South America, Mediterranean and Asia, some companies still list the requirement of an International Smallpox Vaccination Certificate although the World Health Organization no longer lists it as a requirement. Check with the U.S. Health Department when in doubt.

Baggage

The number of suitcases you take on a cruise is not really limited. Most ships do not have luggage storage rooms or space to stack your lug gage during the voyage, so you'll be living with suitcases in your cabin. You should block-print your name and cabin number on baggage tags and firmly attach them to your luggage before arriving at the port of embark ation. And you might want to consider soft-sided luggage that will fit under beds. (It helps stretch the size of the cabin if you don't have to trip over luggage.) If you have more luggage than you can hide in your room and out of the way, ask your room steward to store it for you. It is surprising how he can find corners you never saw.

Bon Voyage Party

Arrangements do not have to be made at the time you book your cruise, but you should notify the cruise line through your travel agent at least one week in advance of sailing as to the number of guests you expect and what you will need in the way of canapes, ice, setups, and liquor. Few companies will allow you to bring your own liquor for these parties. There will be no charge for the ice and glasses, but setups and canapes will be charged to you, and you should know what it costs at the time you make your arrangements. (A tray of hors d'oeuvres could run up to $35 on some ships.) Your room steward will be helping with your party if it is held in your stateroom. You do not have to tip him for these efforts, but he should be remembered at the end of the voyage for "service beyond the call of duty." If your party is large and a public room on board ship is used, you will not be allowed to bring your own liquor under any circumstances, and you will be expected to pay for and tip waiters serving your party.

Visitors Before Sailing

Visitors will need passes to board the ship, and it is a good idea to request the required number of visitor passes from your travel agent or the cruise line in advance of sailing day. Should a guest show up at the dock without a pass, a cruise line representative is always on the dock before sailing, and the guest should have no problem getting aboard.

Some lines have put the lid on visitors and are limiting the number of guests, so prevent embarrassment by making advance arrangements for visitors and guests expected at your bon voyage party.

I have had difficulty boarding a number of ships recently. Cunard and Royal Caribbean Cruise Lines have tough policies when it comes to guests. I can understand their reluctance particularly in California and New York ports where sailing days have become bon voyage days to parting crowds and they come aboard in droves. On a recent sailing from San Francisco, the ship looked empty once the visitors were piped ashore. Incidentally, if visitors miss the last call to go ashore and accidentally sail with the vessel, they are "stowaways" and will be required to pay for passage and their own return plane fare from the next port of call.

EMBARKATION (BOARDING YOUR SHIP)

Embarkation begins three or four hours before sailing, so plan your port arrival accordingly. You will be greeted by longshoremen who will take the luggage out of the vehicle and stack it with other baggage to be loaded on the ship. The next time you see your baggage will be in your cabin. The longshoremen or porters on the dock handling the luggage ex pact to be tipped, although signs usually say "tipping is not necessary." Depending on the port from which you are sailing and the number of bags, your tip will vary from 50 cents to $2. Secured parking for your car is available at all ports of embarkation. When transfers are included in air sea packages, no luggage-handling at the pier is required.

TTT: No baggage-claim checks are issued when you hand the porter your baggage at the pier, but few bags (if any) ever go astray between pier and cabin. However, I'm told most cruise lines assume responsibility for your baggage once it is turned over to their representative on the dock. Long shoremen have a passenger manifest, and when they take your baggage from you, they check your name on the list and note the number of bags you have given to them.

Procedure

You will have received an embarkation form (sometimes called an immigration form) in the same envelope with your cruise tickets. This must be completed for the ship's manifest and immigration purposes.

TTT: To avoid delays and unhappy stares from other passengers, complete this form before you get to the check-in counter. Some of the questions on the immigration form are personal, so if you don't feel like telling your age, leave it blank. The required information is: name, address, place of birth, marital status, sex, occupation, passport or alien-registration number (where required for entry), and your signature.

When you arrive at the pier, a clerk will take your documentation and cruise tickets. Check-in procedure is very much like what you expect at an airport. At the ship entrance (sometimes up a flight of stairs), stewards or members of the cruise staff direct you or escort you to your stateroom. Your room steward usually introduces himself shortly after you arrive, and there's nothing more to do except join parting passengers until your baggage is delivered to the cabin. This sometimes takes until sailing time, or even later, then it's time to unpack and settle down into your "home away from home."

Dining Room Reservations

Whenever possible, reserve your dining room table and seating at the time you book your cruise. This avoids standing in line when you board your ship. Some companies pre-reserve by early or late seating only, and require that passengers check with the dining room for specific table assign ments. Others reserve specific tables at early or late seatings and the information is waiting for passengers in their cabins at embarkation. If there is any doubt, check with the dining room as soon as you embark. If you are traveling with friends, make sure you list their names and they list yours as requested table-mates. I have seen families separated because of confused requests. Even if you have made specific dining room requests, if your table assignment card is not waiting for you in your cabin when you embark, check immediately with the dining room. There's many a slip between requests and sailing day and if a problem develops, don't be timid. You are well armed when your sailing confirmation also confirms all of your shipboard special requests, including dining room seating.

Special Diets

At the time your cabin is confirmed, arrange for and order special foods you will require during your cruise. Ask your travel agent to write to the cruise line, listing your requirements, and ask for a copy of the letter and reply confirming your request. Most ships will cater to salt-free diets, reducing diets, diabetic diets, some kosher meals, and other special needs, but it is advisable to make all arrangements prior to sailing. (See "Ship Profiles" chapter.) However, some ships are not equipped to handle special food requirements or requests, and you should check before you book.

Deck Chairs

Deck chairs are reserved on some ships, and if this is the procedure, reserve your chairs and decide whether you want sun, shade, solitude, or companionship. The chief deck steward will help with the decision. Deck chair charges run between $2 and $6 per week on some ships. Ships that do not charge do not reserve deck chairs.

Mal de Mer, or Will I Get Seasick?

Most people don't these days! Modern cruise ships are equipped with stabilizers that are activated when the seas kick up. Stabilizers are used at the captain's discretion to make for a better ride and to keep the ship from rolling with the waves. But stabilizers are not too effective against forward and backward motion (called pitching); so if you experience a light-headed feeling, a queasy tummy, and a slight headache, don't despair. Motion-sickness tablets have been known to correct the symptoms within an hour or so.

To put some horror stories to rest: These non-prescription medicines haven't been around that long, and nothing short of privacy compares with sea sickness when it comes to discouraging sea travel. Boredom, scurvy, claustrophobia, hijacking, sun stroke, malaria, shipwreck, ice or fog do not compare with the dread of suffering from *mal de mer*.

Anyone who has ever been seasick — I mean really seasick, not just "squeamish" — knows it is the only and ultimate kind of seasickness. Early sea travelers tried everything: Mothersill's Seasick Remedy, morphine with atropine, pork fried with garlic, sea water, arrowroot and wine, tomato sauce, mustard leaf, cocaine, a belladonna plaster on the stomach, sodium phenobarbital. Like Mothersill's, these remedies worked for the most part only for those who thought it did.

Scientific investigation over a period of years indicated that seasickness could not really be blamed entirely on psychogenic factors, but until about thirty years ago, the time-honored method of medical treatment of seasickness were the words: "It's all in your mind."

The true remedy for seasickness (apart from the contributions made by engineering and construction of ships that take the waves a lot better because of bow, beam, and stabilizers) came abruptly and quite by accident. The cure was discovered at the allergy clinic of Johns Hopkins University Hospital in Baltimore. A couple of doctors were researching the use of several drugs for the relief of allergenic conditions. One of the drugs used was a synthetic antihistimine, $C_{17}H_{22}No.C_7H_6ClN_4O_2$, called "dimenhydrinate" (later known as Dramamine). They were giving it to pregnant patients afflicted with allergies. Their patients soon began reporting that the drug also was soothing car sickness and nausea.

When Dr. Leslie Gay and Dr. Paul Carliner reported their findings to the U.S. Army, they decided to test it for seasickness aboard a troop transport ferrying military personnel and their families between New York and Germany. The ship was the *USAT* (U.S. Army Transport) *General Ballou,* a 13,000-tonner carrying some 1,400 passengers. The voyage selected for the trial was in November 1945, when the seas are normally obligingly rough. Doctors Gay and Carliner divided the five hundred men selected into two groups. The first group was then subdivided and each man was given a 100-milligram capsule of Dramamine just as the ship left New York Harbor. The second part of this group received a sugar capsule. Only the doctors knew which pills were Dramamine. Similar capsules were distributed six hours later, and each man received another before each meal and before retiring at night. Of the 135 who took Dramamine, not a single passenger complained of nausea or vomiting. Of the sugar-takers, 35 became seasick within twelve hours of sailing, and they, too, recovered within three hours after taking the Dramamine. More than 65 percent of the remaining passengers on the ship were seriously seasick in the turbulent waters of the Atlantic.

I did not know of the *General Ballou's* contribution to sea travel until I began my research for this chapter of THE TOTAL TRAVELER BY SHIP. I sailed the *Ballou* from New York through the Panama Canal to Tokyo and was introduced on board to Dramamine whenever the seas kicked up. Too bad the ship and crew were not awarded a plaque for historic contribution to sea travel.

The discovery of Dramamine suddenly made obsolete other remedies for the prevention, cure, and endurance of *mal de mer.*

There have been improvements in the original Dramamine formula, and a number of drug companies offer non-prescription and prescription motion-sickness medicines. Should you board the ship without them, your room steward, the purser's office, or the ship's hospital will dispense them without cost. If you want to bring your own, there are the likes of Bonamine, Dramamine, or Marezine in the non-prescription section of most drugstores. In severe cases the ship's doctor will administer an injection that I have seen cure motion sickness in time for the passenger to enjoy his next meal.

Now comes a bandage instead of a pill to cure seasickness. It doesn't go on your stomach, nor on your sweating brow, but behind the ear. Transderm-V is a small, bandage-like product that goes behind the ear. It re leases, by absorption into your blood stream, medication that supposedly blocks responses from that portion of your nervous system responsible for *mal d'mer*. What it releases is actually a continuous dose of scopolamine for 72 hours. It resembles a flesh colored band aid about the size of a dime. A prescription is required and most doctors know about it.

After much research, developers of the product say motion sickness results because of "multidirectional acceleration a deceleration while riding in a car, ship or airplane and that affects our normal balance which is maintained by visual cues and from the inner ear." The balance half of the inner ear (the other half's for hearing) has structures monitoring linear acceleration and semi-circular canals for turning movements. When motion sickness occurs, nerve impulses are moving rapidly from the inner ear to the brain. So, when you are sitting in a cabin, looking at walls which appear stationary while the ship is constantly rocking, motion sickness is likely to develop.

What Scopolamine does is slow the outpouring of these impulses and this helps calm the inner ear's response to the disparity of balance.

Encouraging news is that studies at sea have shown Transderm-V to be very effective in reducing drowsiness, motion sickness and other unpleasant affects of sickness at sea.

The patch is attached to a hairless portion of the skin behind the ear, an area of high pore concentration. Constant minute amounts of scopolamine permeate the intact skin directly into the bloodstream. Usually by the time the Transderm-V effectiveness has worn off, travelers have become accustomed to the motion of the ocean, but a new patch can be applied for seasickness which persists.

There could be some side effects so it is recommended you consult your physician before using the system. It costs about $3.50 for a two-disc package.

There are other approaches to motion sickness that, mixed with common sense, may effect a cure without medication. Lots of fresh air, deep breathing, and no over-indulging in tempting food and drink. Motion sickness has a tendency to make you feel as though your clothing is tight. When the seas swell, you may have a tendency to expand in the same direction. If you're included toward motion sickness, wear your loosest garments and try a couple of meals of dry soda-crackers. I know an old salt who says the best cure is a good shot of brandy to go along with the soda crackers.

SHIPBOARD FACILITIES

Although facilities and conveniences vary from ship to ship, most offer similar, if not identical, services. The degree and quality of these services differ. Every attempt has been made to detail the services and differences in the "Ship Profiles" chapter.

Banking

The U.S. dollar is legal currency on ships sailing from U.S. ports. On ships sailing from Mediterranean, British, or other ports, currency used on board is usually based on either the ship registry or ownership. The purser's office maintains a bank for cashing travelers checks, but his supply of cash is often limited on non-U.S.-based ships. Caribbean cruising vessels always have enough greenbacks on hand to take care of demand. Some vessels allow passengers to sign for their bar tabs and then settle accounts on the last day of the voyage. In those cases most major credit cards will be honored. Check this point in the "Ship Profiles" chapter and again with your travel agent, because ships sometimes change procedures in midstream. The information will serve as a guide as to the amount of cash or traveler's checks you will need for the journey. Personal checks are not cashed on board most cruise ships.

TTT: Should you run short of cash, use your credit cards in ports of call for the allowable cash. Visa and American Express and others allow you $250 with your card. Carte Blanche and American Express allow up to $500. Gold Cards and VIP cards allow more. Also, where other than U.S. currency is used on board ship, you can expect about a 10 percent differential in favor of the ship on the exchange,as compared to the official rate. The purser calls this "breakage," but it's more like extra revenue for the ship. If you learn that the ship you will be sailing will be using English pounds, for instance, you might want to exchange your money in a bank en route to the ship. You'll be pence and pounds ahead, and there's no problem converting back if you have extra. If you follow my advice, when you decide on how much to convert, remember that tipping is in whatever currency is "official" on board but dollars are always accepted. Many ships bring local bank representatives on board when the ship arrives in port. This is a great convenience to passengers and the exchange is at bank rates. The bank representative usually stays on board until an hour or so before the ship sails so passengers can convert leftover local currency back into dollars. When this system is used, passengers are advised of hours and exchange rate in the daily bulletin or newspaper.

Safety Deposit Boxes

Most ships have them. They are available to passengers from the purser in charge of the ship's bank. It is advisable for passengers to deposit valuables and large sums of money in safety deposit boxes, particularly when the ship is in port. Some ships have 24 hour access to the vaults; others 12 hours.

Bars

Opening and closing times of bars are announced. Bar prices are listed and alcoholic mixed drinks are priced close to the two-dollar mark. The sale of alcoholic beverages may be restricted by U.S. Customs while the ship is in port and in territorial waters, or the price may be higher during that time period because of taxes. The good old days when a Scotch and soda cost 35 cents have disappeared. It's hard to find a ship charging less than $1.85 per drink, and, sorry to say, it's getting easy to find ships where drinks are going for more than $2.50 per.

Letters, Parcels, and Telegrams

These will be delivered to your cabin shortly after they are received on board. Your packet of travel documents should have names and address of the shipping company's port agents who receive the ship mail and deliver it to the vessel when it arrives in port. If your packet does not include contact at sea addresses, ask your travel agent to get it for you or contact the cruise line if you want to receive letters from home while you are cruising. Leave this information with family, friends or the office and include the ship's radio call-letters for emergency purposes.

Keeping In Touch

Just because you're out at sea doesn't mean you must be out of touch with family, friends or business. All ships are equipped with radio and telegraph facilities, and, depending on sophistication of the equipment, it is possible to telephone anywhere in the world from the radio room, and on some ships from the telephone in your stateroom. The radio operator will assist you with rates and placing calls. You may be asked to pay in cash for your telephone call immediately upon completion, and you will not be allowed to reverse the charges. On some of the new ships, passengers have the option of placing telephone calls through the marine operator or through satellite communications networks. Prices vary. On one ship, it cost me only $15 to telephone Miami from somewhere off the coast of China. On another, it was $30 to call Miami from somewhere off the coast of Colombia. Due to International Law, the Radio Station is closed while the ship is in port. Ship information office will assist you in locating communications facilities on shore. Almost all ships have intra-vessel telephone service so you can telephone other passengers and ship offices.

News Bulletins

Daily broadcasts on the ship's radio or loudspeaker system and a printed daily program keep passengers advised of port arrival times, entertainment, scheduled meal-hours, and limited news of the outside world. Read them if you want to know what's happening on board. There is also a brief headline type of newspaper but it's enough to highlight important news and sports events.

Electricity on Board

Most ships have a 110/115-volt AC outlet in the bathroom for the exclusive use of electric shavers. Your hair dryer will not operate from this outlet. Voltage current and cycles vary from ship to ship, and plugging in without checking could destroy your appliance. Some of the newer ships have 110-volt outlets in staterooms, but most do not. If that's the case, ask your room steward for the loan of a converter that will step the 220 volts down to 110, or ask him where you can safely use your curler or dryer. I travel with voltage convertible appliances and only need adapters to use whatever current is available. Adapters are available in ship store's or from room stewards.

TTT: There's a handy converter-adapter on the market that weighs about 3 ounces and converts the current in your stateroom. My hair blower works more slowly, but it saves me the embarrassment of walking down plush hallways to a laundry room to plug in the hair dryer.

Don't forget that special adapter so your two-prong plug will fit into the three-prong socket.

TTT: Contact lens wearers who need to clean lenses electronically, should try using the shaver outlet. It has worked for me. I'm told the cycles are slower and that's why it works. But keep an eye on the process and turn it off after 25 minutes. Also, bring extra lens supplies with you. Very few ships stock even the basic necessities like cleaner or lubricant and it is sometimes hard to get on small islands.

Hairdressing

All ships have hairdressing salons for men and women. The beauty shop gets mighty busy halfway through a cruise, and early appointments are suggested. Expect to pay about $15 for a shampoo and set, plus a $2 tip. Same for men.

Sauna and Massage

Saunas are available at no charge to passengers on some ships; others charge a nominal $4 or $5 fee. Massage is usually by a masseuse or masseur who takes care of both sexes, and the charge is from about $15 for a half-hour rubdown.

Laundry

Ships on cruises longer than one week offer valet laundry service, and price lists and laundry bags are available from your room steward. Others have laundry rooms with electric washers and dryers for the use of passengers, at no charge. Some ships even furnish the soap. There is also an iron and ironing board available for passengers' use in laundry rooms, and the room steward will arrange to have your clothes pressed, as needed, by professionals for a reasonable fee. Some machines require a token, obtainable at the purser's office for about 50 cents.

Library

Ships' libraries range from fair to excellent, but most ships have adequate reading material at no cost. Most require a deposit of a dollar or two, which is intended as a tip to the librarian when the last book is returned. Some are now asking for $5 deposits.

Medical Services

All cruise ships have medical facilities, but they are not required to provide more than emergency care, which is usually no problem on Caribbean, Mexican and Alaska cruises because the next port of call is never more than twenty-four hours away. There is always a doctor on board, sometimes two, and at least one nurse. Some ships are equipped with small hospitals. There is no charge for treatment of mal de mer (seasickness), but doctors do charge for treatment of conditions unrelated to shipboard travel. The fee is generally $15 for treatment in the hospital and $20 if the doctor visits you in your stateroom. Only limited amounts of prescription medicines are available on board ship, so passengers are advised to take an adequate supply with them.

TTT: If you suffer from a chronic ailment that may require special care during your cruise, be sure to ask your home town doctor for a brief medical history, just in case. It will help the ship's doctor treat you. This also is true if you are allergic to specific foods or medicines. Remember, the ship is equipped to handle first-aid care on an emergency basis. More serious conditions may require hospitalization, in which case the ship's doctor has the authority to hospitalize you in the next port of call, or the ship will arrange for your transportation back home. This will be at your own expense, and there is no refund due you for the unused portion of your cruise. Insurance is available through your travel agent for this type of trip cancellation.

TTT: Be sure your teeth are in good condition if you're off on a long cruise. Very few ships have dentists on board, and a ship's doctor can do little more for your toothache than prescribe a couple of aspirins.

Church Services

Most ships have a minister, priest, or rabbi who officiates at all denominational services. Announcements are made daily on board ship.

Ship Shops

Every ship has shops. Not surprisingly, the ships stock items passengers are bound to forget, such as toothbrushes, toothpaste, hair spray, and the like, but more interesting are the luxury items carried in ship stores. These shops are duty-free, which means the shopkeeper did not pay duty on the items he is selling, but you will have to declare what you buy in the ship store on your customs declaration. Perfumes, crystal, cameras, and jewelry are sometimes cheaper on board ship than on shore, and it pays to check them out. Some shops are lavish, other stock little more than essentials.

DINING AT SEA

I like to compare a cruise with a summer camp for grownups — a summer camp where you can have seconds and thirds of all your favorite foods. You can eat when you like and what you like. A cruise is really a movable feast. I have yet to know a cruise passenger who disembarks and complains that he is hungry. The opposite is true — most passengers complain they eat too much. That's part of cruising! Cruise lines go to great lengths to tempt you with gourmet delicacies, three regular meals, several buffets, and extra goodies every day of the cruise. Every dish served may not be your favorite, but the passenger with an open mind is bound to find something to satisfy his or her taste buds. If you sail a Greek vessel, expect Greek food. The same goes for ships of other nationalities, but most serve ethnic dishes from all over the world in addition to their own.

In an extensive survey conducted by a major cruise line trying to determine what makes a passenger select a specific ship, it was discovered that nothing influences the travelers' choice more than food. So if when you go out for dinner you prefer a French restaurant, look for a ship specializing in rich French food. Italian? Greek? Scandinavian? if you have a special fondness for specific ethnic foods, let that preference influence your choice of vessel and you'll be happy for the length of the voyage.

This is not to say that an Italian ship serves only spaghetti and pizza, but there's a better than even chance the specialty of the house will equal the best available in an Italian restaurant back home or in an excellent restaurant in Italy.

If you like plain food and not much spice, your best bet may be a British ship. The food is plentiful and uncluttered by rich sauces, and you can even get plain boiled potatoes and plain roast beef. You can, of course, order plain boiled potatoes with plain roast beef on any ship and have it for just about every meal if you like but if you're sailing a French ship or one that prides herself on food, the chef might be tempted to quit his job in mid-ocean and your waiter may abandon ship.

Norwegian and Swedish cruise ships are likely to dazzle you with smorgasbords, and on Dutch ships you may get a sampling of such well-known Dutch colonial specialties as the spicy Javanese rijsttafel and nasi goreng.

I have selected several menus from different ships for your inspection, but let's assume there's nothing on the menu that appeals to your taste buds. Any recourse: Summon the head waiter (captain) assigned to your section of the dining room and request a special order of anything you like. There's no assurance he will be able to whip up pheasant under glass within twenty minutes, but there's usually steak or chicken available on most ships (on some it may be cheese and crackers).

Not all ships accommodate special food requests, but if they do, special orders for crepes, caviar, lobster, flaming dishes, or the like should be placed the day before. Birthdays, anniversaries, or just plain "I love you" parties should be arranged twenty-four hours in advance on board ship. There is no charge for these special orders and no charge for birthday cakes. In fact, there's no extra charge if you order every single thing on the menu every day of your cruise. You may end up paying something to the ship's doctor for stomach treatment, but not for the food.

Ships stake reputations on their chefs. Some cuisines follow the ethnic and cultural personalities and images portrayed by the cruise line. Most ships advertise "international cuisine," which can mean anything from a menu featuring dishes from different countries to gourmet chefs and flaming dishes. With rising costs of food and labor, many ship lines have turned food and beverage departments over to catering firms. They pay these companies a fixed price per passenger and per crew member for the food, and the bars are part of the concessionaire's domain. In such instances special orders may be limited.

There are two seatings in the dining rooms where passenger capacity is greater than dining-room capacity. Usual dinner hours are 6:30 and 8:30, lunch is at noon and 1:30 p.m., and breakfast is anytime until 9:30 or 10:00. Dining times are known as the first and second seatings or the main and late sittings; when you eat is a personal choice, and the decision must be made at the time you make your dining-room reservations. There are advantages to both seatings. Earlier dining allows time for a movie and entertainment in the evening. Later dining allows time for a cocktail party before dinner.

TTT: Don't let tablemates spoil your appetite. If you have been seated with people who make you feel uncomfortable or your food tastes differ dramatically, ask the maitre d'hotel (or captain) to change your table before you have eaten too many meals together and a change might be embarrassing. Hearty eaters can have their cruise ruined if they sit with picky snackers and vice versa. Don't be timid in the dining room (or any place else on board ship).

Room Service

This is a variable. Some ships serve no food in staterooms; others pride themselves on a twenty-four-hour cabin service. As a general rule, breakfast is served in staterooms and other meals by special request only. In some instances, breakfast service may be restricted to uncooked items juice, coffee, rolls), called "Continental Breakfast".

Diets

If you have forgotten to advise the cruise line about dietary requirements or medical diet requirements in advance, contact the purser or the maitre d'hotel immediately after boarding. If there is any problem with the food being served, the chief purser is the man who can change or influence the dining-room scene, if your efforts in the dining room have failed.

Cruise and Lose (Weight)?

TTT: "Cruise" is synonymous with "food," and many a traveler resists the lure of the seas because he or she says, "I eat too much and gain weight." But, say experts, you can feast on gourmet foods, satisfy your most discriminating taste buds, enjoy the service and atmosphere, and disembark at the end of the voyage without damage to your waistline. I consulted diet authority Dr. Abraham Friedman, author of Fat Can Be Beautiful, for advice on how a cruise-ship passenger can enjoy the bountiful and beautifully displayed gourmet delicacies without gaining weight.

Dr. Friedman says it is possible to face the palate-tempting delectable dishes like cannelloni, quiche Lorraine, pate de foie gras, and beef Wellington and come away without popping your buttons. His advice is to "exercise portion control; be a gourmet and not a gourmand; a gourmet savours his food, takes small portions and lingers over it; he eats slowly, letting his taste buds enjoy every mouthful; taste the many delectable and exotic foods and enjoy them in small amounts without consuming a tremendous number of calories. " However, says Dr.

Friedman, "if you cannot exercise portion control because temptation is too much for you, don't even swallow a teaspoon of any of the calorie-loaded sweets, starches, pastas, fats and pastries." Another alternative is: Skip one of the meals. If you sleep late, skip breakfast and enjoy a protein-laden brunch. If noontime catches you topside at the pool deck, pass the six-course luncheon being served in the dining room and settle for the hamburger (without the bun) and a cold drink out in the balmy breezes. Dr. Friedman also says if weight problems are keeping you on land, cut out the midnight buffet. In fact, don't even look at the tantalizing display of food if there's one chance in a million you can't resist this kind of temptation.

Desserts, of course, are every dieter's downfall. While your tablemates are eating baked Alaska, instruct the waiter to serve you grapefruit or melon. And order only one entree. You can have fish, poultry, and meat, but substitute "or" for "and". One portion, no matter how good it tastes, is enough.

Dr. Friedman offers a couple of other suggestions: Budget your calorie intake. If you anticipate all the goodies bound to be served at the captain's dinner, limit yourself to a salad for lunch or omit the main course the next day. Increase your physical activity. Exercise, run, walk, swim, dance, especially before meals. The doctor says it tends to diminish your appetite.

Dr. Friedman also is the author of the book "Sex Can Keep You Slim", but I will omit his suggestions on that subject.

I am not an authority on dieting, but I have found my own system for leaving the ship in the same shape as I boarded it. I have juice and coffee served in my cabin in the morning by the room steward; I always order a salad for lunch; then I enjoy my dinner. I don't have mixes with my alcoholic beverages, which eliminates a few calories, and I stick to dry wine with my dinner. Desserts? At my first encounter with my waiter I lay it on the line. If he expects a tip at the end of the voyage, absolutely no desserts, other than fruit, can be served to me no matter how much I beg. You would be surprised at how well that works! And, I limit my indulgence at the midnight buffet to fruit and tea.

DRINKING AT SEA

The water is safe, and although liquor prices on board ship have increased, drinking is still relatively cheap and readily available, so many passengers feel they can't afford not to take advantage of the prices. Mixed alcoholic drinks run from $1.85 to $3.00 on all ships, and the sommelier is the man you should get to know in the dining room. He's the one who wears the large key and tasting cup around his neck and asks nightly whether you would care for wine with your dinner. He's the wine steward, and he has a wine cellar guaranteed to liven up the party. Wines are impressive extras for that special meal at sea. The price of wines is not included in cruise rates, but good wines cost as little at $8 for a bottle. Wine stewards are tipped when they serve or at the end of the voyage.

TTT: Drinking water is safe on all ships sailing U.S. ports of embarkation, and the ship will inform passengers as to whether tap water is potable, or whether drinking water is supplied in thermos pitchers. All water is not potable on board all ships you board in foreign countries. On the Nile, for example, don't drink the water! Same is true on some Greek cruising vessels. Trust only bottled, capped, distilled water. See **TTT** "Nile Cruising".

Lounges

There is usually more than one lounge, and on board ship a lounge is a bar that serves alcoholic beverages. Lounges are also great meeting centers for passengers. Singles should have no hesitancy about sitting at the bar alone. No one considers a single woman a pickup at a ship's bar. After all, everyone's in the same boat, and somehow that makes conversation on board ship, at either a bar or the swimming pool or on deck, an accepted part of the lifestyle.

ACTIVITIES

First-time passengers have difficulty realizing the complete scope and range of possible activities and indulgences on a ship. Seasoned travelers stroll around the ship with an air of confidence, while neophytes tend to ramble off and study deck plans so they can plan the most direct route to the dining room.

A typical daily activity program lists something to do almost every minute. No passenger intends to participate in every activity. Select what turns you on, be it dancing, bridge, or swimming, and allow yourself time to relax and enjoy the luxury of doing nothing.

TTT: If you are traveling alone and want to meet people, attend the very first "for singles only" party and let the cruise-staff hostesses know

American Dinner

Hsingang, Saturday, May 19, 1984

APPETIZERS

ASSORTED RELISHES
MELANGE OF MELONS IN PORT WINE
BEEF TARTAR ON RYE BREAD,
GARNISHED WITH DANISH CAVIAR
JUMBO PRAWN COCKTAIL WITH
AMERICAN SAUCE

SOUPS

MANHATTAN CLAM CHOWDER - COCK A LEEKY
CHILLED PUMKIN BISQUE

FISH

POACHED ALASKAN SALMON STEAK WITH MOUSSELINE SAUCE
STEAMED POTATOES

ENTREES

ROAST YOUNG VERMOUNT TURKEY WITH CHESTNUT DRESSING
GIBLET GRAVY, MASHED POTATOES
BROCCOLI MIMOSA

SUGAR GLACED VIRGINIA COUNTRY HAM WITH FRESH PINEAPPLES
SWEET POTATOES - BROCCOLI MIMOSA

ROAST CHOICE PRIME RIB OF KANSAS BEEF WITH NATURAL GRAVY
CREAMED HORSERADISH
GRILLED TOMATO - CORN O' BRIEN - BAKED POTATO WITH GARNISH

SALADS - DRESSINGS

CURLEY ENDIVE - CUCUMBER - CAESAR SALAD
CAESAR - PRINCESSE - BLUE CHEESE

DESSERTS

CHERRY JUBILEE FLAMBÉ - PUMKIN RUM PIE
APPLE IN THE JACKET, VANILLA SAUCE - PETITS FOURS

ICE CREAMS

PISTACHIO - RUM RAISIN - STRAWBERRY - PINEAPPLE

FRUITS - CHEESE

SELECTION OF FRESH FRUITS FROM THE FRUIT BASKET
CHEDDAR - EMMENTHALER - BOURSIN PEPPER - BRESSE BLEU
ASSORTED CRACKERS

America - The Beautiful

Chefs Suggestion

MELANGE OF MELONS IN PORT WINE
COCK A LEEKY SOUP
ROAST CHOICE PRIME RIB OF KANSAS BEEF,
NATURAL GRAVY, CREAMED HORSERADISH
GRILLED TOMATO - CORN O' BRIEN
BAKED POTATO WITH GARNISH
CAESAR SALAD
CHERRY JUBILEE FLAMBÉ

From Our Wine Cellar

MAY WE RECOMMEND
WHITE
Johannisberg Riesling 1980/81
Beaulieu Vineyards $ 9.00
RED
Cabernet Sauvignon 1979,
Beaulieu or R. Mondavi $12.00

Captains Welcome Dinner

APPETIZERS
ASSORTED RELISHES
RUSSIAN SEVRUGA MALOSSOL CAVIAR WITH CONDIMENTS, MELBA TOAST
JUMBO PRAWN COCKTAIL, SAUCE AMERICAN
HOME MADE PATE "CHAMPAGNE" WITH CUMBERLAND SAUCE

SOUPS
CLEAR OX TAIL SOUP "AMONTILLADO", CHESTER STRAWS
BOULA BOULA SOUP WITH CROUTONS
JELLIED CONSOMME "MADRILENE"

FISH
CREAMED LOBSTER "NEWBURG" SERVED IN A PUFF PASTRY
SHELL, VAPEUR POTATOES
• • • • • • • • • • • •
FRESH KIWI SHERBET
• • • • • • • • • • • •

ENTREES
ROAST CRISPY LONG ISLAND DUCKLING WITH OREGON BING
CHERRY SAUCE, BUTTERED BRUSSEL SPROUTS, SAUTEED WILD RICE
BROILED FILLET OF CHOICE BEEF "ROSSINI" MADEIRA SAUCE,
BRAISED LETTUCE, GLACED CARROT STICKS, CHATEAU POTATOES

SALADS AND DRESSINGS
TOSSED GREENS - WATERCRESSE - TOMATO - CUCUMBER
THOUSAND ISLAND - FRENCH - ROQUEFORT - CHIFFONADE

DESSERTS
MANGO FLAMBE (FLAMED IN THE DINING ROOM)
FRESH STRAWBERRIES "ROMANOFF" - SACHER CAKE WITH WHIPPED CREAM

ICE CREAMS
PISTACHIO - RUM RAISIN - VANILLA - PINEAPPLE

FRUITS
SELECTION OF FRESH FRUITS FROM THE FRUIT BASKET

CHEESE
CHEDDAR - EMMENTHALER - BRIE - BRESSE BLEU
ASSORTED CRACKERS
PETITS FOURS

IRANIAN SEVRUGA CAVIAR ON ICE THRONE, AMERICAN DRESSING

PROSCIUTTO E MELONE   VENISON PATE ST. HUBERT

BEEF BOUILLON WITH PROFITEROLES   BISQUE OF LOBSTER

COLD AVOCADO CREAM SOUP

GOLDEN SAUTEED FILLET IF SOLE AMANDINE, PARISIENNE POTATOES

SHRIMP NEWBURG, RICE PILAF AND FLEURONS

ROAST ROYAL PHEASANT, FLAMBE WITH COGNAC

SAUTEED TOURNEDOS OF BEEF WITH CREAM AND MUSHROOMS

BRAISED SPRING PEAS WITH ONIONS   BUTTERED GLAZED CARROTS

DUCHESSE POTATOES

HEARTS OF LETTUCE SALAD
Vinaigrette Dressing

GATEAU SAINT HONORE   PETIT FOURS   CHOCOLATE SOUFFLE, VANILLA SAUCE

ICED BOMBE TROCADERO

TRAY OF SELECTED CHEESES

BASKET OF FRESH FRUIT IN SEASON

COFFEE

CAP-TRA/EB

you want to meet the opposite sex (if that's what you want). No one ever met anyone by spending the cruise in his stateroom.

Entertainment

Diversity is the word that best describes shipboard entertainment experiences. This past season alone, cruise passengers had the opportunity to choose from Las Vegas-style revues, Broadway musicals, big band sounds, or jazz festivals. For a change of pace they could decide to study up on foreign policy or financial planning, or attend a classical music concert, or sample wines from Italy or California. Top name entertainers performed, magicians astounded audiences. There were film festivals, theme parties, lectures by famous figures in sports. And while not all of the these options were available on every cruise, there is a variety offered on every ship and everyone on board is invited to everything scheduled.

Only exceptions are parties hosted by the captain for VIP passengers, repeat passengers, and others singled out by the cruise line for special treatment. On ships where main-lounge seating capacity is less than the passenger count, it is usually a scramble for seats before show time.

There is no minimum beverage charge nor is any beverage purchase required in the nightclubs or lounges, and seats are on a first-come basis for shows. Movies are shown at announced times. Passengers can dance without drinking, laugh at the comedian without sipping, sit on a bar stool drinking coffee. Everyone is entitled to participate in all the entertainment offered.

Those special parties? If you have sailed on the ship before, you will be invited to at least one, but if you enjoy special attention, have your travel agent inform the cruise line of your qualifications for VIP status. Some companies have eliminated VIP parties and invite all passengers to a cocktail party hosted by the captain. Others continue the tradition with very small gatherings in the captain's quarters.

SPORTS AT SEA

When taking a cruise, pack the athletic gear. The newest kind of activity on board ships is sports. Responding to the steadily growing interest in maintaining physical fitness, even while on vacation, cruise lines have modernized old facilities and built new ones, added sports programs on board and ashore, even expanded restaurants menus to offer health-conscious cooking. One company even has an Olympic program for passengers. It is in this area of physical fitness that cruise ships have made the most dramatic changes in recent years.

Today, many ships, and all the new ones, have the latest in exercise equipment, weight training devices, and trained staffs to supervise their use. Jogging is encouraged, and many vessels have special decks for this purpose.

Many cruise lines have developed exercise programs, dancercize classes, aerobics, and training schedules for vacationers who want to either continue a program started at home or perhaps start a new one. Some ships have personnel on board who can help plan individual exercise programs in cooperation with shipboard nutritionists and medical staff.

In addition, land activities are available to cruise vacationers. Increasing numbers of passengers are taking their golf clubs along, for example. Not only can they practice putting and driving on board several ships, but they can sample some of the finest golf courses in the world while in port. One cruise line has organized a golf tournament in which passengers on a 14-day cruise in the Orient compete on several of Asia's best known courses.

Tennis players, too, are finding that a cruise need not mean putting away the racquet. Most ships spend part of all of many days in resort-oriented ports or major cities and tennis buffs can play the courts in the Caribbean, Mexico, Europe, Asia and the United States.

The *Queen Elizabeth 2* has almost gone overboard on fitness. It has the most comprehensive health program at sea and a full spa on board. It's the Golden Door, designed and operated by *Deborah Szehely*, founder of the posh California spa of the same name. Sixteen different exercise classes run from 7:30 a.m. to 5 p.m. Each class is the same as at the California spa where a week could set you back $2,500 but on board the Queen it's all included in the cruise fare.

WHAT TO WEAR WHEN

Gone are the days when taking a cruise meant buying a new wardrobe. Cruise ships reflect clothes-trends of the decade, and life aboard ship is casual, informal, and easy. Shipboard rules are flexible. People take a cruise to have fun, and if wearing a tuxedo is going to ruin the cruise, leave it at home. On the other hand, if the tux has been hanging in the closet and could use an airing, by all means take it along.

Cruise travel is a delight for heavy packers. When in doubt about whether to take something on a cruise, don't hesitate—take it along!

Part of the fun is to dress up for a special "night on the town" on board ship, and those nights can come as frequently or as infrequently as you like.

Recommended dress code is specified in the ship's daily newspaper, and there is a code used on all ships. On nights designated as "formal," a dark business suit or a tuxedo with white, dark, or fancy jacket is appropriate. Women can wear anything from dressy pants suits to an evening gown (depending on the ship) or long or short cocktail clothes. "Informal" indicates jackets and ties or leisure suits for men, and women feel comfortable in cocktail dresses, pants, outfits, long skirts, or whatever they would wear in the evenings in a resort hotel. "Casual" designates the night when the men leave jackets and ties in cabins and the women show up at dinner in slacks, jeans, patio clothes — anything but shorts or a swim suit.

TTT: The more expensive the cruise and the longer the voyage, the more formal the atmosphere. On the *QE 2* Caribbean cruises the daily activities bulletin suggested formal dress every night, but fewer than half the passengers wore black ties except on 'formal" nights.

Remember that a cruise ship is a floating resort, and daytime clothes or whatever you would wear at a nice resort in your cruising area of the world are appropriate. Swim suits for sunning are a must, but wear a robe for cover-up en route to the swimming pool. Evenings can be breezy at sea, and it is recommended that stoles, sweaters, or wraps be included even on Caribbean cruises. Ships are air-conditioned, and the wrap may feel good in some corners of the theater. Leave your furs at home; they are cumbersome and not generally worn at sea. However, if you are heading toward Alaska or the North Cape, take a fur jacket or even a coat. It might make the difference between comfort and a chill.

Women have fewer questions than men do about what to wear where or when on board ship. "Casual" to the distaff traveler could mean a slack suit: "informal" could stretch from a dressy pants suit to a long or short cocktail-type dress. "Formal"? From dressy pants to anything short of a beaded evening gown (and you'll see a few of those on some of the round-the-worlders like the Sagafjord or the Royal Viking vessels).

TTT: So you want to sit at the captain's table in the dining room? Impossible on some ships, limited possibility on others. The policy varies. One company says "every passenger is a VIP and no one is ever invited to dine with the Captain." Another company seats VIPs with the captain for the entire trip, and since this limits the number of VIPs to no more than four, chances are slim for this "honor." On some lines VIP passengers are invited on a rotating basis.

CRUISING WITH CHILDREN

Robert Benchley once said: "In America there are only two ways to travel—first class and with children." Pundit Benchley would be surprised to learn that ship travel makes available first-class vacations with children at prices and conditions families are finding very appealing.

Although cruises are designed by the nature of the dream experience to make mom feel like Grace Kelly and dad take on a Cary Grant aura, cruising is becoming a family affair long remembered. For most travelers it's as close as we will get to vacationing on a fabulous estate complete with swimming pools, screening rooms for movies, a staff of governesses to cater to kids, a team of professional chefs delivering menus without price lists, an assemblage of crew members delighted to look after the whims of the entire family and no discussions as to who helps with the dishes or makes the beds. Major decisions of the day center on choice of foods and activities.

Add constantly-changing scenery, learning experiences that come with visits to interesting ports of call where life styles and languages contrast with back home and a know-before-you-go price tag, and it's easy to find valid reasons why families are heading out to sea. An indication of just how popular family cruising is becoming is best illustrated by numbers. If all the kids who took a cruise in 1984 had done so at the same time, they would have filled 131 luxury, ocean-going cruise ships.

About 100,000 North Americans under the age of 18 were part of sea-going families last year and the industry anticipates healthy increases in those numbers. There are many aspects of cruising that attract families, not the least of which is that welcome relief from vacation cash flow worries. Once on board, almost everything is included and there are no expensive surprises.

Most cruise lines offer special family rates. Generally, children sharing a cabin with two paying adults receive a substantial discount, often 50 to 65 percent of the minimum fare, sometimes a percentage of the applicable adult fare. Qualifying ages vary with each line with different rates for infants, children and teenagers. Some cruise lines even take children free when they are sharing cabins with two paying adults.

Cruising with children isn't a new trend, although it is developing at a quickening pace. Even during those fabled years when ship travel was reserved for the very wealthy, children were part of the family entourage. Although times and life styles have changed, children seem to stay the same. Regardless of age and stage, they are the first to find their way around a ship; first to love the motion of the ocean; and last to disembark at the end of the cruise. Almost all ships welcome families, but some spread a more appealing welcome mat in the form of planned activities, professional counselors and special bargain children's rates.

Selecting the right ship is the magic key to a successful cruise with children. If you happen up the gangplank of a vessel with a couple of toddlers or teenagers and they are the only juniors on board, your dream vacation could become a nightmare before the first meal is finished. Conversely, if a holiday at sea means leaving the patter of little feet and loud music back home and you find yourself sailing a family-oriented vessel during school vacation times, you may be tempted to jump ship at the first port of call.

Segregating family from non-family-type vessels is not difficult. Ships with special facilities and activities for children brag about them boldly in their multi-colored brochures. Children's rates are published and advertised. Ships preferring adult passengers usually say "children's rate available on request", and that's a pretty good sign they would prefer the under 14-year-old crowd left shoreside. If there isn't a single photo of a youngster in the ship's brochure, tread carefully when making reservations that include pre-teenagers.

Good examples of non-children ships are the three plush liners operated by Royal Viking Line. They offer limited special rates, and under-16-year-olds pay one-half adult rate. They must occupy the cabin with two full-paying adults, but three or four-berthed cabins are very scarce on these vessels. The company readily admits they do not encourage children as passengers, and they offer no special supervision or entertainment. However, they will provide a counselor when the manifest shows 10 or more pint-sized travelers will be on board.

Royal Cruise Line's *Golden Odyssey* and *Royal Odyssey* sail the Mediterranean during summer months and the Caribbean in winter months. Company execs allow as how youngsters under eight "are too young" for their ships and they would "prefer not to have children as passengers". Cunard/Norwegian American Cruises' brochures selling their classy *Vistafjord* and *Sagafjord* don't have a single, childish face showing, and for good reason. They are not overly enthusiastic at the prospect of sharing facilities with junior passengers, although they do offer a rate of a little less than half for passengers under 12.

Caribbean cruises are the best place to find rate and ships sure to bring smiles to the face of the family breadwinner. A quick check of brochures turns up some exceptional bargains ranging from half minimum fares (depending on ages) to free. All children's rates are based on sharing cabins with two full-fare adults. Ships welcoming children not only offer special rates, but brag about children's playrooms, activities and Mary Poppins-type staffs devoted to turning younger passengers into cruise addicts. Usual routines on one cruise line is for parents and children to meet with counselors at the beginning of the voyage when schedules and responsibilities are outlined. Schedules are apt to keep youngsters occupied from dawn to dusk, with parents taking over at dinner mealtime.

Family cruise season is traditionally during school holidays, and air fares are included in some package offerings. When air is not part of children's fares, transfers and baggage handling are included with family arrangements. The question of clothing for cruising shouldn't worry parents. Requirements vary from ship to ship, and parents are surprised to find their jeans-clad kids don't resist wearing a jacket a couple of nights during the week. Daytime dress is comparable to what they would wear ashore for any sports activity.

Ships seem to be made for children. They are the first to find their peers and adjust to new surroundings. There's nothing confining about 10 decks of open space. They are quickly involved in planned activities, between-meal snacks, parties, bingo and shipboard-style horse-racing. They are the first to learn the Italian words that bring the fastest response in the dining room, the Jamaican dialect that turns a grouchy waiter into a smiling friend, and they become positively cosmopolitan as they make friends with fellow travelers from all parts of the world. They acclimate quickly to Baked Alaska, Eggs Benedict and service. The major adjustment comes when it is time to disembark and the realities of daily living hit home.

A working parent who rarely spends much time with his (or her) family finds cruising an ideal way to get to know each other again. It's togetherness, free of the strains of day-to-day living. Families swim together, movie together, share shore experiences, dine together and come away closer. Cruising is a guilt-free holiday without the anxiety that follows parents when they leave the kids at home or the worries that come with taking teenagers to a land-locked resort. Ship captains tell me they have never lost a child at sea, and that's a comforting thought.

Even Robert Benchley would approve of programs designed to keep pint-sized and teenage travelers almost out of sight. There's baby-sitting available to take over where the counselors leave off. Sitters are reserved through room stewards on most ships for about two dollars and hour. Clever programming keeps children at arm's length from adults in public rooms. Deck games are scheduled, while most adults are indoors or on tours. Kids get their turn at the movies, disco and pizza grill about an hour before those activities show up on the grown-up schedule. Imagine the childish delight of a pizza and/or ice cream parlor, or a disco where there are no cash registers. It's all on the house . . . enough to delight passengers of any age!

All things considered, it's little wonder that cruising is becoming a family affair. I'm reminded of a friend who finds the first week back home the most difficult for the whole family. He tells about his two daughters, ages 8 and 10, who have a hard time adjusting to scrambled eggs at the family breakfast table after a week at sea. Seems they prefer their eggs on toast, topped with cheese and bacon. Eggs Benedict can easily become a habit.

TTT: For childrens' rates and facilities, check Ship Profile Chapter. Family facilities, baby sitting and rates are listed for each ship.

TTT: If the patter of little feet on board a cruise ship doesn't excite you or you have convinced grandma to baby sit while you second honeymoon on board a ship, avoid cruise lines that advertise childrens' rates during summer months and other school vacation periods (Christmas holiday, Easter, etc.) Although there are supervised programs, short of throwing the kids overboard, there's no way to avoid them and like they say, children will be children.

SANITATION AT SEA

Ever since a 1978 New York Times front-page article reported that a "majority of cruise ships failed Public Health inspections," the traditional "sparkling clean ship" syndrome has been surviving under a cloud. After reading the headlines, many a passenger has been more concerned with kitchen cleanliness than with ship facilities, amenities and itineraries.

Even veteran cruise buffs are asking questions, and the Public Health Service in Miami, which issues monthly reports on cruise-ship inspections, is receiving almost fifty inquiries a day. These reports cover some aspects of the ship sanitation story, but when interpreted as a total overview, they can be misleading.

The factual side is a lot brighter and less confusing. Of the ships based in U.S. ports on year-round service, 90 percent pass Public Health inspections with flying colors. True, publicity and inspections may have shined up a few galley sinks, but 30 of the 34 ships calling the United States "home" rated between 85 and 100 on their inspections as THE TOTAL TRAVELER BY SHIP was completed.

Until recently, monthly reports issued by the Public Health Service included latest inspections of all ships calling at American ports, and they listed ships like the Yugoslavian-registered *Dalmacija,* which made a single call in the United States last year. The 5500-ton vessel carries 165 passengers and usually sails between Italy and Yugoslavia at a daily rate of about $40. More important, the ship did not board passengers in the Florida port she visited. Other ships that do not board passengers in the United States were also included in monthly summaries. Their failure to meet high sanitation standards were grouped with our regular fleet, and resultant averages help to muddy statistics and confuse passengers.

For example, ships like the *Zvir, Tuhobic,* and *Klek* are included, but these ships are not listed in the most current ship-directories, and they do not board passengers on our shores. What's more, they may never again return, but they do change the total picture as reported by Public Health inspectors.

Herein lies the root of the confusion. When headlines and lists readily available to the public report that 50 percent of the vessels failed inspection, there's no need to cancel reservations. Public Health inspects all ships entering U.S. ports, and that list includes freighters, tankers, and passenger vessels. John Yashuk, the man in charge of inspection teams that check vessels for cleanliness, now separates our regular passenger fleet from infrequent visitors and non-passenger-carrying vessels, so headlines have been defined but more research is required if you are going to let sanitation reports influence your choice of a floating holiday.

A passenger is entitled to ask, "Can cruising be hazardous to my health?"

For answers, I went to Yashuk. He allowed as to how "cruising is not going to be a danger to anyone's health and no one should fear taking a cruise for that reason." He does say ships that meet his department's stringent requirements are safer when it comes to ship-related illness.

The modern vessel-sanitation program began in 1970 after an outbreak of typhoid on a ship. The program was revised in July 1975 when a severe dysentery outbreak on board a passenger vessel required toilet paper and medicine be helicoptered to the ship out at sea. An investigation followed, and authorities decided the inspections program at the time was not doing an adequate job shining up sinks and reporting on ship cleanliness. These are facts of travel the public has a right to know.

The program was revised, and when it was instituted not a single ship met Public Health Service standards. It took three months before the first vessel scored 98 percent. In order to rate a passing grade, ships had to change food-handling procedure and had to install water-disinfecting equipment. Some had to rebuild food storage facilities completely; others had to purchase new refrigeration units.

But there's good news for the traveler. A recent inspection showed only three of the year-around fleet with less than the required 85 percent score.

Contrary to what negative publicity may imply, cruise lines welcome Public Health inspectors, and some companies — Carnival Cruise Lines, Commodore Cruise Lines, Norwegian Caribbean Lines, Royal Caribbean Lines, Holland America Cruises — have employed sanitation consultants to sail with the ships on a full-time basis. Their sole job is to maintain Public Health Service standards at all time. On the other hand, inspectors are not "out to get" the ships. When a deficiency is noted, ample time is allowed for immediate correction. When it is accomplished while the inspector is still on board, no points are subtracted from the score card. Follow-up inspections are made within two weeks, when possible, on ships with serious deficiencies. The most common problem area on board ships is ice machines. Failure to have a chain attached to the ice scoop could mean the loss of 20 points and a failing grade. Almost all ships have roach and bug problems, but a cockroach or two only means a 2-point loss in an inspection.

The old adages about cleanliness don't seem to hold true when it comes to ships that pass or do not pass stringent sanitation inspections. A careful check of the number of gastrointestinal infections requiring medical attention on board ships gave no clues as to the ships' sanitation ratings. One ship earned 100 on a Saturday inspection following a cruise on which 67 passengers needed medical treatment for diarrhea. Another ship came off with a 98-point inspection on the day the ship returned to Miami with 55 diarrhea cases on board.

According to ship medical logs, gluttonous indulgence is responsible for almost all gastrointestinal upsets on board ships these days. However, the Public Health program of unannounced regular inspections has helped reduce incidences of mass outbreaks of diarrhea. One such outbreak a few years ago was blamed on seepage of sea water into potable-water tanks. This is a carefully checked item on all inspections, and potable-water samples are sent to the Atlanta Center for Disease Control for analysis.

Public Health inspectors pay careful attention to water supply and food. A single infraction of 32 items checked is enough to deduct 20 points from a ship's rating, enough to publicize a failing mark. The inspection system is not very different from shoreside restaurant sanitation inspections, where high priority is assigned to specific areas termed "disqualifying."

Fresh and potable water, the method of disinfection, and connections between the two systems are of great concern to inspectors. Public Health requires certain devices to protect the water supply so there is no back-siphoning, for example, between the water you drink and the water used for scrubbing the decks. Also checked are engine-room water lines to make sure there is no contamination from bilge fluid.

Crew galleys are inspected just as closely as passenger kitchens. A recent investigation revealed that an intestinal outbreak among passengers originated in the crew galley. That particular vessel voluntarily canceled a cruise. All crew members were examined and the ship did not resume sailings until she received a clean bill of health.

A two-year check of inspection reports gives no hint that older ships or new vessels have a better record of passing inspections. Neither does the flag flying from the mast have much influence on the outcome of inspections.

Public Health inspectors also take a good hard look at swimming pools. If you've wondered why the water is drained from pools when your ship is in a U.S.-mainland, Hawaiian, Alaska, or Virgin Islands port, it's because the vessel is complying with requirements, and that means a recirculating system using either a sand filter or other type of filtration system with chlorination, and that's hard to accomplish for vessels alongside for just a few hours.

Public Health recommends against using swimming pools on board ship when the vessel is in a foreign port or harbor because of possible contamination. Many ports around the world are polluted, and when the pool is filled with that kind of water there's a possibility of water-borne illness.

On-board illnesses must be reported to the Center for Disease Control in Atlanta, and when the incidence or type of illness indicates a trend, inspectors board the vessel at the first U.S. port. But, neither the Public Health Service or the Center for Disease Control has the authority to detain a vessel should it fail sanitation standards set by the local, state, or national agency. They can recommend cancellation of voyage to the cruise line and most ship operators take these recommendations very seriously. Unlike the S. Coast Guard, the inspecting agencies can detain a vessel only when there is an indication of a disease epidemic.

Public Health officials say most ships are immaculate and live up to ship-shape traditions. They say the most frequent health problem posed on board cruise ships is the common cold that spreads among passengers.

Yashuk adds more encouraging words. He says that, all things considered, ships do a good job when you think that kitchens are in constant use and clean-up time allowed between arrival and departure at home port is sometimes less than six hours.

Should you want to check the rating of a particular ship, individual reports on most recent inspections, write to Vessel Inspection Division, Public Health Service, Room 111, 1015 North America Way, Miami, Florida 33132. Monthly reports listing passing and failing of inspections are available from the same source.

TOWARD THE JOURNEY'S END

No matter how much you want to postpone it, the end of the cruise is bound to come. At the final captain's party he usually makes his farewell speech, inviting passengers to cruise the vessel again. Invariably, the cruise director stands up and says he has a special message for the passengers: 'The captain wants me to announce that you have been so nice, we are turning around and repeating the cruise. " At which point everyone stands up and cheers. But as with all good things, the end of the cruise means showing how much you appreciated the service extended, and this is called a "gratuity."

Tipping

How much, when, and to whom is the most frequently asked question about cruising. Tipping is a personal matter, but cruise lines make it less personal by recommending how much, when, and to whom at a session called a "briefing" toward the end of the cruise. In the "Ship Profiles" chapter, recommended amounts are indicated for every ship.

The list of how much and to whom has grown in the last couple of years and contemporary one-class cruising has changed the way we tip. The couple sailing in a top suite for $3,500 a week eat in the same dining room, enjoy the same entertainment and visit the same ports as the couple paying under $2,000 for an inside cabin with upper and lower berths. Yet, recommended tipping for both couples is the same. No longer does the total tip represent a percentage of the cruise fare.

Tipping rules of the sea vary little from ship-to-ship. Basically, all recommendations are per passenger, per day of the voyage which really means per night. Even if you boarded at midnight and disembarked at 8 a.m. a week later, count the nights, not the days in calculating gratuities. With very few exceptions, cruise lines and ship personnel expect passengers to tip, but they allow as how no passenger has ever been thrown in the brig for defying the tipping codes. Cruise directors admit non-tipping passengers must be very good at avoiding the room steward who miraculously appears even though you may not have seen him for days and dining room waiters whose service is exemplary on the last night of the voyage.

Few Americans object to tipping for services rendered. On board ship, however, recommended tips have little to do with degree and quality of service. In fact, cruise directors point out that recommended amounts are "basic" and if you received outstanding service you might want to up the amount.

Also interesting to note that recommended tipping does not correspond to price category of the ship, except for ships at the top of the price scale. Tipping policies do depend greatly on nationality of the service crew. Surprisingly, higher priced ships frequently recommend less tipping than budget and moderately priced vessels. Italian union crews, for example, command high salaries so tips are not as major a factor in employment agreements. Caribbean and Indonesian crews depend almost entirely on tips and very little on meager salaries.

Sitmar Cruises is recognized as a moderately-upscale company, yet recommended tipping is less than on board lower priced Norwegian Caribbean Lines.

Your waiter and his assistant expect to be tipped. Most ships recommend between $2.50 and $3.50 per person, per day, to each of them. Some recommend $2.50 per person, per day, for the waiter, and he takes care of his assistant. Holland America Cruises (HAC) says "tipping is not required and is included in the cost of your cruise." However, when HAC first introduced the no-tipping policy, it was "no tipping permitted." They have bowed to pressure by the American traveler who insists on showing his gratitude personally and with cash. HAC found there was no way to overcome the American tipping syndrome, and passengers continue to tip, but not as much as they would ordinarily."

If the dining room captain in your section has cooked up special dishes, tossed a Caesar salad, and extended himself, you might want to give him about one dollar a day per person. If the maitre d'hotel has been super and the service has been far beyond the call of duty, half of what you give the captain would be fair. Some companies suggest as much as two dollars a day to each of these supervisors, but unless they have really gone overboard for you, it seems excessive.

Bar and wine stewards who have not been tipped with each order will expect 15 to 20 percent of what you have spent with them. Deck stewards who serve bouillon and tea get about 50 cents per person per day.

Room stewards expect anywhere from $2.50 to $3.50 per person, per day, depending on the ship and the service. He takes care of his assistants.

A good rule of thumb is to count on about eight dollars a night for tips on budget priced ships; at least $10 on higher priced vessels and $15 on luxury ships. It is recommended that you distribute all gratuities on the last night of a one or two-week cruise. On longer cruises it's appropriate to tip at the end of each week and at the end of the cruise.

Waiters say they sleep better if they are tipped the night before the ship reaches home port. Passengers have been known to skip the last breakfast and skip passing a few bucks to the waiter who served them during the cruise.

North Cape cruising vessels follow similar guidelines. Mediterranean and Greek-island ships (except for the few in the luxury category) recommend between $3.50 and $4.50 as the total tip required in the dining room and cabin, per person, per day. Some Greek-flag ships follow an old island custom and pool their tips. Passengers are requested to place their gratuities in an envelope, and the monies are then divided among service and such behind-the-scenes personnel as cooks and dishwashers. Americans find this procedure impersonal, so they continue to tip according to their own experience. Europeans follow suggestions and like the idea of pooling. They say it takes the "commercialism" out of tipping.

Seasoned cruisers sometimes tip half the recommended amount to the waiter, captain and room steward at the beginning of the voyage. At the end of the cruise they over-tip the other half by about 20 percent. They say it tends to improve the service.

TTT: Contemporary cruise trends have also changed service customs on board and added still another person, if not with his hand out, at least expecting to be tipped. Cabin service in one form or another is offered by almost every ship, but it not like it was in the old days when your room steward answered your call for breakfast in bed. Few of the new ships even have call buttons. Instead, passengers telephone "room service" and a bell boy delivers breakfast, drinks or sandwiches. He is not included in the "regular" list to be tipped, so he expects a gratuity every time he delivers. One dollar per person served seems adequate. These little niceties which are touted in brochures as "all included" cost a little more these days but most passengers consider them well worth a few extra dollars.

If room service is provided by your own room steward, do NOT tip each time he does something for you, including food service in your cabin. Tip him/her at the end of the voyage, remembering with special consideration to the special services provided.

As for the longshoremen, when the sign at Port Everglades, for instance, reads "Tipping Not Required," I remember the high wages being paid these porters, and I never tip more than a dollar. They carry the bags less than 30 feet to a loading machine. I know the situation is different in such ports as New York and I have had reports that passengers who undertipped found their baggage on the wrong ship headed for a different part of the world. So, in New York one dollar per bag should satisfy existing greed; but don't tip any more than that. Over-tipping is just as bad as undertipping, and inflation is pushing amounts upward without help from insecure travelers.

DEBARKATION

No matter what the brochure lists as the arrival time in home port, if your ship has visited foreign islands, it will take a minimum of two hours for baggage to be unloaded and for customs and immigration officials to clear the ship for passenger debarkation (also known as disembarkation). If you are making a plane connection, plan accordingly. Allow four to six hours from scheduled arrival time for airplane connections.

You will be asked to place your packed luggage outside your stateroom door at a specific time on the last night at sea. Save a small carry-off bag for your night clothes and toilet articles. On the morning of arrival, eat your breakfast in leisure and wait until the purser announces that the ship has been cleared before you vacate your cabin. Don't congregate in public areas or near the gangplank. It's the surest way to ruin a pleasant cruise.

Most ships have efficient systems for getting passengers off quickly. It is done by the letter of your last name or by color-coded cards. You disembark when they call your group. Then you find your luggage by color or the first letter of your last name, assemble it, and face the customs inspector, if you have not been pre-cleared on board.

Most people who have trouble with customs inspectors bring it on themselves, either through disregard or ignorance of customs laws. Customs is a serious business, and it's not time to joke around. Customs inspectors are stricter on citizens of their own country than they are on foreigners. The "Customs—U.S. and Canadian" chapter details duty-free allowances ($400 per person, including one quart of alcoholic beverages, except from the U.S. Virgin Islands). This includes everything you bought on board ship or received as a gift. It will help if you have your receipts with you when you go through customs. It will also help if all of your purchases are in one suitcase and you can produce them quickly, should the inspector ask to see them. (See U.S. Customs declaration form).

Once the inspector has cleared you, a baggage handler will carry your luggage to your transportation. He expects a tip similar to what you would tip an airline porter.

The Ship's Family or, Who's Who on Board

If you boarded with visions of "Captain Steubing" of "Love Boat" fame dancing in your head, forget it! The Captain of your cruise ship didn't get his master's papers in a school for actors or through a mail-order mill. He and the rest of his officers are professionals. While it is fun and games for passengers, tending to your safety and catering to your requirements is serious business for the crew. Although titles, duties and services vary from ship to ship, the basic responsibilities of care and feeding of passengers remain the same.

Cruise-ship deck officers have usually been trained in their own countries and received their education and seamen's papers from an internationally-recognized maritime school. While it may sound glamorous and perhaps inviting, there's practically no way a dishwasher can ever climb the ladder to captaincy without fulfilling educational and legal requirements. Not to say that many a ship master didn't go to sea at a tender age, but you can bet your passport there were many years in between during which he completed lengthy study and training requirements.

For the most part, ships are organized into three main departments: deck, engine room and purser's office. Some Norwegian vessels have added a Hotel and Services Department which operates much as it would in a resort or hotel on shore. Here's a run down on the ship's family and what you can expect from each.

CAPTAIN: He is absolute monarch on board. His responsibility is the safety and welfare of his passengers as well as their pleasure, although he relegates the latter to subordinate departments and doesn't get directly involved, except in emergency situations. He is judge, jury, sheriff and king, and he is usually the most genial and outgoing member of the ship's family. You won't make points if you call him "Skipper". 'Sir" or "Captain" are more acceptable forms. While the crew calls him "The Old Man" behind his back, passengers are not afforded the same privilege.

STAFF CAPTAIN: He is second in command and deals with all matters relating to the crew. He is sometimes called "Chief Officer" on Norwegian and English ships. When you meet him at dinner or on deck, his proper title also is "Captain'.

CHIEF ENGINEER: He reigns supreme in the engine room and holds the same maritime rank as the Captain. His department is responsible for moving the ship through the waters comfortably and for keeping arrivals and departures as close to scheduled times as possible. His department also is responsible for almost all other machinery on board, and he has engineering officers and an engine-room crew to help him keep the propellers turning.

STAFF ENGINEER: He is second man in the engine department.

CHIEF PURSER: He's the head of the department that handles the ship's finances and hotel operations. His office and staff serve as the general information center and clearing house for immigration and customs formalities in all ports. He and his staff of assistant pursers supervise entertainment, accommodations, meal services, printed material distributed on board, special requests and the like.

HOTEL MANAGER: His is a fairly new position at sea, and his duties vary greatly from ship to ship and overlap with the Chief Purser. He usually wears a uniform only on formal nights, and dresses like a hotel manager the rest of the time. He does what the Chief Purser does on most vessels (bed, board, entertainment).

DOCTOR: He and his staff (usually a nurse) are available on a 24-hour basis, as needed.

CHIEF RADIO OFFICER: He supervises your link to the outside world. His staff monitors the ship's radio and arranges for cablegrams and telephone calls between ship and shore, and shore and ship. They also receive cablegrams and deliver them to passengers and crew.

Non-Uniformed Members of the Family

The cruise director and his staff are key to on-board entertainment, shore excursions, activities, fun and games on board. They don't wear seamen's uniforms, but are easily identified because they dress in company-approved classic sea-going sports attire. They are genial, outgoing and will talk to you first on deck.

The Food and Beverage Manager is becoming a familiar face on board many ships which are finding it practical to divide ship operations into maritime and passenger services. The Hotel Manager decides what you are going to eat, how it is served, and he is in charge of all guest services on board ship. He may or may not wear a uniform, so he may appear in black tie in the dining room; in sports clothes on deck.

TTT: Uniform insignia varies by country. For instance, Italian officers have gold stripes on a red background for the engineers' and pursers' departments, green in the communications department. Norwegian and British insignia are gold on black epaulettes. Color braid between the stripes tells you the department. The number and width of the stripes tell the rank. There is no color used for deck officers. Gold braid is used on blue sleeves; epaulettes on white shirts.

TTT: Don't hesitate to talk with officers on board ship. They are interesting people who know a lot about the vessel and the ports you will be visiting. They know the best restaurants and beaches on shore and they'll be happy to share the information.

WHO'S WHO ON BOARD SHIP

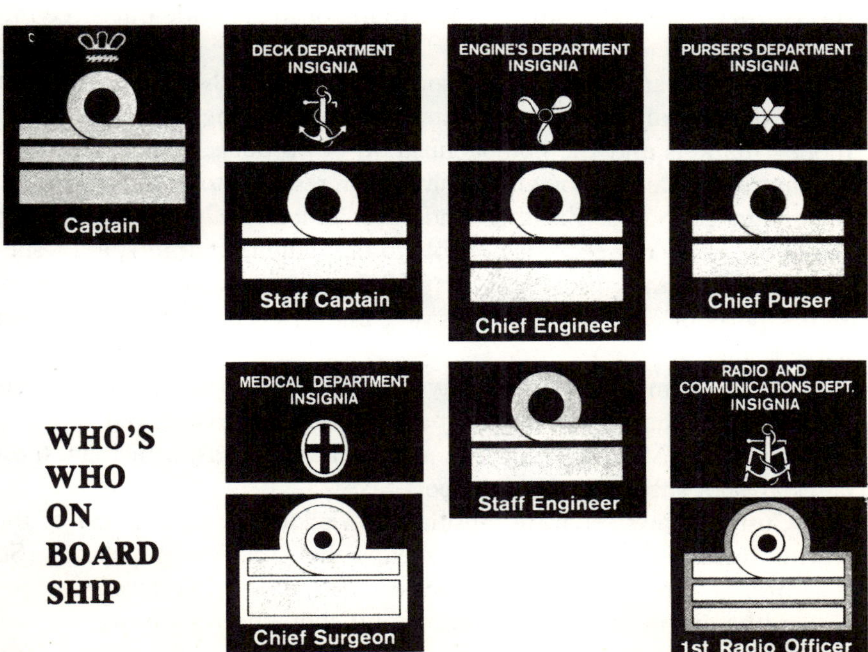

Customs—U.S. and Canadian

Ships offer the inveterate shopper myriad enticements. It's a lot easier to transport bulky purchases by sea and there are few travelers who can resist "bargains" that seem to come with every sightseeing experience.

Recent changes in U.S. import laws are of special benefit to the shopper who opts for the sea lanes. Travel by ship eliminates size and weight limitations still enforced by airlines and makes it easier to succumb to the temptation of lugging home that six-foot-high wooden figure from islands like Haiti.

Lawmakers in the United States considered inflation trends when they liberalized duty-free exemptions, but economists, eyeing the changes, worry about increased deficits on our balance-of-payment sheets; they objected loudly to the tripling of world-wide duty-free imports for travelers.

As a comparison shopper of some repute, my advice is: Worry not about dollar balance of payments. With the strong dollar in world money markets and the homogenization of products, much of the joy and many bargain opportunities have been restored to serious shopping in foreign countries. Exciting finds are almost unlimited, and price savings have increased. It is possible to buy china, perfumes, and especially liquor at savings of more than 50 percent in Caribbean and West Indies ports of call, but as they say: "Buyer, check it out before you leave home."

It's a common sight these days to find cruise passengers with lists in hand, comparing home town prices with bargains offered in every faraway port. Most exciting are native-made goods, which in most cases are not subject to U. S. import taxes.

Customs laws separate "insular possessions" from the rest of the world. Insular possessions? That means the U.S. Virgin Islands (St. Thomas, St. Croix, St. John), American Samoa, and Guam.

Although inventories are similar on shop shelves throughout the Caribbean, prices are far from identical. Signs offering "duty-free" and "tax-free" merchandise lure shoppers, and those two inducements also vary from island to island. The terms "duty-free" and "tax-free" refer to the shopkeeper's purchase price and the laws of the land or country. For instance, in Jamaica there is no duty or tax assessed on merchandise brought into the island for resale to visitors who are taking the merchandise out of the island. In most countries true duty-free merchandise cannot be sold over the counter and must, by law, be delivered to the purchaser at his or her departure point (airport or ship). "Duty-free" and "tax-free" have no bearing on what U.S. or Canadian Customs services will assess the traveler on return to home shores.

Cruise ship passengers are wise to avoid mailing bulky items whenever possible. Not only are shipping costs high, but even with more liberalized laws (covered later in this chapter), delayed shipments, inspections, and dual documentations can be frustrating, to say the least.

Shoppers traveling by ship don't necessarily literally carry their purchases back home. Since there is no limitation on size of your purchases, almost every shoreside merchant will deliver bulky crates to the ship. On most vessels, parcels (small and oversized) will share your cabin for the remainder of the voyage; on others, room stewards will arrange for safe storage until the night before you disembark. With proper pre-arrangements, ship personnel help get the loot to the customs area. But from there on, you're on your own for arrangements with airlines, if your sea travel is a flight away from home.

Cruise passengers in the market for such big-ticket items as cameras, porcelain, silver, crystal, quality Swiss watches, and the like, would do well to check prices at home before purchasing in foreign ports. If you're planning to buy china, for instance, you should check whether the particular pattern is available in your home town. Gold jewelry should be purchased only from reliable merchants and offers too good to be true made by street merchants should be avoided. The same holds for cut semi-precious stones. On a trip to Rio, I succumbed to the brilliance of the stones and the sales talk of a handsome street vendor, who took me behind a building for a semi-secret display of faceted "tourmalines, emeralds, aquamarines, and topaz." I now own the most extensive collection of colored glass this side of Rio.

Moral of the story, and good advice: Shop only at reputable and long-established stores. In some, look for the approval stamp or logo of the tourism association. In Hong Kong, for instance, should you find you paid for less than the shopkeeper says you bought, there is recourse. If the shop is a member of the Hong Kong Tourist Association, that organization's consumer force will take action and represent you in the dispute. Resist when in doubt.

On the other hand, a bargain really depends upon personal likes and dislikes. Show me a cruise passenger, and I'll show you someone who can not resist the booze in the Virgin Islands, the perfume in Martinique, the handicrafts in Mexico. And those are just a few of the worthwhile items available on some of the more popular routes.

IMPORTANT RECENT CHANGES

Significant benefits for international travelers are part of recent changes detailed in the Customs Procedural Reform and Simplification Act. Highlights of the new law affecting both U.S. residents and non-residents are:

1. Your duty-free allowance has been increased to $400 based on the fair retail value in the country of acquisition.

2. The number of cigarettes allowed in your exemption is 200 (one carton; five cartons from U.S. Virgin Islands).

3. The exemption from the U.S. Virgin Islands, American Samoa, and Guam has been increased to $800.

4. Articles in excess of the personal exemption will be assessed at a flat 10 percent rate of duty up to $1,000 and at regular and varying rates when the amount exceeds $1,400 except from the Virgin Islands, and so on. The rate assessed on the first $1,000 of excess is a flat 5 percent.

5. It is now possible to include merchandise shipped from the Virgin Islands or Samoa in your duty-free exemption.

6. Unsolicited gifts mailed to the United States enter duty-free when the fair retail value is $50 and from the Virgin Islands the limitation is $100.

U. S. CUSTOMS REGULATIONS

In clearing U.S. Customs, a traveler is considered either a "returning resident of the United States" or a "nonresident. " You are a returning resident if you leave the United States for purposes of travel, work or study abroad and return to resume residency in the United States. Nonresident regulations are covered in the section on "Canadian Customs Regulations."

Articles acquired abroad and brought into the United States are subject to applicable duty and internal revenue tax, but as a returning resident you are allowed certain exemptions from paying duty on these items.

Articles totaling $400 may be brought into the United States without duty if:

1. You bring the articles with you at the time of your return to the United States (except from insular possessions) and they are properly declared to Customs. (Articles purchased and left for alterations or other reasons cannot be applied to your $400 exemption when shipped to follow at a later date.)

2. You are returning from a stay abroad of at least 48 hours, except from Mexico or the Virgin Island. For example: passengers on a ship leaving Miami on Friday at 4 p.m. would be eligible for the exemption if the ship returns to the United States on Sunday at 4 p.m. or later. If, however, the ship left the United States on Friday at 4 p.m. and returned on Sunday at 9 a.m., the exemption would not apply. In this case, or in the event you have used part or all of your exemption within 30 days prior to returning to the United States, your exemption is limited to $25. In other words, exemptions are not cumulative and are valid every 30 days.) If you cannot claim the $400 or $800 exemption because of the 30-day or 48-hour minimum limitations, you may bring in, free of duty and tax, articles acquired abroad for personal or household use, if the total fair retail value does not exceed $25. This is an individual exemption and may not be grouped with exemptions of other family members on one customs declaration. You may include any of the following: 50 cigarettes, 10 cigars, 4 ounces of perfume. If any article brought with you is subject to duty or tax, or if the total value of all dutiable articles exceeds $25, no article may be exempted from duty or tax.

Cigars and Cigarettes

Not more than 100 cigars and 200 cigarettes (one carton) may be included in your exemption. Excess quantities are subject to tax and duty. Products of Cuban tobacco may be exempted if purchased in Cuba. Unlike restrictions on liquor imports, the tobacco exemption is available to all travelers, regardless of age.

Alcohol

Alcohol may be included in exemptions if the quantity does not exceed one liter (33.8 fluid ounces) and, if you are 21 years of age, it is for your own use or for use as a gift, and if it is not in violation with the laws of the state in which you arrive. Information about state restrictions and taxes should be obtained from state governments, as laws vary from state to state. Alcoholic beverages in excess of the one-quart limitation are subject to duty and internal revenue tax. (See the alcohol tax chart on page 90.) Shipping alcoholic beverages by mail is prohibited by U.S. postal laws.

TTT: Customs officers cooperate with state officials, so California residents arriving by ship (or air) in California ports may find their liquor confiscated or taxes collected on the spot. The same applies to Texas. However, Californians landing at Florida ports, for example, will not be taxed or subject to laws other than those enforceable in Florida. Conversely, Floridians landing in California are subject to the same laws as returning California residents; but customs officers are allowing in-transit passengers to land their liquor quotas without any problem if they present airline tickets for a connecting flight. This is a touchy subject, and neither state nor U.S. officials will commit themselves on an "official" policy, but few travelers encounter difficulty. What if Californians arrive at domestic air terminals within your state with five bottles of booze landed in a Florida port. Unless you are spot-checked, let your conscience be your guide.

You may import articles in excess of your customs exemptions, unless they are prohibited from entering the United States. Items not entitled to free entry will be subject to customs duty calculated by the Customs Inspector. A simplified method is now in effect (see "Rates of Duty'). Duty assessed will be based on "fair retail value in the country of origin." Payment of duty may be made by personal check in the exact amount drawn on a national or state bank or trust company of the United States and made payable to the "U.S. Customs Service', by money order or by traveler's checks, if the value does not exceed the duty charged by more than $50. Not accepted are checks with second endorsements and foreign currency of any kind. Cash in the form of greenbacks is the only means of payment that will not require such personal identification as a passport or social security card.

Duty-free Shops

Articles bought in duty-free shops in foreign countries are subject to U.S. Customs exemptions and restrictions. Articles purchased in U.S. duty-free shops (airport transit lounges) are subject to duty when re-entered into the United States. If you return directly or indirectly from St. Thomas, St. Croix or St. John (U.S. Virgin Islands), American Samoa, or Guam, you are entitled to a customs exemption of $800 based on fair retail value of the articles in the country where acquired.

Not more than $400 of this exemption may be applied to merchandise obtained elsewhere than in these islands. Residents 21 years of age or older may enter four liters of alcoholic beverages (128 fluid ounces) free of duty and tax, provided not more than one quart of this amount is acquired elsewhere than in these islands. (Example: your ship visits St. Thomas, St. Maarten and Martinique. You spend $400 in St. Thomas, $200 in St. Maarten, and $300 in Martinique, for a total of $900. Your exemption includes the $400 spent in St. Thomas and $400 of the $500 spent in St. Maarten and Martinique. Your $100 excess is subject to duty.) Since few ships visit American Samoa or Guam, hereafter "Virgin Islands" will be substituted for "insular possessions."

TTT: U. S. Virgin Islands, American Samoa, Guam (also known and referred to as "insular possessions")Articles acquired in and sent from these islands to the United States may be included in your duty-free exemption if properly declared. (See later section on "Shipping Purchases Back from the Virgin Islands.)

Customs Declaration

You must declare to U.S. Customs, either orally or in writing, all articles acquired abroad and in your possession at the time of your return if you plan to claim the items in your exemption. You must also declare items shipped (other than $25 gifts) from the U.S. Virgin Islands. The wearing or use of an article acquired abroad does not exempt it from duty, and it must be declared at the price you paid for it. The customs officer will make an appropriate reduction in value for wear and use. An opened bottle of liquor, even partially consumed, must also be declared. The customs officer will approximate the number of ounces and include it in the total of your alcoholic imports. Your declaration also must include items you have been asked to bring home by another person, any article you intend to sell or use in your business, alterations and repairs made to articles taken abroad, and gifts presented to you while abroad.

Customs declaration forms are distributed on vessels and should be prepared in advance of arrival for presentation to the immigration and customs inspectors. Fill out the identification portion of the declaration form (see sample form) You may declare orally to the customs inspector of the articles you acquired abroad, if you have not exceeded the duty-free exemption allowed. A customs officer may, however, request that you prepare a written list, if he thinks it necessary.

WELCOME
TO THE
UNITED STATES

DEPARTMENT OF THE TREASURY
UNITED STATES CUSTOMS SERVICE

CUSTOMS DECLARATION

FORM APPROVED
OMB NO. 1515-0041

Each arriving traveler or head of family must provide the following information (only **ONE** written declaration per family is required):

1.   Name: __*BLUM*__________ __*MILTON*__________ __*R*__
      Last   First   Middle Initial

2.   Number of family members traveling with you ---- *2* ----------

3.   Date of Birth: __*4*_|_*30*_|_*1931*_ 4. Airline/Flight: __*QE 2*__
                       Month   Day   Year

5.   U.S. Address: --*5838 Collins Ave*-------------
Miami, Fl 33140

6.   I am a U.S. Citizen   YES [X]   NO [ ]
       If No,
       Country: ----------------------------

7.   I reside permanently in the U.S.   YES [X]   NO [ ]
       If No,
       Expected Length of Stay: ---------------

8.   The purpose of my trip is or was
           [ ] BUSINESS   [X] PLEASURE

9.   I am/we are bringing fruits, plants, meats, food, soil,   YES [ ]   NO [X]
       birds, snails, other live animals, farm products, or
       I/we have been on a farm or ranch outside the U.S.

10. I am/we are carrying currency or monetary   YES [ ]   NO [X]
       instruments over $5000 U.S. or the foreign
       equivalent.

11. The total value of all goods I/we purchased
       or acquired abroad and am/are bringing
       to the U.S. is (see instructions under
       Merchandise on reverse side; visitors
       should report value of gifts only): $ *800* XX
                                                        U.S. Dollars

SIGN ON REVERSE SIDE AFTER YOU READ WARNING.

(Do not write below this line.)

INSPECTOR'S NAME	STAMP AREA
BADGE NO.	

Customs Form 6059B (051184)

A written declaration is required if the total fair retail value of articles acquired abroad exceeds your personal exemption; includes more than one quart of alcoholic beverages, one carton of cigarettes, or 100 cigars; includes items not intended for your personal or household use, such as commercial samples, items for sale or use in your business or articles you are bringing home for another person; includes articles acquired in the U.S. Virgin Islands and being sent to the United States; or if customs duty or internal-revenue tax is collectible on any single article in your possession.

FAMILY DECLARATION: The head of a family may make a joint declaration for all members residing in the same household and returning together to the United States. For example, a family of four may bring in free of duty articles valued up to $1,600 ($3,200 from the Virgin Islands) retail value on one declaration, even if the articles acquired by one member of the family exceed the personal exemption allowed. Infants and children are entitled to the same exemption as adults, except for alcoholic beverages.

AVOIDING CUSTOMS PENALTIES: It's hard to fool Uncle Sam's customs officers. Not even nice little old ladies escape the scrutiny of customs agents assigned to some 300 points of the entry along about 96,000 miles of U.S. borders and at posts in Canada and the Bahamas. After years of people-watching and baggage inspections, agents say there is no "profile" of a typical smuggler. Very few, if any, cruise ship passengers are professional smugglers, and most give themselves away by nervousness, by being too helpful or talkative, or by simply doing "stupid things," according to my friends in the Customs Service. French-made gowns, for instance, are easy to spot. They say zippers are a dead giveaway.

The best way to avoid penalties is to declare everything! If you understate the value of an article or if you otherwise misrepresent an article in your declaration, you may have to pay a penalty in addition to payment of duty, to say nothing of the possibility the article will be seized and forfeited if the penalty is not paid. If you fail to declare an article, not only is it subject to seizure and forfeiture, but you will be liable for a personal penalty in an amount equal to the value of the article in the United States. And you may also be liable to criminal prosecution. It's just not worth the embarrassment and possible problems. Besides, duties have been simplified and taxes decreased, and if an article is worth purchasing overseas, it's worth paying assessed duties.

Another bit of advice: Don't rely on know-it-all persons outside the Customs Service. Cruise directors usually have up-to-the-minute information available for passengers, but merchants abroad are more interested in selling than they are in repeat business, so they frequently come up with bad advice leading to violations of customs laws and costly penalties. Some merchants offer travelers invoices or bills of sale showing false or understated values. This can be another costly route. Customs inspectors know the fair retail value of all popular items and are aware of the reliability and practices of shopkeepers throughout the Caribbean.

If in doubt about whether an article should be declared, declare it, then ask the customs inspector for advice in establishing the value. Customs inspectors handle tourist items day in and day out and are acquainted with normal foreign prices. Current commercial prices of foreign items are available at all times, and on-the-spot comparisons of these values can be made.

CUSTOMS EXEMPTIONS: If you take foreign-made articles (watches, cameras, and so on) out of the United States, these items should be registered with U.S. Customs before departure, because they are dutiable each time they are brought into the country, unless you have proof of prior possession. To obtain a certificate of registration, take the article to the customs office nearest you (they are at all international airports and major ports of embarkation). If you have not registered these items before boarding ship, check with the purser. There is usually a customs officer on board ship until sailing time, and he has necessary forms for registration. He will want to see the items and check serial numbers of cameras and the like. The certificate will expedite free entry of these items when you return to the United States.

GIFTS: Bona fide gifts of not more than $50 in fair retail value may be mailed to friends and relatives and may be received by them free of duty and tax provided the the same person does not receive more than $50 in gift shipments in a single day. The "day" is the day on which a parcel is received for customs processing. This amount goes to $100 if the parcel is shipped from the U.S. Virgin Islands. These shipped gifts need not be declared and are not included in your personal exemption. Perfume containing alcohol valued at more than $5 retail, tobacco products, and alcoholic beverages are excluded from this gift-mailing provision.

When shipping gifts back home, be sure the outer wrapping of the package is marked (1) "unsolicited gift," (2) with a description of the nature of the contents, and (3) with the fair retail value. If any one item in a gift parcel is subject to duty, the U.S. Postal Service will collect the duty plus a handling charge in the form of "postage due" stamps. In case you're wondering—duty cannot be prepaid. And you cannot send a "gift" to yourself. Gifts ordered by mail from the United States do not qualify under this duty-free gift provision an are subject to duty.

PAYING FOR YOUR DUTY-FREE EXCESS: Articles imported in excess of your customs exemption will be subject to duty, unless the items are entitled to free entry or prohibited. Here's how it works: The inspector will place the items having the higher rate of duty under your exemption, and duty will be assessed upon the lower-rated items. After he deducts your exemption and the value of any articles that are duty-free, a flat rate will be applied to the next $1,000 (fair retail value of the merchandise). Any dollar amount of an article or articles over $1,000 will be dutiable at various rates based, in most cases, on wholesale value.

TTT: Take no chances. If your purchases exceed the duty-free limitation, itemize them, starting with the highest dutiable items and continuing on down to lowest. For instance, leather and china have high duties, so I list them first to make sure they enter in the duty-free category, just in case the customs inspector is busy or doesn't take time for a careful analysis of my purchases.

The flat rate of duty is 10 percent, based on fair retail value in the country of acquisition, including Communist-bloc countries. Articles must accompany you, except if they were acquired in the U.S. Virgin Islands. In that case, the flat rate of duty on the additional $1,000 is five percent, regardless of whether the articles accompany you or are shipped.

For example: You acquire goods valued at $1,500 from countries other than the Virgin Islands. The first $400 is duty-free; the next $1,000 is taxed at 10 percent, and the remaining $100 is assessed at various rates of duty. If you acquire goods valued at $1,900 from the Virgin Islands, the first $800 is free of duty, the next $1,000 is taxed at the rate of 5 percent, and the remaining $100 is assessed at various rates of duty.

RESTRICTED ITEMS: Fruits, vegetables, plants, cuttings, seeds, unprocessed plant products, and certain endangered plant species either are prohibited from entering the country or require an import permit. Canned or processed items are admissible. Applications for import permits should be sent to Quarantines, USDA-APHIS-PPQ, Federal Building, Hyattsville Maryland 20782.

"Pirated " copies of copyrighted books (those produced without authorization of the copyright owner) are prohibited. These include photo-offset copies of American best sellers and expensive textbooks produced and sold in the Far East for a fraction of what their cost would be if they were produced in the United States.

Meats, livestock, poultry (including pet birds) are either prohibited or restricted, depending on disease conditions in country of origin. Fresh meat is generally prohibited, but canned meat is permitted if the inspector determines that it is commercially canned, cooked in the container, hermetically sealed, and can be kept without refrigeration.

MONEY: There is no limitation in terms of total amount, but if you transport more than $5,000 in monetary instruments in or out of the United States, you are required to file a report (Customs Form 4790) with U.S. Customs. Ask a customs officer for the form on arrival or departure. Monetary instruments include U.S. or foreign coins, currency, traveler's checks, and money orders.

GOLD: Gold coins, medals and bullion, formerly on the prohibited list, may be brought into the United States, but copies of gold coins are prohibited if not properly marked as "copies.'

TRADEMARKED ARTICLES: Foreign-made trademarked articles may be limited as to the quantity brought into the United States, if the registered trademark has been recorded by the American trademark-owner with U.S. Customs. Types of articles usually of interest to tourists are lenses, cameras, binoculars, optical goods, tape recorders, jewelry, perfumes, and watches and clocks. You are allowed one article bearing a protected trademark. The article must accompany you and must be for personal use.

TTT: Customs inspectors are on the look-out for clones of personal computers manufactured and sold in the Far East. Prices are about 75 percent less and the PC's are marketed under names that are a tip-off on compatibility. If it's an "Orange," you know which machine has been ripped off. Inspectors are authorized to confiscate the machines.

Shipping Purchases Back from the Virgin Islands

Let's say you wanted to buy a set of china while your ship visited St. Thomas and there was no way you could handle the crate from ship to plane to home. There's good news in recent customs regulations. You may send from the U.S. Virgin Islands purchases acquired there if they are properly declared and processed, but there is a routine that must be followed: Up to $800 worth can enter the United States under your personal exemption, but all of it must have been purchased in an "insular possession" to qualify for the total exemption. The amount of duty-free purchases that came into the United States with you when you entered will be subtracted from what you ship. A flat five percent duty rate applies to the next $1,000 purchased in the Virgin Islands and regular duty applies to purchases in excess of that amount ($800 plus $1,000). However, to obtain the special five percent rate on articles shipped in excess of the exemption, the following step-by-step procedure must be followed:

1. List all articles acquired abroad on your baggage declaration (Customs Form 6059B), except those sent under the $100 bona fide gift provisions. Indicate which articles are being sent; complete a Declaration Of Unaccompanied Articles (Customs Form 255) for each package to be sent. This form is available when you clear U.S. Customs, if it was not available where you made your purchase.

2. The customs inspector at the time of your return will collect duty and tax if owed on the goods accompanying you, will verify your unaccompanied articles against sales slips, invoices, and the like, and will validate Form 255 as to whether goods are free of duty under your personal exemption. Two copies of the three-part form will be returned to you.

3. Send the yellow copy of the form to the shopkeeper (or vendor) holding your purchase, and keep the other copy for your records. You are responsible for advising the shopkeeper at the time you make your purchase that your package is not to be sent until he receives this form.

4. The shopkeeper should place the form in an envelope and attach the envelope securely to the outside of the package, which must be clearly marked UNACOMPANIED TOURIST PURCHASE. This is very important in order for you to receive the duty-free allowances.

5. The Postal Service will deliver the package, if sent by mail, after customs clearance. Any duty owed, plus a postal-handling fee, will be collected by the Postal Service. If your purchase is being sent to you through a freight handler, you will be notified by the carrier of the arrival of your shipment, at which time you will go to the customs office processing your shipment and complete the entry process. Any duty or tax owed will be paid at that time. Freight and express packages delivered without prior arrangements for acceptance will be placed in storage by U.S. Customs after five days. This is at the expense and risk of the owner. Items remaining unclaimed for one year will be sold. Mail parcels not claimed within 30 days are returned to the sender unless a duty assessment is being protested.

RATES OF DUTY: Various rates of duty for some of the more popular items imported by travelers are listed below for use as an advisory guide only. Rates of duty depend on country in which the item was manufactured and purchased, and rates vary as much as 90 percent on products from Communist-dominated or -controlled areas. The following assessments are averages in most cases:

	Internal Revenue	Customs Duty
Alcoholic Beverages *(per gallon 128 fluid ounces)* Brandy, Gin, Liquers, Rum, Vodka, Whiskey	$10.50	.31 to $3.40
Wine (sparkling)	$2.40 to $3.40	$1.17
(still)	.17 to $2.25	.31 to $1.00
Antiques *(produced prior to 100 before entry certificate required)*		*Free*
Bags *(hand, leather)*		*8.5–10%*
Beads *(imitation, precious, semi-precious).*		*7–13%*
Books *(foreign author or language)*		*Free*
Books *(foreign author or language)*		*Free*
Cameras:		
motion picture (valued over $50)		*6%*
still (valued over $10)		*7.5%*
lenses		*8.8%*
China:		
bone		*11.6%*
nonbone		*14.1%*
tableware		*30.7%*
Clocks *valued over $10 (10%, plus 3.9 cents per jewel, and*		*.70*
Figurines *(china)*		*12.5–22.5%*
Fur *(wearing apparel)*		*7.4–11.6%*
Golf balls		*3.8%*
Ivory		*4.9%*
Jade (cut but not set)		*2.5%*
Jewelry *(average)*		*12.5%*
Perfume *(in addition to 3 cents per pound)*		*plus $10.50 per gallon excise tax*
Radios *(transistor)*		*7.7%*
Shoes *(leather)*		*2.5–20%*

More and New Exemptions

Another boon for the shopping traveler is a little-known law that permits duty-free entry of certain articles brought into the United States from some 100 developing countries and 40 dependent territories under the U.S. Generalized System of Preferences (GSP). It is intended to help developing nations improve their financial or economic conditions through export trade. It allows duty-free importation of a wide range of products otherwise subject to customs duty. The law went into effect on January 1, 1976,

About 2,700 items have been designated as eligible for duty-free treatment. For your guidance, I'll list the most popular tourist purchases. Many items, such as footwear, textile articles (including clothing), watches, some electronic products, and certain glass and steel products, are excluded from duty-free entry. This exemption list is determined by the effect importation has on U.S. industry.

To take advantage of GSP, you must have acquired the eligible article in the beneficiary country where it was grown, manufactured, or produced. Articles may accompany you or may be shipped from the developing country directly to the United States, and the same duty-free GSP status applies.

To play safe, request that the merchant complete a certificate of origin or reasonable facsimile. Remember that most items purchased in duty-free shops will not be eligible for GSP treatment unless the merchandise was produced in the country in which the duty-free shop is located. You can't purchase a Brazilian gem in Jamaica, for instance, and claim a GSP exemption. You can purchase the same gem in Brazil and receive the exemption.

GSP items are not exempt from Internal Revenue taxes. If you bring back Barbados rum, for example, there won't be any duty, but there will be IRS tax due.

Duty-free items brought back from the designated countries will not affect your normal $400 duty-free allowance ($800 from the Virgin Islands). But remember, you must list all items brought into the United States, no matter whether they are subject to duty or come under GSP. If articles fall into the GSP category, note country of purchase and origin on your declaration.

Visitors and non-residents are entitled to bring in articles that are duty-free under GSP, in addition to their basic customs exemption.

The list below is an advisory guide to items designated as eligible for duty-free treatment under GSP. Note that certain items from particular countries may be excluded. The list of exclusions and countries changes annually, so check with your nearest customs office or the American Embassy or consulate in the country you are visiting. The information quoted here is projected as accurate for 1985.

ITEMS EXEMPT FROM U. S. DUTY WHEN PURCHASED AND MANUFACTURED IN LISTED GSP COUNTRIES

Cameras (motion picture; still; lenses; other photographic equipment)
Candy
Chinaware (bone, nonbone; tableware not included)
Cigarette Lighters (pocket; table)

Cork (except from Portugal)
Earthen Tableware or Stoneware (available in 77-piece sets and valued not over $12 per set; except from Rumania)
Figurines (china)
Flowers (artificial, of plastic or manmade fibers)
Furniture (wood or plastic)
Furs (wearing apparel; gloves; excluded from Argentina)
Games (played on boards: chess, backgammon, darts, mah-jongg)
Golf Balls and Equipment
Ivory (beads and other ivory articles; except from Hong Kong)
Jade (cut but not set for use in jewelry; other jade articles)
Jewelry (of precious metal, stones, or silver) and flatware not valued at more than $18 per dozen; all other, except from Hong Kong)
Motorcycles
Music Boxes
Musical Instruments (except pianos)
Paper (manufactures of)
Pearls (cultured or imitation, loose or temporarily strung and without clasp)
Perfume
Printed Matter
Radio Receivers (solid state, not for motor vehicles; except from Republic of Hong Kong, Singapore, and Korea)
Records (phonograph; tapes)
Shavers (electric)
Shells and articles made from shells (except from the Philippines)
Silver (tableware and flatware)
Skis and Ski Equipment (ski boots not included)
Stones (sapphires and rubies, cut but not set, suitable for use in Jewelry — except from Thailand; emeralds and diamonds not included; semi-precious stones, cut but not set, suitable for use in jewelry)
Tape Recorders
Toilet Preparations (except bay rum and bay water from Bermuda)
Toys (dolls not included, except from Hong Kong)
Wood (carvings)

Beneficiary Countries

The countries listed have been designated as beneficiary developing countries in the U.S. Generalized System of Preferences:

INDEPENDENT COUNTRIES

Angola
Argentina
Bahamas
Bahrain
Bangladesh
Barbados
Belize
Bhutan
Bolivia
Botswana
Brazil
Burma
Burundi
Cameroon
Cape Verde
Central African Empire
Chad
Chile
Colombia
Congo (Brazzaville)
Costa Rica
Cyprus
Dominica
Dominican Republic
Egypt
El Salvador
Equatorial Guinea
Fiji
Gambia
Ghana
Grenada
Guatemala
Guinea
Guinea Bissau

Guyana
Haiti
Honduras
India
Indonesia
Israel
Ivory Coast
Jamaica
Jordan
Kenya
Korea, Republic of
Lebanon
Lesotho
Liberia
Malagasy Republic
Malawi
Malaysia
Maldives
Mali
Malta
Mauritania
Mauritius
Mexico
Morocco
Mozambique
Nauru
Nepal
Nicaragua
Niger
Oman
Pakistan
Panama
Papua New Guinea

Paraguay
Peru
Philippines
Portugal
Rumania
Rwanda
Sao Tome and Principe
Saint Vincent and Grenadine
Senegal
Sierra Leone
Singapore
Somalia
Sri Lanka
Sudan
Surmam
Swaziland
Syria
Tarzania
Thailand
Togo
Tonga
Trinidad and Tobago
Tunisia
Turkey
Upper Volta
Uruguay
Venezuela
Western Samoa
Yemen
Yugoslavia
Zaire
Zambia
Zimbabwe

NON-INDEPENDENT COUNTRIES AND TERRITORIES

Afars and Issas, French
   Territory of the
Antigua
Belize
Bermuda
British Indian Ocean
   Territory
British Solomon Islands
Brunei
Cayman Islands
Christmas Island (Australia)
Cocos (Keeling) Islands
Comoro Islands
Dominica
Falkland Islands (Malvinas)
   and Dependencies

French Polynesia
Gibraltar
Gilbert Islands
Heard Island and
   McDonald Islands
Hong Kong
Macao Wallis and
   Futuna Islands
Montserrat
Netherlands Antilles
New Caledonia
New Hebrides
Condominium
Niue
Norfolk Island

Pitcairn Island
Portuguese Timor
Saint Christopher—Nevis—
   Anguilla
Saint Helena
Saint Lucia
Saint Vincent
Seychelles
Spanish Sahara
Tokelau Islands
Trust Territory of the
   Pacific Islands
Turks and Caicos Islands
Tuvula
Virgin Islands, British

CANADIAN CUSTOMS

Canadians planning a trip outside Canada should take a close look at the amount of exemptions allowed and the restrictions imposed on them when they return home to Canada. It is strongly recommended to register such valuable items as cameras, jewelry, and electronics with Canadian Customs at departure points. This will facilitate re-entry of these items.

Exemptions

Any resident of Canada returning from abroad may qualify for personal exemption and bring into Canada goods up to a specific value, free of duty and taxes. There are no age limitations, and even an infant can qualify.

The personal exemption, however, has limitations on the frequency of its use, on the length of stay abroad, and, concerning alcoholic beverages and tobacco products, on the age of the individual.

Goods brought in under a personal exemption must be for personal or household use, souvenirs, or gifts for friends or relatives. The exemption is a very personal thing for which an individual qualifies at a given time. It cannot be pooled with or transferred to other individuals. You cannot, for example, combine your quarterly and yearly exemptions and claim the total as a special exemption. Nor can you use half of your yearly exemption and save the remainder for another trip six months later.

Details

After 48 hours or more of absence for an unlimited number of times during a year, you may bring in goods valued up to $10, and only an oral declaration is required. Once in every calendar quarter you may bring in goods valued up to $50, and a written declaration may be required. After seven days' absence or longer, once every calendar year you may bring in goods valued up to $150, and a written declaration will be required. You can claim a yearly ($150) and a quarterly ($50) exemption in one calendar quarter, provided these are claimed for separate trips.

Tobacco and Alcoholic Beverages

You may bring in alcoholic beverages and tobacco products free of duty and taxes, if you are eligible for the quarterly ($50) or yearly

116

($150) exemption. The dollar value of these items will be part of your personal exemption. Any person 16 years of age or older may bring in 200 cigarettes, 50 cigars, and two pounds of tobacco. Additional quantities may be brought in but are subject to duty and taxes on the excess amount.

If you meet the age requirements set by the province or territory through which you re-enter Canada, you may bring in 40 ounces of wine or liquor or 24 twelve-ounce cans or bottles of beer or ale (288 fluid ounces). All provinces, except Prince Edward Island and the Northwest Territories, allow you to exceed the normal allowance up to 2 extra gallons, but the cost is high, and a special permit is required. All tobacco products and alcoholic beverages must accompany you in order to qualify for exemptions.

You may send gifts from abroad to friends or relatives in Canada as long as these parcels are not valued at more than $15 Canadian and do not contain alcoholic beverages, tobacco products, or advertising matter. Duty and taxes will be assessed on gifts valued over $15 Canadian. Make sure a gift card is enclosed to avoid misunderstanding. Gifts mailed from abroad are not declared on re-entering Canada and are not counted in your exemption.

Canadian Declarations

When you re-enter Canada, you must declare to Canadian customs everything acquired abroad, purchases as well as gifts. You must also declare all goods you brought before you left at Canadian duty-free stores and are still carrying with you. Goods should be easily accessible for inspection, and it is a good idea to have receipts available.

Goods brought in under any of the exemptions must accompany you in hand or checked luggage, no matter what countries you have visited. It is advisable to declare all "goods to follow," meaning you should declare purchases being mailed to you in Canada. When you are notified that your parcel has arrived, you have 30 days to clear it through customs. You must present your copy of the declaration form.

EXCEEDING THE EXEMPTION: There is no law that prevents you from bringing back any quantity of goods, provided you are willing to pay the full rate of duty and taxes. On the first $150 worth, there is a special rate of 25 percent, if you have been away from Canada for 48 hours or more. On quantities over that, regular duty and taxes will be assessed.

TTT: If you are bringing in far less than your allowable personal exemption, the customs officer will advise you if it would be to your advantage to clear the goods under the 25 percent special rate and save your personal exemption for another trip.

DUTY AND TAXES: Customs assessments depend on what you buy and where you buy it. Canada's trade agreements list "British preferential" and the "most favored nations." The "British preferential" tariff rate applies to goods purchased in Britain and in most Commonwealth countries. The United States is listed as one of the "most favored nation" group.

The following items are free of duty and all taxes: coin and stamp collections, signed original paintings valued at more than $20, original sculptures and valued at more than $75.

A 12 percent sales tax is imposed on the following, regardless of whether the items are included in your exemption: camera accessories, electric razors, and some musical instruments.

Duty, but no sales tax, is imposed on the following items. They must have been purchased in a "most favored nation."

Clothing:
Cotton. 22½%
Wool, knitted. 27½%
Man-made fibers 25%

Most audio-visual equipment (radios, TVs, and so on) are taxed, and duty is assessed at an average of 15 percent; sporting goods can cost returning Canadians as much as 20 percent, and jewelry up to 25 percent.

Hints and Tips

Although uniforms have a tendency to intimidate, travelers should be aware that "customsphobia" is a highly-overrated condition. Misconceptions aside, customs inspectors are not ogres. They are simply interested in getting their job done without harassment of innocent travelers. Their job is simple: to prevent the smuggling of narcotics and other contraband and to provide the federal government with the import revenues to which it is entitled.

Nevertheless, customs inspectors do not like smart alecks and, being human, will sometimes be tougher with the occasional traveler who tries to outsmart them. Unless you like to play games and are trying to bring in a barrel of diamonds, it makes little sense to try to avoid paying duty.

Facing U.S. Customs is a lot easier if you keep your sales slips, invoices, and other evidence of purchase available, should the Inspector ask for verification. Pack your baggage so inspection of purchases is easy. Try to pack separately the articles you acquired abroad. When the Customs Officer asks you to open your luggage, don't hesitate or try to talk him out of it.

If you know before you go, and follow the rules, clearing U.S. Customs is a breeze.

Preclearance and Registration

A couple of new wrinkles have been added to the system, and both make clearing Customs a lot faster. First: before you leave the country, you can register only items with a serial or registration number. No jewelry or other items without these numbers can be registered, since they are difficult to identify.

The second new procedure is made to order for cruise passengers and speeds debarkation by a couple of hours. With cooperation by the Customs Service and the cruise lines, most ships requiring clearance on arrival in Florida enjoy clearance on board ships. What happens is simple. Customs and immigrations officers board vessels as they enter the harbor. Passengers are given forms to complete and one member of each family meets the Inspector, declares his goods. If there is a tax to be paid, the amount is determined by the Inspector and paid by the traveler on debarkation. Once you have been cleared on board ship, you need only collect your luggage on shore and be on your way. A word of caution is in order. Don't try to cheat U.S. Customs and make a false declaration on board ship. Taxes are very low on items exceeding duty-free quotas, but the embarrassment and fines can be mighty expensive.

Also, be sure you have your customs form completed before you get into a line for clearance. This holds true on board ship or in airports. Nothing is sharper than the edge created when a traveler holds up a line while he completes a simple form.

TTT: If there is some larceny in your soul, you should know that a preclearance is a matter of honor, but spot checks are made by inspectors in the customs area. If you are caught and have cheated on your declaration, penalties and seizure can be imposed. Preclearance speeds debarkation and helps passengers and cruise ships. It also avoids mob scenes in small customs areas. More ships are eyeing preclearance systems, and you will be told at the pre-debarkation briefing whether your vessel uses on-board preclearance or whether you will have to show and tell your luggage and purchases.

TTT: Frequently travelers want to know about:

PASSPORTS: Contact the Passport Field Agency nearest you at the following zip codes: Boston 02203; Chicago 60604; Detroit 48226; Honolulu 96850; Houston 77002; Los Angeles 90261; Miami 33130; New Orleans 70130; New York 10021; Philadelphia 19106; San Francisco 94102; Seattle 98174; Stamford CT 06901; and Washington, D.C. 20542. Some Clerks of Court and Postal Clerks also issue passports.

VISAS: Get in touch with the nearest appropriate Embassy in Washington, D.C. or nearest consular office. Or, have your travel agent handle all visas for you. Or, use a visa service. I have been satisfied with prompt service by Travel Agenda, 119 West 57th St., New York, NY 10019 (212) 265-7887. For a small fee, plus visa charges, the company handles multiple visas. Well worth it when you are in a hurry and cannot spare your passport for any length of time.

INOCULATIONS: Contact your local or state health department. They keep up with U.S. Center for Disease Control advisories.

FOREIGN CURRENCY: Your local bank can give you the information, or check your Sunday newspaper business or financial section. The national airline of the country to which you are traveling also is up on exchange rates.

Ports of Embarkation

BALTIMORE Dundalk Marine Terminal

Location: On Broening Highway. By car, exit from I–95.
Parking Facilities: Dockside parking in guarded park-and-lock lot opposite terminal, $1.00 per day. Visitor parking free.
Transfers: City bus service to terminal from any point in Baltimore area, 75 cents. Taxi from city, about $10.00, from airport, $15.00. Ride takes 20 minutes from downtown Baltimore, 25 minutes from Baltimore-Washington International Airport.
Ships: Periodic calls by *Oriana, Royal Viking, Bermuda Star, Rhapsody.*

BOSTON Commonwealth Pier 5

Location: In South Boston. By car, easily reached from Central Artery via High Street exit or Northern Avenue-Atlantic Avenue ramp. Pier is about 1,200 feet away from the airport, opposite.
Parking Facilities: Indoor secured parking available to cruise passengers for $2.50 per day, payable in advance. Outside guarded lot opposite terminal, $1.00 per day. Free visitor parking.
Transfers: Taxi from Logan International Airport to pier, about $8.00 for 10-minute ride; from downtown Boston, about $5.00 for 5-minute ride.
Ships: Periodic calls by *Carnivale, Oriana, Mardi Gras,* and *Royal Viking Sea.*

CHARLESTON Passenger terminal

Location: On Concord Street at foot of Market Street, in city's peninsular area.
Parking Facilities: Secured long-term parking for cruise passengers, $3.00 per day. Shuttle service provided. Visitor parking free.

Transfers: Limousine service from airport, $7.00. Taxi, $13.00.
Ships: Seasonal cruise ship visits include: *Galileo, Mermoz, Rhapsody, Veracruz.*

LOS ANGELES   San Pedro/Wilmington terminals

Location: By car, Harbor Freeway, 25 miles south from downtown Los Angeles to San Pedro or Wilmington. For Royal Viking and Sitmar Cruises, off at C Street, east to Avalon, south to Berth 195. For Carnival Cruise Line's *Tropicale,* Princess Cruises, *QE2,* and others, take Harbor Freeway to Harbor Boulevard to Berth 95.

Parking Facilities: Cars picked up and returned dockside for storage rate of $25 for 3 to 4 days; $40 for 7 days; up to $70 monthly. No long-term parking within terminal. Reservations required: Central Garage, 127 West "B" St., Wilmington, CA (213)834-3123 or, Seventh St. Garage, 777 S. Center St., San Pedro, CA (213)832-4335 (about $5 per day).

Transfers: Bus transportation poor and undependable. Taxi from down town Los Angeles to port, about $25; from airport, about $25.

Ships: Regular schedule — *Fairwind, Pacific Princess, Royal Viking Sea, Royal Viking Sky, Tropicale.*

PORT OF MIAMI   Passenger terminals
(Dodge Island)

Location: On island in protected Biscayne Bay, connected with downtown Miami by drawbridge. By car, easily reached from Biscayne Boulevard at N.E. 5th Street. Complete directions to piers available at port entrance. Separate, air conditioned lounges for each of nine passenger terminals. (Saturday is busiest day of the week.)

Parking Facilities: Secured lots opposite each terminal. Long-term parking, $3.00 per day. Visitor parking, $1.00.

Transfers: Bus transportation provided, with departures every half hour from airport and downtown Miami. Limousine from airport, $6.00 per person; from Miami Beach. $5.50 per person. Taxi from airport, $12.00 from Miami Beach, $8.00. Ride takes about 20 minutes from Miami International Airport and Miami Beach.

Ships: Home port for *Caribe I, Carnivale, Dolphin, Emerald Seas, Festivale, Mardi Gras, Nordic Prince, Norway Skyward, Song of Norway, Southward, Song of America, Starward, Sun Viking, Sunward II.* And new *Holiday.*

NEW ORLEANS

Location: At foot of Poydras Street on the river, next to the Hilton Hotel.

Parking Facilities: Indoor parking at the Rivergate, opposite the terminal, $3.00 per day. At the Rivergate Building $3.00 per day. At north wharf and south wharf, $12.00 per week. Visitor parking free.

Transfers: Limousine service from airport, $4.00. Taxi from airport, $7.00, from mid-city hotels, $4.00

Ships: Bermuda Star

NEW YORK   Passenger terminal

Location: New port facilities on Hudson River at West Houston Street. By car or taxi, easily reached from exits on the West Side Highway between 42nd and 57th streets.

Parking Facilities: Open roof-top parking for 1,000 cars for visitors on sailing and arrival days. Reached by automobile ramp at 55th Street and 12th Avenue. Visitor parking charge, about $6 (charged by hour). Long-term, covered parking next to Passenger Ship Terminal at Pier 94; free courtesy car to and from terminal. (For parking reservations, write Kinney System, 711 Twelfth Avenue, New York, New York 10019.) A convenient service also offered by Oil Market Garage, Inc. Attendants, on the street level in front of ships, will pick up cars and deliver them when ship returns to port. All indoor parking in protected building. Minimum charge covering five days of parking, $25 ($6 each additional day). Long-term rates for more than 30 days. Typical rate covering 22 to 30 days, $80. (For service, write Oil Market Garage, Inc. 575 Eleventh Avenue, New York, New York 10036).

Transfers: Metered taxis from midtown hotels, $7.00. From La Guardia Airport, limousine service, $8.00 per person; taxi, $15.00 to $17.00, plus tolls. From John F. Kennedy International Airport, limousine service, $10.00; taxi, $20.00 to $25.00, plus tolls. Limousines from airports to East Side Airline Terminal, than taxi to pier, about $12.00. Ride takes a few minutes from midtown Manhattan; about 45 minutes from Kennedy Airport; about 30 minutes from La Guardia and Newark airports.

Ships: Atlantic, Oceanic, Queen Elizabeth 2, Royal Viking ships, Bermuda Star, Nordic Prince, Veracruz.

PORT EVERGLADES (Fort Lauderdale, FL)   Passenger terminals

Location: In southeast Fort Lauderdale. Main entrance at intersection of
   Route 84 and U.S. 1 (Federal Highway). Easy access from I–95,
   Route 7 (U.S. 441), or Florida Turnpike. Located five miles from
   Fort Lauderdale/ Hollywood International Airport.
Parking Facilities: Vehicle outdoor-storage at piers, $3 per day (payable
   in advance). No charge for visitor parking.
Transfers: Intercity buses from Miami and Palm Beach, city buses to
   port entrance. Limousine from Miami Airport, about $8.00 per per-
   son. Taxi from Fort Lauderdale Airport, $6.00; from Miami airport,
   about $25; from downtown Fort Lauderdale, about $5.00. Ride
   takes about an hour from Miami International Airport; 10 minutes
   from Fort Lauderdale Airport.
*Ships: Amerikanis, Atlantic, Canberra, Danae, Fairwind, Rotterdam, Oceanic,
   Queen Elizabeth 2, Rhapsody, Royal Viking* ships, *Sagafjord, Vistafjord,
   Stella Solaris.*

SAN FRANCISCO   Passenger terminals

Location: Adjacent to downtown area and Fisherman's Wharf along the
   Embarcadero. By car, easily reached from San Francisco Bay Bridge
   (Main Street exit to Mission Street) and Golden Gate Bridge. Most
   ships leave from Pier 35 at foot of Bay Street.
Parking: Cars and taxis allowed on pier to discharge passengers, but no
   vehicle storage available in area. Advance arrangements with local
   garages or parking lots on daily or weekly basis recommended. Lim-
   ited visitor parking between piers 31 and 33 for $5.00. *Transfers:* Taxi
   from St. Francis Hotel (midtown), about $5.00; from air port, about
   $20.00. Ride takes about 45 minutes from airport.
*Ships: Fairsea, Fairsky, Pacific Princess, Royal Viking, Santa Magdalena, Santa
   Maria, Santa Mariana, Santa Mercedes, Sun Princess, Nieuw Amsterdam,
   Sagafjord, Noordam.*

SAN JUAN (PUERTO RICO)   Passenger terminal

Location: In the old San Juan waterfront district, within walking distance of Old City center.
Parking Facilities: Difficult for long-term parking. Rates at Pier 3, fifty
   cents first hour; 25 cents each additional hour; No parking charges
   at other piers. Limited visitor parking.

Transfers: Most air-sea passengers are transferred by air conditioned bus from airport. Metropolitan public transport by bus available. Taxi rate, depending on use of meter, about $8.50.

Ships: Among vessels using this port of embarkation (increasingly popular because of Puerto Rico's proximity to other Caribbean ports of call): *Daphne, Danae, Britanis, Carla C,* Cunard's *Countess* and *Princess, Mermoz.*

RATING PORTS OF EMBARKATION

TTT: Our panel of experts who participated in rating ships was also asked to rate ports of embarkation based on accessibility, transfer service between airports and port, waiting rooms, baggage handling, Customs, attitude of dock workers, tipping and general appearance and facilities. Evaluation was based on the same 1 to 10 system used to rate ships. The Port of Miami received the top overall rating (8.9). *Vancouver, *Hong Kong and Port Everglades (Fort Lauderdale, Florida) tied for second place with 8. Others were rated as follows: Baltimore 5; Boston 5; Los Angeles 4.5; New Orleans 6.5; San Francisco 7.5; San Diego 7.5; Piraeus 4.5; Savannah 6.5; Charleston 7 and Philadelphia 6.7.

*Hong Kong and Vancouver were not profiled in Ports of Embarkation Chapter because almost all passengers arrive on air-sea packages and do not use port facilities except for embarkation and debarkation.

The Shipping Companies

In these times of economic uncertainty, passengers and other travelers show increased concern about stability of cruise lines holding their money for months prior to scheduled sailings. And, these concerns are understandable, particularly after the demise of airlines as respected and reputable as Laker, Air Florida and Braniff.

All cruise companies with vessels sailing from U.S. ports and selling passage in the United States are bonded for default and must abide by State laws covering consumer rights. But travelers have a right to know a little more about these companies, their financial stability, their history, and experience with ships.

For those reasons and others (like a natural curiosity about the people behind the operation of the companies), THE TOTAL TRAVELER BY SHIP includes a chapter covering "The Shipping Companies." While researching, I learned that many are being operated by second and third generation shipping families; others have the financial and business backing of European companies with centuries of experience in passenger and cargo vessels.

AMERICAN HAWAII CRUISES
3 Embarcadero Center
San Francisco, CA 94111

Headquartered in San Francisco, American Hawaii Cruises operates the only inter-Hawaiian Island cruises. Both ships are of U.S. registry and employ U.S. crews. How this came about is an interesting story.

The keel of the first Independence, a United States Naval vessel, was laid in 1813 and was, at the time, America's foremost maritime defense vessel.

The second half of the 20th century produced an all new *Independence*. Constructed in the Bethlehem Quincy Ship Yard in Massachusetts in 1951, it was the largest passenger ship built in the United States for more than a decade. The now famous *SS Independence* was built for

American Export Lines, designed and constructed to be the fastest, safest and most comfortable cruise liner ever to fly the American Flag. More than $50 million was expended for the planning, building, furnishing and equipping of the ship, and the Nation's most outstanding ship building and allied talents were employed in its creation, using thousands of craftsmen from almost every state in the Union.

The ship was designed to carry over 1,000 passengers on long cruises between New York and the Mediterranean and boasted 23,000 feet of open deck space along with large and sumptuously appointed public lounges and staterooms.

In 1974 the ship was purchased by Atlantic Far East Lines (part of the well known C.Y. Tung Group of Hong Kong) and entered cruise services in South Africa.

In 1978, with the demise of the Pacific Far East Line, a number of Americans decided they would not allow America's great maritime traditions to cease, and they set about obtaining the necessary Federal legislation, which influenced the Congressional Act passed in November, 1979. This opened the way for the ship to be redocumented under the United States flag although the vessel had been operating under Panamanian registry. This was done and the vessel was renamed the *SS Oceanic Independence*. President Carter signed this bill into law on November 15, 1979 and American Hawaii Cruises was in business.

Immediately, a team of interior designers and craftsmen was put to work on the ship to restore and renew its former elegance. The job was finished in June, 1980, and the vessel re-entered American cruise operations on a year around program of seven day cruises sailing from Honolulu every Saturday.

The *Independence* was joined in 1982 by the *Constitution* which underwent similar redocumentation, refurbishing and reconstruction and both ships sail on regular Saturday and Sunday departures from Honolulu.

BAHAMA CRUISE LINE
4600 West Kennedy Blvd.
Tampa, FL 33609

Bahama Cruise Line is a wholly owned subsidiary of Common Brother, Ltd., a company in the shipping business since 1890 when it was formed to transport troops to Hindustan. Bahama Cruise Line was a one-ship fleet (*Veracruz*) until 1984 when Holland America's *Veendam* was purchased by the C.Y. Tung Group of Hong Kong and Bahama

Cruise Line became the operator. Company has announced an on-going refurbishment plan for both vessels.

CARNIVAL CRUISE LINES
5225 N.W. 8th Ave.
Miami, FL 33136

Carnival Cruise Lines is a family owned and operated company formed in 1972 specifically to operate the *T.S.S. Mardi Gras*. Owner Ted Arison had just separated business interests from Norwegian Caribbean Lines when he acquired the *Mardi Gras*. Within a short time, she was transformed from a two-class transatlantic ship to a one-class vessel geared to Caribbean cruising on a year around basis.

Carnival's intention was to bring cruising to middle America, to the cross section of Americans who had never seen the ocean and never thought of sailing an ocean liner. From those marketing dreams, evolved the "Fun Ship" concept of cruising. By 1975, she was carrying more passengers than competing vessels and Carnival purchased her almost identical sister ship, the *T.S.S. Carnivale*, formerly the *Empress of Britain*. Demand was so great, the ships set occupancy records in 1976.

In 1977, the company purchased the *s.a. Vaal*, rebuilt and refurbished her in a Japanese shipyard at a cost of more than $20 million and expanded the fleet to three one-week ships sailing from the Port of Miami. The vessel was renamed the *Festivale*.

One year later, at a time when oil prices were dramatically increasing and cruise lines were concerned about operational costs, CCL began construction of a new superliner, the *M.S. Tropicale*. She inaugurated service in January, 1982 and launched a new generation of passenger ships. (See Tropicale profile).

Expansion and growth of the Miami-based company is not finished. Three additional ships are under construction. The *Holiday* goes into service in mid–1985 and will be followed in 1986 and 1987 by the *Jubilee* and *Celebration*. All three ships will be 48,000 tons. Construction of a fourth vessel, still unnamed, will probably begin in early 1985 at the same Danish shipyard that built the *Holiday*. She'll be an almost exact sister-ship and be completed by 1987. Vessels cost in excess of $150 million each, representing a total commitment to the cruise industry of almost a billion dollars by a company that was not in business 15 years ago.

Carnival Cruise Line has racked up an enviable record in the cruise industry. For 10 consecutive years, the ships have averaged better than 100 percent occupancy. Much of the credit is given to the aggressive, young marketing and sales team. I give much of the credit to the close-knit, family type of operation. The president, Micky Arison, is a third generation shipping man. His grandfather, Ted's father, operated passenger and cargo ships in the Mediterranean.

The marketing team is responsible for many of the free air and reduced rate offerings that spur other companies into competing rate structures.

The "Fun Ship" image, bolstered by around the clock activities, is carried over on all CCL vessels. It is realistic to look for a 10-ship moderately priced, contemporary fleet by the end of the decade.

CHANDRIS, INC.
666 Fifth Ave.
New York, NY 10019

John D. Chandris purchased his first vessel, the sailing ship *Simitrios* in 1915, an event which marked the founding of Chandris Cruises. He followed that with purchase of steamers, and entered the passenger shipping industry in 1922 with the *Chimara*. But the Chandris family, still actively involved in operation of the vast interests, says real entry into the passenger side of shipping came with purchase in 1936 of the 1,705 ton *Corte II* from the French. Chandris promptly renamed her *Patris*. She carried 161 one-class passengers to Venice, the Greek Islands and the Holy Land. John Chandris died at the end of the war, and his two sons, Dimitios and Antony, took over. They built one of the largest shipping companies in the world.

Some of the highlights in the growth pattern of the company include purchase of the *Lurline*, today's *Ellinis*, operated around the world to Australia, through the Suez Canal on her outbound voyage and through the Panama Canal on the way home. More purchases and conversion followed: the *President Hoover*, (purchased and renamed *Regina Prima*); the *Queen Frederica*; *America* renamed the *Australis* (now sailing as the *Italis*); *Kenya Castle* converted and renamed *Amerikanis*; *Amsterdam* became the *Fiorita*; *Aurelia* is the *Romanza*; *President Roosevelt*, the *Atlantic*, *Lurline*, the *Britanis*, and the *Victoria*.

Chandris doesn't operate all of their own vessels. A number have been chartered out to other companies and it is sometimes difficult to keep up with which are Chandris owned and operated, and which vessels are not. Most Chandris ships on charter to other companies remain manned and staffed by Chandris' Greek crews, which adds to confusion in the marketplace. For example, Fantasy Cruises, an American company, operates the Chandris owned *Amerikanis*, *Britanis* and recently purchased *Galileo.* What passengers get is a mix of Greek and Italian nationalities on board.

Chandris also is involved in land resort operations and owns two hotels on Corfu, hotels on Chios and Crete and the Chandris Athens Hotel.

CLIPPER CRUISE LINE
7711 Bonhomme Ave. St. Louis, MO 63105

Headquartered in St. Louis, Clipper Cruise Line is owned and operated by Barney Ebsworth who also owns and operated INTRAV, a highly successful wholesale tour company. Ebsworth formed Clipper with the intention of building and operating small vessels to cruise America's inland waterways. The first of three 100–110 passenger vessels, the *Newport Clipper,* went into service in 1983 and was followed by the *Nantucket Clipper* in late 1984. The *Charleston* Clipper is under construction and due to begin service in 1986. Vessels are well run with all American crews and service. They operate seasonally in New England and Southeast and Florida waters. Yacht-like in personality and size, they are not for travelers looking for casinos and round-the-clock entertainment. Nor are they for the budget priced traveler. They are for travelers who enjoy a quiet, relaxed atmosphere in large staterooms cruising through almost still waters. Since vessels are in a different port every day and evening, entertainment is based on shore-side lecturers and what is available in each port.

COMMODORE CRUISE LINE
1007 North America Way
Miami, FL 33131

Commodore Cruise Line was founded in 1966 when hotelier Sanford Chobol chartered the *m/s Princess Leopoldina* for a series of Caribbean cruises. The venture was very successful and Chobol decided the Caribbean could support regularly scheduled one-week cruises from Miami. In 1968 he brought the *m/s Boheme* into service. The vessel was built in Finland and especially designed for cruising warm waters.

The vessel's success was immediate and Commodore was having difficulty meeting demands. So, in 1973, the *m/s Bolero* was added to what looked like a growing fleet. The Bolero pioneered the western Mexico itinerary on a regular one week schedule. Interesting to note, this itinerary is now being followed by a half dozen vessels. In 1976, the Bolero returned to European service and was replaced by the *Cariber.*

The *Caribe* was sold by the owners in 1981 and now sails as the *Scandinavian Sun* and Commodore Cruise Line found a replacement vessel for her in the former *Olympia*. She was named the *Caribe I*.

Headquartered in Miami, Commodore was sold to Lion Ferry of Helstadt, Sweden, a joint venture-type of operation between Swedish and German companies engaged in ferry services in Europe. This transfer of ownership in the mid-1970's was followed by another sale of the company in 1980 to Sally Shipping Co. of Finland. Present owners are very large ferry operators with more than 15 vessels in their fleet. Flags on the *Boheme* have changed from German to Panamanian.

COSTA CRUISES
One Biscayne Tower
Miami, FL 33131

Costa Cruises is one of the oldest privately owned maritime firms in Italy, established in 1924 with the purchase of the freighter *Ravenna*.

Costa traces its beginnings even farther back to 1860 when Giacomo Costa founded an olive oil manufacturing concern which succeeded because of his original methods of refining and packaging.

In its growth years, Costa Cruises paralleled expansion begun by Giacomo. It is estimated that the wide interests held by the company and affiliated companies have about 100 Costa relatives and offspring managing and assuring its success.

In 1968, Costa pioneered Caribbean sailings from San Juan and today, the embarkation port remains important for the Line. In the same year, Costa is credited with revolutionizing the cruise industry through introduction of the air-sea concept.

Also in 1968, the Costa family made a major commitment to the U.S. market and Costa Cruises (nee Costa Line, Inc.) was formed and the first corporate office was opened in New York.

Going back a number of years, in 1948 the *Anna C.* came on line. This 12,000-ton vessel was the first air conditioned luxury Italian passenger ship of the post war period. *Anna C.*'s maiden voyage to South America was followed six months later by acquisition of two more passenger ships, the *Andrea C.* and the *Giovanna C.* The first passenger ship to be built by Costa was the 20,416-ton *Federico C.* in 1958 and in 1966, Costa's flagship, the 30,000-ton *Eugenio C.* was completed.

Costa is as loyal to its vessels as it is to its passengers and Italian crews. While the *Federico* has been sold to Premier Cruises and now sails as the *Royale,* the *Eugenio* remains part of the fleet and operates in the Mediterranean and South American waters.

Although Costa's passenger cruise line began officially with the *Anna C.* in 1948, the company's first U.S. cruise program started in 1959 with 13-day cruises from Miami on the *Franca C.* (My first cruise from the Port of Miami was on this one). The Mediterranean program began with Genoa departures in 1959; Venice sailings were introduced in 1967. From Miami, three and four-night cruise patterns to the Bahamas were initiated on the *Anna C.* in 1964, followed in 1966 with 10 and 11-day cruises on the Federico C. In 1984, names of ships in the Costa fleet were changed to include the word "Costa" instead of the familiar "C".

In mid–1983, Costa moved its corporate headquarters to Miami and changed marketing concepts with emphasis on seven day and longer cruises, including a 96 day World Cruise on the Danae. The *Costa Riviera* (ex *Marconi*) begins Caribbean service from Port Everglades, Florida in late 1985.

In addition to ships owned by Costa, the company operates on charter the *Danae* and *Daphne.* Ships owned by Costa fly Italian flags and are staffed by all-Italian crews. Vessels under charter arrangements are staffed by crews furnished by owners of the vessels (Greek on those mentioned above) but food and service is supervised by Costa representatives on board each ship.

CUNARD LINE
555 Fifth Ave.
New York, NY 10017

By some strange coincidence of history, Cunard, which was the first company to provide regular transatlantic passenger steamship service, is now the last.

The first Cunard vessel was the tiny, 1,154-ton paddlewheel steamer *Britannia,* which made her maiden transatlantic voyage in 1840. The last is the 67,107-ton *Queen Elizabeth 2,* which for 30 weeks of each year carries passengers across the Atlantic between Europe and America. Between the first ship in 1840 and the *QE 2* today a vast armada of passenger vessels filled the Atlantic. Among them, Cunard Line was always a leader, operating more than 175 ships in 138 years.

Samuel Cunard conceived the idea of regularly scheduled transatlantic steamship service in the late 1830's. It was his belief that ships could run on schedules like trains, and without dependence on wind and sail, steamships could offer regular advertised service. He was convinced ships could sail on specified dates, from specified ports to specified destinations.

For its time, it was a historic and monumental concept. It was an idea whose time had come. And, not only did he have the vision, but he also had the ability to bring it to fruition. Samuel Cunard was a Halifax merchant with American roots. As a young man he worked in shipping in Boston and may have sailed on Fulton's early steamboat, the *Clermont*. He prospered in various enterprises, including shipping, and was a mature man of 53, already successful and relatively wealthy, when he embarked on his new enterprise.

The basic plan, which was successful for the next 100 years, was to have steam ships operating in tandem so that regularity could be insured. He began with four near-sister ships, the *Britannia, Arcadia, Caledonia,* and *Columbia.* These vessels could make the Atlantic voyage in 14 days at 8 1/2 knots and maintain a weekly departure schedule from Liverpool.

As the speed of ships increased, fewer vessels were required and the ultimate dual service was reached with the *Queen Mary* and *Queen Elizabeth* making transatlantic crossings in less than a week and carrying nearly 2,000 passengers a voyage. Today, the *Queen Elizabeth 2* makes the voyage eastbound in five days and westbound in six (the time change and docking schedule accounts for the difference).

In the glory days of transatlantic passenger shipping, Cunard ships were household words. There was the *Aquitania, Mauretania, Berengeria, Luisitania, Carmania, Franconia, Queen Mary* and Queen Elizabeth. And, at one time, the Cunard advertising slogan, "getting there is half the fun," was known throughout the world.

In an earlier period, Cunard switched from wooden paddlewheel ships to iron hulled, screw driven vessels. The first of these was the *Andes* in 1852. She was a little larger than the *Britannia* and had a "stupendous" apartment 55 feet long. In 1856 Cunard built the famous *Persia,* and because the screw propeller was not yet proven, used a paddlewheel. The *Persia* was the largest ship in the world at the time. She was 390-feet long and 3,300 gross registered tons.

The *Servia* was built in 1881. She was a massive 7,392 tons and was the first Cunarder to be fitted with electric lights. Among the many Cunarders to come along were the 12,950-ton *Campania* in 1893 which was the first Cunard ship with two propellers; the *Carmania,* in 1905 which opened a new era in sea propulsion when she was built as the first turbine driven ship in the fleet.

The last great transatlantic liner, the *Queen Elizabeth 2,* entered service in 1969. She was designed to be a luxury Atlantic liner half the year and a cruise ship the other half. She is the last bastion of a mode of travel and way of life, that for most of the world, can only be experienced vicariously.

The future of transatlantic travel rests solely with the *Queen Elizabeth 2* and an occasional positioning voyage by one or the other of the world's smaller cruise ships. Beyond the *QE 2* lies only conjecture and a dream. Perhaps there will be a technological advance that will make a new great passenger ship possible. It's a remote likelihood, but it's a dream ship lovers cling to.

So, for now, enjoy, the *Queen Elizabeth 2*. She's the last of her kind.

CUNARD/NAC
555 Fifth Ave.
New York, NY 10017

Devotees of Norwegian American Cruises were concerned when Cunard Line announced the purchase of Norwegian American Cruises. The *Sagafjord* and *Vistafjord* had developed a loyal following and it took a great deal of assurance by Cunard that the product would not change and every effort would be made to improve them. And, that's what happened. Cunard spent $15 million to build additional deluxe accommodations and kept most of the trained deck and service crews. As a ship follower, it is always sad to see a company like Norwegian American go out of business. In operation for 70 years, it had made a name in the marketplace for service and ambience. Norwegian America Line first began in 1910 as Den Norseke Amerika-linje. It built its first vessel, the *Kristianiafjord,* which carried passengers between Norway and New York in 1913. Before it closed its doors, NAC had eight ships serve the company. The *Kristianiafjord* was joined in 1913 by the *Bergensfjord.* Both were 10,650 tons and carried passengers in three classes. In 1917 came the larger, 12,977 ton *Stavangerfjord* to replace the *Kristianiafjord.* Between wars, the *Bergensfjord* and *Stavangerfjord* maintained Norway-New York service, carrying over 400,000 passengers. In 1937, the two ships were joined by the 18,650 ton *Oslofjord.* During World War II, the *Bergensfjord* was a troop carrier for the Allies and the *Stavengerfjord* was commandeered by the Germans as a troop depot ship. After the war, she went back into transatlantic service alone. The *Bergensfjord* had been sold and the *Oslofjord* destroyed and replaced by a new *Oslofjord* in 1949.

When pleasure cruising gained in popularity after the war, the company offered Caribbean, Pacific and Mediterranean cruises. In 1956 a new *Bergensfjord* joined the fleet. The *Stavangerfjord* was retired in

1962 after 45 years of service, 770 Atlantic crossings, and having carried over half a million passengers.

In 1965 the *Sagafjord* made her inaugural voyage. The *Vistafjord* joined her in 1973 replacing the *Bergensfjord* and the *Oslofjord* and completing the fleet was before Cunard bought the company.

In 1981,the *Sagafjord* was completely refurbished and renovated and passenger capacity increased. Both the *Vistafjord* and *Sagafjord* are luxury ships, and Cunard continues to operate them with appeal to the up-scale traveler who can afford the best.

Cunard/NAC could have increased passenger berths to accommodate more than twice the present capacity, but opted instead to maintain the high ratio of service personnel to passengers and the quality of service.

EASTERN STEAMSHIP LINES/ WESTERN STEAMSHIP LINES

1220 Biscayne Blvd.
Miami, FL 33101

Eastern Steamship is a pioneer when it comes to cruising from Miami. It has had vessels in continuous service on three and four-day cruises to the Bahamas since 1953. In those days, its two ships (*Yarmouth* and *Evangeline*) included calls at Havana. The ships were replaced in the 1960s by the *Ariadne* and the *Bahama Star* and in 1970s by the *Emerald Seas*. The company maintains its image of "party cruising" and many of the original employees are still on staff.

A western subsidiary, Western Cruises, operates the *Azure Seas* out of San Pedro (Los Angeles) on Monday and Friday sailings to Ensenada (Mexico). The party and gambling theme is maintained on both east and west coast sailings.

Continuous refurbishing programs on both vessels are in place and company enjoys a high rate of repeat passengers.

HOLLAND AMERICA CRUISES

300 Elliot Ave, West
Seattle, WA 98119

Holland America Cruises influenced passenger shipping history from its very beginnings. Since 1872 when the first *S.S. Rotterdam* sailed on her maiden voyage from The Netherlands to New York City, there have been 136 Holland American vessels in service. The early links between Holland and America began a rich heritage and partnership maintained by Holland America Cruises.

Today, Holland America has a modern and integrated three-ship fleet, slated for expansion to four within the next few years. Officers are Dutch, crew from Indonesia. Holland America is unique in the industry with its "no tipping policy." Passengers may sign for most on-board purchases and even pay with a personal check in most cases. The vessels all offer informal daytime food services and there are no-smoking areas in all Holland America dining rooms.

When Holland America named its two new vessels, *Nieuw Amsterdam* and *Noordam,* it was following company tradition. Some of the oldies include vessels of both names as well as *Potsdam, Ryndam, Maasdam, Statendam* (recently sold to Paquet and renamed *Rhapsody*), all ending in "dam."

Talking of oldies, the first *Rotterdam* was an iron vessel carrying eight passengers in first class, 380 in steerage, plus 1500 tons of cargo. Two young Dutchmen commissioned the ship because they wanted to make sure she would remain in Rotterdam as home port. That maiden voyage was so successful, a new company was formed—Netherlands-American Steam Navigation Company. It became Holland America Line in 1896. Holland America Cruises is one facet of The Netherlands based company. HAC operates the North American cruise business.

Westours is a major subsidiary of HAL's extensive involvement in tourism and specializes in Western U.S., Alaska and Canada. It operates seven hotels, four day boats, a motorcoach fleet of nearly 200 vehicles. Westours' operations in the Yukon and Alaska have set industry standards for 38 years. Deluxe escorted motorcoach operations in the Canadian Rockies have been expanded in 1985 to include helicopter rides from Banff and golf at Jasper Park Lodge.

HOME LINES
1 World Trade Center
New York, NY 10611

Home Line's history goes back a little more than 30 years. Operations began in 1947 with the *S.S. Argentina* running between Italy and South America. Two additional passenger ships were added in 1948, the *S.S. Brazil* and the *M.V. Italia.* By late 1949 Home Lines also had the *S.S. Atlantic* in regular service

Other highlights in the company's history include addition to the fleet of the *S.S. Homeric* in 1955. While she was in Canada and Caribbean cruising service, the *Atlantic* was renamed the *Queen Frederica* and deployed into regular service between New York, Italy and Greece.

Home Lines was one of the first companies to enter the 7-day cruise market. In December, 1960, the *Italia* inaugurated highly suc-

136

cessful one week cruises between New York and Nassau; a service which has continued on other Home Line ships. The *Italia* was followed on this route by the *Homeric* (ex *Mariposa*) and later the *S.S. Oceanic*.

Home Lines' style was expanded in 1965 when the 39,241-ton *S.S. Oceanic* was put into service. The company terminated its transatlantic passenger services and concentrated exclusively on year around cruising. For the next several years, until the end of 1972, the Home Lines' program revolved around alternating the *S.S. Oceanic* and the *Homeric* in Caribbean and Bahamian cruise service. With growth in Florida-originating cruises, the *Homeric* moved winter headquarters to Fort Lauderdale for a year prior to being withdrawn from service. To fill that void, the company purchased the 25,300-ton *S.S. Hanseatic* (ex *S.S. Shalom*), refurbished her and rechristened her the *S.S. Doric*. She joined the fleet in 1974.

Home Lines, an American company headquartered in New York, is owned by a charitable foundation which supports a maritime school in Greece. It entered a new chapter in its history with construction and operation of the *S.S. Atlantic* which entered service in mid 1982. A new vessel is under construction in France and will enter service in mid–1986.

The company has an excellent reputation for service and quality. Also, a loyal following with passengers repeating voyages on an annual basis. Flags from the masts are Panamanian, but all deck and service personnel are Italian which is in keeping with the traditions of the company.

Up until the past couple of years, Home Lines did little marketing or advertising outside the northeastern United States and Eastern Canada. With addition of the $100 plus million *Atlantic,* and in anticipation of the new ship, marketing efforts have been expanded to the rest of the country.

On board, service is excellent. Most employees have been with the company for more than 10 years and are as loyal as the cadre of repeat passengers.

NORWEGIAN CARRIBEAN LINES
One Biscayne Tower
Miami, FL 33131

Ice and coal appear to have little in common with Caribbean cruising, but not to a family named Kloster. That family of three generations of Norwegian seafarers represents the past, present and the future for a company which has become one of the most important in America's cruise industry. Klosters Rederi A.S of Oslo has come a long way since 1906 when Lauritz Kloster purchased the 830-ton *Sjogutten* to haul ice and coal between Norway and Great Britain.

Today, doing business in the United States as Norwegian Caribbean Lines (NCL) and sailing in far warmer waters, NCL's fleet of five modern vessels carries over 250,000 passengers annually from the Port of Miami to the Bahamas, the Caribbean and Mexico, making it one of the largest cruise companies in North America just 18 years after its entry into the North American passenger market.

Growth and success is not new to the company. The pattern was first set at the outbreak of World War I when Lauritz Kloster built his merchant fleet up to a total of 135,000 deadweight tons. Even two World Wars did not diminish the activity of the Klosters fleet, although in both instances its utilization was diverted from business to government service. One of its ships, the cargo carrier *Lidvard* gained immortality during World War II when it escaped from the occupied port of Dakar and carried its officers and crew safely to London.

In the mid–1960's Knut Kloster entered the Miami-Caribbean one-week cruise market with his *M.S. Sunward.* Operating the company was Ted Arison (now owner of Carnival Cruise Lines). Between the two shipping geniuses, the one-week world of cruising from Miami was born. The NCL fleet rapidly increased to four vessels and Arison and Kloster ended their association in 1971. But the concept they created is a permanent part of cruising and is likely to remain so in the foreseeable future—one class, unstuffy, comfortable cruising. Both men were instrumental in the growth and development of the Port of Miami.

NCL's biggest gamble was investment of over $100 million in the purchase and transformation of the *S.S. France* into the *S.S. Norway.* No other ship in recent history created more headlines and coverage.

Not all of the family interests have been diverted by the Klosters to passenger shipping. Growth has continued in cargo transportation and it continues to expand in both areas. The U.S. operation is headquartered in Miami. Kloster says fleet expansion is not complete and he is studying feasibility of a super-ship of the future. (See Ships of the Future) He is not ruling out more conventional liners to the fleet before the end of the decade. Recent purchase of Royal Viking Line is an indication of the kind of expansion NCL may have in mind.

OCEAN CRUISE LINES
Two Executive Drive
Fort Lee, NJ 07024

The New Jersey-based company was organized in 1984 and is a division of Travellers, one of Europe's largest tour operators. In rather a complicated set-up, official owner of the company is a Swiss corporation named the 2000 Corporation. Company purchased the *Italia* and *City of Andros* and renamed them *Ocean Princess* and *Ocean Islander*, respectively. Spent a few million on putting them in shape and sent them out to sea. The *Ocean Princess,* in better condition to start with, went into immediate service in the Mediterranean. The *Islander* took more time in the shipyard and entered Caribbean service in late 1984. Company says a third ship will join the fleet in 1985 and it will be named the *Ocean Ambassador.*

Although original intention was to sail the vessels round trip from Piraeus, Greek law prevents ships not registered in Greece to follow this itinerary. So they will sail from Venice and Piraeus on alternate departures.

Company president is former Sitmar executive, Rick Williams, and he brings a lot of know-how to Ocean Cruise Lines. Inaugural season has brought problems relating to fast start-up and should be straightened out quickly. Inaugural price incentives warrant a close look by travelers bent on catching a bargain.

PAQUET CRUISES
1007 North America Way
Miami, FL 33132

A French company with a 120 year history in shipping, Paquet U.S. headquarters has moved from New York to Miami. Like many of the leading lines, Paquet was founded to provide ferry operations. Nicola Paquet in 1860 began passenger service with a chartered 350-ton vessel named the *Languedoc.* His company shuttled passengers between Marseille and Morocco. Within a few years, he and a few associates formed Compagnie de Navigation Paquet. Service was extended to the Canary Islands and Senegal. Routes to the eastern Mediterranean and other ports were added.

Paquet belongs to a French transportation conglomerate with shipping interests that still offer regular ferry service to North Africa. For some years, Paquet's fleet consisted of more than a half dozen ships, but in 1985, the company operates the *Azur* in Europe, the *Mermoz* in the Mediterranean and Caribbean from San Juan, and the *Rhapsody* (ex *Statendam*) which sails from Port Everglades during winter months and from Vancouver the rest of the year.

The European and U.S. companies are independently operated subsidiaries of Chargeurs S.A., the Paris-based parent company with diversified industrial interests, including air, sea and land transport, household products and textiles, among others, with annual gross revenues of two billion dollars.

Paquet has established a solid reputation of reliability and outstanding food services. Cuisine is French, for the most part, although international foods are served. Paquet continues its tradition of complimentary wines at dinner on all vessels.

The *Azur* runs out of Toulon to Mediterranean ports. She was built in 1971 (ex *Eagle*) and caters to a young European crowd. Paquet's ferry service is on the 10,500-ton passenger/car vessel *Massalia*. She sails out of Marseille to North Africa on a weekly basis.

PEARL CRUISES OF SCANDINAVIA
1700 Montgomery St.
San Francisco, CA 94111

A joint venture between two major Scandinavian shipping companies, Pearl Cruises of Scandinavia was formed in 1981 and purchased the *Finnstar*. While she was being converted and up-graded in a Danish shipyard, the new company researched cruising grounds and determined cruising from Hong Kong had a future. The vessel was renamed *Pearl of Scandinavia* and ownership changed during the first year of operation. It is now owned by Lauritz en A/S, a respected name in shipping, which also owns a major interest in DFDS.

Company is marketing club-like on board atmosphere (Club Pearl) and offers interesting itineraries between Hong Kong and Kobe (Japan) as well as to Indonesia and Singapore. It is also operating the 330-passenger *Princess Mahsuri*.

PRINCESS CRUISES
P&O
2029 Century Blvd.
Los Angeles, CA 90067

From very modest beginnings in 1965, Princess Cruises has emerged as one of the leading cruise companies in North America. The line's first ship was a 6,000-ton ferry chartered from Canadian Pacific Railway. She was the *Princess Patricia* from which the company name emerged. During the winters of 1965–66, the *Princess "Pat"* pioneered cruising Mexico's West Coast Riviera.

Demand soon outreached capacity on the *Princess Patricia* and two years later, Princess Cruises chartered the newly completed Italian ship *M/S Italia* and renamed her *Princess Italia.* She entered service in the fall of 1967 and the company expanded operations out of Los Angeles and San Francisco to Alaska and Canada.

As demand continued to exceed capacity, the *S.S. Carla* was chartered and renamed *Princess Carla.* In 1971, Princess Cruises negotiated with the Norwegian owners for charter of the new 20,000-ton *Island Venture* which was renamed *Island Princess.*

As part of the company's expansion, in 1974 Princess Cruises sold the company to P&O, one of the world's largest shipping companies. The agreement allowed retaining the "Princess" company name. As a member of the vast P&O Group, the *Island Princess* was purchased and the modern 17,000-ton *Spirit of London,* owned by P&O, was renamed the *Sun Princess* and joined the *Island Princess* under the Princess flag.

In 1975, the twin sister to the *Island Princess,* the *Sea Venture,* was purchased by P&O for Princess Cruises. She was renamed *Pacific Princess* and joined with the *Island* and the *Sun* to form the present three-ship fleet which cruises the waters of the West Coast Mexican Riviera, the Caribbean, trans Panama Canal, Mediterranean and Alaska and Canada.

In November, 1984, the fleet expanded to four ships when the new "state-of-the-art" super-Love Boat, 45,000-ton *Royal Princess* entered service. Princess Cruises has received international attention since "Love Boat" scenarios are placed about the company's ships.

P&O—Established at the turn of the 19th century, the Peninsular and Oriental Steam Navigation Company is England's largest shipping company. The company pioneered service in many areas of the world and added a tone of luxury and "snob appeal" to sea travel.

P&O operates the *Canberra, Oriana* and *Sea Princess* under its own banner and owns Princess Cruises which does sales and marketing for P&O in the U.S. In 1983, P&O purchased the Swan Group which operates Mediterranean and Nile cruises.

ROYAL CARIBBEAN CRUISE LINE
903 South America Way
Miami, FL 33132

Royal Caribbean Cruise Line is the Miami-based operator of four cruise ships owned by Royal Caribbean Cruise Line A/S, a Norwegian company founded in 1968 by I.M. Skaugen & Company and Anders Wilhelmsen & Company, commercial ship owners from Oslo, Norway. Later that same year, they were joined by another prominent shipping company, Gotaas-Larsen, Inc., of New York.

I.M. Skaugen, oldest of the three companies, was founded in 1912 by Captain Isak Skaugen, and Anders Wilhelmsen formed the company bearing his name in 1939. In 1940, Harry Irgens Larsen and a companion escaped from Nazi-occupied Norway by sailing to America in a 15-foot dingy in a grueling 52-day transatlantic crossing. In 1946, Harry Larsen and Trygve Gotaas founded their company in New York City. It is now headquartered in Bermuda.

Royal Caribbean pioneered the concept of offering seven and 14-day cruises every Saturday year around from Miami. The line's four ships were built specifically for Caribbean cruise vacations at Wartsila Yard in Helsinki, Finland. Each ship is easily recognized by the distinctive circular Viking Crown Lounge, making them the only ships in the world to offer a panorama of the sea from a lounge 10 or 11 stories above the water.

RCCL has built a solid reputation for consistency of product and has developed a loyal following among passengers. While waiting for construction to be completed on the *Song of America,* RCCL was the first major cruise line to lengthen a cruise ship by slicing the mid-section and adding a new middle to the vessel. This was first successfully accomplished on the *Song of Norway* then followed by similar mid-section surgery on the *Nordic Prince.* Similar expansions have been accomplished since then by other companies.

A few words about the parent ownership—it is a joint venture where each of the participants is heavily involved in other aspects of shipping (freight, cargo, ferry, passenger cruising). In recent years, they have become more involved either together, with additional participants, or individually in other major cruise passenger operations and ownership. It is somewhat difficult to sort out and doesn't concern passengers. Companies in which they are involved have heavy financial backing and are being organized and developed along good solid business lines. Involvement is in Scandinavian World Cruises and Pearl Cruises of Scandinavia, also in Eastern and Western Cruise Lines.

ROYAL CRUISE LINE
One Maritime Plaza
San Francisco, CA 94111

Royal Cruise Line, Ltd., is headquartered in Piraeus, Greece. It was founded for the explicit purpose of constructing a fleet of new super-deluxe cruise ships and operating cruises in the Mediterranean, Scandinavian and Western Hemisphere waters for North American cruise passengers. Founder P.S. Panagopoulos, well known in the Greek cruise industry, is president of the company and retains overall responsibilities for the line's activities.

Royal Cruise Line (USA), Inc. was formed in 1974 and is responsible for sales and marketing. Company headquarters is in San Francisco.

First ship in the fleet was the 460-passenger *Golden Odyssey*, launched in Denmark in 1974. She was joined in mid–1982 by the *Royal Odyssey* (ex *Doric*) after an estimated $20 million transformation.

Royal Cruise Line markets its vessels primarily in the California and West Coast areas and published brochure rates include air transportation from Los Angeles to and from the vessels. In the last couple of years, with expansion of the fleet, the company has expanded sales efforts into the rest of the country and brochures now list "cruise only" rates with allowances for passengers who provide their own air transportation.

ROYAL VIKING LINE
One Embarcadero Center
San Francisco, CA 94111

Royal Viking Line was purchased by Norwegian Caribbean Lines in mid–1984 but both companies are operating independent of each other. Royal Viking remains based in Oslo, with North American operations and sales handled by its San Francisco corporation which serves as headquarters for the global organization.

Founded in 1970 as a mutual endeavor of three Norwegian steamship companies — F. Klaveness, Bergen Line and Nordenfjeldske, Royal Viking operates three very deluxe vessels. The background of the founding companies is testimony to a long established link with the sea and shipping, although RVL itself is quite new as passenger shipping companies go. All of the founders' companies were organized more than a century ago and achieved prominent roles of leadership among Norwegian ship operators. With this heritage, it has been the aim of

Royal Viking Line from the very beginning to provide the "quintessence of contemporary cruising" for the ocean voyager of today.

The *Royal Viking Star* was introduced in 1972 as the first of these streamlined and identical sister ships built in Helsinki. She was joined by the *Royal Viking Sky* in mid–1973 and later that same year by the *Royal Viking Sea*. All three are outstanding vessels catering to the sophisticated, luxury traveler with the tastes, money and time to demand the best.

SCANDINAVIAN WORLD CRUISES
(Sea Escape)
1080 Port Blvd.
Miami, FL 33132

Scandinavian World Cruises is a Miami-based company, owned by DFDS which was founded 114 years ago in Copenhagen, Denmark. Its four letters stand for Det Forenede Dampskibs-Selskab, which in English means The United Steamship Company.

DFDS is one of the largest passenger carrying companies in Europe. Its vessels link ports in the North Sea, the Atlantic, the Baltic and the Mediterranean. DFDS carries over three million passengers a year on its routes, making it one of the most experienced companies in the world. It has a total of 12 passenger vessels and 16 modern cargo ships. Many of the vessels are designed to utilize the roll-on/roll-off system that was invented by DFDS for container shipping, a concept that revolutionized freight handling worldwide.

DFDS is part of the well known Lauritzen Group, also of Copenhagen. Lauritzen is a conglomerate with interests in shipping, shipbuilding and industry.

Scandinavian World Cruises started operations in North America in 1981 when it introduced the *Scandinavian Sun,* followed by the *Scandinavian Sea* and then the 30,000-ton *Scandinavia.* 1984 wasn't a very good year for the company. The *Sea* caught on fire and was declared a total loss. The *Scandinavia* was withdrawn from North American service and taken back to Europe and the *Sun* also had difficulties. 1985 looks better for the company. A refurbished and upgraded *Scandinavian Sun* is back in service and another vessel has been put into service and named the *Scandinavian Sea.* It sails on day cruises to Nowhere from Florida's West Coast.

SITMAR CRUISES
10100 Santa Monica Blvd
Los Angeles, CA 90067

Sitmar Cruises is an American company headquartered in Los Angeles and owned by the "V" Group, a multi-national, diversified company with major shipping interests. Owner is Boris Vlosov, a second generation shipping person who runs the company from a Monte Carlo base formed by his father. Tankers, cargoliners, freighters and passenger cruise service comprise the fleet. The American operation is run by former airline marketing and sales persons doing a good job selling the vessels.

Sitmar Cruises was founded by the "V" Group when it entered the North American cruise market in 1971. But, long before that the parent company was involved with passenger liners.

The Societa Italiana Transporti Marittimi of Genoa, known as Sitmar Line, began North American transatlantic passenger service in 1954 when it repositioned the *Castel Felice* from South American runs to service between Bremen and Quebec. The *Castel Felice* was built in 1930 as the British India Steam Navigation Co.'s *Kenya* for East African service; purchased by Sitmar in 1951; refitted and renamed *Castel Felice* for Italy-South America service. After 1958, she operated primarily on Italy-Australia service with occasional transatlantic sailings. She went out of service in 1970.

The first *Fairsea* was built in 1941 in Pennsylvania as the *Rio de la Plata* for Moore McCormack Line and served as an escort aircraft carrier to the *U.S.S. Charger* during the war. Sitmar Line bought her in 1949, had her refitted as an emigrant carrier and chartered her to the Australian Government for emigrant service in 1955. She was broken up in 1969.

Today, Sitmar Line operates the *Fairstar* from Australia. She was built in 1957 as the troopship *Oxforshire* and withdrawn from government service in 1962. She was converted and made her first emigrant voyage from Southhampton in 1964. She is currently on a passenger cruise schedule from Australia to the South Pacific.

Sitmar Cruises' purpose was to operate the *Fairwind* and *Fairsea* when they came into the North American market in 1971 and 1972. Original plans called for them to cruise between Fort Lauderdale and Los Angeles. Itineraries of both vessels have changed dramatically during the intervening years.

Pride of the Sitmar fleet is the 1984 addition of the $150 million *Fairsky* which has more than doubled the company's passenger capacity in North America. Sitmar also has spent $26 million to completely up-grade and reconfigure the *Fairwind* and *Fairsea* bringing all three vessels to the same top level. Although Sitmar is an America company, owned by a Monte Carlo firm, its vessels are associated with Italian-flavor and atmosphere because of the Italian crews. All three ships are registered in Liberia. The company is in the planning stages for two additional vessels which will give Sitmar a five ship fleet operating out of East and West coast ports.

SUN LINE
One Rockefeller Plaza
New York, NY 10021

Sun Line was incorporated as a Greek Company in 1961. Its first vessel was the *Stella Maris I,* used exclusively for Aegean cruises from Piraeus. But the concept really started before that. Cruising in the Aegean was always a unique experience for yachtsman and privileged travelers. In the early 1950s, sophisticated Europeans found that the romance of the Greek lslands was dimmed by the choice of a cargo or a small mail boat as a means of travel.

Realizing this, Mr. CH. A. Keusseoglou decided that elegance, combined with the magic of the sea and the romance of imaginative ports of call could provide pleasurable experiences for the discerning traveler. He put his concept into cruising when he acquired his first vessel.

Keusseoglou had already established a reputation as an enterprising young shipping executive as the head of Home Lines. Now he brought yacht-style cruising to the Aegean. The *Stella Maris* was joined by the *Stella Solaris,* then the *Stella Maris II* and the *Stella Oceanis.*

In 1971, the Marriott Corporation acquired an interest in Sun Line, but Keusseoglou and his son retained management of the company. The company enjoys an excellent reputation and is the best in Aegean cruising; also operate the best Greek flag vessels afloat. They are luxurious. They are not cheap, but then, nothing is.

Ship
Profiles

RATING THE SHIPS

For the past 10 years THE TOTAL TRAVELER BY SHIP has been under pressure to 'rate" the ships. I remain true to my conviction that cruising is for everyone; that there is a ship for every traveler and every traveler, with a little research, can find his/her ship. A decade ago, choices of vessels were limited. The first edition of this book profiled 40 ships. The 1985–1986 edition covers some 127 cruise ships. With so many tempting "bargains" being advertised, and with so many new companies entering the sea lanes, the time has come to offer more critical evaluations to assist readers in finding their own special ships. How to arrive at impartial evaluations was a major problem.

Firm in my conviction that no one person's opinion and preference should influence ship ratings, I invited 20 travel writers who specialize in cruise reporting, 18 travel agents who book thousands of passengers annually and 20 travelers who have cruised at least eight ships in the past four years to participate in a detailed survey. Using a scale of 1-to-10 with "10" being "excellent" and "1", "poor", they evaluated ships in 23 different categories based on personal knowledge and experiences.

Assuming you should get what you pay for, a ship charging $500 a day should deliver five times as much and should be five times better than a ship charging $100 a day. So, it would be unfair to lump all ships into a single category and compare them regardless of prices charged for days at sea. In fairness to lower and medium priced vessels and to allow for a better comparison of ships charging comparable rates, four categories based on price were developed.

Ships were categorized by "average daily rates" printed in brochures. A.D.R. (average daily rate) was used because of varying cruise lengths. Air-sea and discounts were not considered in categorizing ships since published rate is what the cruise line has decided the cabin should be selling for in normal times, when demand catches up with supply.

When that happens, that's the price passengers will be paying for the cruise but the price ratio between ships will likely remain the same.

READING THE RATINGS

CATEGORIES

Ships were divided into the following categories:

Budget: Under $110 per day
Moderate: From $111 to $185 per day
Up-scale: From $186 to $295 per day
Luxury: From $295 per day

AVERAGE DAILY RATE (A.D.R.)

Rate was determined by adding rates of average inside and outside cabins to minimum and maximum rates, excluding suites, unless the ship has a large number of these superior accommodations. Total was divided by number of price categories and then by cruising days. Seasonal increases were considered but free air and discounts were not included in A.D.R.s, which the price most passengers pay, per day of the voyage.

RATINGS

Using the scale of 1-to-10, (see Rating Chart below), evaluations by **THE TOTAL TRAVELER** were tallied, averaged and final ratings reached. Different values were assigned each participant, depending on experience and number of vessels cruised during past five years. In reading the ratings, remember the ships were evaluated within the category and are compared against each other. A ship rated "7" in the Budget Category does not offer the same product as a ship rated "7" in the Moderate, Up-scale or Luxury Category.

RATING CHART

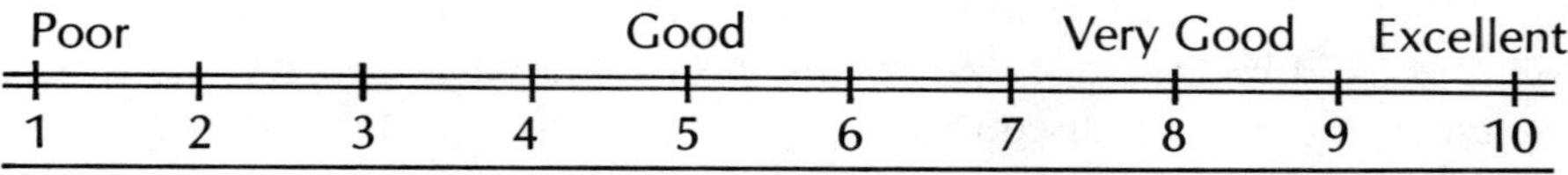

IN A WORD (OR TWO)

The Rating Panel was asked to list the first word, or two, that comes to mind when they think of the ship. The ones most frequently mentioned appear at the end of each ship profile. Choice of words included crowded, fun, tacky, up-beat, luxury, budget, food, bingo, disco, busy, bargain, relaxing, beautiful, old, new, party, European, pleasant, nice, itinerary, spacious, interesting, value, enjoyable and any others.

(✔✔✔✔✔) Outstanding features noted by the panel are ✔ checked.

OTHER EVALUATIONS

Favorite Ship:

Using the same scale of 1 to 10, the panel was asked to name their favorite ships. Every major vessel was named and only three duplicate 'favorites" showed up.

Moneys Worth:

Using the same scale of 1 to 10, the panel rated shipping companies on (1) money's worth; (2) accurate brochures; (3) passenger satisfaction. Ninety percent of the companies rated above "7" in all three areas. Highest ratings went to Carnival Cruise Lines, Cunard/NAC, Home Lines, Norwegian Caribbean Lines, Royal Caribbean Cruise Line, Royal Viking Line and Sitmar Cruises. They were all rated above 8.8, which means cruise lines are delivering superb products and passengers are satisfied they are getting their money's worth.

GOLDEN ANCHOR AWARDS

Top rated ships in all four categories were eligible to be selected

1985–1986

GOLDEN ANCHOR vessels

BUDGET: The panel's ratings of ships in this category indicated the vessels could be doing a lot better even at these low rates.

MODERATE: Carnival Cruise Lines' *TROPICALE*

UP-SCALE: Sitmar Cruise's *FAIRSKY*

LUXURY: Cunard's *QUEEN ELIZABETH 2*

KEY TO READING SHIP PROFILES

Specifics

Include tonnage, medical services, and other details.

Space Ratio

Computed by dividing the gross tonnage by the maximum passenger capacity on board ships. Space ratio is a good indication as to whether public areas on board will be crowded. For example, a ship is 20,000 tons and carries 500 passengers. Space ratio is 40. Another ship is 20,000 tons and carries 1500 passengers for a space ratio of 13.3. The higher the space ratio of passengers-to-facilities, the more spacious the vessel.

Facilities

These include toilet, shower and/or tub and wash basin. Where there are limited or no private facilities, it has been noted.

Itineraries

Ports of call mentioned cover published or planned itineraries planned by cruise lines. It is impossible to name every port of call, so typical routes are listed. Brochures with specific cruise dates and ports are available from travel agents or from cruise lines. Itineraries are subject to change with little or no notice.

Tipping

The amount quoted is the amount recommended by the cruise line. Passengers should tip based on quality and quantity service. Small gratuities should also be given to deck stewards, tearoom waiters and the like, if they have extended themselves. When the recommended tip suggests an amount for the cabin steward or the dining room waiter, it is not necessary to tip their assistants. They are included in the single tip. Bar tips are based on shoreside recommendation of 15 to 20 percent and tips are given when service is rendered. Tip in cash or add it to running tab if ship has a charge system. It is sometimes difficult to figure 15 percent of an odd amount, so 25–50 cents is an accepted minimum at bars. Ship's officers are never tipped. All tips are per person, per day (more accurately per night), unless otherwise noted.

Rates

All rates quoted are per person, based on two persons occupying the same cabin (double occupancy), except where otherwise noted. The number of single cabins available on each ship, without an additional surcharge, is indicated wherever the information was available. Rates are subject to change and fluctuation. Rates are influenced by oil prices and inflation, and have a tendency to continue on an upward slant, except for "soft" sailing periods, usually at the beginning or end of a season. All third and fourth passenger rates, as well as childrens' rates are based on sharing the same cabin with two full fare adult passengers.

TTT: Unless otherwise noted, there is no charge for deck chairs. All ships are air conditioned and all cabins have private facilities (toilet, wash stand, shower or tub) unless otherwise noted. Where cabins have individual air conditioning controls, it is noted. Otherwise, air conditioning is central and controlled by the ship's engineer.

TTT: For passenger guidance, the number of ship elevators and information as to whether the ship tenders in some ports is noted in profiles of the ships.

M.S.:	Motor Ship (uses diesel oil)
M.V.:	Motor Vessel (has piston engine)
R.M.S.:	Royal Mail Ship (sometimes referred to as Royal Majesty Ship)
S.S.:	Steamship
T.S.:	Turbo Ship (similar to T.S.S.)
T.S.S.	Turbo Steamship (turbo engines; uses heavy fuel oil)

M.V. AMERICA
M.V. AMERICAN EAGLE
M.V. INDEPENDENCE
M.V. SAVANNAH
(American Cruise Lines)

Category: Moderate
A.D.R.: $160
Rating: 6

From Baltimore, Savannah, Haddam (CT), Washington, D.C. through inland American waterways. Built 1983 and 1984. Registry: U.S.A. Capacity: 130 passengers; 29 crew (American deck and service). Space ratio: 8.5

Specifics: Tonnage: 1,000-1100; length: 220 feet; beam: 45 feet; cabin climate controls; 3 sun decks, 7 public rooms; picture windows all cabins; no elevators, swimming pool, shops, casino or hospital.
Electric Current: 110 volts A.C.
Entertainment: Local entertainment from ports visited; jazz band; historians, lecturers.
Dining: 1 dining room, single seating; reservations in advance. American-style menus.
Itinerary: Varies. Typical 7-day itinerary from Baltimore visits Crisfield, Williamsburg, Cambridge, St. Michaels.
Tipping: No recommended amount. "At passengers' discretion."
Rates: From $945 to $1155, depending on itinerary and season

TTT: These are fine inland coastal cruise ships with a casual, relaxed on board atmosphere. Nicely appointed, each cabin with a picture window to give passengers to see American communities bordering inland waterways. Six cabins with double beds; no single cabins without surcharge. Company plans to expand Mississippi River itineraries. Number of cabins varies from ship-to-ship. American Eagle has only 24 cabins.

In a word (or two): Very interesting

Category:	Budget
A.D.R.:	$100
Rating:	5

M.S.ALEXANDR PUSHKIN
(International Cruise Center)

From Leningrad, Bremerhaven, London (Tilbury), Le Havre and sometimes Montreal. Built 1965. Registry: U.S.S.R. Capacity: 700 passengers. 315 crew (Russian). Space ratio: 28.

Specifics: Tonnage: 20,000; length: 577 feet; beam: 69 feet; stabilizers; 2 elevators, swimming pool, duty-free shops, beauty/barber shops, lounges, 6 bars, medical services, 9 decks.
Electric Current: 220 volts A.C.
Entertainment: 2 dance orchestras, movies, entertainers, nightclub.
Dining: 1 dining room, 2 seatings. Can reserve table when booking. Russian specialties.
Tipping: Not required.
Itinerary: Transatlantic sailings from Montreal. Winter cruising in Europe. Tenders at some ports; docks in most.

TOTAL
TRAVELER
Golden
Anchor
Awards
1985

TOTAL
TRAVELER
Golden
Anchor
Award
Moderate
Category

TOTAL
TRAVELER
Golden
Anchor
Award
Up-Scale
Category
1

TOTAL
TRAVELER
Golden
Anchor
Award

Luxury
Category

Queen Elizabeth 2
SOUTHAMPTON

Rates: Transatlantic minimum about $600; All rates based on double occupancy, except minimum, which is based on four persons in a cabin (two uppers, two lowers). Special student discounts for transatlantic. Interport fares available.

TTT: Cabins on Russian ships are small (they call them "compact"), but average cost is lower than on comparable ships. Food is hearty and adequate. Caviar is superb! For more TTT's, see Mikhail Lermontov profile. No cabins with double beds: 26 single cabins without surcharge. Minimum cabin and others do not have private facilities. Cars are carried transatlantic.

TTT: Service from New York was discontinued in 1983 because of embargo on Russian transportation from and to U.S.

In a word (or two): No frills, Budget

	Category:	Budget
S.S. AMERIKANIS	*A.D.R.:*	under $100
(Chandris, Inc./Fantasy Cruises)	*Rating:*	4

From Port Everglades (Florida). Built 1952 as *Kenya Castle;* named *Amerikanis* 1967; rebuilt 1968; refurbished 1971. Registry: Greece. Capacity: 910 passengers; 250 crew (Greek). Space ratio: 32.

Specifics: Tonnage: 19,377; length: 576 feet; beam: 74.4 feet; stabilizers; individual cabin climate controls; 2 elevators, 2 swimming pools, duty-free shop, beauty/barber shops, 3 lounges, 5 bars, discotheque, sauna, gymnasium, children's game room, library, hospital, facilities, 8 public decks, casino.

Electric Current: 220 volts A.C.

Entertainment: 2 orchestras, movies, entertainers.

Dining: 2 dining rooms, 2 seatings. No reservations when booking. Few special dietary requests possible.

Tipping: $2.00 to waiter; $1.25 to helper and $2.50 to cabin steward. Cash bar: with service.

Itinerary: From Port Everglades, 1 day cruise to nowhere and some overnight cruises just going out to sea; 5 night cruises to Bahamas and Ocho Rios, Jamaica. Sunday departures.

Rates: Hard to figure because some cruises do not include cabins. Average around $100 per day with cabin and food. Day cruises without cabin but with meals run $39 to $49 depending on day; overnights without cabin are priced the same and cabins are priced by number of occupants.

TTT: This ship is a surprise. She has very large cabins, spacious decks, public areas and two dining rooms. She was built to sail transatlantic and is much more than a ship designed for an overnight run. She has all the comforts of a 'higher priced vessel, but could use redecorating and brighter colors. Tender Loving Care would do a lot to improve the vessel. No cabins with double beds; no single cabins without surcharge. Food is fairly good; so is entertainment. Big draw is gambling action in the full casino.

In a word (or two): Bargain and Old

<table>
<tr><td></td><td>Category:</td><td>Up-Scale</td></tr>
<tr><td>M.S.ASTOR</td><td>A.D.R.:</td><td>$250</td></tr>
<tr><td>(United Cruise Lines)</td><td>Rating:</td><td>7</td></tr>
</table>

From Southampton to Las Palmas; South African ports and the Seychelles. Built in 1981 as *Berlin,* renamed *Astor* prior to inaugural voyage. Registry: South Africa. Capacity: 550 passengers; 220 crew (mixed English-speaking) Space ratio: 31.

Specifics: Tonnage: 18,800; length: 538 feet; beam: 74 feet; stabilizers, individually controlled air conditioning, color television every cabin, bars, lounges, dining room, library, heated indoor pool, outdoor pool, sauna, gymnasium, solarium, hospital with x-ray, 7 dialysis machines and water therapy; all cruise ship amenities, 3 elevators, 6 passenger decks, television all cabins.
Electric Current: 220 volts A.C.
Entertainment: orchestra, movies, live entertainment, small casino.
Dining: 1 dining room; 2 seatings, international cuisine. Special requests available from dining room captain.
Tipping: $2.50 to waiter; $2.50 to room steward. Cash or charge bar.
Itinerary: Varied length voyages from European ports. U.S. sailings not included in 1985 itineraries. Length of voyages varies from 10 to 21 days. Tenders some ports.
Rates: Vary with itineraries. Typical 11-day minimum $2,002; maximum $4,696. (10 minimum cabins; (3 super-sized suites)

TTT: Ship was sold in 1983 to South African Marine Corporation and South Africa is "home port." Vessel had a $4 million renovation in

1984. In addition to reducing passenger capacity from 630 to 550, 36 new suites were built and six lounges added on the top deck for use by passengers for private parties or conferences. A childrens' activities center and satellite communications were also added. The all-German speaking crew been replaced by an English-speaking international crew and staff. Cabins are smaller than they should be on a vessel offering this quality of service and food (which is outstanding!) Picture windows in outside cabins, beautiful decor.

In a word (or two): European

M.V.ATLANTIC
(Home Lines)

Category: Up-Scale
A.D.R.: $200
Rating: 8

From New York to Bermuda and West Indies; from Port Everglades to Caribbean, West Indies and transcanal. Built 1982. Capacity: 1069 passengers; 500 crew (Italian). Registry: Liberia. Space ratio: 29.

Specifics: tonnage: 33,800; length: 671 feet; beam: 90 feet. Stabilizers; individual cabin climate controls; 4 elevators, 2 swimming pools, shopping center, beauty/barber shop, valet, laundry, sauna, gymnasium, 33 public rooms, medical, casino.

Electric Current: 110 volts, A.C.

Entertainment: Orchestras, movies, nightclubs, sports program.

Dining: 1 dining room, 2 seatings.

Tipping: $2.00–2.50 to waiter and to cabin steward; $5 per week to table captain; $3 per week to maitre d'. Cash or charge bar.

Itinerary: From New York, 7-day Saturday sailings to Bermuda, Spring, Summer, early Fall. From Florida to Caribbean, West Indies and transcanal, Fall and Winter. Cruises of varied durations. Tenders some ports.

Rates: Typical 7-day sailing to Bermuda: $905 minimum; $1410 maximum; Suites $1915. Typical 11-day $1790 to $3,630.

TTT: The Atlantic inaugurated service in April 1982. Ship was built at the La *Seyne-sur-Mer* shipyards in France at an estimated cost of well over the $100 million mark. Italian-style service, very good food and entertainment with a beautiful ship at a fair price makes for very, very good cruise experiences. Seven architects and interior decorators from three countries created a variety of environments which ends all possibility of monotony and uniformity of design. 30 single cabins without surcharge; 160 deluxe cabins with sitting rooms; $3.50 charge for deck chairs.

SPECIAL RATES: Third and fourth cabin occupants of any age pay half the minimum rate. Children's activities and counselors on board during winter West Indies cruises. Handicapped travelers must travel with non-handicapped passenger. Caribbean cruise rates usually include air and are priced higher on average than Bermuda sailings.

In a word or two: Traditional and Nice

✔✔✔✔ Food and Service

	Category: Moderate
M.S.AZUR	*A.D.R.:* $120
(Paquet Cruises)	*Rating:* 5.5

From Mediterranean ports to Red Sea and Mediterranean. Built 1971 for Southern Ferries (division of P&O); sailed as *Eagle* until 1975 when Paquet purchased the vessel and named her *Azur*. Rebuilt 1976. Registry: France; Capacity: 687 passengers, 206 crew (French). Space ratio: 22.

Specifics: Tonnage: 15,000; length: 466 feet; beam: 72 feet; stabilizers, 2 swimming pools, barber/beauty shop, 3 elevators, gymnasium, hospital, laundry, 7 passenger decks, radios all cabins. theater, lounges, bars. No casino

Electric Current: 220 volts A.C.

Entertainment: Sports oriented, carries bicycles, sail boats, wind surfing boards, water skis, etc. on board for passenger use. disco, variety shows.

Dining: 2 restaurants. Intimate Eden Roc Grill is for passengers in more expensive cabins. Food throughout is French, continental and Nouvelle Cuisine. No advance reservations.

Tipping: $2.50 to waiter, $1.00 to helper; $2.50 to room steward. Cash bar.

Itineraries: Varied itineraries, 7 to 12 days from Toulon, Rhodes and Nice to Red Sea ports of Aqaba, Hugada, Safaga, Eilat and Sharm el Sheikh. Eastern Mediterranean to Israel and Egypt; other voyages from Nice.

Rates: Depending on itinerary, 7 days $625 minimum, $1,165 maximum.

TTT: Paquet recently spent $20 million to up-grade the ship and is now marketing the *Azur* in the U.S. as well as in Europe. Vessel appeals to young passengers who are water sports enthusiasts. English is primary language on board. Complimentary wines with lunch and dinher.

In a word (or two): Continental, Fun

S.S. AZUR SEAS
(Western Cruise Lines)

Category:	Moderate
A.D.R.:	$167
Rating:	5

From Los Angeles to Mexico on 3 and 4-night cruises. Built 1954 as *Southern Cross,* rebuilt, refurbished under Ulysses Line flag 1975 and sailed as *Calypso:* additional refurbishing 1979. Sold to Western Cruise Lines (a subsidiary of Eastern Cruise Lines) 1979. Completely refurbished and entered California service 1980. Registry: Panama; Capacity: 734 passengers; 345 crew (mixed). Space ratio: 27.

Specifics: Tonnage: 20,000; length: 603 feet; beam: 78 feet; stabilizers; 1 elevator, shops, lounges, bars, casino, 8 decks, whirlpool spa, gymnasium, casino.

Electric Current: 110 and 220 volts A. C.

Entertainment: 2 orchestras, movies, entertainers; disco, casino.

Dining: 1 dining room, 2 seatings. Reservations when booking or after boarding. International cuisine.

Tipping: $2.00 to waiter; $1.00 to busboy; $2.00 to room steward. Cash bar. Tip maitre d' for special requests. Major credit cards accepted for on board expenses.

Itinerary: 3 and 4-night Monday and Friday sailings to Ensenada, Mexico. Docks at Ensenada and San Diego on Tuesdays.

Rates: 3-night: minimum $415 (23 cabins): maximum $570 (66 cabins); 4-night minimum: $475 maximum $620.

TTT: This is the only ship operating on short cruises between California and Mexico and is a popular itinerary. Last refurbishing was extensive. She is a good riding vessel. Before becoming the Azur Seas, she plied North Sea waters for many years and took the waves very well.

In a word (or two): Party

S.S.BERMUDA STAR
(Bahama Cruise Line)

Category:	Moderate
A.D.R.:	$157
Rating:	6

From New Orleans to Caribbean (winter, fall); from New York to Bermuda (spring, summer). Built 1957 as *Argentina;* purchased from

Moore McCormack Lines by Holland America Cruises and rebuilt as *Veendam* 1973. Sailed as *Monarch Star* 1976–78; returned to Holland America and renamed *Veendam* 1978. Purchased in 1983 by Tung Group of Hong Kong and operates on long term charter to Bahama Cruise Line; refurbished same year and renamed *Bermuda Star*. Registry: Panama. Capacity: 738 passengers; 340 crew (mixed deck and service). Space ratio: 33.

Specifics: Tonnage: 23,500; length: 617 feet; beam: 84 feet; stabilizers, individual cabin climate controls, 3 elevators, swimming pool, gift shop, newsstand, beauty/barber shops, dry cleaning, laundry, gymnasium, sports deck, lounges, hospital facilities, 9 decks, casino.

Electric Current: 110 volts A.C.

Entertainment: Orchestras, theater, nightclub, disco, name entertainers. No smoking section in lounges.

Dining: 1 dining room, 2 seatings. Reservations when booking, special dietary requests when booking. Special Brass Grill Restaurant for deluxe cabin passengers but same food and menu as other dining room.

Tipping: $2.00 to waiter, same to room steward; $1.00 to busboy; Cash bar.

Itinerary: 7-days cruises from New Orleans to Key West, Cozumel, Playa del Carmen. Summer from New York to Bermuda.

Rates: 7-day minimum, $895 (7 cabins); maximum, $1,440 (44 cabins); 9 single cabins without surcharge but at maximum rates.

TTT: 286 outside cabins, 72 inside. Minimum cabins on Navigation Deck are very good buys. They are larger than some higher priced cabins and are located across the hall from higher priced deluxe cabins. About $1.5 million has been spent improving the ship and some of the new features include a special restaurant for upper-category passengers and a Lido buffet area. Menu is the same but environment and service makes it special. She's a nice old ship and cabins are extra large.

In a word (or two): Nice

	Category:	Budget
M.S. BOHEME	A.D.R.:	$117
(Commodore Cruise Line)	Rating:	5.5

From St. Petersburg, Florida to the Caribbean. Built 1968; refurbished 1978. Registry: Panama. Capacity: 448 passengers; 210 crew (German deck; Caribbean, European and Korean: service). Space ratio: 24.

Specifics: Tonnage: 11,000; length: 450 feet; beam: 65 feet; individual cabin climate controls; stabilizers; 2 elevators; swimming pool, shopping arcade, beauty shop, 5 lounges, ballroom, 3 bars, medical services, 7 decks,casino.
Electric Current: 110–220 volts A.C.
Entertainment: 2 orchestras, movies, entertainers, nightclubs.
Dining: 2 dining rooms, 2 seatings. Reservations when booking. Special dietary arrangements in advance or on board.
Tipping: $2.00 to waiter; $1.00 to busboy: $2.00 to cabin steward. Cash bar.
Itinerary: Every Saturday from St. Petersburg to Key West, Port Antonio and Cozumel. Docks in all ports.
Rates: Minimum $639 (8 cabins), maximum $9959 (1 cabin). Air-sea available. Third and fourth passengers in cabins pay $295.

TTT: Commodore Cruise Line offers the lowest priced 7-day cruise rates out of Florida. Known as "The Happy Ship" the *Boheme* has a fine reputation for homogenizing passengers into one happy family. Six cabins with double beds; no single cabins without surcharge. Theme cruises cater to special interests. For example, September cruises are "Oktoberfests Afloat," and that means beer and lots of hoopla; Country & Western Jamborees are complete with hoe-down orchestras and entertainers.

In a word (or two): Good, Value

S.S. BRITANIS
(Chandris, operated by Fantasy Cruises)

Category: Budget
A.D.R.: under $100
Rating: 3.5

From Jamaica to Southern Caribbean (winter months); from New York (summer months). Built 1932 for Matson Line; sailed as *Monterey;* served as troop ship in World War II; in service as *Matsonia* 1957; renamed *Lurline* 1964. Purchased by Ajax Navigation of Greece 1971 and sailed under Chandris flag until charter a couple of years ago to Fantasy Cruises. Refurbished 1970. Registry: Greece. Capacity: 1,600 passengers; 400 crew (Greek deck, mixed service). Space ratio: 25.

Specifics: Tonnage: 25,245; length: 642 feet; beam: 79 feet; stabilizers; 3 elevators, swimming pool, 16 public rooms, lounges, bars, large ballroom, children's facilities, gymnasium, 9 decks, casino.
Electric Current: 110 volts D.C.

Entertainment: 2 orchestras, movies

Dining: 2 dining rooms, 2 seatings. Reservations when booking. No off-the-menu special orders. Tables seat from two to eight.

Tipping: $2.00 to waiter and to cabin steward; $1.00 to bus boy. Cash bar.

Itinerary: from Montego Bay, Jamaica every Saturday 7-night cruises to Aruba, Cartagena, and San Blas Islands. Summer months from New York on varied cruise lengths similar to Amerikanis schedule from Port Everglades. Some cruises to Bermuda and Nova Scotia.

Rates: Caribbean cruises only. 7 nights minimum about $750 (35 cabins); maximum $1,310 (2 suites).

TTT: *Britanis* retains very little of the pleasing decor of a Matson liner. New York cruise rates slightly higher. Casino attracts passengers on New York cruises. This is first year sailing from Montego Bay and passenger acceptance remains to be seen. Refurbished, freshened up 1980 but she still looks old and could use more work. Read advertising very carefully. Minimum advertised rates usually refer to cabins without facilities (and there are more than 30) and to four persons sharing a cabin. Fine print should be enlarged. Passengers who know what they are buying and are happy to buy a very, very low priced cruise disembark satisfied. Those who expect more are disappointed. Food is surprisingly good, as is entertainment.

In a word or two: Tacky, Budget

S.S. CANBERRA	*Category:* Moderate
(P&O Cruises)	*A.D.R.:* $240
	Rating: 5.5

Sails from Southampton to North Sea and Mediterranean. Built 1961 in Belfast as *Great Britain*. Ordered by P&O Lines but completed for P&O-Orient Lines. 1966 transferred to P&O Lines, named *Canberra* for capital of Australia. Refurbished 1982. Registry: United Kingdom; Capacity: 1,750 passengers; 800 crew (British deck, international service). Space ratio: 26.

Specifics: Tonnage: 45,000; length: 819 feet; beam 107 feet. Stabilizers, air conditioned, theater, 3 swimming pools, 5 elevators, children's playroom, 14 public rooms, beauty/barber shop, gift shops, casino, 10 passenger decks.

Electric Current: 220 volts A.C.

Entertainment: Orchestras, night clubs, shows, movies.

Dining: 2 dining rooms, 2 seatings. Table assignments on board. Special dietary requests when booking.

Tipping: $2.00 to waiter, $1.00 to helper; $2.50 to cabin steward. Cash or charge bar.

Itineraries: Varied itineraries with some including transatlantic. Mostly from Southampton to Mediterranean. Cruise lengths from 7 to 22 days with one 40 day voyage to Australia. Also sold in segments. Interesting unusual itineraries with air-sea packages from some U.S. cities. (See Air-Sea Chapter)

TTT: *Canberra* has large percentage of inside and outside cabins without private facilities. (Listed in brochure as "With facilities nearby.") Rates are not all that much cheaper than cabins with facilities so it's a case of early bookers getting the private bathrooms. Single cabins without surcharge available. Ship was third largest cruise ship behind the QE2 and Norway until recent construction of a few superliners. Lots of open space. Dining room assignment depends on cabin price. Passengers are international with the vessel's most loyal following from Great Britain and Australia. Talk is vessel will be moved to permanent home in Australia and that's where she is cruising at press time. Scheduled to return to Southampton in late spring. *Canberra* got a lot of publicity when she was involved in Falklands/Malvinas conflict. Ship could do with a complete overhaul but passengers register few complaints. Rates are very reasonable for mileage covered and service rendered.

In a word (or two): Big and Old

Category:	Budget
A.D.R.:	$110
Rating:	6

M.S. CARIBE I
(Commodore Cruise Line)

From Miami to Caribbean. Built 1953 as the *Olympia* in Scotland, sailed under Greek flag until 1983 purchase by Commodore Cruise Line. Rebuilt in 1971 and again totally reconstructed and refurbished in 1983. Registry: Panama. Capacity: 900 passengers; 330 crew (mixed international deck and service). Space Ratio: 28.

Specifics: Tonnage: 23,000; length: 610 feet; beam: 79 feet; stabilizers, individual cabin climate controls, 3 elevators, swimming pool, 11 public rooms, 8 passenger decks, theater, 2 jacuzzis on pool deck, casino, hospital, shops, beauty/barber shops, casino.

Electric Current: 110 and 220 A.C.

Entertainment: 2 orchestras, movies, disco, casino

Dining: 1 very large dining room; 2 seatings. Reservations at time of booking. Special dietary requests when booking or on board.

Tipping: $2.00 to waiter; $1.00 to bus boy; $2.00 to room steward; Cash bar.

Itinerary: Every Saturday from Miami to Puerto Plata, St. Thomas, San Juan, Cap Haitien.

Rates: 7-day minimum $639 to maximum of $959. Third and fourth cabin passengers pay $295 each.

TTT: Five single cabins without surcharge. Childrens' counselors on board for supervised activities during holiday and summer sailings. Not all cabins have telephones. Double deck theater. See TTT: Boheme for comments regarding Commodore Cruise Line food, service, etc.

In a word (or two): Friendly

	Category:	Up-Scale
M.S. CARLA COSTA	*A.D.R.:*	$218
(Costa Cruises)	*Rating:*	4.7

From San Juan to West Indies and the Caribbean. Built 1952 as *Flandre;* refurbished and rebuilt 1968; refurbished 1976. Registry: Italy. Capacity: 748 passengers; 370 crew (Italian). Space ratio: 27.

Specifics: Tonnage: 20,477; length: 600 feet; beam: 80 feet; stabilizers, duty-free shops, beauty/barber shops, lounges, ballroom, sauna/massage, card room, hospital facilities, 8 passenger decks.

Electric Current: 127 volts, 50 cycles, A.C.

Entertainment: 3 orchestras, movies, nightclub shows, casino, cooking classes, wine tasting.

Dining: 1 dining room, 2 seatings. Can make reservations when booking. Special diets available through maitre d'.

Tipping: $2.00 to $2.50 to waiter; $2.00 to cabin steward; $15 for 7 days to maitre d'. Cash bar.

Itinerary: Every Saturday from San Juan, one-week cruises to Curacao, Caracas, Grenada, Martinique and St. Thomas. Tenders at some points.

Rates: Minimum $995 (6 cabins), maximum $2,320 (2 suites). Air-sea available.

TTT: 10 cabins with double beds; no single cabins without surcharge. Deck chairs $5 per week. All cabins with private facilities. Over-priced at $218 per day. Ship would compare better with a lower A.D.R., putting her in the "Moderate" category. Many Latin passengers board in Caracas and don't seem to mind the rate. Lots of South American children during December to March.

In a word or two: Food and Old

	Category:	Moderate
T.S.S. CARNIVALE	*A.D.R.:*	$150
(Carnival Cruise Lines)	*Rating:*	7.5

From Miami to the Caribbean. Built 1956 as *Empress Of Britain;* sailed transocean as *Queen Anna Maria;* refurbished and rebuilt 1976. Registry: Panama. Capacity: 1,350 passengers maximum; 950 normal cruise; 550 crew (Italian deck; mixed Spanish/Caribbean: service). Space ratio: 29.

Specifics: Tonnage: 27,250; length: 640 feet; beam: 87 feet. Stabilizers; individual cabin controlled air conditioning; 4 elevators; 1 indoor, 3 outdoor swimming pools; duty-free shipping arcade, 3 nightclubs, 5 lounges, ballroom (capacity 550), health club, children's game room, hospital facilities, 9 passenger decks, very large casino.

Electric Current: 110 volts A.C.

Entertainment: 4 orchestras, movies, nightclub shows.

Dining: n1 dining room, 2 seatings. Reservations when booking; table assignments after boarding. Special dietary arrangements when booking

Tipping: $2.50 to waiter; $1.25 to busboy; $2.50 to cabin steward. Cash bar.

Itinerary: Every Monday and Friday from Port of Miami, 3 and 4-day cruises to Nassau. Docks in port.

Rates: Minimum $290 (20 cabins); maximum $595 (5 suites). Children's rate: $95 for under 16 year olds occupying same cabin with two adults. Some single cabins without surcharge. Air-sea and air-sea-land packages available.

TTT: 61 cabins with double beds; 12 single cabins without surcharge. All cabins with private facilities.

TTT: Carnival Cruise Line ships enjoy the well-deserved "fun ships" reputation. Atmosphere is relaxed, informal. Entertainment outstanding. Food and service way above the norm. There is something going on someplace on board around the clock. Because of the size of the ships, there is still plenty of space for quiet relaxation. All five ships (Carnivale, Mardi Gras, Festivale, Tropicale and the new Holiday) have full-sized Las Vegas-style casinos on board which operate when ships are at sea. There are craps, roulette, black jack and slots. Seven-days of cruise activities are packed into three and four-day voyages and the vessel spends one full day at sea so passengers have 24 hours of non-stop shipboard partying. A good choice to test the waters before embarking on a longer cruise if you aren't sure the pace and tempo are for you.

In a word (or two): Fun and Value
✔✔✔✔✔ Activities, Entertainment

S.S. CONSTITUTION
(American Hawaii Cruises)

Category: Up-Scale
A.D.R.: $220
Rating: 6.2

From Honolulu to neighboring Hawaiian Islands. Built in 1951 as *Constitution* for American Export Lines, she inaugurated service in 1951 from New York to Mediterranean; refurbished 1959 with 110 first class berths added; hull repainted white in 1960; laid up in 1968; sold to Atlantic Far East (C.Y. Tung Group) 1974 renamed *Oceanic Constitution,* but she never sailed for the company. Purchased by American Hawaii Cruises, 1980; refurbished and refurbished, entered service 1982. Redocumented under U.S. flag as *S.S. Constitution.* Registry: U.S.A. Capacity: 800 passengers; 340 crew (American deck, engine and service). Space ratio: 37.

Specifics: Tonnage 30,090; Length: 682 feet; Beam: 89 feet; stabilizers, 2 swimming pools, conference facilities, golf range, theater, lounges, all amenities, 4 elevators, hospital.

Electric Current: 110 volts

Dining: 1 dining room, 2 seatings. American and international specialties.

Tipping: $2.50 to dining room waiter; $1 to $1.50 to assistant; $2.50 to room steward. Cash bar.

Rates: Depend depend on season and range from $995 minimum (16 cabins). Third and fourth passengers, $695. Children under 16, $395. 30 single cabins without surcharge.

Itinerary: Sunday departures, 7-day cruises from Honolulu to Lauai, Kona, Hilo, Kahului, Molokai.

TTT: See *Independence* comments for cruise style and services. Ship has 43 cabins with double beds, 16 with king size beds. No casinos on either ship.

In a word or two: Up-beat, Enjoyable
✔✔✔ Itinerary

M.V. CUNARD COUNTESS
(Cunard Line, Ltd.)

Category:	Moderate
A.D.R.:	$195
Rating:	5.5

From San Juan to Caribbean and West Indies. Built specifically for Caribbean cruising in 1976. Registry: Britain. Capacity: 750 passengers each; 350 crew each (British deck; mixed Caribbean, service). Space ratio: 23.

Specifics: Tonnage: 17,586; length: 536 feet; beam: 74 feet. Stabilizers; 2 elevators, swimming pool, shopping arcade, beauty salon, 4 lounges, main lounge seating 350, top-deck bar, meeting rooms, library, health and fitness facilities, sauna, medical services, 8 decks.

Electric Current: 115 volts A.C./D.C.

Entertainment: Orchestras, movies, entertainers, nightclub, special interest theme cruises, new indoor/outdoor center for "Theatre-in-the-Round", disco, jacuzzis.

Dining: 1 dining room, 2 seatings. Special dietary requests and dining room reservations in advance when booking.

Itinerary: Year-round from San Juan, 7-day cruises to Caracas, Grenada, St. Thomas alternating with cruises to St. Maarten, Antigua, Martinique, Guadeloupe, St. Thomas and Tortola. Docks in all ports.

Tipping: $2.00 to waiter; $1.00 to busboy; $2.00 to cabin steward. Cash bar.

Rates: 7-day cruises: minimum $889 (10 cabins); maximum $1949 (22 cabins), depending on season. Third passenger in cabin, $459 to $549 also depending on season. Special price for second week of cruising, $299 seasonal

TTT: Cabins, each with push-button telephone, convert to sitting rooms for daytime living. Cabins "compact", every inch of space used. Good light in bathrooms. Comfortable for short cruising. Entire deck allotted for public areas. Observation decks open up over bridge for better views when entering ports. Seven million dollar renovation project was completed in 1973. Most waiters from Caribbean Islands. Ship is prototype of ships of the 1970s. No cabins with double beds. Single cabin surcharge is 175 percent of per person rate, but singles who do not want to share may book at the "per person, double occupancy" rate on a wait list with confirmation 30 days before sailing). Per person fare for singles available and guaranteed on a "share" basis; cruise line finds you a cabin mate (same sex).

TTT BARGAIN: Cunard sometimes runs a "sale" where passengers may stay on for a second week of cruising at a very nominal rate. In 1984, it was as low as under $400. Look for this offer during "off season" months in early spring and late fall. Company also offers terrific package with one week on shore in Barbados or St. Lucia and one week on board ship for minimum of $1,248. See *Cunard Princess* **TTT**.

In a word (or two): Busy
✔✔✔ Itinerary

	Category:	Moderate
M.V. CUNARD PRINCESS	*A.D.R.:*	$230
(Cunard Line, Ltd.)	*Rating:*	5.5

From Los Angeles to Mexico (from Fall through Spring); from Vancouver to Alaska (summer months). Designed and built specifically for Caribbean cruising. Built 1977. Registry: Britain. Capacity: 750 passengers each; 350 crew each (British deck; mixed Caribbean, service). Space ratio: 23.

Specifics: Tonnage: 17,586; length: 536 feet; beam: 74 feet. Stabilizers; 2 elevators, swimming pool, shopping arcade, beauty salon, 4 lounges, main lounge seating 350, top-deck bar, meeting rooms, library, sauna, medical services, 8 decks, casino.
Electric Current: 115 volts A.C./D.C.
Entertainment: Orchestras, movies, entertainers, nightclub, special interest theme cruises, health and fitness program.
Dining: 1 dining room, seats 500, 2 seatings. Special dietary requests and reservations in advance when booking.
Tipping: $2.00 to waiter; $1.00 to busboy; $2.00 to cabin steward. Cash bar.
Itinerary: Mexico itinerary can be taken as 7 or 14 days from Los Angeles or Acapulco. Visits Cabo San Lucas, Mazatlan, Puerto Vallarta,

Manzanillo and Acapulco. Sailing north itinerary is reversed and includes Zihuatanejo. Tenders some ports.

Rates: Mexico 7-day cruises: minimum $899 (10 cabins); maximum $1,799 (22 cabins). Third passenger in cabin, $589. Second week of cruising for total from $1,088 to $2,098. Alaska 7-days from $975 to $2120, depending on season. Special price for second week cruising $299, seasonal.

TTT: See *Cunard Countess* **TTT** for comments on facilities, cabins, entertainment, etc. Ships are identical in construction and facilities.

In a word (or two): Busy
✔✔ Itinerary

mts DAPHNE	*Category:*	Up-Scale
mts DANAE	*A.D.R.:*	$220
(Costa Cruises)	*Rating:*	4.8

Daphne: from Fort Lauderdale to Caribbean, West Indies (winter months); from Vancouver to Alaska (summer months). *Danae* from Venice to Mediterranean and in Caribbean. *Daphne* built 1955 as *Port Melbourne;* sailed as *Therisos Express* 1972; *Danae* built 1956 as *Port Sydney,* sailed as *Akrotiri Express* 1972–1974. Both vessels used as refrigerated cargo ship before purchase by Carras 1974, rebuilt and refurbished; renamed *Daphne* and *Danae;* chartered to Costa 1978. Registry: Greece. Capacity: 420 passengers; 225 crew (Greek). Space ratio: 32.

Specifics: Tonnage: 16,000; length: 533 feet; beam: 70 feet. Swimming pool, stabilizers; shopping arcade, beauty/barber shops, library, children's playroom, lounges, 3 bars, theatre, discotheque, 7 decks, including 3 promenade decks, casino.

Electric Current: 220 volts, 60 cycles, A.C.

Entertainment: Theatre, movies, nightclub, casino.

Dining: 1 dining room, 1 seating. Advance reservations encouraged, but not necessary. Greek and Italian specialties.

Tipping: $2 to $2.50 to waiter and helper; $2 to cabin steward. Cash bar. $5 for 7 days to maitre d'.

Itinerary: Daphne: Winter, early spring, every other Saturday from Port Everglades on 14-day cruises to San Juan, St. Croix, Antigua, St. Lucia, Barbados, Martinique, St. Kitts, St. Maarten and St. Thomas. Summer cruises 7-days from Vancouver top Wrangell, Endicott Arm, Juneau, Skagway, Davidson and Rainbow Glaciers and

Ketchikan. Spring and fall 16-day positioning voyages through the Panama Canal.

Danae: Spring and Fall from Venice to Greece, Egypt, Israel, Turkey and Yugoslavia. Summer 14 to 18-day Northern Europe/Baltic cruises. Vessel making around-the-world voyage in 1985. Tenders at some ports.

Rates: Two-week minimum $2,035 (7 cabins); maximum $4,725 (6 suites with verandahs). One week minimum $1,325 (7 cabins); maximum $2,645 (6 cabins with verandahs). Children under 12 sharing cabin with two adults charged $1,095 in Caribbean; $665 in Alaska. Rates slightly lower on Danae.

TTT: 18 cabins with double beds; no single cabins without surcharge. Almost all cabins are outside, most with bathtubs. Deck charges have been removed. One dining room seating most voyages makes for very friendly environment. Good service, food.

In a word (or two): Food and Service
✔✔✔ Single seating dining

	Category:	Moderate
S.S. DOLPHIN	*A.D.R.:*	$135
(Dolphin Cruises)	*Rating:*	6

From Port of Miami to Bahamas. Built 1956 for Zim Lines; sailed as the *Lion;* sailed as *Amelia de Mello* 1966 to 1972; purchased by Ulysses Line 1972; rebuilt, refurbished same year; name changed to S.S. Dolphin January 1979. Still owned by Ulysses, but operated by Paquet Cruises until late 1984. Now operated by Dolphin Cruises. Registry: Panama. Capacity: 684 passengers; 185 crew (Greek deck; Caribbean/Indonesian, service). Space ratio: 22.

Specifics: Tonnage: 12,500; length: 501 feet; beam: 65 feet. Stabilizers; 1 elevator, shop, beauty shop, lounges, small casino, 6 decks.

Electric Current: 110 volts A.C.

Entertainment: 2 orchestras, movies, entertainers, disco, casino.

Dining: 1 dining room, 2 seatings. Reservations after boarding or when booking. Limited special dietary requirements.

Tipping: $2.00 to waiter; $1.00 to bus boy; $2.00 to cabin steward. Cash bar.

Itinerary: Monday and Friday sailings from Miami, three and 4-day cruises. to Nassau and Dolphin Cove (a Bahamas island); Freeport added on 4-day cruises.

Rates: 3-day minimum: $285 (7 cabins); maximum $555 (20 cabins); 4-day minimum; $370 (7 cabins); maximum $680 (20 cabins).

TTT: Ship has reputation for very good food. Dolphin Cruises continues Paquet tradition serving free red and white wines at dinner. Table assignment for evening meal only. Open seating at breakfast and lunch. Younger passengers like the Dolphin. 13 cabins with double beds; no single cabins without surcharge. Not all cabins accessible to elevator. Check deck plan carefully.

In a word (or two): Buffet
✔✔ Food and complimentary wine

Category:	Moderate
A.D.R.:	$162
Rating:	6.7

S.S. EMERALD SEAS
(Eastern Steamship Lines)

From Miami to Bahamas. Built 1944 as *General W.P. Richardson;* sailed as *La Guardia,* 1949 to 1956; *Leilani,* 1956 to 1961; *President Roosevelt,* 1961 to 1970; *Atlantic,* 1970 to 1972; changed ownership and named Emerald Seas 1972. Registry: Panama. Capacity: 960 passengers; 400 crew (mixed). Space ratio: 31.

Specifics: Tonnage, 24,459; length: 627 feet; beam: 75 feet. Stabilizers; 3 elevators, outdoor swimming pool, sun deck, duty-free shop, beauty parlor, sports area, 1 ballroom (capacity 450), 5 lounges, 2 outdoor French cafes, 9 passenger decks, full casino.
Electric Current: 220 volts D. C.; A.C. for razors only.
Entertainment: 3 orchestras, movies, nightclubs, discotheque.
Dining: 1 dining room, 2 seatings. Special dietary arrangements in advance.
Tipping: $2.00 to waiter; $1.00 to bus boy; $2.00 to room steward. Cash bar.
Itinerary: 3-night Friday sailings to Nassau and Little Stirrup Cay; 4-night Monday sailings to Nassau, Freeport and Little Stirrup Cay. Tenders some ports.
Rates: 3-night cruises, minimum $290 (10 cabins); maximum $610 (7 cabins); 4-night cruises, minimum $385 (10 cabins); maximum $725 (17 cabins). Air-sea-land available. BARGAIN: second and third cabin passenger, sail free

TTT: *Emerald Seas* has the largest cabins in the short cruise market. Ship is very well maintained and appointed. Twelve cabins have double beds; 33 have queen size beds. New casino has blackjack, roulette and craps with $2 minimums. Special childrens' programs, video arcade, movies.

In a word (or two): Old and quality

<table>
<tr><td>T.S.S. FAIRSEA</td><td>Category:</td><td>Up-Scale</td></tr>
<tr><td>T.S.S. FAIRWIND</td><td>A.D.R.:</td><td>$215</td></tr>
<tr><td>(Sitmar Cruises)</td><td>Rating:</td><td>8.2</td></tr>
</table>

Fairsea from Los Angeles to Mexico; from San Francisco to Canada and Alaska; from West Coast transcanal to San Juan. *Fairwind:* from Port Everglades to Caribbean, South America and transcanal to Acapulco. *Fairsea* built 1955 as *Carinthia;* completely refurbished, rebuilt and recommissioned 1971. *Fairwind* built 1956 as *Sylvania;* completely refurbished, rebuilt and recommissioned 1972. Ships identical except for decor colors. Structural changes and complete redecorating both vessel 1984. Registry: Liberia. Capacity: 925 passengers each; 500 crew members each (Italian and Portuguese). Space ratio: 27.

Specifics: (both ships): Tonnage: 25,000; length: 608 feet; beam: 80 feet. Individual cabin climate controls, 3 elevators, 3 swimming pools, laundry, valet, medical services, closed-circuit TV (in deluxe cabins, lounges), shopping arcade, complete on-board youth program, youth counselors, sauna-massage, gymnasium, 6 bars, 5 lounges, library, wide-screen theatre, card rooms, 11 passenger decks, casino.

Electric Current: 220 volts D.C.

Entertainment: Professional entertainment, orchestra, quintet, dance team, chorus line, variety-format nightclub shows, movies.

Dining: 2 dining rooms, 2 seatings. Reservations when booking. Special dietary arrangements when booking or at least two weeks before sailing. Special orders through dining room captains. Pizzeria; Italian specialties.

Tipping: $2.50 to waiter (includes helper); $2.00 to cabin steward. Passenger discretion to dining room captains for special services. Cash or charge bar. Major credit cards accepted to settle bills at the end of the voyage.

Itinerary: Fairsea: September through May, from Los Angeles 7, 10, 11-days to Mexico, calling at Puerto Vallarta, Mazatlan, Acapulco, Zihuatanejo and Cabo San Lucas. June through August 12 and 14-days from San Francisco to Canada/Alaska calling at Vancouver, Alert Bay, Ketchikan, Sitka, Glacier Bay, Valdez (some voyages) and Astoria. *Fairsea* also has 14-day, one-way Panama Canal cruises from Los Angeles or San Francisco to San Juan or San Juan to Los Angeles or San Francisco. *Fairwind:* From Port Everglades, year-round, 7, 10, and 11-day Caribbean cruises, varied itineraries to San Juan, St. Thomas, Nassau, St. Croix, Curacao, Caracas, British Virgin Islands. *Fairwind* also has 14-day Caribbean cruises with partial transit of the Panama Canal; 12-day Panama Canal transits. Tenders most ports.

Rates: 7-day minimum (23 cabins) $1200; maximum $2150 (6 suites); 10-day minimum $1,550, maximum $3115; 12-day Canada-Alaska minimum $2,175, maximum $4,370; trans-Panama Canal, 12-day minimum $1,995, maximum $4,280. Third and fourth passengers charged about 60 percent of minimum and includes free air; children under two free; under 18 pay substantially reduced rate depending on voyage and season.

TTT: Bookkeeping system comparable to a large resort. Passengers may use major credit cards to settle bar and service bills for which they have signed during the voyage. Two cabins with double beds; no single cabins without surcharge. If you like Italian cuisine and atmosphere, you'll love the *Fairsea* and *Fairwind.* Cabins are larger than average; service warm and friendly. Sitmar enjoys one of the highest repeat passenger percentages in the business.

TTT: Both ships have been totally refurbished and up-graded at a cost of about $25 million. They are contemporary in design and colors but maintain Sitmar feeling on board. Colors are brighter and up-beat. Casinos have been installed on all Sitmar ships but they have under-estimated demand and they are too small. Six double beds in suites only. Some single cabins without surcharge. Sitmar encourages family cruising and has a full children's program, playrooms and activities for all age groups. They do an excellent job but if the patter of little feet leaves you cold, think twice before sailing during school holiday periods.

In a word (or two): Upbeat
✔✔✔ Food and service

Category: Up-Scale
A.D.R.: $239
Rating: 9.2

T.S.S. FAIRSKY
(Sitmar Cruises)

From San Francisco to Alaska and Canada (summer months), from Los Angeles to Mexico rest of the year. Built 1984. Registry: Liberia. Capacity: 1200 passengers, 550 crew (Italian deck, Italian and Portuguese service) Space ratio: 38.

Specifics: Tonnage: 46,000; length: 789 feet; beam: 91 feet; stabilizers, individual cabin climate controls; state-of-the-art electronics, gymnasium, drug store, shops, beauty/barber shop, telephones all cabins, 3 outdoor swimming pools, spa/sauna, television all cabins, laundromat, dry cleaning services, 11 passenger decks, youth center, theater, casino.

Electric Current: 110 and 220 volts A.C.

Entertainment: Orchestras, cabaret-type shows, theme cruises, movies.

Dining: 2 dining rooms, 2 seatings. Reservations in advance. Special requests in advance, but possible on board with dining room captain. Pizzeria

Tipping: $2.50 to waiter (includes his helper. Passenger discretion to dining room captains for special services. $2.00 to cabin steward. Cash or charge bar. Major credit cards accepted to settle bills at the end of the voyage.

Itinerary: Summer months, 12-day cruises from San Francisco to Alaska and Canada to Vancouver, Ketchikan, Juneau, Sitka, Glacier Bay, Victoria. Rest of the year from Los Angeles on 7, 10, 11 and 12-day cruises to Acapulco with stops in Puerto Vallarta, Mazatlan, Cabo San Lucas.

Rates: Although "common rated" with other Sitmar ships, *Fairsky* has fewer price categories and minimum is higher than on other Sitmar vessels. 7-day Mexico minimum is $1,130 (14 cabins); maximum (exclusive of suites) $2,130 for (28 mini-suites). 12-day Alaska minimum $2,295 to $4,370 for mini-suites.

TTT: *Fairsky's* innovations are for the most part refinements of traditional ship designs rather than revolutionary. Contrary to trends of the 1980's, the vessel is powered by steam turbines instead of diesel engines. Result—the smoothest, quietest new ship afloat. There is no vibration anywhere and it is sometimes difficult to remember you are on a cruise ship. There are full service pantries on every deck which provide excellent cabin service delivered by room stewards. The word "compact" was not used in designing this $150 million vessel. Cabin size is reminiscent of a bygone era. Bathrooms and showers are also large, towels fluffy and public lounges huge. Dining rooms have picture windows and the Observation Lounge affords comfortable and unobstructed leisurely viewing of where the ship is heading. Overall design concentrates gives passengers a traditional feeling of sailing a ship, not vacationing in a land-based resort and Sitmar-addicts are happy with this updated, state-of-the-art big sister to the Fairwind and Fairsea. Colors are easy to live with. Service is excellent. Stewards bring fresh fluffy towels twice daily, turn down beds, seem to be always present and happy to have you on board. Continental-style food service tastefully prepared by master chefs. Total experience is comparable to luxury-priced vessels. See *Fairwind/Fairsea* **TTT** for more about Sitmar service and amenities.

In a word (or two): Smooth, Traditional
✔✔✔✔✔ Food, Service, Facilities

	Category: Moderate
T.S.S. FESTIVALE	*A.D.R.:* $175
(Carnival Cruise Lines)	*Rating:* 8.5

From Miami to Caribbean. Built 1961 as *Transvaal Castle;* sailed same route (England to Africa) as *S.A. Vaal.* Purchased by Carnival Cruise Lines 1978, renamed *Festivale;* extensive rebuilding and refurbishing 1978. Registry: Panama. Capacity: 1,400 passengers; 580 crew (Italian: deck; mixed Caribbean: service). Space ratio: 33.

Specifics: Tonnage: 38,175 (original tonnage was 30,000, but extension of three decks and reconstruction added tonnage to vessel); length: 760 feet; beam: 90 feet; stabilizers; 4 elevators, individual cabin controlled air conditioning, 3 swimming pools, sauna, gymnasium, 10 public lounges, ultra modern electronic bridge, all cruise amenities, full gambling casino.

Electric Current: 110 volts A.C.

Entertainment: 3 orchestras, movies, entertainers, disco.

Dining: 1 dining room, 2 seatings. No advance reservations but special requests accommodated when made with booking. International specialties.

Tipping: $2.50 to waiter; $1.25 to bus boy; $2.50 to cabin steward. Cash bar.

Itinerary: Sunday departures beginning mid–1985; 7-day cruises to Nassau, San Juan, St. Thomas. Docks in every port.

Rates: Minimum $895 (5 cabins); maximum $1,795 (10 cabins). Children's rates: $195 for under 16 year olds occupying same cabins as two adults; singles $495 per person, four to a cabin.

TTT: The *Festivale* is one of the most beautiful ships afloat. She has been totally rebuilt but retains old-world glamour of the sea in a contemporary environment. Cabins are large and well appointed. 33 percent (146) of the cabins have queen-sized beds; 14 singles available without surcharge. All cabins have telephones. Original art works and tapestries are worthy of an inspection trip and a cruise. Colors throughout are bright and cheerful with no garish overtones. Cabins are over-sized, particularly outside cabins, in all price categories. In spite of her capacity of 1,400 passengers, space ratio is 33, giving the ship one of the largest space-per-passenger ratios afloat. See **TTT** *Tropicale* for additional comments; 24 hour cabin food service.

In a word or two: Upbeat and fun
✔✔✔ Food, entertainment, activities

S.S. GALILEO	*Category:*	Moderate
(Fantasy Cruises)	*A.D.R.:*	$138
	Rating:	3.5

From Miami to Bahamas winter months; summer from New York to nowhere, Bermuda and Nova Scotia. Built 1963 for Italian Line. Was laid up for several years before purchase in 1984 by Chandris and immediate charter to Fantasy Cruises. Remodeled in 1984 and began service in October 1984. Registry: Panama; Capacity: 1,60 passengers, 200 crew (Italian deck, mixed service). Space ratio: 26.

Specifics: Tonnage: 27,887; length: 427 feet; beam: 94 feet; stabilizers, 2 elevators, air conditioned, theater, large casino, gift shops, 2 swimming pools, 8 passenger decks; beauty shop, 2 elevators, casino.
Electric Current: 110 volts A.C.
Entertainment: orchestras, bars, revues.
Dining: 1 dining room, 2 seatings. Try special requests when booking. Table assignment on boarding. Italian-staffed dining room influences specialties.
Tipping: $2.00 to waiter; $1.00 to busboy; $2.00 to room steward. Cash bar.
Itinerary: Winter months from Miami 2 and 5 day (Sunday and Friday) sailings to Key West, Playa del Carmen and Cozumel on longer

cruises and to Nassau on others. Summer months from New York, Boston and other East Coast ports to Nowhere, Bermuda and Nova Scotia.

Rates: Minimum 2 nights $425 minimum (10 cabins); $935 maximum suites (2 with sitting rooms). 5-night minimum $875; maximum $935. Rates depend on season. Third and fourth cabin passenger pay $99 for 2-nights; $199 for 5-night cruises. Children charged $80 for 2-nights; $199 for 5-nights.

TTT: 1984 remodeling brought vessel up to U.S. Coast Guard requirements. Also added 74 cabins to increase capacity. Terms of ship sale to Chandris require that a specific number of Italians be employed on board. So chefs are Italian but service crew is mixed. Very large casino replaced a main lounge. No single cabins without surcharge but the new cabins all have double beds.

In a word (or two): Busy

Category:	Moderate
A.D.R.:	$220
Rating:	7.9

M.S. GOLDEN ODYSSEY
(Royal Cruise Line)

From Singapore and Hong Kong winter months to the Orient. Summer months from Piraeus to Mediterranean and Black Sea, Built: 1974. Registry: Greece. Capacity: 460 passengers; 200 crew (Greek) Space ratio: 23.

Specifics: Tonnage: 10,500; length: 427 feet; beam: 63 feet; All cabins with telephones, three channel radio; 5 bars, 3 lounges, boutique, beauty/ barber shops, theater, 2 saunas, swimming pool, gymnasium, stabilizers; 2 passenger elevators; special propeller system that reduces vibration; 7 passenger decks, small casino.

Electric Current: 110 volts A.C.

Entertainment: Movies, bands, live entertainment.

Dining: 1 dining room; 2 seatings; reservations and special dietary requests when booking.

Tipping: $7 a day, per person, at the end of the cruise. Tips are pooled and divided among the crew.

Itinerary: Winter months 15 days between Hong Kong and Singapore; Summer months Mediterranean from Lisbon and Athens to North Africa and Baltic ports on 14, 15-day cruises. Docks most ports.

Rates: Cruise only minimum, Orient 15 days, $2,898 (7 cabins); maximum $3,548 (8 deluxe suites). From Los Angeles, add $950 for package. (See Air-Sea); Cruise only Mediterranean 14 days $1,550 (7 cabins); maximum, $3,548 (8 deluxe suites). Third or fourth persons, about 30 percent discount on minimums. Rates are seasonal.

TTT: Totally deluxe; almost all cabins are outside and good sized. Air-sea packaging is based on Los Angeles departures and there are additions or subtractions allowed, depending on point of origin. Company enjoys an excellent reputation. I have never received a negative letter or report from a passenger, and that makes this company one of the few in that category. Ship is ship-shape at all times, well operated, professionally organized.

In a word or two: Beautiful and Yacht-like

✔✔✔✔ Itineraries

	Category:	Moderate
M.S. HOLIDAY	*A.D.R.:*	$181
(Carnival Cruise Lines)	*Rating:*	Not rated

Built 1985 in Aalborg, Denmark. Begins service July 1985. Registry: Panama; Capacity: 1,760 (including upper berths), normal cruise 1,452 passengers, 660 crew (Italian deck; mixed international service. Space Ratio: 31

Specifics: Tonnage: 45,000 plus; length: 728 feet; beam: 92 feet; stabilizers; individual cabin climate controls, 8 elevators, 3 outside swimming pools, beauty/barber shops, hospital, boutique, massage room, 9 passenger decks, childrens' playroom, closed circuit T.V., sauna, drug store, stereo in all cabins, golf driving platform, 2 whirlpool spas, 11 lounges-bars; enclosed promenade, very large full casino.

Electric Current: 110 volts A.C.

Entertainment: orchestras, musical revues, round the clock activities, most complete casino afloat.

Dining: 2 dining rooms, 2 seatings. Special requests when booking. Table assignments after boarding.

Tipping: $2.50 to waiter; $1.25 to bus boy; $2.50 to cabin steward. Cash bar.

Itinerary: From Miami, 7-day cruises every Saturday to St. Maarten, St. Thomas and Nassau.

Rates: Common rated with other Carnival Cruise Line ships which means that minimum and maximum cabins are priced the same, but this vessel has more medium priced cabins so average is slightly higher. 10 minimum cabins $945; 10 suites with verandahs $1,695 (slightly higher in season). Average outside cabin on Main Deck $1,270.

TTT: Ship was selected for the cover of the 10th Anniversary Edition of THE TOTAL TRAVELER BY SHIP because this vessel sets the stage for the style in which middle-America is going to cruise for at least the next decade and probably longer. Built at a cost of more than $150 million, she is the second in Carnival's new generation of ships (the first: *M.S. Tropicale*) and she will be followed by three more vessels scheduled to be completed within the next three years. Contemporary in design, cabins are identical in size and design, depending on whether they are insides or outsides. Minimums have a different configuration and maximums are deluxe with verandahs and jacuzzi bathtubs. Public rooms and restaurants take up two full decks. Dining rooms have picture windows; main lounge (American Lounge) is multileveled and the Gaming Club casino looks more like a gambling salon than a floating crap game. Design, use of space and colors is ingenious. Interior architect Joe Farcus has done a fine job. Designer Carole Farcus, who also designed the *Tropicale* and *Festivale* interiors, has outdone herself in creativity and imagination. One of the first women (and maybe the only one) specializing in ship design, she understands what passengers want and she builds the features into ships in up-beat designs that wear well. One lounge is in the style of an underground grotto. The piano bar has the old-time feel of Casablanca, and a double-decker London bus is a snack bar strategically placed on the largest shipboard promenade. Reflections Discotheque, Rick's American Cafe, outdoor bars, an indoor Lido area called The Wharf, Tahiti Lounge, Blue Lagoon and childrens' areas have names which match decor. Casino is very large, beautifully decorated and still has $2 minimum chips at black jack tables. No single cabins without surcharge. Suites have bathtub jacuzzis; over 60 percent of the cabins are outside, all lower beds can be converted to doubles.

State-of-the-art electronics, design and facilities added to Carnival Cruise Line's entertainment policy, moderate prices, free air packages makes the *Holiday* "The Ship of 1985", a ship for travelers looking for their money's worth in the Moderate Category.

In a word (or two): Beautiful, New, Fun

S.S. ITALIS
(Chandris, Inc.)

Category: Budget
A.D.R.: $100
Rating: 4

Originally built 1940 as *America;* refurbished, purchased by Chandris 1965 and sailed as *Australis;* sold to the now defunct Venture Cruises 1978 but never completed a voyage as a reborn *America;* repossessed by Chandris; put into Mediterranean service and renamed *Italis* 1979. Registry: Panama. Capacity: 1,500 passengers; 600 crew (Greek). Space ratio: 24.

Specifics: Tonnage 34,449; length: 723 feet, beam 93 feet; stabilizers; 5 elevators, swimming pool, shops, gymnasium, lounges, bar, 21 public rooms, 8 passenger decks.

Electric Current: 110 and 220 volts. A.C. and D.C.

Entertainment: Orchestras; large movie theater; shows; disco; taverns.

Tipping: $5 a day to chief steward at the end of the voyage for distribution to entire crew. Cash bar.

Itinerary: 14-day cruises from Barcelona to Malta, Alexandria, Haifa, Kusadasi, Piraeus, Naples, Genoa. Air-sea available.

Rates: Cruise lengths vary. 14-days from New York sometimes include transatlantic air and transfer between airport and pier in Barcelona, minimum cabins without private facilities. $1,346 (4 berth cabins); minimum cabins with private facilities (2 berth cabins), $1,609; maximum $2,428.

TTT: Large and comfortable in rough seas, but she isn't the America of old. Refurbished in part by Venture Cruises and then again by Chandris when she was repossessed. Deck chairs $5 per week.

In a word or two: Tacky and bargain

M.S. KAZAKHSTAN
(International Cruise Center)

Category: Budget
A.D.R.: under $100
Rating: 5

From European and Russian ports to Caribbean, South Africa, Orient. Built, 1976. Registry: U.S.S.R. Capacity: 475 passengers; 265 crew (Russian). Space ratio: 35.

Specifics: Tonnage: 16,000; length: 515 feet; beam: 71 feet; stabilizers;

fully air-conditioned, 3 elevators, swimming pool, beauty/barber shops, lounges, theater, casino, medical services, 7 passenger decks.
Electric Current: 220 volts A. C.
Entertainment: 2 orchestras, movies, nightclub shows, casino.
Dining: 1 dining room, 2 seatings, no special diets, Russian specialties.
Tipping: Not required.
Itinerary: Varied from London, North Sea ports to European, Mediterranean and longer voyages. Tenders at some ports.
Rates: Average just under $100 per day even on very long voyages.

TTT: No single cabins. All cabins have private facilities. 150 percent of per person rate charged for single occupancy. Sailing from U.S. ports discontinued in 1982. No word on resumption at press time. Food is meat and potatoes, AND caviar and vodka.

In a word (or two): Old and Bargain

T.S.S. MARDI GRAS	*Category:* Moderate
(Carnival Cruise Lines)	*A.D.R.:* $175
	Rating: 7.5

From Miami to Caribbean. Built 1961 as the *Empress of Canada;* purchased by Carnival Cruise Lines, refurbished 1973 and again in 1982. Registry: Panama. Capacity: 1,240 passengers; 510 crew (Italian deck, mixed service); Space ratio: 30.

Specifics: Tonnage: 27,250; length: 650 feet; beam: 87 feet; stabilizers; individual cabin controlled air conditioning, 4 elevators, 1 indoor, 2 outdoor swimming pools, duty-free shopping arcade, health club, children's game room, 3 nightclubs, 5 lounges, ballroom (capacity 550), hospital facilities, 6 passenger decks, large casino.
Electric Current: 110 volts A. C.
Entertainment: 3 orchestras; movies, nightclub shows; disco.
Dining: 1 dining room, 2 seatings. No reservations when booking. Special dietary requests in advance.
Tipping: $2.50 to waiter; $1.25 to bus boy; $2.50 to cabin steward. Cash bar.
Itinerary: Every Sunday from Port of Miami, 7-day cruises Ocho Rios, Grand Cayman, Cozumel. Docks all ports.
Rates: Minimum $895 (20 cabins); maximum $1,795 (6 suites); children's rate $195 for under–16-year-olds sharing cabin with two adults. Single rate: $395 per person, four to a cabin.

TTT: A full casino operates when the *Mardi Gras* is at sea. Plush red velvet decor, casino play at Las Vegas odds with craps, roulette, blackjack, and slots. 104 cabins with double beds; 8 single cabins without surcharge. See "**TTT**" *Carnivale* for additional comments on atmosphere, service and ambience. 24-hour cabin food service. Quoting from a personal report published in *TRAVEL TRADE MAGAZINE,* "It's day six on board the *Mardi Gras* and we're heading back toward the Port of Miami. The mood on board is much like a party winding down or maybe a happening that has climaxed and not quite ready to settle down to the real world. The *Mardi Gras* is different from other one-week cruise ships. She appeals to travelers seeking the casual, informal, comfortable approach to vacations at sea; the traveler who wants the style and service offered by cruise experiences but wants it in a style that carries over from his own lifestyle on shore. The Mardi Gras is no replica of TV's Love Boat in elegance and style, but passengers sure have more fun than their television counterparts. Not to say she's not a pretty ship. This follower of the sea lanes appreciates her handsome paneled walls, wide promenades, excellent theater, well lighted dining room, spacious decks and oversized cabins. She's a grand lady of the sea who serviced the transocean traveling crowd from the time of her launching in 1961 to her purchase by Carnival in 1972. The *Mardi Gras* is a ship in motion. She moves easily through the waters and her passengers move to the orchestras, entertainment, on-board activities."

In a word (or two): Fun and Disco
✔✔✔✔ Activities, entertainment, experience

	Category: Up-Scale
M.S. MERMOZ	*A.D.R.:* $290
(Paquet Cruises)	*Rating:* 7.2

From San Juan to Caribbean winter months; from European ports to North Cape and Black Sea. Built 1957 as *Jean Mermoz;* refurbished and rebuilt 1970. Registry: France. Capacity: 550 passengers; 230 crew (French and Indonesian). Space ratio: 25.

Specifics: Tonnage: 13,800; length: 530 feet; beam: 66 feet; stabilizers; individual cabins climate controls, 2 elevators, 2 swimming pools, shopping arcade, beauty/barber ships, gymnasium, sauna, card room, laundry-valet, Grand Salon, medical services, 10 decks, casino.
Electric Current: 110 volts A.C.

Entertainment: International orchestra; movies, discotheque; pool bars, cabaret; special-interest cruises; annual Classical Music Festival at Sea.

Dining: 1 dining room, 2 seatings in Caribbean; 1 seating in Europe and for Music Festival. Reservations when booking. Special dietary requests must be made in advance. French cuisine; complimentary wines with lunch and dinner.

Tipping: $5.00 per person, per day, covers waiters and cabin steward.

Itinerary: From San Juan 10 and 11-days to St. Barthelemy, Guadeloupe, Curacao, La Guaira, Martinique, Antigua, St. Croix. Some cruises visit Tobago, St. John, two ports not usually included in ship itineraries. Summer months in the Mediterranean.

Rates: 10 day minimum $1,655 (21 cabins); maximum $4,345 (4 cabins), 11-day minimum $1,825, maximum $4,785. Music Festival Cruise rates are higher.

TTT: 16 cabins with double beds; 17 single cabins without surcharge. Has excellent reputation for French gourmet cooking. Paquet's *Music Festival at Sea* is an outstanding cruise experience. Famous artists perform every night of the cruise. For a better idea of what is offered on these very special cruises, 1984 voyage featured flutist James Galway, trumpeter Maurice Andre, cellist Yo Yo Ma, the English Chamber Orchestra and leading dancers of the Paris Opera, plus more than 20 other artists.

In a word or two: Food and Music

✔✔✔✔ French food and complimentary wines

M.S. MIKHAIL LERMONTOV	*Category:* Budget
(International Cruise Center)	*A.D.R.:* Under $100
	Rating: 4

Sails from Leningrad, Bremerhaven, London (Tilbury), Le Havre to Baltic countries, Mediterranean. Built 1971. Registry: U.S.S.R. Capacity: 700 passengers; 315 crew (Russian). Space Ratio: 28.

Specifics: Tonnage: 20,000; length: 577 feet; beam: 78 feet; stabilizers; 3 elevators; swimming pool; beauty/barber shops; gymnasium, sauna, laundry service, 6 lounges, bars, medical services, 9 decks.

Electric Current: 220 volts A. C.

Dining: 1 dining room, 2 seatings. Russian specialties.

Tipping: Not required.

Itinerary: During summer and fall from European ports on varied itineraries. Also does some long voyages to Orient.
Rates: Average daily rate runs just under $100 per day, depending on
itinerary and season. Sometimes makes transatlantic voyage to Canada. Special student discounts for transatlantic sailings. Inter-portport fares also available.

TTT: If you're headed for Russia on any U.S.S.R flag ship you may
stay aboard while the ship is in Leningrad for about $50 per passenger,
per day. This includes all on-board services, food, and two Intourist
tours daily; that's about what the tours would cost if you purchased
them separately. Arrangements for stay-aboards must be made prior to
sailings.

TTT: Russian ships sailing transatlantic will transport automobiles accompanied by passengers. Charges are based on car weight. It pays to
ship and sail Russian-style if you plan to drive around Europe. Your
trip discount of 20 percent for two would make the price of shipping
your car a bargain! 22 single cabins without surcharge. 107 cabins
have private facilities. All calls at U.S. ports discontinued in 1982. No
information available at press time regarding resumption of service
from North America.

In a word or two: Bargain
✓✓✓ Caviar and Vodka

NANTUCKET CLIPPER	*Category:*	Moderate
NEWPORT CLIPPER	*A.D.R.:*	$190
(Clipper Cruise Lines)	*Rating:*	6

From St. Thomas (winter months); from Savannah, Baltimore, Washington, D.C., Boston (rest of year). Built 1983 (Newport Clipper), 1985
Nantucket Clipper; Registry: U.S.A.; Capacity: 102 passengers, 28
crew (all American); Space ratio: 10.

Specifics: Tonnage: 100; length: 207 feet; beam: 37 feet. observation
lounge, bar, 4 decks. No elevators, beauty/barber shop, hospital,
swimming pool. 51 outside cabins all with picture windows.
Electric Current: 110 volts A.C.
Entertainment: Movies on video system; cultural enrichment program,
light musical. Passengers may go ashore in ports since most itineraries call for evenings in port.

Dining: 1 dining room, single seating. American cuisine. Reservations in advance.

Tipping: $7 per week, per passenger paid at the end of the cruise. Tips are pooled and divided among entire crew.

Itinerary: Varies, but typical 7-day cruise from St. Thomas visits Tortola, Norman Island, Virgin Gorda, Jost Van Dyke, St. John. Inland U.S. cruises visit historic East coast cities.

Rates: From $1,195 to $2,990. East Coast U.S. cruises run about $100 less.

TTT: Ships are beautifully appointed and designed for shallow water cruising. Draft allows entry into ports not visited by large cruise ships. Food is very good and service is personal and excellent. It's like sailing a private yacht. Ships are not for travelers looking for the Love Boat experience. They are for those seeking relaxation and unusual ports of call.

In a word (or two): Relaxing and Enjoyable

S.S. NIEUW AMSTERDAM
S.S. NOORDAM
(Holland America Cruises)

Category: Up-Scale
A.D.R.: $220
Rating: 8

Both ships built in France. *Nieuw Amsterdam* completed 1983; *Noordam* in 1984. Both vessels are representative of $150 million generation of new cruise ships. Registry: Netherlands Antilles. Capacity: 1,200 passengers; 559 crew, (Dutch officers, Indonesian service). Space ratio: 27.

Specifics: Tonnage: 33,930; length: 704 feet; beam: 88 feet; stabilized, equipped with every modern convenience for navigation, individual cabin climate controls, shops, barber/beauty shops, laundry, dry cleaning services, infirmary, worldwide telex system, gymnasium, sauna, theater, 2 swimming pools, closed circuit television in every room.

Electric Current: 110 Volts A.C.

Entertainment: Revues, orchestras, movies, string ensembles.

Dining: 1 dining room, 2 seatings, plus Lido and outdoor Bar-B-Que. Can make reservations when booking. Special attention paid to dietary requirements; make arrangements when booking. International cuisine. No smoking section. Two private dining rooms for parties.

Tipping: Not required (See Rotterdam Tipping)

Itinerary: Both vessels sail from Vancouver to Alaska on 7-day summer cruises; winter months, *Nieuw Amsterdam* from Tampa 7-day cruises to Western Caribbean. *Noordam,* 14-day cruises from San Francisco to Mexico with turn around in Acapulco for a 7-day leg.

Rates: From Tampa, 7-day $1,499 minimum, (22 cabins); $2,699 maximum (20 deluxe cabins). Rates higher during season. Similar from San Francisco.

TTT: As each new ship starts making waves, she brings with her innovations never before offered at sea. The *Nieuw Amsterdam* and *Noordam* are no exceptions. Push button telephones with message indicators and closed circuit color television in cabins; daily stock quotations, casinos. Nieuw Amsterdam is themed to Old New York and colors are bright and alive. Noordam is more somber and themed to Dutch Trading Company. Both vessels are spacious and average cabins are good size. Minimums are minimum sized. Twenty cabins have king size beds; 103 with queen size. Full childrens program with supervision during holiday seasons. Also video game room and Arts and Crafts program for all ages. Both vessels have fully equipped health spas.

TTT: Both ships have vibration problems which company says are being solved but I advise against booking last 10 cabins aft from Main Deck down.

TTT: Holland America is the only cruise line that allows seeing eye dogs and has wheelchairs available for rental. Elevators and all public rooms have been built for easy accessibility by handicapped.

In a word (or two): Beautiful and New

	Category:	Up-Scale
M.S. NORDIC PRINCE	*A.D.R.:*	$194
(Royal Caribbean Cruise Line)	*Rating:*	7.8

From Port of Miami to the Caribbean and West Indies. Built in 1970/71. Registry: Norway. Capacity: 1,038 passengers; 400 crew (Norwegian deck; mixed service). Space ratio: 22.

Specifics: Tonnage: 23,200; length: 635 feet; beam: 80 feet; stabilizers, individual cabin controlled air conditioning, 4 elevators, swimming pool, shopping arcade; beauty/barber shops, saunas and gymnasium, 3 lounges, 2 bars, medical services, 8 passenger decks.

Electric Current: 110 volts A.C.

Entertainment: 2 quintets, 1 quartet, 4-piece calypso band; first run movies; nightclub acts.

Dining: 1 dining room, 2 seatings. No reservations when booking. All tables assigned after boarding. No special diets.

Tipping: $2.50 to waiter; $1.25 to busboy; $2.50 to cabin steward; Cash bar.

Itinerary: Varied: 7 days days to Bermuda summer months; 8 days Miami to Nassau, San Juan and St. Thomas; 10 days Miami to St. Croix, Martinique, Barbados, Antigua, St. Thomas.

Rates: 10 day minimum $1,700 (36 cabins), maximum $3,765 (1 deluxe suite); 8 days minimum $1,225, maximum $2,670; 7 days (Bermuda) minimum $1,140, maximum $2,585. Third and fourth cabin passenger: 10 days $750; 8 days $525; 7 days $525.

TTT: 51 cabins with double beds; no single cabins without surcharge. See *Sun Viking* **TTT** for children's facilities. See **TTT's** *Song of America, Sun Viking, Song of Norway* for more information on RCL amenities and on-board facilities.

In a word (or two): Food and service
✔✔✔ entertainment

	Category:	Up-Scale
S.S. NORWAY	A.D.R.:	$228
(Norwegian Caribbean Lines)	Rating:	8.5

From Florida ports to Caribbean. Built as the *S.S. France* in 1961, she was heralded as the "grandest ship of all time." Retired from service in 1974; purchased for use as a floating hotel, but she never left Le Havre until July 1979, when she was bought by Norwegian Caribbean Lines and renamed *S.S. Norway.* Complete refurbished, cabins added, new facilities and updated late 1979, early 1980 at a total cost of about $100 million. Caribbean service mid–1980. Registry: Norway; Capacity: 2,000 passengers; 800 crew (Norwegian deck; mixed service). Space ratio: 35.

Specifics: Tonnage: 70,202; length: 1,035 (3.5 football fields); beam: 110 feet. Two pairs of stabilizers; individual cabin climate controls, 8 elevators, international shopping arcade, walking plaza, beauty/barber shops, gymnasium, saunas, numerous lounges, meeting rooms, discos, gaming area, library, two decks of public rooms, 11 passenger decks, refrigerators most cabins, childrens' playroom, large casino.

Electric Current: 220 and 110 volts A.C. and D.C.

Entertainment: Closed-circuit television, stereo every cabins, nightclubs;

orchestras; live entertainers; movies; discos; casino; 2 complete Broadway musicals.

Dining: 2 dining rooms, 2 seatings; advance reservations when booking handled by computer. Special dietary requests when booking through Passenger Courtesy Department.

Tipping: $2.00 to waiter; $1.00 to bus boy, $2.00 to room steward; Cash bar.

Itinerary: Saturday 7-days to St. Thomas, with a stop at a Bahamas Out Island and Nassau Saturday sailing. Because of her size, ship will not dock in most ports. Special passenger tenders and multiple gangways were designed so passengers can be ferried easily and quickly ashore at St. Thomas and the Bahamas. She docks in Florida and her bow thruster system simplifies maneuvering.

Rates: Although minimum and maximum rates are the same as on other NCL ships, there are more higher priced cabins on the Norway and average daily rate is higher. How much higher depends on your choice of cabins. Minimum, $1,095 (42 cabins); maximum, $2,710 (8 suites, excluding those two super suites left over from the S.S. France days). Third and fourth cabin passengers, $570; children under 17, $335.

TTT: Comparing the Norway with the QE2, the two giant liners afloat:

	Norway	Queen Elizabeth 2
tonnage:	70,202	67,107
length:	1,035 feet	963 feet
beam:	109 feet	105 feet

Single cabins with 150 percent surcharge; 305 cabins with double beds. 8 with king size beds; 2 with queen. Honeymoon suites are really royal complete with mirrored ceilings.

TTT: She may have been the *S.S. France* at one time, but she is now the *Norway* and passengers coming on board expecting the *France* will be disappointed. She is an excellent vessel, but she is not the *France.* Whatever decor is left over from those days is pure nostalgia. The rest of the ship has been redone in a different way. The *Norway* is in today's style without many of the frills for which the *France* was famous. Food is in NCL style and is the same as on the other ships in the fleet. (*Starward, Skyward, Southward, Sunward II*) Public facilities are outstanding. My favorite area is the double promenade with coffee shop, ice cream parlor, sidewalk cafes and shops. Delightful! Full scale musical revues are another highlight. Two dining rooms are not identical and it is hard to say which is more desirable. The Windward is the old first class dining room and is elegant. My husband prefers the Leeward with her beautiful winding stairway. The *Norway*'s destination on one week cruises is secondary to the cruise experience. At press time there were rumors around the docks that the itinerary may be changing. There aren't too many ports that can handle a vessel the size of the *Norway* and with the amount of fuel she burns, choices for one week or shorter cruises, are limited. She's very expensive to operate. A final word of advice if you're going to sail her — she's too big to dock at most ports and she anchors in St. Thomas. Don't line up to disembark when she drops that anchor and the tenders are lowered into the sea. It takes a couple of hours to move some 2,000 passengers and best advice is to relax and take a later tender. There's no big line up coming back to the ship because passengers seem to stagger returns and the ship won't leave without you if you are waiting at the tender dock before the posted final departure time.

TTT: Although N.C.L. has done a lot to improve the *Norway,* there's nothing it can do about cabins designed and built to be sold in two categories. While former first class cabins are large, minimum cabins are very minimum-sized. New decor does a lot to make them look larger, but they are very, very small.

TTT UPDATE: The *Norway* completed a series of Northern European cruises tied in with scheduled drydock in summer 1984. Although company says voyages were well received, a repeat is not planned for 1985. Look for another series of Northern Europe cruises and two transatlantic crossings in 1986 when she is again due for a major drydocking. About $15 million was spent on her and all of the cabins have now been totally redecorated. Owner Knut Kloster says the *Norway* is now "finished," and the ship is the way he visualized her when he spent his original millions on the purchase. Refrigerators have been added to almost all cabins; colored television is installed and working in every cabin and the ship's teevee studio keeps passengers abreast of the news with regularly scheduled broadcasts. Two suites have been redecorated in the style in which honeymooners are expected to honeymoon (silver, mirrors, etc.). They are dream (or maybe fantasy) suites, so you'll have to book far in advance. Seems honeymooners, first or 31st, are booking quickly. New decor throughout the ship is bright, cheerful and has the look of a hotel rooms, rather than a cruise ship. AND, in 1982 NCL installed their first casinos afloat on board the Norway. Craps, black-jack, roulette and rows of slots.

In a word (or two): Big and Beautiful
✔✔✔✔✔ Entertainment

Category:	Moderate
A.D.R.:	$190
Rating:	8

S.S. OCEANIC
(Home Lines)

From New York to Bermuda and West Indies. Built 1965; Refurbished 1973 and 1981; Registry: Panama; Capacity: 850 to 1035; 600 crew (Italian). Space Ratio: 38.

Specifics: Tonnage: 39,241; length: 784 feet; beam: 97 feet; stabilizers; individual cabin controlled air conditioning, 4 elevators, 2 swimming pools, beauty/barber shops, laundry, gymnasium, sauna, 18 lounges, ballroom (575 capacity), casino, medical services, 10 decks.

Electric Current: 110 volts A.C.

Entertainment: 4 orchestras; movies, nightclub; disco.

Dining: 1 dining room, 2 seatings. Reservation when booking. Dining: 1 very large dining room, 2 seatings. Advance reservations suggested. Special dietary requests in advance or with maitre d' on board. Italian specialties.

Tipping: $2.50 to waiter and cabin steward; $5 per week to table captain; $5 per week to maitre D'; Cash or charge bar.

Itinerary: One week from New York to Nassau and Bermuda spring, summer and fall. Winter to Caribbean. Tenders some ports.

Rates: Seven day cruises from New York to Bermuda, from $900 to $1,775. (8 deluxe suites); 14 single cabins without surcharge.

TTT: The *Oceanic* was built for ocean cruising and is the most popular ship sailing out of New York for Bermuda. One of the most unusual facilities found at sea is the Lido area which covers 13,000 square feet and houses 2 swimming pools. The area is topside and is protected by a sliding sunshine cover that shields it from winds an sprays. No cabins with double beds. Deck chair charge is $3.50; 24 hour cabin food service is excellent. Home Lines is a pace setter in maintaining high quality of service and food. Most of the on-board staff has been with the company for years; some into the second generation. Same service and food as on the Atlantic.

* Oceanic is borderline—Moderate and Up-scale. Vessel rates the same in either category.

In a word (or two): Food and Beautiful
✔✔✔✔ Food and Service

	Category:	Up-Scale
	A.D.R.:	$220
	Rating:	5.5

S.S. INDEPENDENCE
(American Hawaii Cruises)

From Honolulu to neighboring island. Built in 1951 as *Independence,* she was the largest passenger ship built in the U.S. for more than a decade. Designed to carry over 1,000 passengers in three classes on long cruises between New York and the Mediterranean, she has 23,000 feet of open deck space along with large well appointed public lounges and staterooms. Purchased by Atlantic Far East Lines in 1974 for South African service; purchased by American Hawaii Cruises 1979, redocumented under the U.S. flag as *Oceanic Independence.* Completely refurbished June 1980 when vessel re-entered American market on a year around program. Registry: U.S.A. Capacity: 750 passengers; 300 crew (American). Space ratio: 27.

Specifics: Tonnage: 20,300, length: 682 feet; beam: 89 feet; stabilizers, 4 elevators, 2 swimming pools, solarium, health spa, gymnasium, 7 public lounges, conference facilities, golf range, card room, barber/beauty salon, hospital, all cruise ship amenities.

Electric Current: 100 volts A.C.

Dining: 1 dining room, 2 seatings. American and international specialties.

Tipping: $2-$2.50 to dining room waiter; $1.00 cents to bus boy; $2 to $2.50 to room steward. Cash bar.

Itinerary: Saturday departures 7-days from Honolulu to Hilo, Kona, Maui; and Nawiliwili. Docks all ports.

Rates: Cruise only rates depend on season, range from $995 minimum (57 upper and lower berth cabins). Third and fourth passenger rate: $695; children under 12: $395.

TTT: Ship accommodates handicapped on all decks from Main and above. A travel companion may be required. There is a nursery on board, children's counselors and playroom. Recreation director assigned to childrens' activities June through August. There are 26 suites; 26 double bedded cabins, three with king size beds; 31 singles cabins available without surcharge. Aloha spirit found both in dress and in services. Poolside breakfasts, tropical menus, Polynesian foods and entertainment, lei making, hula lessons, ukulele lessons. It's a cruise in stateside comfort, Hawaiian style. Food is good (not gourmet); atmosphere on board—American.

In a word or two: Up-beat and Enjoyable

M.V. OCEAN ISLANDER
(Ocean Cruise Line)

Category: Moderate
A.D.R.: $180
Rating: Not Rated*

From Barbados to Caribbean winter months; summer months from Venice and Piraeus in Mediterranean. Built 1956 as *San Giorgio* for *Adriatica Cruises;* rebuilt for Cycladic Cruises in 1980 and renamed *City of Andros.* Purchased by Ocean Cruise Line in 1984 and named *Ocean Islander.* $3.5 million spent on refurbishing and reconstruction. Registry: Panama. Capacity: 260 passengers; 125 crew (Greek deck, mixed international service; Space Ratio: 19.

Specifics: Tonnage: 5,000 tons; length: 368 feet; beam: 51 feet. Stabilizers, 2 elevators, swimming pool, barber/beauty shop, sauna, health center, 3 lounges/bars, 4 public rooms, casino.

Electric Current: 220 volts A.C.

Entertainment: orchestra, floor shows, disco.

Dining: 1 dining room; 2 seatings; special requests in advance of sailing; table assignments on board.

Tipping: $2.00 to waiter; $1.00 to bus boy; $2.00 room steward. Cash bar.

Itinerary: Every Sunday from Barbados (November to April) 7-days to Tobago, cruises Orinoco River to Ciudad Guyana, Grenada, Union and Palm Island, Bequia, St. Vincent and Martinique. Spring and summer sailings to Kusadasi, Mykonos, Santorini, Corfu, Bay of Kotor, Dubrovnik and Zadar.

Rates: 7-day minimum $995 (4 cabins); $1595 maximum (4 cabins). Average around $1345 for Mediterranean one week cruise.

TTT: Vessel inaugurated service under Ocean Cruise Line banner in November 1984.

    *Too early to rate. Early reports include comments on some nice facilities and programs, like shore-side sports activities available to passenbers. Ship has 101 outside cabins, 6 deluxe cabins with double beds, and only 17 inside rooms. Yacht-like atmosphere. No singles without surcharge.

M.V. OCEAN PRINCESS
(Ocean Cruise Line)

Category: Moderate
A.D.R.: $180
Rating: 4.8

From Montego Bay to Caribbean winter months; summer months from Nice and Venice in Mediterranean. Built 1966 as Italia for Costa Cruises, she was later leased to Princess Cruises and sailed as the Princess Italia.; refurbished and up-graded by Ocean Cruise Line in 1983 and renamed Ocean Princess. Registry: Panama. Capacity: 460 passengers; 225 crew (Greek deck, mixed international service); Space Ratio: 26.5.

Specifics: Tonnage: 12,200 tons; length: 438 feet; beam: 77 feet. Stabilizers, 6 elevators, swimming pool, barber/beauty shop, sauna, health center, 3 lounges/bars, 4 public rooms, casino.

Electric Current: 220 volts A.C.

Entertainment: orchestra, floor shows, disco, casino

Dining: 1 dining room; 2 seatings; special requests in advance of sailing; table assignments on board. Also a cafe for buffet lunch.

Tipping: $2.00 to waiter; $1.00 to bus boy; $2.00 to room steward. Cash bar.

Itinerary: Every Saturday from Montego Bay (November to April) 7-days to Aruba. Cartagena, Cristobal, partial transit of Panama Canal, and Grand Cayman. Other months from and Venice on 7 or 14-day cruises to Mediterranean and Black Sea ports.

Rates: 7-day minimum $795 (4 cabins); $1795 maximum (17 cabins). Average around $1345 for Mediterranean one week cruise.

TTT: Ship was completely re-done in contemporary style by internationally known ship design team of Agni and Michael Katzourakis. Very Scandinavian look instead of the Italian look of the vessel's former life. Her inaugural Mediterranean season in 1984 was well received. Cabins are very comfortable but cabin service is limited. Deck space is good. Colors are easy to live with but may not wear too well over the years. Itineraries are excellent and prices include free air from some Florida cities. Nice feature is large bathrooms but about half the cabins are inside. No singles without surcharge. Food service during first year of operation needs to be improved.

In a word (or two): Wait and See

S.S.ORIANA
(P&O Cruises)

Category:	Moderate
A.D.R.:	$145
Rating:	4.5

From Australia to South Pacific. Built 1960 for Orient Line but completed for P&O Orient Lines. Transferred to P&O 1966. Completely refurbished and converted to one-class cruise ship 1973. Registry: United Kingdom. Capacity: 1,750 passengers, 500 crew (British deck, mixed service). Space ratio: 24

Specifics: Tonnage: 41,910; length: 804 feet; beam: 97 feet; 3 swimming pools, 15 public rooms, barber/beauty shop, medical, gymnasium, 11 passenger decks, children's playroom, theater.

Electric Current: 220 volts A.C./D.C.

Entertainment: Orchestras, varies with every cruise

Dining: 2 restaurants, 2 seatings. Few special dietary requests possible. Seating assignments after boarding.

Tipping: suggested amounts not available, but safe to count on $5 a day.

Itinerary: Varies, but usual sailings 10 to 14 nights from Sydney, Australia to South Pacific islands including Fiji, Pago Pago, Moorea.

Rates: Typical 12-day minimum with facilities $2,927; maximum $3,455

TTT: Difficult to figure number of cabins without facilities because rate is the same for outside without facilities and inside with facilities. Large number of cabins do not have facilities and there are a number of cabins for four. When the *Oriana* was built, she was the fourth largest passenger ship and sailed as a two, and sometimes three-class vessel. Atmosphere on board is informal. Passengers are mostly Australian and British, although marketing efforts are being directed to North America and air fare from San Francisco or Los Angeles is included in cost of the cruise.

In a word (or two): Casual

M.S. PEARL OF SCANDINAVIA
(Pearl Cruises of Scandinavia)

Category:	Up-Scale
A.D.R.:	$188
Rating:	6.5

From Hong Kong and Kobe to People's Republic; from Singapore to South Pacific. Built 1967 as Finnstar; rebuilt and refurbished 1979 and again in 1981. Registry: Bahamas; Capacity: 425 passengers, 217 crew (Scandinavian deck, Filipino service). Space ratio: 29.

Specifics: Tonnage: 12,400; length: 502 feet; beam: 66 feet; individual cabin climate controls, stabilizers, many cabins with tubs, all with private facilities, music system, deluxe suites, large cabins, 2 swimming pools, sauna, 2 casinos, 8 passenger decks, 2 elevators.
Electric Current: 220 volts
Entertainment: orchestra, tv, movies, lecturers
Dining: 1 restaurant, 2 seatings; written special dietary requests accommodated if received one month in advance of sailing.
Tipping: $2.00 to waiter; $1.00 to bus boy; $2.50 to room steward. Cash or charge bar.
Itinerary: Far East and Pacific on four different 14-day itineraries from Hong Kong, Kobe, Singapore to People's Republic, Thailand, Bali and other exotic ports.
Rates: Typical 14 days Hong Kong-Kobe with calls at China ports $2,570 minimum (3 cabins), $6,000 maximum, (16 super suites) Additional 12 suites being added. Low air add-ons to join the ship in rhe Far East.

In a word (or two): Up-beat and Interesting
✔✔✔ Itinerary and Service

M.S. PRINCESS MAHSURI
(Pearl Cruises of Scandinavia)

Category: Up-Scale
A.D.R.: 267
Rating: 7.2

From Sydney Pacific Islands and Coral Sea. Built 1980 as *Berlin,* rechristened Princess Mahsuri in 1983. Registry: West Germany. Capacity: 300 Passengers, 140 crew (German). Space ratio: 26.5

Specifics: Tonnage: 8,000 tons; length: 402 feet; beam: 57 feet, stabilized, individual cabin climate controls, tv, telephones, refrigerators all cabins, casino, boutique, beauty shop, fitness center, sun deck, swimming pool, 2 elevators, theater, disco, 6 passenger decks.
Electric Current: 220 volts A.C.
Entertainment: orchestra, movies, entertainers, lecturers
Dining: 1 dining room seats all 300 passengers in a single seating. Special dietary requests at least one month in advance of sailing in writing.
Tipping: $2.00 to waiter; $1.00 to busboy; $2.00 to cabin steward; cash bar.

Itineraries: From Sydney, Australia to Pacific islands and New Zealand and to interesting ports in Australia. Varied itineraries from 11 to 24 days.

Rates: 15-day typical voyage $2,650 minimum (11 cabins); $4,450 maximum (8 deluxe cabins), plus 4 super deluxe suites for $5,950. All cabins are twin bedded. No double beds. No single cabins without surcharge.

TTT: She is a beautiful ship built for deluxe cruising. Her itinerary is unusual enough to warrant the flight to join her in Australia. Low air fares in conjunction with cruises. She's a small ship with amenities associated with much larger vessels.

In a word (or two): Very Nice

M.V. PACIFIC PRINCESS
M.V. ISLAND PRINCESS
(Princess Cruises)

Category:	Luxury
A.D.R.:	$305
Rating:	7.8

From Los Angeles to Mexico. *Pacific Princess,* San Diego to Mexico; summer and spring from Athens to Mediterranean. *Island Princess* built 1972 as *Island Venture; Pacific Princess* built 1971 as *Sea Venture* for Flagship Cruises. Sold to P&O (owners of Princess Cruises) 1974, repositioned for West Coast cruising. Registry: Britain. Capacity: 626 passengers each; 350 crew each (English officers, Italian dining room and service); Space ratio: 32.

Specifics (both ships): Tonnage: just under 20,000; length: 550 feet; beam: 80 feet; stabilizers, individual cabin controlled air conditioning, 2 outdoor swimming pools (one with retractable sun roof), gift shop, beauty salon, gymnasium, sauna, lounges, bars, theater, library, casino.

Electric Current: 110 volts A.C.

Entertainment: 2 orchestras; movies; nightclubs; special interest cruises.

Dining: 1 dining room, 2 seatings. Reservations when booking. Special dietary requests with Princess Cruises' Special Services Department prior to cruise or with dining room captains.

Tipping: $2.50 to waiter; $1.25 to helper; $2.50 to room steward. Charge system on board, so tips may be added to tab in lounges and bars. Also appropriate tips to dining room captains for special dishes and attention.

Itineraries: Pacific Princess: Winter from San Diego to Acapulco, 12-day spring and summer from Athens to Naples visiting Egypt Israel, Greek islands. Also transatlantic on positioning voyages with stop in Lisbon. *Island Princess:* From Los Angeles to Acapulco with stops in Mexican ports either 7 or 14-day cruise. Summer from Vancouver to Alaska 7-day cruises.

Rates: Typical 7-night Mexico cruise, minimum $1,449 (28 cabins); maximum $3,101 (4 suites), depending on season. 12-day Mediterranean cruise $2,784 minimum, $6.624 maximum. Third cabin passenger 50 percent of minimum.

TTT: Ships are well appointed and very popular. *Pacific Princess* is better known as TV's Saturday-night favorite *Love Boat.* See **TTT** *Sun Princess.* 4 cabins with double beds; 3 with king size and 1 queen size each ship. Singles pay only 10 percent above per person rate as a supplement to occupy the cabin alone. All cabins have telephones.

TTT FARE ALERT: Princess has fare reductions and offerings called "Bonus Plans". For example, passengers who make full payment six months before cruise departure date, receive a five percent discount on cruise fares. Singles pay only 10 percent above cabin rate and do not have to share the cabin. Limited availability so book early for this one. Company offers "bargains" periodically and it pay to read the ads.

In a word (or two): Food and Exciting
✔✔✔✔ Food and service

	Category:	Luxury
R.M.S. QUEEN ELIZABETH 2	*A.D.R.:*	$400
(Cunard Line, Ltd.)	*Rating:*	9.6

From New York Boston, Norfolk, and Port Everglades. Built 1969. Registry: Britain. Capacity: 1,740 passengers; 1,000 crew (British). Space Ratio: 38.

Specifics: Tonnage: 67,107; length: 963 feet; beam: 105 feet; stabilizers, individual cabin climate controls, 13 elevators, 2 indoor, 2 outdoor swimming pools, 6 cocktail lounges—Queen's Room (400 capacity), Double Down Room (500 capacity), Q–4 Room (150 capacity), shopping arcade, beauty/barber shops, men's and women's saunas, gymnasium, Turkish bath, laundry-valet service, children's rooms, 2 libraries, kennels (only on transatlantic voyages), medical and dental services, 30 public rooms, 13 passenger decks, casino, Golden Door Spa at Sea.

Electric Current: 110-volt outlets in deluxe cabins; 220 volts in other cabins; A.C. and D.C.

Entertainment: 4 orchestras; two first-run movies daily; nightclub shows; full-length variety shows; special-interest cruises, Golden Door Spa, computer room.

Dining: 4 dining rooms, one and two seatings, depending on cabin. Reservations when booking recommended. Dining-room assignment according to cabin category price. Flaming dishes, French cuisine, gourmet dining in grill rooms.

Tipping: $3.50 to waiter and to cabin steward. Cunard says "at discretion of passenger". Suggests additional gratuities to dining-room captain, deck stewards, and others for extra services rendered. Higher priced and first class passengers are expected to tip more.

Itinerary: Varied cruises and long voyages. Sails transatlantic from April to November; 7, 8, 14 days from New York and Port Everglades to Caribbean; also short cruises from Southampton to Canaries; holiday cruises from New York to Caribbean December and January; annual World Cruise 80 days from New York with stops for additional passengers at Port Everglades and Los Angeles. Sold in segments with some free air. Tenders at most ports.

Rates: Too wide a difference to quote. Transatlantic includes free return air in opposite direction. From $1100, includes weekend in Europe. Special discount for roundtrip. Sample Caribbean, 10 days, from $1,945; World Cruise (89 days) from New York, minimum $22,850, maximum $275,000 (luxury suite). Number of minimum cabins changes with cruise. Two-class ship for transatlantic voyages. Deck chair charge: $5.

TTT: The *QE2* is not in the same category as other "floating resorts". She is a sophisticated city afloat. The *Queen* is the only super-sized ship with complete hospital, medical, and dental facilities, a 500-seat theater, and dining room space large enough to allow all passengers the luxury of dining in a single seating. There are new kitchen and dining room facilities. Public space is immense, and the *QE2* reigns as the undisputed "Queen of the Seas."

However, even Queens run specials when beds are available, and it is possible to catch a "sale" on *QE 2* sailings on certain cruises advertised a couple of months before sailing. Good bets are the *QE2*'s offer to fly passengers one way if they cruise the Atlantic during the summer months and the "business traveler's" offer where second passenger pays a reduced rate. Student special of 50 percent of minimum fare for transatlantic crossings. Nursery, baby-sitting: $2.50 per hour.

Many cabins have beds that convert to doubles. All cabins have private facilities. Single passengers occupying luxury or deluxe rooms charged two fares. Single occupancy of standard two-bed room, charged at 150 percent; 125 single cabins without surcharge. No deck chair charges for cruises; $6.00 charge for trans-atlantic crossings. And, in keeping with the you-get-what-you-pay-for principle, top category passengers get to dine in the Queen's or Princess' grills and that's a treat! Off-the-menu orders are routine; food and service in the tradition of yesteryear. The monied are lucky. Other passengers don't have quite the same choice in dining rooms. Menus are extensive, however. There is after all, only one "Queen."

TTT: Cunard suggests tips to head waiters in dining room — $20 to $30 per couple all restaurants. In Queen's and Princess Grill waiters expect $5 per person, per day. Also, depending on the dining room you're eating in, room stewards expect more. Night stewards should get $1.50 per day, if used, and the swimming pool attendant who hands out the towels expects $2.50 a week. Third and fourth passengers get a rate break, but amounts vary depending on season and cruise itinerary. Same with children's rates. Sailing on the *QE 2* is an experience; one that may fade away with the Queen.

The *QE 2* really is royal looking. Contemporary touches have been added like unlimited learning opportunities in the computer learning center, and the Golden Door Spa at Sea. A mew Magrodome indoor/outdoor center with retractable roof is used for Theatre-in-the-Round-at-Sea. Area is very popular day and night. Service is excellent in all cabin categories but menus vary depending on voyage. Same kitchen caters food in both grill rooms and the Colombia Dining Room.

In a word (or two): Luxuriously Elegant
✔✔✔✔✔ Food, Facilities, Service

Category:	Moderate
A.D.R.:	$180
Rating:	5.9

S.S. RHAPSODY
(Paquet Cruises)

From Port Everglades to Eastern Caribbean (winter months); from Vancouver to Alaska (late spring and summer months). Built 1957 as *S.S. Statendam* for Holland America Cruises; partially rebuilt (new promenade deck) 1972; purchased and refurnished by Paquet 1982 and renamed *S.S. Rhapsody*. Registry: Bahamas. Capacity: 850 passengers, 430 crew (French officers, mixed service crew). Space ratio: 27.

Specifics: Tonnage: 24,500; length: 642 feet; beam: 79 feet; stabilizers, individual cabin controlled air conditioning; 3 elevators, 1 indoor, 1 outdoor swimming pool, fashion boutique, newsstand, drug store, gift shop, beauty/barber shops, laundry, pressing service, library, gymnasium, lounges; 3 bars, hospital-medical facilities, 9 decks, casino.

Electric current: 110 volts A.C.

Entertainment: Orchestras, theater performances; can-can revue; nightclub, disco.

Dining: 1 dining room, 2 seatings. Reservations when booking or after embarkation. Special dietary requests must be made at least two weeks prior to sailing. Suggest requests be reconfirmed with maitre d' during embarkation.

Tipping: $2.00 to waiter; $1.00 to bus boy; $2.00 to cabin steward; cash bar.

Itinerary: From Port Everglades 7-days to Nassau, St. John, St. Thomas (fall, winter months); Summer from Vancouver to Alaska, 7-days; Panama Canal positioning voyages.

Rates: 7-day minimum $995 (10 cabins), maximum 2,385 (20 cabins); third and fourth cabin passengers $314-$340; seasonal changes.

TTT: Wide selection of cabins with double beds. Number of single cabins from $1,235 to $1,490 depending on choice of cabin and season. Cabins are extra large. She's a very nice ship. Food is very good and in the Paquet tradition, complimentary red and/or white wines served with dinner meals. Master Chef is French and specialties are also French. Delicacies include almost everything considered "sinful" in French cuisine. Good entertainment program. Lots of variety. Recent redecoration gives the ship a "fresh" and "new" look.

In a word (or two): French-flavored and Enjoyable
✔✔✔ Food and complimentary wines

	Category:	Moderate
S.S. ROTTERDAM	A.D.R.:	$165
(Holland America Cruises)	Rating:	8

From Port Lauderdale to Caribbean and West Indies; from San Francisco to Alaska; New York and San Francisco on trans-Canal cruises, and annual Around-the-World cruise. Built 1959. Registry: Netherlands Antilles. Capacity: 1,110 passengers; 550 crew (Dutch officers, Indonesian crew). Space ratio: 34.

Specifics: Tonnage: 38,000; length: 748 feet; beam: 94 feet; stabilizers;

individual cabin climate controls, 7 elevators; indoor and outdoor swimming pools; duty-free shop; drug store; beauty/barber shops; laundry-valet; gymnasium; sauna; library; ballroom (capacity 470); outside cafes and numerous bars; sky room; sun room; smoking room; card room; medical services; 10 passenger decks, casino.

Electric Current: 110 A.C.

Entertainment: Orchestras; movies; entertainers; 2 nightclubs; disco; casino.

Dining: 2 dining rooms, 2 seatings. Reservations and special dietary requests in advance. Special orders available from maitre d'.

Tipping: "Not required." Holland America makes no tipping recommendation and stops short of discouraging gratuities. However, most passengers tip in the dining room waiters and cabin steward but tips are about 25 percent less than on comparable quality ships.

Itinerary: 7-day cruises September-November, April, May from Port Everglades to St. Thomas, St. Maarten, Nassau; 10, 17-days transcanal spring and fall; 7-days from West Coast ports to Alaska spring and summer. Annual around the world voyage January-March, sold in segments or complete 87–90 days.

Rates: Varies with cruise and season. Example: 7-day Caribbean, minimum $815, maximum $1,425 (low season); 14 days; minimum $2,020, maximum $3,370; around-the-world 90-days (approximately) $22,000 to $40,000 (sold in four segments or as a complete voyage). Tenders most ports .

TTT: The *Rotterdam,* an outstanding ship with a very loyal following, is still the flagship of the Holland America fleet. She makes one spectacular voyage every year. In 1985, it was available in four segments from 14 to 27 days or for the entire voyage. Passengers select the portion of the itinerary that interests them most, and HAC offers a fare that includes air transportation to join or leave the vessel at some distant point. For example, you might select the 27-day cruise between Los Angeles and Hong Kong and HAC would fly you back to Los Angeles free. The Rotterdam is one of the remaining "grande dames" of the seas. She is as comfortable, luxurious and well maintained as she was over two decades ago. 1985 marked her 27th annual world cruise. Amenities, service, and food are typical of HAC and a mite above other vessels in the fleet. Great ship!

TTT: "Tipping Not required" means exactly that. You don't HAVE to tip unless service was beyond what you feel you were entitled to. However, we Americans are afflicted with what I call a "tipping syndrome," and we insist on leaving a monetary token of appreciation. After lengthy discussions with shore and HAC ship personnel and executives, I have concluded passengers might be well advised to leave tips amounting to half of what is expected on other ships. A total of about $1.50 in the dining room, same in cabins, will be appreciated. Although if you ask any HAC officer or cruise director he will repeat company policy—"No gratuities are required." See *Nieuw Amsterdam/ Noordam* **TTT** for more about Holland America service and amenities.

TTT: At the rates now being charged for the Rotterdam, she's a bargain.

In a word (or two): Old World

	Category:	Moderate
S.S. ROYALE	*A.D.R.:*	$167
(Premier Cruise Lines)	*Rating:*	4.8

From Cape Canaveral (Florida) to the Bahamas. Built 1958 for Costa as *Federico C.,* purchased by Premier, rebuilt and refurbished 1984. Registry: Panama; Capacity: 760 passengers; 450 crew (Italian). Space ratio: 25.

Specifics: Tonnage: 21,000; length: 606 feet; beam: 70 feet; stabilizers, individual cabin climate controls; 4 elevators; 3 outdoor whirlpools, swimming pool, duty free shops; barber/beauty shops; 7 lounges; ballroom; card room; medical services; 8 decks, 11 public rooms, casino.

Electric Current: 110 volts A.C.

Entertainment: 3 orchestras, movies, nightclub, specialty acts, cabaret.

Dining: 1 dining room, 2 seatings; outdoor cafe, ice cream parlor; table assignment on board. Special dietary requests in writing to Customer Service in advance of sailing. Reservations possible when booking.

Tipping: $2.00 to waiter; $1.00 to busy boy; $2.00 to room steward. Cash or charge bar. Credit cards (and cash) accepted for on-board expenses.

Itinerary: Monday and Friday 3 and 4-night cruises from Cape Canaveral, Florida to Nassau and a Bahamas Out Island.

Rates: Three-days from $295 minimum (6 cabins) to $650 (8 suites). 4-days from $330 to $ $830 depending on season. Ship has about 20 cabins without facilities which sell for much less. These cabins connect to cabins with facilities and are recommended for families. Special rates for this arrangement.

TTT: Some cabins with beds that convert to doubles. No singles without surcharge but company "guarantees" single rate which means it will find a cabinmate or single passenger sails at the per person, double rate and does not share the cabin.

TTT: It is difficult even for cruise ship followers to realize the *Star/Ship Royale* as the former *Federico*. She has been re-done from top to bottom into a contemporary-looking vessel. Many features on board are more than reasonable facsimiles of what we have come to expect on higher priced vessels. The Royale is easy to identify. If you happen to pull up alongside a ship with a flaming red hull, you'll know she's the Royale.

In a word (or two): Happy

S.S. ROYAL ODYSSEY
(Royal Cruise Line)

Category: Up-Scale
A.D.R.: $218
Rating: 7

From London, Athens, Lisbon (summer and fall) to Black Sea, North Sea and Mediterranean. Winter transcanal, Mexico and Caribbean. Built 1964 as *Shalom,* sold and named *Hanseatic;* sold, refurbished and rebuilt 1976 as *Doric;* sold, refurbished and refurbished, as the *Royal Odyssey* 1982. Registry: Greece. Capacity: 850 passengers; 400 crew (Greek). Space ratio: 35.

Specifics: Tonnage: 25,500; length: 625.9 feet; beam: 82 feet; stabilizers; individual cabin climate controls, 5 elevators; 2 outside, 1 inside swimming pools; shopping center; beauty/barber shops; laundry; sauna; gymnasium; 11 lounges; ballroom; bars; medical services; 11 passenger decks; 16 new penthouse suites; 22 deluxe suites; 279 outside staterooms; 63 inside; casino.

Electric current: 110 A.C.

Entertainment: Orchestras; movies, nightclub.

Dining: 1 dining room, 2 seatings.

Tipping: $7 per person, per day. Tips are pooled, Greek style and divided among entire crew. Total amount given to Purser at the end of voyage.

Itinerary: Summer months varied sailings from Athens to Malta, Capri, Livorno, Nice, Palma, Cadiz 14 days; Athens to London 15 days with calls at Malta, Capri, Nice, Palma, Lisbon; London 14 days to Leningrad, Helsinki, Stockholm, Copenhagen, Gothenburg, Bergen. Tenders some ports. Winter months: between San Juan, Curacao and Acapulco via Panama Canal and Caribbean ports, also Miami to Acapulco, similar route.

Rates: Mediterranean, 14 days (cruise only) minimum $1,898 (11 cabins); maximum $3,698 (14 super deluxe suites). Trans-Panama from Miami 12 days, minimum $1,948; maximum $3,548. Reductions for third and fourth cabin passengers.

TTT: The vessel managed to keep her identity through her life as the *Shalom, Hanseatic* and *Doric* but became an entirely different ship with a different atmosphere when she became the *Royal Odyssey.* She is a pretty ship but much of the old art work and all of the Deco furnishings have been replaced with light colored wood Scandinavian-modern. The physical plant is outstanding. Cabins are comfortable and former first class cabins are spacious. Public rooms are large. No double or king size beds. No single cabins without surcharge. Wheelchair passengers find no ledges leading in to staterooms.

TTT: Ship has a "Host Program" which pleases women traveling alone. About 15 men ranging in age upwards from 50's are employed to socialize with single women. It works. The gentlemen agree to work by a set of rules which discourages "hanky panky" and must circulate amongst the women. They dance with them, talk with them and generally socialize. Backgrounds are checked carefully and most are retired Army and Navy officers and businessmen. They are not gigolos but a few left the ship with bulging little black address books.

In a word (or two): Pleasant and Relaxing

M.V. ROYAL PRINCESS
(Princess Cruises)

Category:	Luxury
A.D.R.:	$329
Rating:	9

From San Juan and Los Angeles transcanal, and to Alaska summer months. Built in Wartsila Shipyard, Helsinki, *Royal Princess* inaugurated service late 1984. She was christened in Southampton by Princess of Wales, Registry Great Britain; Capacity: 1200 passengers, 500 crew (British deck, Italian service); Space ratio: 37.5

Specifics: Tonnage: 45,000; length: 761 feet; beam: 95 feet; stabilizers, state-of-the-art appointments and electronics, individual cabin climate controls, all outside cabins, 10 passenger decks, 4 swimming pools, 2 whirlpool jacuzzis, complete health spa, theater, color T.V.

and refrigerators all cabins, medical center, beauty/barber shops, 16 public rooms, 3 banks of elevators, full casino

Electric Current: 110 and 22 Volts

Entertainment: Orchestras, casino, theatrical performances, Love Boat style

Dining: 1 dining room; 2 seatings; table and seating requests when booking; special requests in advance or on board through maitre d'.

Tipping: $2.50 to waiter; $1.25 to helper; $2.50 to room steward . Charge system on board, so tips may be added to tab in lounges and bars. Also appropriate tips to dining room captains for special dishes and attention.

Itineraries: Winter season 10 and 14-day transcanal between Los Angeles and San Juan. Summers from San Francisco 10-day cruises to Alaska and Canada.

Rates: Typical 14 day transcanal minimum $3,556 in outside cabins (about 70 cabins, but company warns that safety equipment "largely obscures view"); maximum $9,114 (2 huge suites with verandahs). Alaska 10-day rates minimum $2,410; maximum $6,500.

TTT: She is a beauty! And well she should—looks like she could have cost more like $200 million rather than the announced $160 million to build her. From top to bottom, from the plush Princess Court to the Crown Casino, the *Royal Princess* is deluxe and should qualify for a future *Golden Anchor Award.* She's the new *Super-Love Boat* and we'll all be seeing and hearing a lot more about her on the tube and from passengers who will taste her pleasures during this inaugural season. She's the only new vessel with ALL outside staterooms which makes it really nice so all passengers view the ocean without paying a premium. Everything about the ship is a departure from what we have come to expect on cruise ships.

Her teak decks cover more than two acres which include several swimming pools (lap, hot spa, fresh and salt water with some heated), a number of bars, sports facilities, and a unique five-island area with a definite South Seas look.

Cabins all have closed circuit television with remote control, large picture windows, private balconies on 154 of the 600 cabins and each has its own refrigerator. Cabins are extra large with minimum space of 170 square feet. Plastic key cards, twin beds that convert to queen-size, large dressing tables, excellent lighting, furniture is natural 1 wood. Bathrooms are tiled, large and every one has a tub and shower.

Design is the most unconventional at sea and deck plan reverses what we have come to consider "traditional". Took a little getting used to on the inaugural voyage but passenger was positive. The Promenade Deck encircles the vessel, purser's area is double tiered with shops and lobby on the upper level but major public area is five decks below. Theory behind design was to devote high space to cabins (except for an extraordinary Panorama Lounge) and put public space on lower decks. All of the major rooms, including the restaurant have windows and putting the dining room mid-ship should make for smoother dining.

Colors are elegant, understated, soft and easy to live with.

It's hard to rate a vessel until after she has been in service for at least six months, but with the Royal Princess we take no chances in rating her excellent in service, food, amenities and facilities. Entertainment is also superior.

TTT: Because of the way ship was built, minimum rated cabins are priced at the same level as on other Princess Cruise's vessels but are outside cabins instead of inside. Singles pay only a 10 percent surcharge for solo occupancy. See Pacific Princess **TTT**

PERSONAL TTT: I spent eight days on board during her inaugural transcanal voyage and it was the next best thing to spending eight days in the Guggenheim Museum being treated like a visiting dignitary.

In a word (or two): Total Luxury

✔✔✔✔ The Ship

	Category:	Luxury
ROYAL VIKING SEA	*A.D.R.:*	$330
ROYAL VIKING SKY	*Rating:*	9.2
ROYAL VIKING STAR		

(*Royal Viking Line*)

From San Francisco, Los Angeles, Port Everglades, New York, Copenhagen, varied itineraries worldwide. *Royal Viking Star* built 1972, *RV Sea* and *Sky* built 1973. Mid-sections stretching completed on all three ships in 1983; lengthened by 93 feet. Registry: Norway. Capacity: 725 passengers, 375 crew (Norwegian deck, European service). Space ratio: 39.

Specifics: Tonnage: 28,000; length: 725 feet; beam: 83 feet. Stabilizers; individual cabin climate controls, 5 elevators; swimming pool (two on Royal Viking Star); beauty/ barber shops; gymnasium; sauna; library; card rooms, 11 public rooms; main lounge seats all passengers; theater; 9 decks, casino.

Electric Current: 110 volts A.C. and D.C. and 220.

Entertainment: Orchestra; movies; special events; nightclub acts; theme nights, lecturers, celebrity guests.

Dining: One dining room accommodates all passengers at one seating. Special dietary requests honored (passengers register requests on embarkation form). Off-the-menu orders encouraged by maitre d'. German, Austrian, and other European chefs, international cuisine.

Tipping: $3.50 to waiter and to cabin stewardess. Major credit cards honored. Settle accounts day before end of the voyage.

Itinerary: Varied cruise lengths; worldwide cruising. Alaska, North Cape, New England/Canada, Baltic, Pacific, Around the World, Caribbean; Mediterranean, Trans-Canal, Orient, South Pacific and Mexico. Most cruises 14 days to 70 days. Sometimes offer 7-day Caribbean cruise. Tenders some ports.

Rates: Typical 14-day cruise: minimum $2,320 (52 cabins), maximum $9,382 (penthouse suites). Average rate just under $300 per day, per person, if you do not include 18 percent of the cabins which are suites. Including suites, average daily rate jumps to $415. Children under 17, pay one-half minimum fare. Also, split voyage possible on very long cruises. RVL encourages back-to-back 14 day voyages with discounts.

TTT: Royal Viking is pure elegance, but these ships are not for everyone. They are for the monied, luxury-loving class who want to cruise in the style to which they are accustomed. Atmosphere is refined; service is low-key and excellent. Ships are well constructed; cabins are good-sized and comfortable for long cruises. Almost all cabins are outside. Limited numbered double-bedded cabins available.

Reservations not accepted for specific cabin by number. Passengers reserve by cabin category and RVL assigns cabins one month before sailings (usually). Consideration is given to location preference, but no guarantee as to cabin number. RVL says cabins within a category are comparable. System is different, but it seems to work well.

TTT: Nine penthouse suites are first to sell out on all cruises. New sports deck, second swimming pool, and brightened decor added. Very few children sail RVL ships but company adds counselors when number booked warrants an activities program. Only weak area on the ships is in entertainment which falls short of excellence in other area.

FARE ALERT: Even the up-scale market is feeling some softness and Royal Viking Line has some outstanding offers (from time-to-time). Air-sea and discounts (called incentives, etc.) are advertised. If you're hankering for this kind of cruise experience, tell your travel agent to keep you informed. He is the first to know and you could be the second. Average priced outside cabins go for around $276 per day and that makes sailing deluxe possible at up-scale category prices. No single cabins without surcharge.

TTT: Royal Viking Line was purchased by Norwegian Caribbean Lines but no changes are anticipated in itineraries, on-board service or amentities. According to the owner of NCL Knut Kloster companies will have the same ownership but will operate independently of each other for the foreseeable future.

In a word or two: Pure Luxury
✔✔✔✔✔ Food, Service, Itineraries

M.S. SCANDINAVIAN SUN
(SeaEscape)

Category:	Budget
A.D.R.:	$89
Rating:	Not Rated

From Miami to Grand Bahama Island. Built 1968 as *M. V. Freeport;* sailed as *Sea Star* 1975; renamed *M.S. Caribe* 1976 and sailed for Commodore Cruise Lines. Purchased by Scandinavian World Cruises 1981; refurbished and partially rebuilt 1982. Registry: Bahamas. Capacity: 434 cabin passengers plus 573 deck passengers for a total of 1,000; crew 200 (Scandinavian deck, mixed service) Space ratio: 11.

Specifics: Tonnage: 11,000; length: 441 feet; beam: 70 feet; stabilizers, air conditioned, 2 elevators, bow thruster system, outdoor swimming pool, lounges, shops, beauty/barber shops, casino.
Electric Current: 220 and 110 A.C. and D.C.
Entertainment: Non-stop on return voyage featuring continuous dancing; full casino, movies, entertainers.
Dining: 2 dining rooms, smorgasbord buffets, assigned times.
Itinerary: Daily Miami departure 8 a.m., Freeport arrival 1 p.m. Return 6 p.m. with Miami arrival at midnight. Air-land-sea packages.
Tipping: Suggested on board.
Rates: Cabins $40 in addition to deck space, roundtrip, $89.

TTT: The *Scandinavian Sun* provides ferry-like service between Miami and Grand Bahama Island and should also be classified as an "attraction" and day trip experience. Unless you only want to spend four or five hours in Freeport, consider a cruise-land, or air-cruise-land package. The ship can carry 200 cars. The *Scandinavian Sun* is a fun way to get to the Bahamas if you are visiting in Florida. The one-day trip is probably one of the best values you'll find anywhere. You board the ship at 7 a. m.; sail at 8. Breakfast is at sailing time; luncheon buffet (hot and cold and as nice as you'll find anywhere) is served from 11:30. You have four or five hours ashore, then the return to Miami. Buffet supper, three choices of shows, music, dancing, a casino. When the ship docks in Miami at 12:30 a.m., they have a hard time getting some of the passengers off the dance floor and on shore. Everything except port taxes (about $12), drinks and the casino is included. I recommend overnighting in Freeport, but if you take the *Sun* roundtrip in one day, cabins are available on board for $40 from the purser. If you have not purchased one before boarding, they go quickly, so act fast.

In a word (or two): A Day of Fun

	Category:	Luxury
M.S. SAGAFJORD	*A.D.R.:*	$335*
(Cunard/NAC)	*Rating:*	9

From New York, Port Everglades, San Francisco on transatlantic, South African, Mediterranean and around-the-world voyages. Built in 1965; refurbished 1981 and again in 1983. Registry: Norway. Capacity: 513 passengers; 300 crew (Norwegian and Northern Europeans). Space Ratio: 50.

Specifics: Tonnage: 24,000; length: 620 feet; beam: 82 feet; stabilizers, individual cabin climate controls, 4 elevators, indoor and outdoor swimming pools, boutique, beauty/barber shops, sauna-massage, gymnasium, library, lounges, bars, ballrooms, medical services, 12 passenger decks, casino, penthouse suites, deluxe suites with verandahs.

Electric Current: 220 and 110 volts A.C. and D.C.

Entertainment: 2 orchestras, movies, theater, travelogues, special interest cruises, name entertainers, Golden Door Spa at Sea.

Dining: 1 dining room, 1 seating. Advance reservations encouraged when booking. Special diets on request.

Itinerary: Summers: 14 day Alaska/Canada voyages from San Francisco; winter: annual around the world cruise; also Hong Kong to Kobe cruises and some Caribbean from Port Everglades; trans-Panama Canal voyages. Cruise lengths range from 6, 14, to 84 days. Split or segments of world cruise possible. Tenders at some ports.

Tipping: $3.50 per person, per day to waiter and to cabin steward.

Charge or cash bar, 15 to 20 percent recommended in cash or on tab. Credit cards accepted for final payment.

Rates: Vary with itinerary and season. Example: 14 day transcanal minimum $2,630 (11 cabins); maximum $10,500 (2 super-luxury suites). *Average daily rate used to categorize ship is an average of outside cabin rate excluding top priced suites. 87-day World Cruise, minimum $19,140; maximum, $71,780. Third and fourth passenger rates available. 51 single cabins without surcharge.

TTT: All but 32 cabins are outside with portholes or windows. 90 percent have bathtubs. Public space is large enough to accommodate a full complement of passengers in the main lounge, theater and restaurant at one time. NAC did a $20 million renovation job in 1982. New terrace sun deck was added and provided space for 15 new suites with terraces and panoramic views. Cunard spent an additional $10 million in 1984 and enlarged the dining room, added a casino and complete spa.

The *Sagafjord* was created and designed for long range, low density cruising with maximum space per passenger. Ship is immaculate, service very good. Both the *Sagafjord* and her sister ship, *Vistafjord,* are not for swingers. There is an elegant atmosphere; enjoyment on the quiet side. Entertainment on both ships is good, but not outstanding. Service in the dining room would be improved if waiters had busboys or assistants to help them. Good news is Cunard has eliminated the annoying surcharge for caviar on days when it is not on menu. Thanks to readers who took the time to write me about the charges. I took the complaints to Vice President Jim Sullivan and the charge disappeared almost over night.

The *Sagafjord* and *Vistafjord* are beautiful ships. Shiny, elegant and classy. But in the not-for-everyone category. They are for the well heeled with a keen desire for a cruise that tends to be sophisticated, slower paced and on the quieter side of the jumping, more active ships. Although in fairness to Cunard, spa and fitness programs are adding a lot to on board entertainment and ambience.

In a word (or two): Luxury and Beautiful
✔✔✔✔ Food and Service

SEA GODDESS I
SEA GODDESS II
(Sea Goddess Cruises Ltd.)

Category:	Luxury
A.D.R.:	$530
Rating:	8.3

Sea Goddess I from St. Croix to Caribbean; *Sea Goddess II* from Monte Carlo and Athens to Mediterranean. *Sea Goddess I* built 1984; *Sea Goddess II* inaugurates service in May 1985. Registry: Norway; Capacity: 116 passengers; 71 crew (Norwegian and European). Space ratio: 33

Specifics: Tonnage: 4,000; length: 340 feet; beam: 47 feet; all accommodations are suites (no cabins) and are nearly identical; sport deck with aft platform for water skiing and snorkeling, health center, swimming pool, hot tub, tropical greenhouse, outdoor cafe, library, card room, Piano Bar, Supper Club, individual cabin climate controls, stereo/video in every cabin, 1 elevator, barber/beauty shop, shops, 5 public rooms, 6 passenger decks.

Electric Current: 110 volts A.C.

Entertainment: Movie video cassettes in every suite, piano bar, local entertainment brought on board in most ports.

Dining: 2 dining rooms, single seating. No reservations necessary. Special dietary arrangements in advance. Off-the-menu orders encouraged. Passengers may eat any time between in a two hour spread of hours and may sit at the same table every night or change.

Tipping: Included in cost of the cruise

Itinerary: Winter: *Sea Goddess I* sails from St. Croix on alternating itineraries with one going to the Grenadines and the other to Eastern Caribbean islands. *Sea Goddess II* on one week cruises alternating from Monte Carlo and Athens to Mediterranean and Greek ports. Goddess I in Mediterranean summer months.

Rates: One week Caribbean $3,600; one week Mediterranean $4,000.

TTT: Suites are almost identical and priced uniformly but some locations are preferable to others because of the motion of the ocean. Suites are very large (about 200 square feet) and sitting rooms have a seven-foot sofa. An expandable table rises for dining. Bedrooms have floor-to-ceiling mirrored walls and large windows. Choice of sleeping arrangement is left up to guest who can decide on queen-size or twin beds. Vessel is beautifully decorated in fine fabrics, white oak, soft colors and unbelievable amenities. Each suite is different and bathroom decor is complete with velvety blanket-size towels. Terry bathrobes and every suite has a tub and shower. Large closets as expected. Rate includes all bar charges, gratuities and a fully stocked refrigerator, including caviar and your favorite wines which are pre-determined on a passenger questionnaire completed before sailing.

TTT: A *Sea Goddess* cruise is different from all other cruises. There is no bingo, no costume party, no horse racing and no talent night. Passengers are sophisticated travelers who want the best and are willing to pay for yachtlike atmosphere with no structured activities. Staff is at the beck and call of passengers and service of all kinds is available on a 24-hour basis. Only negatives reported indicate food preparation is less than the gourmet quality promised in brochures. Also some passengers find the vessel confining unless you happen to be a water sports enthusiast.

In a word (or two): Different, Expensive

✔✔✔✔ Concept

M.S. SKYWARD
(Norwegian Caribbean Lines)

Category:	Moderate
A.D.R.:	$185
Rating:	6.2

From Miami to the Caribbean. Built 1969. Registry: Norway. Capacity: 724 passengers; 300 crew (Norwegian: deck; mixed Caribbean: service). Space ratio: 22.

Specifics: Tonnage: 16,254; length: 525 feet; beam: 75 feet; stabilizers, individual cabin climate controls, 4 elevators, 2 swimming pools, casino, shopping arcade, beauty/barber shops, sauna, health center, skeet shooting, 3 lounges, 3 bars, medical services, 5 decks.

Electric Current: 110 volts A.C. and D.C.

Entertainment: Orchestras, theater performances, nightclub shows, special-interest cruises, casino.

Dining: 1 dining room, 2 seatings. Encouraged to make reservations at time of booking. Special dietary requests through Passenger Courtesy Department or through travel agent.

Tipping: $2.00 to waiter, $1.00 to bus boy; $2.00 per person, per day to cabin steward. Cash bar.

Itinerary: Every Sunday, all year, 7-day cruises to Western Caribbean ports of Cancun, Cozumel, Key West, Bahamas Out Island. Tenders most ports.

Rates: Minimum $975 (4 cabins, uppers and lowers); maximum $1,965 (9 suites). Third and fourth passengers in cabins, $495; children under 17, $295. Most cabins are outside with twin lower beds.

TTT: Double-bedded cabins are available, both inside and outside, and some beds can be moved together. But watch out for what the company calls "oversized lower bed"; two full-grown passengers are in for lots of togetherness and probably little sleep. Decks were extended, cabins refurbished in 1978 and again in 1984. 185 cabins described as having "double" beds, but they are narrower and are closer to "junior doubles". Makes for togetherness. No single cabins without surcharge. Dining-room reservations by computer prior to sailing.

In a word (or two): Busy and Enjoyable
✔✔ Entertainment

S.S. SEA PRINCESS
(P&O Cruises)

Category:	Up-Scale
A.D.R.:	$255
Rating:	7

From Southampton and Venice to Northern Europe and Mediterranean. Built 1966 as *Kungsholm* for Swedish American Line, sold to Flagship Cruises 1975; sold in 1978 to Sea Leasing Corporation and operated by P&O Cruises. Rebuilt and refurbished 1978. Name changed to *Sea Princess*. Registry: United Kingdom; Capacity: 844 passengers; 400 crew (British deck, mixed international service); Space ratio: 33

Specifics: Tonnage: 27,670; length: 660 feet; beam: 86 feet. Stabilizers, air conditioned. 310 of 402 cabins are outside, 18 public rooms, 2 outdoor and 1 indoor swimming pools, gymnasium, medical, beauty/barber shop, disco, sauna, 4 elevators, children's playroom, outdoor cafe, 7 passenger decks, theater.

Electric Current: 220 volts A.C.

Entertainment: Orchestras, cabaret, disco, movies

Dining: 1 restaurant, 2 seatings. Reservations in advance but assignment on board. Special dietary requests when booking.

Tipping: Suggestions on board, but count on $5-$7 a day.

Itineraries: 13 and 14-days from Southampton to Northern European ports to Mediterranean; from Venice and Piraeus to Mediterranean ports including Turkey, Egypt and Israel. Also Around the World voyages.

Rates: Vary by season and itinerary. Typical 14 day Northern Europe cruise minimum $2,639 (14 cabins), maximum $4,093 (4 deluxe cabins).

TTT: Ship is beautiful. *Sea Princess* retains the woods and fine look of a luxury vessel. Spacious and offers very interesting itineraries. Air-sea packages from major cities. See Air-Sea Chapter. Passengers are mostly British but more Americans are discovering the *Sea Princess.*

In a word (or two): International Experience

M/S SONG OF NORWAY
(Royal Caribbean Cruise Line)

Category: Up-Scale
A.D.R.: $203
Rating: 7.5

From Port of Miami to the Caribbean and West Indies. Built 1970. Registry: Norway. Capacity: 1,040 passengers; 400 crew (Norwegian: deck; mixed: service). Space ratio: 22.

Specifics: Tonnage: 23,005; length: 635 feet; beam: 80 feet; stabilizers, individual cabin climate controls, 4 elevators, swimming pool, shopping arcade, beauty/barber shops, sauna, 3 lounges, 2 bars, medical services, 8 passenger decks.

Electric Current: 110 volts A.C.

Entertainment: 2 quintets, 1 quartet, 4-piece calypso band, first-run movies, nightclub acts, casino.

Dining: 1 dining room, 2 seatings. Cannot make advance reservations when booking. All tables assigned after boarding. No special diets.

Tipping: $3.75 to waiter ($2.50 waiter, $1.25 busboy); $2.50 to cabin steward. Cash bar.

Itinerary: 7-day cruise every Saturday to Grand Cayman, Montego Bay, Cozumel/Cancun. Tenders some ports.

Rates: 7-day cruises: minimum $1,225 (38 cabins); maximum $1,975 (10 deluxe cabins); third and fourth cabin passengers, $525 (children included). Year-round rate schedule.

TTT: 58 cabins with double beds; no single cabins without surcharge. No playrooms. Children's programs during summer and holiday cruises. RCCL ships (see *Sun Viking* and *Nordic Prince*) are consistent in high quality of food, entertainment and service. The *Song of Norway* and *Nordic Prince* were stretched to increase capacity. New cabins are identical to old cabins and increase of 30 percent in passengers has not affected service or space ratio. New lounges and a larger dining room actually increased the space ratio. Additional **TTT**'s, see *Song of America, Sun Viking, Nordic Prince.*

In a word or two: Up-beat and Food
✓✓✓✓ Food and Entertainment

<table>
<tr><td></td><td>Category:</td><td>Up-Scale</td></tr>
<tr><td>M/S SONG OF AMERICA</td><td>A.D.R.:</td><td>$201</td></tr>
<tr><td>(Royal Caribbean Cruise Line)</td><td>Rating:</td><td>8</td></tr>
</table>

From Port of Miami to the Caribbean. Built, 1982; inaugurated service December, 1982. Registry: Norway. Capacity: 1414 passengers; 500 crew (Norwegian: deck; mixed service) Space ratio: 27.

Specifics: Tonnage: 37,584; length: 705 feet; beam: 94 feet; stabilizers, individual cabin climate controls, 7 elevators, shopping arcade, 2 swimming pools, theatre, 6 lounges, all modern amenities, medical services, 11 passenger decks.

Electric Current: 100-volts A.C.

Entertainment: Orchestras, musical revues, movies, nightclub acts, Calypso band.

Dining: 1 dining room, 2 seatings. No reservations when booking. All tables assigned after boarding. No special diets.

Tipping: $2.50 to waiter; $1.25 to busboy; $2.00 to cabin steward. Cash bar.

Itinerary: 7-day cruises every Sunday to Nassau, San Juan, St. Thomas. Tenders some ports.

Rates: 7-day cruise minimum $1,225 (96 cabins); maximum, $1,2,105 (1 super deluxe suite), other maximums $1,905 (20 deluxe outside staterooms). Year around rate. Third and fourth cabin passengers $525, including children.

TTT: Ship cost over over $140 million and offers the same consistent, quality service routine on her smaller sister ships in the Royal Caribbean fleet. Several features are worthy of special mention. The Viking Lounge is 12 decks above the sea and offers a 360 degree round the world view, much like the crow's nest above fabled Yankee Clippers. There's even an elevator to take you straight up for a special view. Intimate lounges, large ballrooms, a land-sized theatre for movies and special performers, ethnic theme nights in the elegantly appointed dining room, and an elegantly designed ship built to meet cruising demands of today. Every innovative maritime feature has been incorporated in her construction. She was built with efficiency in mind and with passenger comfort uppermost on the list of priorities. Too bad cabins are so small. It is hard for two people to maneuver unless one bed is pulled up into the wall. The rest of the ship is extremely spacious and delightful. For children's programs, on board amenities, style of cruising, see Sun Viking profile.

In a word or two: Up-beat
✓✓✓✓✓ Entertainment and food

M.S. SOUTHWARD
(Norwegian Caribbean Lines)

Category:	Moderate
A.D.R.:	$192
Rating:	6.4

From Miami to Caribbean and Mexico. Built 1971. Registry: Norway. Capacity: 762 passengers; 358 crew (Norwegian: deck; West Indian, mixed Caribbean: service). Space ratio: 23.

Specifics: Tonnage: 16,607; length: 536 feet; beam: 75 feet; stabilizers, individual cabins air condition controls, 4 elevators, swimming pools, shopping arcade, beauty/barber shops, sauna, work-out machines, 3 lounges, 3 bars, medical services, 6 decks, casino.

Electric Current: 110 volts A.C. and D.C.

Entertainment: Orchestras, movies, theater, nightclub revues, casino.

Dining: 1 dining room, 2 seatings. Reservations when booking. Special dietary requests in advance through Passenger Courtesy Department or through travel agent.

Tipping: $2.00 to waiter, $1.00 to bus boy; $2.00 to cabin steward. Cash bar.

Itinerary: Every Saturday all year. 7-day cruises to Puerto Plata, St. Thomas, San Juan, Nassau. Tenders at some ports and Out Island.

Rates: Minimum $975 (19 cabins, uppers and lowers), $1,995 maximum (8 suites). See Skyward **TTT**. Third and fourth cabin passengers, $495; children's rate, $295 (under 17 years of age).

TTT: 157 cabins with double beds, both inside and outside; 9 single cabins without surcharge. Like other NCL ships, cabins are small, but entertainment is very good. Special childrens program during summer months and holidays for nursery age and older.

In a word or two: Busy and Enjoyable
✓✓✓ Entertainment

Category:	Moderate
A.D.R.:	$190
Rating:	6.7

M.S. STARWARD
(Norwegian Caribbean Lines)

From Miami to the Caribbean and the Bahamas. Built 1968. Registry: Norway. Capacity: 758 passengers; 325 crew (Norwegian: deck; mixed Caribbean: service). Space ratio: 22.

Specifics: Tonnage: 16,107; length: 525 feet; beam: 75 feet; stabilizers, individual cabin climate controls, 4 elevators, 2 swimming pools, shopping arcade, beauty/barber shops, sauna, baby-sitting services, 3 lounges, 3 bars, medical services, 6 passenger decks, casino.

Electric Current: 110 volts A.C.

Entertainment: Orchestras, movies, theater, nightclub revues, casino.

Dining: 1 dining room, 2 seatings. Reservations when booking. Special dietary requests in advance through Passenger Courtesy Department or through travel agent.

Tipping: $2.00 to waiter; $1.00 to bus boy; $2.00 to cabin steward. Cash bar.

Itinerary: Saturday s 7-days to Bahamas Out Island, Ocho Rios, Grand Cayman, Cozumel. Tenders some ports and Out Island.

Rates: Minimum $975 (12 cabins), maximum $1,795 (4 suites); third and fourth cabin passenger $495; children 12, $295.

TTT: Decks extended so ship has space for the 110 new cabins built in 1978; dining room enlarged, new main lounge, nightclub, other public rooms; 49 cabins with double beds, both inside and outside, no single cabins without surcharge. Refurbished and up-graded in 1984 (See Skyward **TTT**)

In a word (or two): Busy and Enjoyable
✔✔ Entertainment

Category:	Up-Scale
A.D.R.:	$245
Rating:	6

S.S. STELLA MARIS
(Sun Line Cruises)

From Venice and Nice around Italy; Piraeus to Greek Islands and Turkey. Built 1944; sailed as *Bremerhaven;* Sold to Sun Lines by Canadian owners 1958; converted and rebuilt 1966. Registry: Greece. Capacity: 180 passengers; 110 crew (Greek). Space ratio: 23.

Specifics: Tonnage: 4,000; swimming pool, laundry, beauty/barber shops, duty free shops, 3 lounge bars. 1 elevator, 6 passenger decks.

Electric Current: 220 volts A.C.

Entertainment: Orchestra, theater, disco.

Dining: 1 dining room, 2 seatings. Special dietary requests in writing two weeks before sailing. International cuisine, Greek specialties.

Tipping: $8.00 per person, per day placed in an envelope at the Purser's desk prior to final debarkation. Tips are pooled and divided among staff. Cash bar.

Itinerary: Alternate Saturdays from Venice and Nice (summer months), 7-day cruises to Dubrovnik, Corfu, Malta, Tunis, Elba, Portofino.

Rates: Typical 7-day cruise: minimum $1,120 (2 cabins); maximum $1960 (16 cabins).

TTT: Ship is large enough for comforts of a larger vessel but maintains a yacht-like atmosphere. No facilities for children; no single cabins without surcharge. 80 outside cabins, 30 inside—all with private facilities and telephones. No double beds. An intimate, personal-service ship best suited for cruise itineraries that visit hard-to-get to unspoiled ports of call.

In a word (or two): Up-beat

M/V STELLA OCEANIS
(Sun Line Cruises)

Category: Up-Scale
A.D.R.: $220
Rating: 7

From San Juan to Caribbean and Leeward Islands (winter months); Mediterranean and Greek Islands (summer months). Built 1966 as Aphrodite; rebuilt and refurbished 1967. Registry: Greece. Capacity: 280 passengers; 140 crew (Greek). Space ratio: 20.

Specifics: Tonnage: 5,500; length: 350 feet; beam: 53 feet; stabilizers, swimming pool, lounges, bar, gift shop, beauty and barber salons, 6 passenger decks, 2 elevators.

Electric Current: 220 volts A.C.

Entertainment: Greek dancers, orchestra, disco, taverns.

Dining: 1 dining room, 2 seatings. Special dietary requirements should be sent in writing two weeks before sailing.

Tipping: $8.00 per person, per day placed in an envelope at the Purser's desk prior to final debarkation. Request passengers do not tip individually during the cruise. Tips are pooled and distributed to all personnel.

Itinerary: Winter months from San Juan, 14 days to St. Maarten, Martinique, St. Lucia, Barbados, Tobago, cruising Orinoco River, Ciudad Guayana (for Angel Falls & Canaima), Bequia, St. Vincent, Guadeloupe, Antigua, St. Kitts and St. Thomas. Summer months from Piraeus, 3 and 4 days to Greek Islands and Turkey. Tenders at some ports.

Rates: Typical 14-day cruise: minimum $2,545 (7 cabins); maximum $4,785 (14 suites or deluxe).

TTT: Itinerary is unusual. Since the ship is small, it can enter harbors larger vessels are afraid to maneuver; 113 cabins are outside, and 38 have bathtubs. All cabins have telephones. No single cabins without surcharge. No double-bedded cabins.

In a word (or two): Friendly, Greek

✔✔✔✔ Unusual itineraries

	Category: Up-Scale
T.S. STELLA SOLARIS	*A.D.R.:* $245
(Sun Line Cruises)	*Rating:* 8.1

From Athens to Greek Islands and Aegean (summer months); from Port Everglades to South America and Caribbean (winter months). Built 1953 as *Camoge;* purchased by Sun Lines 1962; converted, reconstructed, ran briefly as *Bunte Kuh.* Entered present service 1963; refurbished and rebuilt 1973. Registry: Greece. Capacity: 620 passengers; 300 crew (Greek). Space ratio: 29.

Specifics: Tonnage: 18,000; length: 560 feet; beam: 72 feet; stabilizers, individual cabin climate controls; twin swimming pools, gymnasium, sauna, 3 lounges, bars, duty-free shop, beauty shop, medical services, 8 passenger decks, 2 elevators, casino.

Electric Current: 110/220 volts A.C.

Entertainment: Orchestras, theater, nightclub, disco.

Dining: 1 dining room, 2 seatings. No reservations when booking. Dietary requests should be made in advance. Greek specialties.

Tipping: $8.00 per person, per day placed in an envelope at Purser's desk prior to final debarkation. Tips are pooled and divided among staff. Cash bar: 15 percent recommended with service.

Itinerary: Varied cruise lengths. 7 to 14 days (summer months) to Greek

Island, Alexandria, Rhodes, Istanbul from Piraeus (Greece); From Port Everglades (winter months) to Amazon River, West Indies, Rio de Janeiro and Panama Canal. Tenders at some ports.

Rates: Depends on cruise. 12 day Panama Canal minimum $2,080 (19 cabins), maximum $4,420 (34 deluxe cabins). Mediterranean cruises, slightly lower priced. No single cabins without surcharge. Third and fourth cabin rates available, depending on cruise itinerary.

TTT: The *Stella Solaris* is the Sun Line's flagship. She's sleek and understated in decor with dark wine velvet and elongated murals of hand wrought bronze, leather upholstery. Cabins are spacious. Atmosphere is personal-attention oriented. Itineraries are unusual. 250 cabins are outside and 218 have full bathtubs. Six cabins with double beds. Beautiful dining room. She's the best in Aegean cruising. No children's programs.

TTT: Sun Line says "Any physical disability that may require special attention or treatment must be reported when reservation is requested. Passage may be refused to anyone whose health or physical condition may constitute a danger to that person or another passenger." Same rules apply on almost every ship, but Sun Lines spells it out very clearly.

In a word (or two): Nice

✔✔✔✔ Service and Itineraries

M. V. SUN PRINCESS
(Princess Cruises)

Category: Up-Scale
A.D.R.: $247
Rating: 7.7

From San Juan to Caribbean (nine months); from Vancouver to Alaska summer months. Built 1972 as *Spirit of London;* is a twin sister to Norwegian Caribbean Line's *Southward.* Registry: Britain. Capacity: 686 passengers; 370 crew (British officers, Italian dining room and service). Space ratio: 25.

Specifics: Tonnage: 17,370; length: 500 feet; beam: 75 feet; stabilizers, individual cabin climate controls, swimming pool, beauty/barber shops, laundry, sauna-massage, 5 lounges, 4 bars, medical services, 7 decks, 2 elevators, casino.

Electric Current: 110 volts A.C.

Entertainment: 2 orchestras, movies, nightclubs, theater.

Dining: 1 dining room, 2 seatings. Reservations when booking. Special dietary requests through Special Services prior to cruise. Off-the-menu requests through dining room captain.

Tipping: $2.00 to cabin steward. Same to waiter; $1.00 to bus boy. Charge bar: tip with service or write tips on check; Credit cards accepted for charge settlement at end of voyage.

Itinerary: From San Juan 7-days alternating itineraries winter, spring and fall to Barbados, Palm Island, Martinique, San Maarten and St. Thomas. Other itinerary includes Curacao, Caracas. 14-day trans-canal between Los Angeles and San Juan, calling at Acapulco, Cartagena, Aruba, Martinique, and St. Thomas. June through September from Vancouver. 7-day cruises to Alaska, visiting Ketchikan, Juneau, Skagway, Glacier Bay and Misty Fjord. Ship tenders in some ports.

Rates: Examples: Caribbean 7-day minimum $1,449 (16 cabins); maximum $3,094 (4 suites). Third cabin passenger pays 50 percent of minimum cruise fare; 7-day Alaska cruises from $1,337 to $3,255.

TTT: 139 cabins with double beds. Singles pay only 10 percent surcharge to occupy cabin alone. Special childrens' counselor on board when more than 25 children are booked. Princess Cruises uses a bookkeeping system similar to that of most resorts. Passengers may sign bar, wine and service bills and settle accounts with purser. All major credit cards accepted. Be sure to take head coverings and extra rain gear for tender rides in Alaska if you're sailing on the Sun Princess. Open life boats are used for the tenders. This is not the case on the Island Princess or Pacific Princess, which carry tenders.

In a word (or two): Upbeat and Pleasant
✔✔✔ Food and Entertainment

M/S SUN VIKING
(Royal Caribbean Cruise Line)

Category: Up-Scale
A.D.R.: $193
Rating: 8

From Port of Miami to the Caribbean and Mexico. Built in 1972. Registry: Norway. Capacity: 728 passengers; 320 crew (Norwegian: deck; mixed: service). Space Ratio: 25.

Specifics: Tonnage: 18,556; length: 550 feet; beam: 80 feet; stabilizers, individual cabin climate controls, 4 elevators, swimming pool, shopping arcade, beauty/barber shops, sauna, 3 lounges, 2 bars, medical services, 8 passenger decks.

Electric Current: 110 volts A.C.

Entertainment: 2 quintets, trio, 4-piece calypso band, movies, nightclub acts.

Dining: 1 dining room, 2 seatings. No reservations when booking. All tables assigned after boarding. No special diets.

Tipping: $2.50 to waiter; $1.25 to busboy; $2.50 to cabin steward. Cash bar.

Itinerary: 14-days with alternate Sunday sailings. Can be broken into 7-day cruises with embarkation/debarkation in Barbados. (Air-sea package available)Ports of call include Ocho Rios, Curacao, Caracas, Barbados, Martinique, St. Maarten, San Juan and St. Thomas. 10 days to St. Croix, Martinique, Barbados, Antigua, St. Thomas; 8 days to Nassau, San Juan and St. Thomas. 8 and 10-day itineraries substitute for Nordic Prince while that ship sails New York to Bermuda run during summer months.

Rates: 14 days, minimum $2,265 (14 cabins), maximum $3,470 (9 deluxe outside cabins); 10 days, minimum $1,700, maximum $2,600; 8-days minimum $1,225, maximum $1,825; 7-days minimum $1,300, maximum $1,825, Third and fourth cabin passengers: 14 days $1,050; 10 days $750; 7 days $755.

TTT: 50 staterooms with double beds, no single cabins without surcharge. Children's programs during school holiday periods. Royal Caribbean's philosophy is to provide supervision and activities for teens (and under) on seasonal cruises, primarily during summer vacation periods. During those times, there is a program supervised by counselors as well as baby sitting services. There are no public rooms exclusively for the use of kids or teens, but during family travel periods, the ship(s) try to schedule pool and public room usage for their activities at times when adult passengers are not using them. Kids go free on shore excursions.

In a word (or two): Food and Enjoyable
✓✓✓✓ Entertainment

	Category:	Moderate
M/S SUNWARD II	A.D.R.:	$170
(Norwegian Caribbean Lines)	Rating:	7.4

Miami to the Bahamas. Built 1971 as Cunard *Adventurer;* purchased by NCL 1977 and refurbished so structure conforms with other ships in fleet. Registry: Norway. Capacity: 674 passengers; 279 crew (Norwegian: deck; mixed Caribbean: service). Space ratio: 21.

Specifics: Tonnage: 14, 100; length: 484 feet; beam: 71 feet; stabilizers, individual cabin air condition controls, elevators, swimming pool, shops, beauty/barber shop, lounges, 4 bars, medical services, 6 passenger decks (10 including those for other uses), casino.

Electric Current: 110 volts A.C.

Entertainment: Orchestras, movies, nightclub revues, theater, casino.

Dining: 1 dining room, 2 seatings. Reservations when booking. Special dietary requests through Passenger Courtesy Department at time of booking.

Tipping: $2.00 to waiter; $1.00 to busboy; $2.00 to room steward. Cash bar.

Itinerary: 3-day and 4-day cruises to Bahamas, all year. Every Monday, to Nassau, Freeport and Bahamas Out Island. Fridays to Nassau and Out Island. Tenders at some ports.

Rates: 3-day cruise: minimum $295 (20 cabins), maximum $615 (20 suites); 4-day cruise: minimum $400, maximum $760. Third and fourth cabin passengers, $240 three-nights; $328 four nights; Children under 17, three-nights, $130 four nights, $165. Air-sea.

TTT: The Bahamas Out Islands port is a beach party; Great Stirrup Cay (Bahamas Out Island) is a privately owned island developed by NCL. The experience is worth the cruise, if clear blue waters excite you. No cabins with double beds; no single cabins without surcharge. NCL's Dive In (snorkeling) program was initiated on the Sunward II. It was so popular, it is now offered on the other vessels. Even water intimidated passengers learn to love the experience.

In a word (or two): Party
✔✔ Entertainment

	Category: Moderate
M.S. TROPICALE	*A.D.R.:* $175
(Carnival Cruise Lines)	*Rating:* 9.1

From Los Angeles to Mexico. Built: 1981, commissioned, 1982. Service inaugurated January, 1982. Registry: Liberia. Capacity: 1,400 passengers; 550 crew (Italian deck; mixed service). Space ratio: 29.

Specifics: Tonnage: 36,674; length: 660 feet; beam: 85 feet; individual cabin temperature controls, closed circuit T.V., piped in music, telephones, 3 outdoor swimming pools, 8 passenger elevators, 10 public rooms, plus lounges, golf driving range, children's playroom, hospital, beauty/barber shops, sauna, spa and sports activities room, large casino.

Electric Current: 110 and 220 volts A.C. and D.C.

Entertainment: movies, theater, live entertainers, disco, very large casino.

Dining: 1 dining room, 2 seatings. Special dietary requests when booking through travel agent. International cuisine, Italian specialties.

Tipping: $2.50 to waiter; $1.25 to bus boy; $2.50 to cabin steward. Cash bar.

Itinerary: From Los Angeles 7-day cruises to Cabo San Lucas, Puerto Vallarta and Mazatlan. Tenders some ports.

Rates: Tropicale is "common rated" with other Carnival Cruise Line ships. (Explanation, see Festivale). 7-day minimum $895 (9 cabins); $1,795 maximum (12 verandah suites). Average cabin, $1,110.

TTT: The *Tropicale* is the first of the current generation of new ships costing more than $100 million. She could well be the prototype of ships of the 80's and 90's. At a cost of more than $110 million, it took better than two years to build her at the *Aalborg Vaerft* of Aalborg Yard in Denmark. She was built as a twin screw passenger liner with raked streamlined soft nose stem, transcom stern, bulbous bow for fuel economy and flared bow. She has one bow thrust propeller for easy maneuvering, a semi-balanced rudder and fin stabilizers for smoother sailing. Navigation bridge is completely enclosed and the main propulsion motors are operated at a constant speed driving controlable pitch propellers from the bridge. What should concern passengers more than her technical capabilities is her beauty, and that she is! She is a work of art. 95 percent of her cabins feature twin beds that covert to full king-size beds. Decor is bright and bold. Lounges and public space designed to relax passengers in soothing colors. If the *Tropicale* is what ships of the future will look like, passengers will find the good-olddays of cruising are yet to come. Rates on the *Tropicale* are comparable to other Carnival Cruise Line ships. All cabins are almost identical in size and appointments, except for verandah suites. Select cabins by location and deck, not by size.

TTT: Best buy on the ship—minimum priced cabins. Size is identical to other inside cabins. Only difference is one bed has been removed and an upper berth added. Ideal accommodations for singles, but there is a 150 percent charge for occupying this cabin or any cabin on the ship on a single basis.

TTT: Sailing the *Tropicale* is a fun party at affordable prices. One of the few ships taking advantage of marvelous nights at sea with parties and happenings out on deck. Mexican party as the ship leaves Puerto Vallarta was the most fun I have had at sea in a long time. While service is not white glove, food is of excellent quality prepared tastefully and served with tender loving care.

In a word (or two): Fun and Beautiful
✔✔✔✔✔ Food, Entertainment, Activities

S.S. UNIVERSE
(World Explorer Cruises)

Category: Budget
A.D.R.: about $100
Rating: 3.5

Varied itineraries world-wide, summer: Alaska cruises. Built 1953 as a fast freighter; sailed as *Badger Mariner;* reconstructed; sailed transatlantic as *Atlantic* under American Export flag; improvements, reconstructed 1960; refurbished, refurbished 1971; refurbished, 1980; entered service 1972 as *Universe Campus;* renamed *Universe* 1976. Registry: Liberia. Capacity: 600 passengers; 200 crew (Chinese and other Oriental). Space ratio: 32.

Specifics: Tonnage: 18,100; length: 564 feet; beam: 76 feet; stabilizers, 1 elevator, swimming pool, library, 5 main lounges, 5 passenger decks. Casino, beauty/barber shops, theater.
Electric Current: 110 volts A.C. and D.C.
Entertainment: Orchestra, movies.
Dining: 1 dining room, 2 seatings. Tables assigned after boarding. Special diets not possible. No off-the-menu orders.
Tipping: $2.00 to waiter; $2.00 to cabin steward. Cash bar.
Itinerary: Varied schedules from Around-the-World to 14-day Hong Kong to Kobe cruises. Summers: from Vancouver, 7- and 14-day cruises to Alaska. Special itineraries sometimes announced. Tenders at some ports.
Rates: Rates not available at press time, but company says "all of our cruises are bargains." Average daily rate estimated at around $100 but varies 10 to 15 percent, depending on itinerary. Alaska 14-day rate from $1,395 minimum (38 cabins); $2,750 maximum (8 cabins). Limited air-sea.

TTT: This is an economy ship, and passengers looking for a bargain never complain. The ship also carries an accredited faculty on board, and classes for audit and academic credit are available. Attracts younger passengers some cruises, much older on others. There is no cabin meal service; no floor shows per se, no telephones in cabins. But, drinks are the lowest priced afloat with average standard alcoholic drinks still selling for $1 and bottles of wine listed from $5 to $20. Alaska itinerary is for passengers in search of "unusual Alaska." Places like Valdez, Lynn Canal, Homer, Wrangell are included, and there is an optional Arctic air tour to Mt. McKinley.

In a word (or two): Tacky and Bargain

S.S. VERACRUZ
(Bahama Cruise Line)

Category: Budget
A.D.R.: under $100
Rating: 4

From New York to New England and Nova Scotia (summer months); from Tampa to Key West and Mexico (winter months). Built 1957 as *Theodor Herzl* for Zim Lines, withdrawn from service 1970 and sat idle for a couple of years before coming under the Bahama Cruise Line banner in 1974. Completely refurbished, 1975. She was named *Carnival,* but never sailed under that name. She did sail briefly between Miami and Nassau, Freeport (Bahamas) as *Freeport II.* Bahamas Cruise Line was purchased by Common Brothers Limited a couple of years ago. The single vessel in the passenger fleet is the *Veracruz.* Registry: Panama. Capacity: 704 passengers. 275 crew (mixed deck, service). Space ratio: 15.7.

Specifics: Tonnage: 10,595; length: 487; beam: 65 feet. 367 cabins with facilities for 704 passengers, full deck of public rooms with lounges, bars, casino, swimming pool, theater, shops, stabilizers, bow thruster, 1 passenger elevator, beauty shop. 8 passenger decks, casino.

Electric Current: 220 volts A.C.

Entertainment: Orchestras, movies, entertainment.

Dining: 1 dining room. 2 seatings. Continental cuisine, kosher menus available if requested at time of booking or at least three weeks prior to departure. Instead of midnight buffet, pizza and other hot snacks served in lounges at midnight. Ship's coffee shop charges minimal amount and is open until 2 a.m.

Tipping: $2.00 to waiter; $1.00 to busboy; $2.00 to room steward. Cash bar.

Itinerary: From New York and Montreal (7-days each direction) to Quebec, Halifax and Nova Scotia, summer months. Every Saturday from Tampa to Key West and Eastern Mexican ports, winter months. Also 2-day cruises to Nowhere from Tampa on selected dates and 5-day cruise to Yucatan.

Rates: Typical 7-day Mexico cruise, minimum $595 (26 cabins), maximum $935 (2 suites). Rates higher in season.

TTT: Cabins with double beds are available, but they go quickly. *Vera-Cruz* isn't the largest or the best, but she is good value with average daily rate around $100 per. She's not pretentious, cabins are small, but single travelers seem to like her. Atmosphere on board is very casual and very friendly. No single cabins without surcharge. "Children sail free" summer offer is a real bargain.

In a word (or two): Tacky and Bargain

Category:	Luxury
A.D.R.:	$330
Rating:	9.2

M.S. VISTAFJORD
(Cunard/NAC)

From Genoa, Hamburg, Venice to Mediterranean and Northern Europe (summer months), Port Everglades to Caribbean and transcanal. Built 1973. Registry: Norway. Capacity: 635 passengers, 370 crew (Norwegian and other European). Space ratio: 37.

Specifics: Tonnage: 25,000; length: 628 feet; beam: 82 feet; stabilizers; individual cabin climate controls, 6 elevators; indoor-outdoor swimming pool; boutique; barber/beauty shops; gymnasium; sauna, card room; library; 4 lounges; ballroom (capacity 700); fully staffed hospital/doctor's office; 8 passenger decks, casino, Golden Door Spa at Sea, casino.

Electric Current: 110 volts A.C.

Entertainment: Orchestra; trio; quintet; movies; theater; nightclub.

Dining: 1 dining room, 1 seating. Reservations when booking. Special diets on request.

Tipping: $3.50 to waiter and to cabin steward. Cash and charge bar.

Itinerary: Winters: 14-day cruises to Caribbean, Mexico. Summer itinerary varies in North Sea and Mediterranean. Also Transatlantic. Tenders some ports. 10 to 20 day cruises.

Rates: Typical 14-day minimum $2,420 (13 cabins); maximum $8,650 (8 cabins). Rates are higher during winter season.

TTT: A classy ship. Ties requested in dining room almost nightly. Cruise season is very dressy. 61 single cabins without surcharge. Cunard/NAC maintains ships at previous high Norwegian American Cruise standards and quality has not changed. Quite the contrary. A number of new features have been added and they make the ship a lot more up-beat and attractive to passengers who like luxury, but also seek some action. Most passengers are ship travel buffs and quite sophisticated. Ships are refined, elegant and small children are not encouraged on board but activities and counselors are on board when the number of young passengers warrants them. Entertainment is not spectacular. Special interest cruises with guest lecturers attract "different" passengers. Ship was refurbished in December, 1981 and Cunard spent $10 on more improvements in 1983 and 1984. An open- air greenhouse look has been adopted. A glass-enclosed area has been built on the uppermost deck and turned into a two-level greenhouse that houses a theater-in-the-round capabilities. The Golden Door Spa at Sea is complete and very popular with a full exercise program. See Sagafjord **TTT:** for more information on cruise style.

In a word (or two): Classy
✔✔✔✔✔ Food, Service and Accommodations

S.S. VICTORIA
(Chandris, Inc.)

Category:	Budget
A.D.R.:	$110
Rating:	3.2

From Amsterdam to North Sea, from Piraeus (summer months); From San Juan to Caribbean (winter months). Built 1937 as *Dunnottar Castle* for Union Castle Lines; completely rebuilt and refurbished 1959; refurbished again 1975. Served as armed merchant cruiser and troopship in World War II; sailed for Incres Lines as *Victoria;* taken over by Chandris 1975. Registry: Panama. Capacity: 654 passengers; 300 crew (Greek). Space ratio: 30.

Specifics: Tonnage: 11,886; length: 575 feet; beam: 72 feet; fin stabilizers; 3 elevators; 2 swimming pools; sauna; lounges; 10 public rooms; 5 passenger decks, casino.

Electric Current: 115 volts A.C.

Entertainment: 2 orchestras, movies; disco; theater; entertainers; casino.

Dining: 1 dining room; 2 seatings. Reservations at time of booking. Limited special dietary requirements possible. Notify when booking try maitre d'.

Tipping: $2.00 to waiter and cabin steward. $15 voyage to maitre d'. Cash bar.

Itinerary: Summer months, 14-day cruises Amsterdam to Northern Capitals and Piraeus to Alexandria, Haifa, Greek islands and Turkey. Winter: Every Monday sailing from San Juan to St. Thomas, Martinique, La Guaira, Aruba. Tenders some ports.

Rates: 7 days, $599 minimum (7 cabins); maximum $999 (4 suites).

TTT: Still a proud lady, she retains much of her charm. Cabins are very large. Deck chairs $5 week.

In a word (or two): Budget and Old

M.S. WORLD RENAISSANCE
(Epirotiki Lines)

Category:	Moderate
A.D.R.:	$155
Rating:	4

From San Juan to the Caribbean, West Indies. Built 1966 for *Paquet Cruises* as *Renaissance;* sold to Epirotiki Lines 1977. Refurbished 1978. Operated under Costa Cruises' charter until 1984. Registry: Greece. Capacity: 426 passengers; 215 crew (Greek). Space ratio: 28.

Specifics: Tonnage: 12,000; length: 492 feet; beam: 69 feet; stabilizers; Individual cabin climate controls; 1 elevator; 2 outdoor swimming pools; boutique shop; beauty/barber shops; gymnasium; sauna; laundry and dry-cleaning facilities; ballroom; bars; library; card room; medical services; 8 passenger decks, casino.

Electric Current: 110 volts A.C.

Entertainment: Theater; disco; special-interest cruises.

Dining: 1 dining room, 2 seatings. Special dietary requirement in advance. Table assignments on board.

Tipping: Amount recommended on board is for total voyage and passengers are requested to give it to the chief purser or chief steward. Tips are pooled and divided among entire service crew. Cash bar.

Itinerary: From Piraeus to Greek Islands and Turkey, 7-day cruises. Tenders some ports.

Rates: 7-day cruises; minimum $775 (13 cabins); maximum $1,390 (10 suites).

TTT: 4 cabins with double beds; 4 single cabins without surcharge. Deck chairs $6.00 per voyage. Ship returned to Epirotiki management summer of 1984 and early reports indicate she is being operated in Epirotiki style. A nice vessel. Atmosphere is now very Greek instead of the French flavor given to her by Paquet. Ship looks old and could use refurbishing.

In a word (or two): Old

FREIGHTER TRAVEL

ADVENTUROUS TRAVELERS curious about the sea, ships, and out-of-the-way places dream of freighter and cargo voyages. Show me a dreamer and I'll show you someone planning (and hoping) for a slow boat to China—a leisurely sailing to a distant island with a strange-sounding name. Talk with half the cruise ship passengers sailing the seas in semi-luxury, and I'll bet they allow as how "Someday, I'm planning to take a freighter cruise around the world." They should know that what they've got on board that cruise ship is not what they are going to get on board a freighter, if they are among the fortunate few who succeed in getting space on a cargoliner.

Freighter travel is not for everyone. It is for people who want to stop the world and get off for a spell. Freighters are for dreamers who visualize slow boats to no place in particular, the world in general. Freighters are for loners who yearn for the peace that comes with solitude and lazy days at sea. Freighters are not for travelers who lean heavily on cruise directors and planned activities, and freighters will be daily and nightly disappointments for passengers who look forward to lavish buffets, service, and companionship.

To dyed-in-the-wool freighter fans, amenities of old liners are nothing compared to the aura of romance and adventure found on working cargo ships. Although today's freighters, like their sister ships designated "cruise," may be a far cry from the tramp steamers of yesteryear that picked up and discharged cargo at random, they still have the timeless appeal of a Hemingway story. To those of us who sail vicariously on the rusted buckets that carried Somerset Maugham across the South Seas, the lure of freighter travel is still a powerful pull.

Although seagoing lifestyles have changed dramatically, to a limited degree, there are still fleets of passenger-carrying cargo vessels. They offer a special shipboard experience appreciated by a dedicated following convinced that passage by freighter is the ultimate trip. If you want to get in on that kind of experience, you had better hurry. Cargo passenger ships may well be the great travel bargains of today, but the choice is narrow and opportunities limited. There are fewer ships handling freight and passengers than ever before in the history of ships. The good old days of boom-loading freighters with long and leisurely days in port have been replaced by the short unloading time it takes to move containerized freight from ship to shore or the reverse. True, the traveler can still almost completely stop time on board a freighter, but a quick look at the way ships of the future are heading will probably make this type of clock-stopping still another chapter in the books filled with tales of the good old days of sailing.

By name alone, freighter-passenger and cargo-passenger vessels separate themselves from cruise ships. By profile, they also differ drastically. Unfortunately for freighter lovers, during the past couple of decades the number of dual-purpose ships has declined dramatically, and there's a good possibility this type of vessel will soon become totally obsolete. During the past couple of years Farrell Lines has discontinued passenger service, Knutson Line was sold to EAG Steamship and they are no longer in business and Delta Line Cruises has announced it is withdrawing its vessels from passenger service in early 1985.

In appearance, freighters are usually smaller versions of cruise ships when it comes to tonnage. Accommodation of cargo-handling gear changes the silhouette, and the super-structure is smaller. Ocean going dry-cargo liners usually have a gross tonnage of between 5,000 and 12,000 and are specifically designed for cargo. The term "liner" is applied to a ship that operates on regular service between ports; and if you're wondering how a tramp steamer got its name, wonder no more. "Tramp" was applied to a ship employed on charter to take cargo from port to port, at any time, anywhere in the world. The cargoliner, referred to as a freighter in some countries, generally has four or five holds and is designed for easy discharge of cargo. The way the ship rides is dependent upon the weight distribution of cargo, so ships are designed to carry the heaviest loads amidship.

According to the International Conventions and Conferences on Marine Safety, a passenger-carrying freighter or cargoliner (the terms are used interchangeably these days) is a vessel principally engaged in transporting goods but licensed to carry a maximum of 12 passengers as well. The most common definition of a passenger freighter is: Ships that carry cargo and take from 2 to 20 passengers along for the ride. Cargoliners generally carry goods, and from 50 to 100 passengers. There last three vessels of this type are being withdrawn from passenger service (Delta Line Cruises) but will continue on cargo runs.

Freighters and cargoliners have other features in common. Cargo is most important on these ships. Cargo governs the ports visited and the length of time in port. Cargo pays the tab and builds company profits. Passengers ride along at the convenience of the company and, some say, to keep sea traditions alive. More and more shipping companies are opting to convert the valuable space occupied by passengers into non-eating, non-service demanding cargo.

Although your dreams of freighter travel may be visions of delight, there are disadvantages you should know about before you opt for this means of sailing the seas.

THINGS TO KNOW BEFORE YOU BOOK PASSAGE

Freighters do not operate on definite time schedules. Some never call at the ports listed in brochures. Ports of call depend on the call of the cargo. Changes are often made midsea, and there's no way passengers can pre-arrange to visit friends at any port. Ports of call are added and subtracted according to loading and off-loading requirements.

There are health and age restrictions on freighters. With 12 or less passengers, freighters do not carry doctors, and each company sets its own requirements and age limitations. Everyone over 65 is usually required to have a medical health certificate testifying to good physical and mental health. One company spells out specifics clearly in their brochure. They will accept no one with a history of heart disease or other serious organic problem; no one who may require continuous medical or personal attention; nor handicapped persons dependent on canes, crutches, or wheelchairs. Some companies raise the age limit to 76, others to 79; few others have no limitations. Check restrictions before booking.

Freighter travel is not for children! Most companies discourage or refuse to accept them as passengers. This is an easy-to-understand rule. Imagine 11 senior-aged passengers climbing the rails after a month and a half at sea with a hyper under–10 year old.

Freighters generally take rough seas very well. Cargo-carrying vessels are broad beamed with low superstructures. This, combined with heavy cargo below the water level, acts as a stabilizing influence. Even in rough seas, with decks awash, cargo keeps the vessel down and reduces the motion of the ocean.

Every passenger goes first class on a freighter because cargo pays ships' operation expenses, making freighter travel one of the best bargains in the marketplace. Rates are on a per day, per person basis, but most companies have found there's little profit in carrying passengers.

Freighters operate on indefinite schedules. So if a freighter's voyage is sold as a 60-day cruise, and it takes 70 days before they deliver you back to port, there's no extra charge for the additional days. On the other hand, if you paid for 60 days and you're back at home port in less time, companies refund a per diem amount based on the number of days you missed on board ship.

It is not uncommon for a freighter to visit one or more ports not on the printed itinerary. Conversely, ships may bypass a listed port of call. Cargo carrying vessels heading for a scheduled port may be rerouted mid-ocean because a lucrative freight hauling contract has been negotiated and is waiting to be picked up halfway around the world. Since freighter travel requires a lot of time and less money, average age of passengers is in the high 60's to mid–70's. Don't expect 12 swingers cruising around the world. Freighter passengers are more apt to get high on a round of bridge than a clandestine meeting with a ship's officer. During summer months average age is lower because many teachers plan ahead for this less expensive route to the world.

TTT: A single woman will not be accepted by most freighter companies for a voyage on which she is the only female booked. Call it what you like, but I call it unfair.

WHICH FREIGHTER CRUISE?

Where do you want to go? A freighter cruise, in addition to the leisurely pace of getting there, is also taking you to a far-away area of the world. Your choice of destinations will determine the length of the voyage and sometimes the flag and registry of the vessel. You won't be hungry on the ship and the flag flying from the mast usually indicates ethnic background of the crew. Chances are good that if the flag is Greek, the moussaka will be excellent.

Naturally, the longer the cruise, the more ports on the itinerary. But remember, containerized cargoliner do not—repeat, do not—spend much time in port. Huge loading cranes lift the containers from trucks to ship or vice versa, and longshoremen work around the clock. Time is money, and that's what freighter and cargo hauling is all about.

A freighter cruise doesn't come with a guaranteed itinerary. The ship may not visit any or some of the ports listed in the brochure, but it will travel in the specified area of the globe. Select the ship going to the Orient, if that's where you want to go, or to the Mediterranean, if those calm, blue waters intrigue you. You may not visit all of the Greek islands, but chances are excellent the ship will put in at a couple of the larger ones.

Along with the area of the world, consider the time you want to spend. Then combine both time and area with ethnic preferences, and you'll come up with one or two ships worthy of further investigation.

TTT: If you are looking for more time in port, select bulk-loading ships. It takes longer to move the cargo. Containerized vessels have speeded required loading and unloading time, so time in ports is shorter. Semi-containerized ships are a compromise.

BOOKING PASSAGE

Not all travel agents are equipped with information needed to book freighters, and few want to spend the time it takes to complete a confirmed booking on a freighter. Most travel agents will honestly tell you they cannot spare the time needed to keep abreast of ever changing freighter schedules and availability. Thus, most of the advance planning and research is up to the traveler. Since time should be discretionary or at least not be listed as a priority to the freighter traveler, you should be willing to spend some of it checking availability, itineraries, and ships. Freighters do not advertise their voyages to the travel trade, and schedules are not published frequently. Select the time of year you prefer to travel, but be flexible. The itinerary of your choice may force you to change your plans to suit the ship.

Be honest with your travel agent about your time schedule. More important, be honest with yourself! Make sure time really is no factor.

Most of the more popular freighter voyages are booked years in advance, but the traveler willing to sail on short notice has an excellent chance of being on board when the ship leaves port. That's what I mean — freighter travel is for the traveler whose lifestyle is flexible. Cancellations come up all the time, and travel agents who register their clients on waiting lists do get called by freighter companies prior to sailings.

If you decide to do your homework and write directly to the freighter company, request brochures with layouts of the ship, up-to-date fares, and cabin availability. They will reply with first available sailing dates, and you'll quickly realize the importance of advance, far-in-advance, planning. If there is no space on the sailing of your choice, ask to be wait-listed, even if you are forced to cancel your plans later on. You are not required to pay a deposit until space is confirmed on a specific voyage. As with all rules, this one has exceptions, and a few companies require substantial deposits when space is requested. When that happens, be sure to purchase cancellation and trip interruption insurance so if you must cancel the trip or return in mid-voyage because of health reasons you will not lose all of your money.

If you decide to be wait-listed, be prepared with passport, required documentation, and inoculations. You may receive a telephone call a few days before sailing saying space is available. You should also request space from more than one company. Second and third choices avoid disappointment.

TTT: At the end of 1984, companies advised me they were accepting reservation requests for late 1985, 1986 and beyond. Space does open up but the ship may not be going in your direction.

PORTS OF EMBARKATION

Certain freighters, like cruise ships, have home ports and other ports where they embark cargo and passengers. Frequently, even though your space on the voyage has been confirmed, the ship will not confirm your port of embarkation. You will be notified a few weeks before sailing of the port and embarkation times. If you arrive in the port city before embarkation day, be sure to contact the ship's port agent and advise him of where you can be reached in case of a last minute change. Passenger carrying freighters sail from Albany, Baltimore, Charleston, Los Angeles, Milwaukee, New Orleans, New York, Norfolk, Philadelphia, Portland, San Francisco, Seattle, Tacoma, Vancouver, and Wilmington. You can and should get the port agent's name, address, and telephone number from the freighter company when you receive your passage tickets and instructions.

TTT: Your port of embarkation is not necessarily your part of debarkation. In most instances, freighter companies reserve the right to return you to your country of origin, but not necessarily to the same city. Check the "conditions" of your passage.

LIFE ABOARD A FREIGHTER

Travel by freighter doesn't mean you'll be roughing it in any sense of the word. There's nothing "tramp" about this type of travel. True, it is less structured and less formal than cruise ship travel, but amenities compensate in many forms. Today's freighters carrying 12 or fewer passengers cruise at speeds comparable to other ocean-going vessels, and many are attractively decorated in passenger areas. The decor is not as plush as on some cruise ships, yet not as drab as on others. A specific area is set aside for passengers' use, and there is always a small lounge for recreational activities. This room sometimes doubles as the dining room. Passengers are free to roam the decks (except for restricted areas) and are free to mix with officers.

Cabins

All cargoliners have outside cabins with facilities, and cabins are generally sold on a per person, double occupancy basis. Cabins are equipped with twin beds (not bunks), table or writing desk, sometimes a small sofa, a chair, and a couple of closets. Newer ships have tubs as well as showers. There is no room service, but cabins will be cleaned daily and made up by a steward. Freighter cabins are generally larger than on newer cruise ships; perhaps not as lavish, but just as comfortable.

Facilities

There is always a lounge and/or bar and a small library. Deck chairs and steamer rugs are provided without charge, and there is plenty of deck space even on container ships for lounging, walking, and exercise. Some freighters even have swimming pools. Valet laundry service is not provided, but most ships have a washer and dryer for passenger use. Ships are heated and air conditioned. There is no beauty shop, no barber shop, no ship store. Passengers are usually permitted to purchase essentials at the crew shop.

Eating on Board

Passengers eat with the officers, and the quality of the food varies from ship to ship. Generally, it is not gourmet dining but it is first class, and service is good. Dining hours are much earlier than on cruise ships. There is no cabin service, but an open pantry is available at most hours and is stocked with do-it-yourself sandwich makings, fruits, and beverages. Because passengers eat what the officers eat and food depends on the tastes of the captain, passengers have reported sailing with captains who have French-trained chefs cooking up gourmet delights. Normal meal hours on a freighter are: breakfast from 7:30 to 8:30; midmorning tea or coffee; lunch from 11:30 to 12:30; tea at 3:00; "happy hour" at 5:00 for cocktails and conversation; and dinner around 6:00 P.M. Special diets cannot be accommodated. There is usually a choice of main courses (perhaps six), but don't expect caviar and lobster. All passengers eat at one seating.

Drinking on Board

Freighters have well stocked bars or cocktail lounges, and drinks are priced lower than on cruise ships. Wine is reasonable and sometimes served with meals at no cost. There's no rule against a bottle in the cabin, if you are so inclined.

TTT: Containerized vessels mean decks covered with containers, and unless you select your cabin carefully, you could spend the voyage with a view of a container instead of the sea. Study deck plans and make sure your cabin doesn't face fore (the bow) of the ship. That's one area always filled with containers.

Ship Safety and Sanitation

All ships boarding passengers in U.S. ports must comply with U.S. Coast Guard and Safety of Life at Sea regulations. Vessels are inspected by U.S. Coast Guard officers, and the same stringent rules applied to cruise ships apply to freighters. This is also true of Public Health inspections. You'll find galley ratings for cleanliness in the same listings that include cruise ships. Very few freighters or cargoliners pass public health inspections with flying colors. The galleys are clean, but they are not set up in the style outlined in these inspections. Galleys on board freighters are too small to have the required footage between edible and nonedible supplies, for instance. I wouldn't worry about sanitation on board freighters. Passengers are in very close contact with the captain, and if conditions are good enough for him and his highly paid officers of the sea, they are good enough for me.

Entertainment

You're on your own, so you and the other 11 passengers better like each other. Bring plenty of reading material and brush up on your bridge and backgammon. There is no entertainment planned except for movies two or three times a week. The crew sometimes puts on a farewell show, and the passengers sometimes entertain the crew, but there's work to do on board a freighter, and officers and crew retire early. (So do passengers.)

Tipping

The only two crew members passengers are obliged to tip are the waiter and the room steward. Some lines recommend a gratuity as low as $1.00 cents a day for each; others recommend you split about 1 percent of your total fare between both.

What to Wear

Casual is the key word. Dress for the weather and comfort. Men should wear jackets and ties when officers dress, but on most freighters this happens once during the voyage. Women can get away with almost anything, but favorites include jeans, skirts, dresses, jackets. Jewelry, furs, and long dresses are out of place on board freighters. The same for tuxedos. Bring wash and wearables and leave the short-shorts at home.

Cruise Lengths

Some freighters will carry passengers only on a roundtrip basis; others traveling the Atlantic, for instance, carry passengers for 10 days into one or two ports in either direction or roundtrip; still others permit passengers to break long voyages and fly back from certain ports. Itineraries and schedules vary greatly, so it is impossible to print a complete guide. It would be outdated before the book could gather a speck of dust on the shelf. At the end of this chapter, THE TOTAL TRAVELER BY SHIP lists typical voyages, names and addresses of freighter lines, and the freighter/cargoliners sailing from U.S. ports of embarkation on a fairly regular basis. Some freighter voyages have been known to last 120 days; some, to terminate after a week.

Rates

Although not as inexpensive as in the old tramp steamer days, freighter travel averages out at between $60 and $85 a day, depending on the ship, facilities offered and accommodations. Cost can go as low as $40 a day and as high as $120. Compared with the current cruise ship average of about $165 a day, freighter travel remains an economical way to float around the world at a leisurely pace.

But Be Sure to . . .

Freighters are not equipped to supply passengers with some of the "necessities" of life available on cruise ships. So, you might want to take items like cosmetics, shampoo, hair blower, transformer, adapters, film, Scotch tape, paper clips, rubber bands, string, pens, playing cards, an alarm clock, a room freshener (if odors bother you), a sewing kit, scissors, cleaning fluid, laundry soap and a wash cloth. Ships have what they call a "slop chest"—a small store that carries basics like toothpaste.

Take a few extra passport photos along. They'll come in handy if the ship puts in at an unannounced port and a visa is required. The port agent will come aboard and take care of those arrangements if it becomes necessary. Also, take your favorite brand of aspirin, writing paper, and lots of reading material. Don't forget a supply of traveler's checks, and you'll find a stack of single dollar bills handy on board ship and in port. You can bank them with the purser while at sea. Of course, bring all of your prescription medicines, sun glasses, and your usual travel gear. You might want to bring a pocketsized dictionary if the ship's crew speaks a language you don't.

IN PORT

Unlike cruise ships, there is no social director to brief you on what to do and see once the ship ties up in a strange port. So good travel guide books are a must. Buy one covering the general area of your voyage, then map your sightseeing plans for the day ashore. Some of your fellow passengers might like to join you, and sometimes the ship's officers plan a sightseeing tour and invite passengers to participate. The ship's port agent is generally on hand to greet you on arrival and will assist with sightseeing plans; but remember, freighters do not dock at passenger terminals. The assigned dock for your freighter could be a couple of miles from where passenger ships land. Tourist information agencies are usually located at the passenger dock or pier, so scrounging for information when there are only 12 passengers on board may become a problem.

To be prepared, write to the tourist offices of the ports listed on the originally scheduled itinerary. Request maps, tours, taxi and bus routes, and prices. Most will be happy to load you down with information. Another approach is to talk with the crew on board the freighter. They probably call at the same ports regularly and will be delighted to share their little-known, offbeat restaurants and retreats with you. I'm told that crew tours are great. They are inexpensive because the total cost of the bus and guide is divided among participants, since it is not a money making proposition for the ship but more a matter of morale.

Ports visited by freighters are sometimes smaller, less well known, and usually still unspoiled by cruise ship passengers who come down gangplanks by the hundreds. "Unspoiled" also means less expensive for shopping and sightseeing. If shopping interests you, check with crew members. They know the best stores and best values.

Time in port is announced by the captain before arrival. He will post the hour by which all passengers must be back on board. This does not mean the ship will sail at the exact time. She may sail six hours later if more cargo arrives, so you should keep checking back with the port agent. All ships will furnish a shore contact telephone numbers and addresses prior to allowing passengers ashore.

TTT: Don't waste time in port; it's probably your most precious commodity. If you decide on public transportation, be sure you know where the bus or streetcar is going and when it is returning. The worst thing you can do is get lost in a country where there are few English-speaking visitors. And as with cruise ships, if you miss the boat, you're on your own!

AFTERTHOUGHTS ON FREIGHTER TRAVEL

In the course of this chapter, I spoke with dozens of companies carrying freight and passengers on their vessels. I was saddened by the rapid phasing out of passenger-carrying freighter-cargo ships. The reason is a matter of economics and convenience. Cargo doesn't talk back; cargo doesn't require service; cargo doesn't eat; and, cargo doesn't complain.

Those four conditions account for diminishing passenger manifests on cargo vessels. Sad, but true. Sometimes the freighter passenger who dearly loves the sea is his own worst enemy and adds to the growing list of all-cargo ships.

Passenger complaints are forcing lines to discontinue passenger service. Looking into one company's mailbag, I found a letter complaining that the cabin didn't have a rug on the floor. Another groused that the officers and crew did not socialize enough; and still another complained that time in a specific port was too short. These letters are enough to drive companies out of the passenger-carrying business on the basis that cargo pays the bills anyway.

Ships are economic realities. As companies build new ships, the tendency is to eliminate the area formerly used for the traditional 12 passengers. As cabins, lounges and dining rooms disappear from deck plans, the space is rapidly taken up by "non-speaking" cargo.

The future of freighter travel? There has been a trend toward merging of major companies. Prudential Lines was bought out by Delta Steamship Lines. American Export has merged with Farrell

Lines. Lykes Bros., an international company, has taken over State Lines. But it didn't save some of the companies nor did these changes do anything to increase the number of cargo ships that accept passengers.

Unfortunately, since the last edition of THE TOTAL TRAVELER BY SHIP, a number of companies have suspended the passenger side of their operations and are limiting shipping activities to cargo. Among them are Black Star Line, Ltd. Up until this year they operated bulk loading vessels that carried cars and freight as well as passengers from Canadian and U.S. Atlantic and Gulf ports to West Africa. Johnson Lines operates Swedish flag ships regularly from U.S. West Coast ports to Europe, but is no longer carrying passengers. Although their limit was six passengers per voyage, the ships were considered luxurious. Food and service was first class. South African Marine Corp. has also discontinued carrying passengers on sailings between New York, Houston and South Africa. Polish Ocean Lines operating plans were questionable at press time, but they are still operating and I have received positive reports from readers who sailed between Canada and Poland.

Lykes has opened offices in California and has expanded itineraries to include People's Republic of China on some of the routes. Other freighters sailing the Orient routes will likely include calls in China. Would-be passengers should know that special visas are required for those visits, and it takes about six to eight weeks to procure them.

So, if you decide your sea route is on the freighter circuit, remember:

1. Officers and crew have a primary duty to the vessel and the cargo.
2. Do not expect luxury cruise service. Pack a sense of humor. You'll need it!
3. When you reach the point of complaint, remember what you bought is what you are getting.

Freighter cruises are for loners, people who don't need a lot of other people around them; people who make friends easily; people who love the sea and want to get more than their money's worth.

Availability changes constantly, and freighter buffs have banded together into a couple of clubs wherein members exchange information. You might want to subscribe to Traveltips, Box 188, 163–07, Deport Rd., Flushing, NY 11358, A year's subscription to the monthly publication costs $19. It costs $12 a year to join the Freighter Travel Club of America, P.O. Box 12693, Salem, Oregon 97309. Membership includes a subscription to a newsletter.

SHIPS OF THE FREIGHTER WORLD

(All rates quoted per person, double occupancy, and based on round-trip, unless otherwise specified. Daily rates quoted are approximate and subject to change.)

AMERICAN PRESIDENT LINES
Passenger Department 1950 Franklin Street, Oakland, CA 94612
American Flag
Age limit: 82 (passengers over 65 require medical certificate)

Sail once or twice a month usually from U.S. West Coast port to a port or ports in the Orient and/or Southeast/Southwest Asia area. Itineraries are indefinite and no specific ports of call nor number of ports can be projected in advance. Voyages vary from one to three months. Sold on a roundtrip basis only. **Rates:** Standard double, $6,800; deluxe double or single, $7,500. For voyages of less than 80 days duration, refunds will be made on the basis of $85 a day in standard cabins, $94 in deluxe. **Ships:** *SS Presidents Adams, Cleveland, Jackson, Taylor, Wilson.* Also sails every other week roundtrip from Singapore visiting Colombo, and Dubal. **Rates:** Roundtrip 28 days $2,155 double, $2,380 single ($77 a day average). One-way on request. One way trans-Pacific passage in combination with South Asia cruise without change of ship is occasionally possible. **Ships:** Containerships *SS Presidents Fillmore, McKinley, Taft* or *Van Buren.*

TTT: All American President Lines ships are air conditioned, have large, comfortable cabins, serve excellent American-style food, have passenger lounges, libraries, cocktail lounges and open snack pantries. Washers and dryers also available. 12-passenger limit each ship. All ships are very well maintained. Company warns that containers may be carried on deck, and may, during some parts of the voyage, obstruct the view from forwardfacing cabins. No way of requesting a specific ship.

BLUE STAR LINE, INC.
701 Sutter Street, San Francisco, CA 94109
British flag
Age limit: 80 (Persons 65 years of age or over must have a doctor's medical certificate)

Bimonthly sailings on two vessels, the *California Star* and the *Columbia Star* (operated in the service of the Johnson Scanstar). From Vancouver, Seattle, Oakland, Los Angeles to London. **Usual ports:** Trans-Panama Canal to Liverpool, London. **Rate:** From Vancouver to United Kingdom, $1,650 per person, double; $200 less from Los Angeles. (Average $68 a day). Also every 24 days from Tacoma, Washington, Oakland, California; Los Angeles; Suva, Fiji Islands; Lyttelton, New Zealand; Wellington and Auckland, New Zealand; Honolulu, Hawaii. One way usually 17 days. **Rate:** New Zealand-U.S. Pacific Coast, $1650 per person, double; between Fiji Island and North American ports, $918 northbound, $1221 southbound. About $200 less with Hawaii as embarkation or final port. Average rate, a little less than $100 per day.

TTT: Ships take only two passengers each. They are accommodated in the owners' suite, which is very nice. Air conditioned, of course. Passengers must embark at last call on Pacific Coast for southbound voyage; last port of call in New Zealand for north-bound voyages. Passengers debark at first port of call on the Pacific Coast or New Zealand, whichever is applicable. On westbound voyages from United Kingdom, passengers may be booked to any of the North American Pacific Coast ports.

DELTA LINE CRUISES
Delta Steamship Lines, Inc.
1 Market Plaza, San Francisco, CA 94106
American flag

(Discontinuing passenger service in early 1985)

EGON OLENDORF
Biehl & Co. (agents)
416 Common St., New Orleans, LA 70130
Various flags (Liberia, Singapore, Panama and Somalia)
Age limit: Not having reached 70th birthday
Bulk loading vessels; 4 to 11 passengers

Sail regularly from one port on the U.S. Gulf, East Coast or Canadian to one port Lisbon/Hamburg range. One-way, 12 to 15 days $487.50 double cabins out of Gulf Coast; $537.50 single. Out of East Coast or Canada $450 double; $500 single. (Average daily rate $32 for 15 days!)

TTT: Six vessels of the fleet are air conditioned and all have swimming pools. Cabins have fans. Ships were built between 1963 and 1974. Most vessels are trampers and sail unscheduled itineraries, so flexibility is a requirement. Ships are bulk carriers that load grain, coal, phosphate, etc., and depending on the port of loading, short notice is given for arrivals and departures. Medical certificates are required of passengers who have reached the age of 65 through 69. No deposit is accepted until space is available. Wait lists are maintained by months of desired sailing. Passengers are contacted by collect phone calls as schedules and space becomes available.

TTT: Cannot be booked through travel agencies. Contact company direct.

FARRELL LINES, INC.
1 Whitehall Street, New York, NY 10004
American flag
Age limit: 75 (passengers over 65 require medical certificate)

(Service discontinued)

HELLENIC LINES
39 Broadway, New York, NY 10006
Greek flag
No age limit

All vessels noncontainerized; no regular sailings from U.S. ports but it is sometimes possible to catch a sailing from New Orleans, Houston or New York to Mediterranean. Voyages are from 50 to 60 days and cost runs about $2,400 ($43.60 a day) One-way and inter-port available but rates change with seasons. Company also has non-scheduled sailings from New York to South and East Africa; 115–125 days, $4,500 ($37.50 day). **Usual ports:** Port Said, Agaba, Jidda, Port Sudan, Djibouti, Mombasa, Tanga, Dar es Salaam, Nacala, Durban. (For embarkation in New Orleans or Houston, add $350 to rate and 20 days to length of cruise.)

TTT: Passage can be purchased on a one-way basis, with open returns. Vessels remain in most ports from two to four days. Ship is passengers' hotel when in port. All ships have lounges and snack pantries. All cabins have private facilities. Washers and dryers available.

IVARAN LINES

U. S. Navigation Co.
One Edgewater Plaza, Staten Island, New York, NY 10305
Norwegian flag.
Age Limit: 73
Ships carry 12 passengers.

Regularly scheduled sailing from Houston and New York to South America. Typical routing from New York includes Baltimore, Norfolk, Charleston, Savannah, Miami, Rio de Janeiro, Santos and Buenos Aires. Roundtrip from Baltimore is 47 days on average. Houston itinerary has changed for 1985. Voyage is approximately 65 days for the roundtrip and typical itinerary includes Tampico (Mexico), Rio de Janeiro, Santos, Buenos Aires, Oaranagua, Montevideo, Barbados, San Juan and return to New Orleans. **Rates:** 65 days $5,082 standard cabin per person, $5,445 single. (Daily average $78).

TTT: Ivaran Lines offers two lovely 12 passenger 14,770-ton freighters, built in 1978, each with double and single cabins with private facilities. Both vessels are fully air conditioned. There is a swimming pool available for passengers' use. lvaran enjoys an excellent reputation. They have been in business since 1902. Ships are more modern than their first one, the 650-ton *Modesta* built in 1892. Official name of the company is A.S. Ivarans Rederi. Today the main interest of the company is the liner trade between the U.S. and Brazil. Ships were built in 1978 and have excellent passenger facilities. English speaking officers and crew.

KNUTSEN LINE

(Sold to EAG Steamship; no longer in business)

LYKES BROS. STEAMSHIP CO.

300 Poydras St., New Orleans, LA 70130
American flag.
Age limit: 79

From U.S. West Coast port to the Orient) Passengers 60 years of age and older must provide a medical certificate of good health from a physicians. Weekly from a Gulf port, usually New Orleans, to west coast of South America: 35–40 days roundtrip, $2,800 ($74 day). One way and inter-port rates available. **Usual ports:** Santa Marta/Cartagena, Cristobal/Balboa, Buenaventura, Guayaquil, Gallao, Matarani or Valparaiso. Also from U.S. Gulf Coast to South and East Africa (4 to 12 passengers) about 60 days; From New Orleans to Rotterdam with return from Bremerhaven to Galveston about 14 days; from California to Far East about 32 days ($2,000) from Gulf Coast to Far East 60 to 80 days $4,500.) Check with company for additional sailings and itineraries.

TTT: There are 44 ships in the Lykes fleet. It is probably the most popular cargo-passenger service available. All vessels are semi-containerized. There are no single accommodations and passage is based on per person, double occupancy. Although New Orleans is the usual U.S. port of embarkation, other Gulf Coast ports are sometimes used. Cabins are roomy, comfortable, outside and with private facilities. Passengers dine with the Captain and officers, and tipping is not encouraged, although extra service is usually rewarded. Ships have lounges, card rooms, excellent food and are air conditioned. Some ships take only four passengers and that is a good indication of differences from ship-to-ship. Itineraries are announced one month in advance. Wise freighter buffs have their names on several lists, then opt for accepting or refusing accommodations when offered. No liquor is sold on board, but no objection to bringing your own. Possible to book port-to-port passage. Average daily rates vary depending on ship and itinerary, but run around $63.

TTT: Lykes has added sailings from New Orleans through the Panama Canal to Balboa, then returning via Canal to Cartagena and Barranquilla. Ships then usually proceed back to New Orleans. Duration about 15 days. Ships are semi-containerized and carry a maximum of 12 passengers in six double cabins. Rate is $1,200 per person. Singles accepted on a share basis. A 75 percent surcharge for exclusive cabin occupancy. Same surcharge in effect for all sailings for single occupancy of a cabin intended for double use. No refund if voyage is shorter than anticipated; no charge if it is longer.

NAURU PACIFIC LINE
North American Maritime Agencies
100 California St., San Francisco, CA 94111
Republic of Nauru flag
No age limit

Ships carry 90–100 passengers and sail approximately every 6 weeks, 40 days, $3,100–4,200 ($87 day), depending on choice of cabin. **Usual**

ports: Honolulu, Majuro, Ponape, Truk, Saipan, San Francisco to Micronesian Islands.

TTT: This vessel is former Holland American Line ship. Entire promenade deck is glass-enclosed public space. Has swimming pool, library, gift and sundry shop. Air-sea arrangements possible. Nauro Pacific Line also operates a 12-passenger ship from Nauru to Australia. Port to port rates available. For example, San Francisco to Truk, from $1,645 to $2,225. Ship is the *Enna G*, designed for passenger-cruise-cargo service so she has amenities associated with passenger ships. All cabins are outside, air conditioned and have private facilities. Nice dining room. Good food and service.

POLISH OCEAN LINES, INC.
Gdynia American Line, Inc.
1 World Trade Center, New York, NY 10048
Polish flag
No age limit

Sails weekly from Canadian East Coast ports to Northern Europe. Semicontainerized; 14 days one-way, $640 ($46 a day); **Usual ports:** Le Havre, Rotterdam, Bremen, Hamburg, Gdynia.

TTT: Roomy cabins, private bath with shower, lounge/hall with semicircular sofa and round table. Basic Polish food. All cabins amidship and air conditioned. Roundtrip passengers must make their own arrangements on shore in Gdynia for about five days. For the past few years, Polish Ocean Lines has not been calling in U.S. ports and board passengers and cargo in Eastern Canada ports.

TTT: Polish Ocean Lines has other vessels sailing from ports in Europe and Far East, Write for availability and schedules. A reader wrote about a 79 day roundtrip voyage he took on the Professor Rylke from Hamburg to Singapore.

PRUDENTIAL LINES, INC.
One World Trade Center, New York, NY 10048
American flag
Age limit: 75 (passengers 65 and over need medical certificate)

About every 18 days, three ships (*LASH Atlantico, LASH Pacifico* and *LASH Italia*) each carrying crew of 34 from New York, Baltimore,

Charleston, Newport News to Mediterranean. 50 days, $3,000 ($60 day). **Usual itinerary:** Spain, Egypt, Israel, Greece, Turkish ports, Romania.

TTT: Very nice ships; four outside staterooms, individual air conditioning controls, every cabin with refrigerator. Movies shown twice a week, card room, deck chairs, alcoholic beverages sold through Chief Steward, washing machine and dryer.

(LASH is acronym for "L"ighter "A"board "SH"ip).

SCHLUSSEL-REEDEREI
Sea and Land Shipping, Inc.
305 N. Morgan St., Tampa, FL 33602
German flag
Age limit: 65

Three times each month, Tampa to Holland: 15 days one way, $750 ($50 day); containerized. **Usual ports:** Tampa, Rotterdam, Vlissingen

TTT: Large cabins, private shower, lounge, smoking room, small pool; not air conditioned. Good food. Passengers should be aware that ship waits at anchor when dockside space is not available, and this wait can be from a few hours to a few weeks. On return, passengers must disembark at first U.S. port. Owner's suite available for $60 additional charge. Book early for that bargain.

STATES STEAMSHIP CO.

(See Lykes Bros. Shipping Co.)

SURINAM LINE
Hansen & Tidemann, Inc.
442 Canal St., New Orleans, LA 70130
Varied foreign flags
Age limit: 55

Every other week, New Orleans to Caribbean: 28–35 days, $400 one way; $750 roundtrip ($23 day). **Usual ports:** Santo Domingo, Port-au-Prince, Paramaribo.

TTT: Ship may be used as your hotel, except in New Orleans and Paramaribo. Hotel arrangements must be made by passenger. Some ships of this line carry only three or four passengers; one ship carries seven passengers.

UNITED BRANDS CO.
1271 Avenue Of The Americas, New York, NY 10020
Varied foreign flags

(Discontinued carrying passengers)

UNITED YUGOSLAV LINE
Kerr Steamship Co., Inc.
1 California Street, San Francisco, CA 94111
Yugoslav flag
No age limit

Monthly sailings, around the world, 150 days or 4 months, $5,500–5,800 ($38 day). **Usual ports,** around world: Piraeus, Beirut, Trieste, Rijeka, Las Palmas, Palma, Cadiz, Barcelona, Latakia, Istanbul, Salonika, Split, Suez, Bombay, Cochin, Madras, Colombo, Hong Kong, Osaka/Kobe, Nagoya, Yokohama, Pusan, to United States. **Usual ports,** Mediterranean: Piraeus, Beirut, Trieste, Rijeka, Las Palmas, Palma, Cadiz/Barcelona, Latakia, Istanbul, Salonika, Split, Puerto Limon, Puntarenas, Corinto, Acajutla, Champerico, Acapulco.

TTT: Some ships carry only 8 passengers. Boarding at last U.S. port, normally Long Beach, California; disembarking at first U. S. port, normally Seattle, Washington. Since the company does not know exact length of voyage at sailing, it collects full around-the-world fare, and passengers sign statements agreeing to accept refund in the event ship is diverted in Mediterranean to return to the U.S. Pacific Coast. Noncontainerized, so port time is usually five to six days.

TTT: Company sells only full-voyage passage. Due to length of voyage, passengers should have a passport in hand, valid for one year from estimated sailing date. Good cabins, twin beds, private bath with shower, lounge, bar, library, radio. Good food; cooperative captain and crew. No laundry facilities available on board. Passengers eat crew food. No check cashing facilities on board, so bring plenty of cash and travelers' checks.

YUGOSLAV GREAT LAKES LINE
180 South Lake Avenue, Suite 335
Pasadena, CA 91101
Yugoslav flag
Age limit: through 82. (Persons 65 and over must have medical statement)

Seasonal sailings, April through November, from Chicago to Yugoslavia and return. Usually 60 to 70 days with calls at Milwaukee, Erie, Toronto, Montreal, St. Johns, Newfoundland, Casablanca, Valencia, Livorno, Naples, Genoa, Trieste, Koper, Split, Rijeka. **Rates:** $2,800 per person, double occupancy; $3,600 single ($47 day).

TTT: Service is operated by two non-containerized sister ships, each carrying 12 passengers in six double cabins. All cabins have private bathrooms with showers. Ships have lounge areas with a bar; small library is available. All cabins and public rooms are air conditioned. Also, year around sailings from Montreal to Yugoslavia and return with ports of call usually the same as those from Chicago. Roundtrip from 40 to 45 days. **Rates:** $2,800 per person, double occupancy; $3,600 single ($65 day).

TTT: Service also is operated with a semi-containerized ship carrying 12 passengers. Ship was built in 1978. Cabins are spacious and have double beds, private bathrooms with showers. There is a passenger lounge and dining area. Ship also has a swimming pool and a small gymnasium available to the passengers.

TTT: I have had excellent reports on this company and the vessels. Surprisingly enough, space was available in June for December sailings. Best time to book is about 10 months in advance of sailing date.

RASHID SHIPPING COMPANY
One World Trade Center, Suite 2045
New York, NY 10048
Egyptian flag
Age limit: none

Rashid Shipping Company operates four sister ships, *MV Abu Rashid, Abu Hosna, Abu Alia, Abu Yussuf.* They each carry 20 passengers in cabins with bath; 28 passengers in cabins without baths. Regular sailings from U.S. East Coast ports (New Orleans, Savannah, Tampa) to Mediterranean with primary ports in Egypt. **Rates:** 35/45 days one way, $1100 with bath, $950 without bath. Special roundtrip cruise fare, $2300 with bath; $2000 without bath. ($31 day).

TTT: Rashid warns passengers that once they have paid and have received passage tickets, no refunds are possible, for any reason whatsoever. Passengers should buy trip interruption and cancellation insurance. Rashid also has an air-sea arrangement with airlines which enables passengers to sail one way, fly the other at money saving options. The company requires full ticket payment six weeks before sailing. Passengers are required to embark at the last U.S. port at which the vessels call. Should they embark at a prior port, there will be a charge of $20 or $30, depending on whether cabin has a bath. Children under 12 sail at one-half fare. Shore excursions of one day to seven days in Egypt are sold on board the vessel. Early reports on the ship(s) were not totally favorable, but a Rashid spokesperson told me two of the vessels were being refitted for greater passenger comfort and the former Yugoslav crew was being rehired. This should improve food and service on board. Destination served by these ships is very popular and the vessel is well priced at around $40 a day. This is a new company. Ships formerly owned by now defunct Jugolinija-Yugoslav Line.

Other Ships,
Other Ports

In addition to the ships profiled in THE TOTAL TRAVELER BY SHIP, there are hundreds of additional vessels plying waters around the world. Space does not permit in depth profiles of all of them, their specifics, itineraries, etc. The most popular ships sailing from North American ports and those ships with the greatest appeal to North American travelers are listed in the Ship Profile Chapter.

Lesser-known, regionally popular vessels and their unusual itineraries are highlighted in this chapter. These vessels are no less attractive, nor do they offer less to passengers. They are "different" from what we have come to expect from Caribbean cruise ships, and they are developing loyal followings. For example, cruising the Nile is an experience quite easily arranged and forever memorable. Sailing on vessels into channels hard to reach by large ships is an adventure attracting more and more travelers in the mid–1980's. What follows is a sampling of vessels Americans find appealing and some the adventurous traveler will enjoy.

Some of the vessels are listed under the names of companies which own and operate them; others under cruising areas. Information included covers year of construction, itineraries, on board ambience, and rates where available.

AMERICAN CANADIAN LINE
461 Water Street
Warren, RI 02885

In business for about 10 years, American Canadian Line operates vessels along the New England coastline and Canadian inland waterways. Two of the vessels are very popular. The *New Shoreham II* was built in 1979 and sails out of Warren, Rhode Island on three to 12-night cruises that sail into the St. Lawrence and Saguenay rivers. Nassau (Bahamas) is home base during winter months for 12-day cruises to the Bahamas

Out Islands. The *New Shoreham II* carries 62 passengers, is 150 feet long and has three passenger decks.

The 80-passenger *Caribbean Prince* inaugurated service in 1983 and from January through April is based in Montego Bay (Jamaica). Voyages are 12-days and itinerary is interesting. She sails about five hours a day and stops overnight in sheltered coves. Summer months, she sails between Detroit and Owen Sound and cruises Georgian Bay.

Both ships are informal, meal service is family style - American. Not much entertainment and there's no need to dress up. No liquor sold on U.S. inland cruises, so a bottle in the room is suggested. Cabins are small but the Caribbean Prince resembles a yacht with teak trim, twin or double beds in cabins, and a choice of inside or outside staterooms. Great feature is the ramp that goes down when ships pull up at a beach. It allows passengers to walk down the slight incline to get ashore.

Luther Blount owns and operates this family-oriented company.

CHANDRIS, INC.
666 Fifth Avenue
New York, NY 10019

Once one of the largest fleets sailing, Chandris started in 1922 when John Chandris put a 300-ton vessel into service off the coast of Corinth. The company is now operated by his sons Antony and Dimitrios, and their flag flies over a half dozen or so vessels plying the Mediterranean and Caribbean.

Chandris has been successful in buying ships no one else seems to want and turning them into highly profitable operations. In addition to Chandris owned and operated ships, the company owns several operated and/or chartered out to other companies. Fantasy Cruises operates and markets the *Amerikanis, Britanis,* and *Galileo. Chandris operates the Victoria.* (See Ship Profiles Chapter) Other Chandris vessels of interest to North American passengers because of attractive air-sea package offerings are listed. Entertainment and food are Greek-flavored on all Chandris ships. Tipping is pooled at the end of the voyage and distributed to all personnel (service and behind the scenes) by the chief steward.

SS Ariane Built 1951, sailed as *Patricia, Freeport II, Bon Vivant;* refurbished 1974. Tonnage: 6,644; passenger capacity 350; swimming pool, air-conditioned, no stabilizers. Sails on Mondays and Fridays on 3 and 4-day cruises from Piraeus to Hydra, Santorini, and other Greek islands.

SS Ellinis Built 1932; was first *Lurline* for Matson Lines; sister ship of *Monterey* and *Mariposa;* major construction and refurbishing in 1963 included new cabins and extra berths in some of the very large rooms. Sails from Genoa on 14-day cruises to Alexandria, Haifa, and Greek ports. Tonnage: 24,000; passenger capacity, 1,100; 9 decks. Some cabins are four-berth; some cabins extremely small and without facilities. Average cabin is very large.

Patris Built 1950 as *Bloemfontein Castle;* refurbished 1974. Tonnage: 16,259; passenger capacity 1,000. Air-conditioned, swimming pool.

Regina Magna Built 1939 as *Pasteur,* sailed as *Bremen;* Tonnage: 23,801; passenger capacity 1,200; stabilized, air conditioned, refurbished, 2 swimming pools.

Regina Prima Built 1939 as *President Hoover,* sailed as *Panama* and *Regina,* purchased by Chandris Group 1965; Tonnage: 10,603; passenger capacity 600. Air-conditioned, swimming pool.

Romanza Built 1939 as *Haucaran,* sailed as *Baeverbrae* and *Aurelia,* pur chased by Chandris in 1970. Tonnage: 8,890; passenger capacity 470. Air-conditioned, swimming pool, theater.

Romantica Built 1936 as *Fort Townshend,* sailed as *El Amir Saud* and *Mansour;* refurbished, 1960; passenger capacity 200. Originally built for Furness Red Cross Line and was the king of Saudi Arabia's per sonal yacht. Air-conditioned, swimming pool.

COASTWISE CRUISE LINE
336 Ocean Street
Hyannis, MA 02601

The name is different, but the company is well known to New Englanders as the Hy-Line. Under the official name of Hyannis Harbor Tours, the company owns 14 small vessels that operate out of New England ports to Florida and has been in business since 1962. Summer itineraries include cruises to Cape Code.

Coastwise Cruise Line's most recent addition to the fleet is the *Pilgrim Belle,* a new 110-passenger steamer which entered service in 1984. It is a mere 95 gross tons, 192 feet in length, 40 feet wide and has one passenger elevator. There is no swimming pool but there are four public lounges and three bars. Special dietary arrangements are possible with three weeks advance notice and there is local entertainment which boards at ports of call.

A single dining room seats all passengers in family-style atmosphere and service. Very informal, there's no need to bring dressy clothing. Cabins are good sized and are all outside which makes for better viewing. There are 10 cabins where beds can be moved together, 4 queen size beds and a single king size in the single suite. Two cabins for singles without a surcharge. Average daily rate is $170 which puts the *Pilgrim Belle* into the "Moderate" price category. Rates go to $187 average in late 1985. Recommended tips total $5 per person, per day.

Decor is in the style of the 1920's and is steamer-type travel in a way that reminds one of that era in riverboat travel. Winter cruises between Alexandria, Virginia and Savannah, Georgia; also between West Palm Beach and Fernandina Beach in Florida.

DELTA QUEEN STEAMBOAT COMPANY
511 Main Street
Cincinnati, OH 45202

In any discussion of ships, the *Delta Queen* and her younger sister, the *Mississippi Queen,* must be included. The romance of Mississippi River cruising was kept alive a few years ago by nostalgic riverboat enthusiasts. The movement was spearheaded by an exceptional woman, Betty Blake, who went on to become president of the company. A personal friend, she died a couple of years ago content in knowing she will always be remembered for her successful efforts to keep traditions of riverboating on the Mississippi alive for future generations. She'll also be remembered for many other things, like her warmth and addiction to ships.

The Cincinnati based Delta Queen Steamboat Co. operates the two vessels. The company is now publicly owned and traces its roots in river history back to 1890 when the Gordon C. Greene Co. was founded to operate packet steamers on the Ohio and Mississippi Rivers.

DELTA QUEEN: She's a venerable 56 year old, first operated on overnight trips between Sacramento and San Francisco. After serving as a U.S. Navy Yard Ferry Boat on San Francisco Bay during WW II, she was auctioned to Tom Greene, then president of the Greene family company. Captain Greene had her towed across 5,000 miles of open sea to New Orleans, then sailed her under her own power to Pittsburgh, where she was remodeled and outfitted for passenger service.

On June 30, 1948, she made her maiden voyage on the Mississippi River system on a round trip between Cincinnati and Cairo, Illinois.

To save the *Delta Queen,* Congress passed six exemptions that protect her through 1988. The Delta Queen is considered an authentic, fully-restored masterpiece and was entered in the National Register of Historic Places in June, 1970.

MISSISSIPPI QUEEN: When new safety requirements made the *Delta Queen*'s future uncertain, company management decided to build a paddlewheeler which would meet all new construction requirements. She would be the largest, most spectacular riverboat ever. The massive undertaking commissioned James Gardner (designer of the *QE 2*) to create the exterior; and internationally known Welton-Beckett for the interiors. She was built in Jeffersonville, Indiana, where about 5,000 steamboats were constructed in the 19th century.

The *Mississippi Queen* inaugurated service on July 25, 1976 from Cincinnati. Her final cost was $27 million. She offers her guests the ultimate in luxury and comfort while keeping close touch with traditions created by her ancestors. Mouldings, mirrors, polished steel and brass, plush carpeting throughout, recall the opulence of great steamboats of the past.

TTT: Both riverboats accommodate 500 passengers in 218 cabins and 12 suites. American crews throughout. Cruise lengths vary and port-to-port bookings are available. They are the only overnight passenger sternwheel steamboats in America and maintain a Dixieland atmosphere in music and entertainments. Itineraries are strictly U.S.A. You sail the Natchez-Vicksburg route or explore the upper Mississippi and Ohio Rivers. Rates average about $170 per day, per person, with special rates for children (about $50 per night). Food is excellent. Service outstanding!

EPIROTIKI LINES
551 Fifth Avenue
New York, NY 10017

The development of increasingly popular Greek Island cruising parallels the growth of Epirotiki Lines. The family-owned company created and pioneered many aspects of Greek Island cruises.

The history of Epirotiki goes back more than a century to the days when the company operated sailing vessels transporting goods and a few passengers between the northern coast of Africa to the Greek mainland. Prime cruise development and involvement dates from 1954.

Until that time, there were no regularly scheduled sea jaunts in the Aegean. Only an occasional millionaire aboard a private yacht was able to experience the pleasures of cruising to the idyllic Greek isles. The islands were always there, but not the ships or the itineraries that allowed for such cruises. Epirotiki operated one special sailing to the islands in the late 1930s. It was the forerunner of present day Greek Island cruising. At the time, the company was primarily concerned with seven small vessels operating an inter-island ferry service.

In 1954, the small liner *Semiramis* was diverted from her usual ferry run and initiated service between Greek Islands. It was the first regularly scheduled Greek Island cruise. Today more than 150,000 people sail the route annually and Epirotiki's main efforts are in this type of cruising. In recent years, as many as 50 percent of the travelers taking these cruises sailed Epirotiki ships.

Epirotiki operates and owns about a dozen ships specializing in the Mediterranean and Greek Islands. Rates are modest on all of their ships and average $85 to $140 per person, per day. All fly Greek flags, carry Greek crews.

Apollo XI—Oldest in the fleet, built originally as the *Oublof* in 1948, renamed Irish Coast; rebuilt as *Apollo XI* in 1970. She's 5,500 tons, carries 300 passengers and a crew of 139; 114 of the cabins are connecting.

Atlas—the largest in the fleet, was built in 1951 and sailed originally as the *Ryndam,* then the *Waterman.* She was purchased by Epirotiki in 1973. She's 16,000 tons, accommodates 700 passengers, has cabins that convert to sitting rooms by day; has all cruise ship amenities with 2 outdoor swimming pools, etc. Rebuilt in 1973, she sails on 7-day cruises from Piraeus to Greek Islands, Israel and Greece spring through November months.

Jason—Built in 1965 as *Ainos,* then sailed as the *Eros* and was chartered to an Arab sheik in 1976 for a few sailings. In addition to Greek Island cruising summer months, she sails winter months between San Juan and Manaus (Brazil) on 12-day Amazon cruises. She's 5,250 tons, has 6 decks, a passenger capacity of 298, good public space, swimming pool.

Jupiter—Built in 1970, she's 9,000 tons, has 7 decks, can accommodate 471 passengers, has a theater, swimming pool, large dining room, good public space. Sails on 3 and 4-day Greek Island cruises.

World Renaissance—(See Ship profile Chapter)

Also in the fleet—The *Orpheus,* a 6,000 tonner built in 1948; the *Neptune,* built in 1955 as the *Meteor.*

TTT: All Epirotiki ships were rebuilt, refurbished and/or redecorated before being put into service. Although ships are small, they travel the calm Mediterranean well and are able to dock in all ports they visit. Greek food specialties; most passengers are European.

EXPLORATION CRUISE LINES
1500 Metropolitan Park Bldg.
Seattle, WA 98101

Exploration Cruise Lines is a unique kind of cruise company, quite different from its much larger counterparts. Vessels are smaller and have been designed specifically to cruise special areas of the world. On most cruises, the ship is almost the total experience with ports of call a secondary consideration.

The ships: Small by oceanliner standards, but their size assures access to unusual places and allows for unusual experiences. Ships are new, meet or exceed all U.S. Coast Guard standards. Shallow-draft design allows for close-up cruising. Vessels have bow thrusters for maneuverability, steel hulls that allow for cruising in ice and up close to glaciers, bow landings for disembarkation at remote attractions. Ships carry inflatable rubber boats to use in launch service and to allow shore stops wherever appropriate. Ships are fully air conditioned and are equipped with the latest navigational and communications systems.

m/v Pacific Northwest Explorer
Gross tonnage: 97.03; length: 143 feet; beam: 28 feet; draft: 7 ½ feet; Registry: U.S.A.; Passenger capacity: 80; crew: 20; Deluxe cabins with double beds and seating areas; other cabins are twin-bedded; dining room; bar, 4 passenger deck.

m/v Majestic Alaska Explorer
Tonnage: 99.7; length: 152 feet; Beam: 31 feet; draft: 8 feet; Registry: U.S.A.; capacity: 88 passengers, 22 crew; same type of cabins as Pacific Northwest Explorer.

m/v Great Rivers Explorer
Tonnage and other specifics same as Majestic Explorer.
Itineraries: Because the vessels are American built and fly the U.S. flag, cruises may originate in any United States port. Explorer ships depart from Ketchikan for 7-night cruises to Alaska during summer months; from Portland through the dams and locks of Columbia River

and Snake River; from San Francisco on three 2-night cruises to Sacramento and San Joaquin Rivers; special cruising for three to seven nights in the wake of Captain Cook between Tahiti and Bora Bora; and Panama Canal cruising for four or five nights visiting the San Blas Islands, Colon, Taboga, Contadora, and other inlets and outlets of the Canal region. Rates vary with cruise itineraries, but average is somewhere between $170 and $195 per day, per person.

HELLENIC MEDITERRANEAN LINES
200 Park Avenue
New York, NY 10017

Hellenic Mediterranean Lines (HML) was formed in 1939 to handle passengers cruising and traveling between the Greek islands. The company is probably partially responsible for starting the first real passenger and car ferry service between Italy and Greece. The service was so successful that the company built two more ships specifically for this run. In 1971, they ordered construction of the Aquarius. All HML ships fly Greek flags and are manned by Greek crews.

T.S.S. Apollonia: Inter-port service Venice, Piraeus, Rhodes, Limassol, and Haifa. Passenger and car ferry; low-cost transportation from Venice to Haifa via Greece. Private cabin facilities; Pullman berths and aircraft seating also available. Space for 60 cars. Built in 1949. Tonnage: 5,300; 420 feet long; 53-foot beam. Carries 619 passengers; 150 crew. No elevators; air conditioned public rooms; no stabilizers. Rates run from $80 to $700, depending on length of journey and termination point. Ship has a self service restaurant, but meals are included in price of passage.

M.S. Aquarius: Spring and summer in the Aegean; Built in 1972. Tonnage: 4,800; 340 feet long; 45-foot beam. Carries 290 passengers; 135 crew. Swimming pool; 1 elevator; air conditioned; 7 decks; lounges. Greek specialties. Rates typical one-week cruise Greek Islands and Turkey from $795 to $1,210

M.S. Castalia: Daily passenger and car ferry service between Patras and Brindisi with stopover privileges in Corfu. Meals and port taxes are not included in passenger rate. Cruise length is one day between ports. Built in 1975. Tonnage: 9,000; 442 feet long; 72-foot beam; 2 elevators; 7 decks; air conditioned; stabilizers; public rooms; private cabins with facilities and deck space. Rates run about $150 per person for an outside cabin.

TTT: Suggested tipping: Five percent of the cost of the voyage given to the chief steward at the end of the passage. He distributes the money collected among the entire crew.

HERITAGE CRUISES
134 East 71 Street
New York, NY 10021

The company was organized to operate and market to the public the magnificent *Sea Cloud,* the sailing yacht formerly owned by socialite Marjorie Merriweather Post. The four-masted vessel was refurbished, refitted and introduced to Caribbean cruisers interested in sampling the good life. The Sea Cloud met with instant success. Vessel was originally built in 1931 as the *Hussar V. Angelina* but gained fame when Mrs. Post purchased her in the 1940s and put her into a class by herself. She is 2,223 tons, 316 feet long and has a beam of 49 feet. Registered in Grand Cayman she accommodates 86 passengers in 41 oversized cabins and two suites, all outside. There are no elevators or swimming pools but there is a club-like lounge with piano music. Entertainment is limited but the ship experience experience satisfies most passengers. What brings luxury class travelers on board is the ship's history. She's a beautiful legendary tall ship. Cruising aboard the *Sea Cloud* while under sail is a breathtaking experience and every passenger feels like the owner of the yacht. It's a chance to live for a short time in a bygone era of luxury. Average daily rate is $420 per person and tipping is recommended at $7 per day. The *Sea Cloud* sails in the Caribbean winter months; Mediterranean summer months. It's a fantasy-like experience; one to be remembered always.

Heritage Cruises added the cruise-yacht *World Discoverer* to its two fleet in 1974 and was completely rebuilt and redesigned into contemporary ship with a few Oriental-design touches. She is registered in Singapore and accommodates 140 passengers and 75 crew. The *World Discoverer* is 3,153 tons, 285 feet long and has a beam of almost 50 feet. She is fully stabilized, has individual cabin climate controls, one passenger elevator and swimming pool; barber/beauty shop, a single restaurant in which all passengers are accommodated in a single seating. Ship offers cruise ship-style entertainment and a small casino. Average daily rate will run a little over $300 per day, per person and that puts her in the "luxury" category. The *World Discoverer* inaugurated service in November 1984 with a 21-day Singapore to Fiji cruise. Regular 12-day winter program calls for sailings between Fiji and Tahiti winter months and spring and summer 11-day China cruises which include a three day stay in Beijing; and fall 12-day Japan cruises. Air-sea-land packages from major gateways are available.

K-LINES HELLENIC CRUISES
645 Fifth Avenue
New York, NY 10022

Philippos Kavounides founded K-Lines in 1910 with a single vessel which grew to five by 1914. Three were lost in World War I and were replaced only to be again destroyed in the Second World War. Today's fleet is again five vessels. The 12,500-ton *Constellation* is considered the flagship and sails twice weekly from Piraeus on short cruises to the Greek Islands. Others in the fleet are the 6,200-ton *Orion,* the 5,500-ton *Galaxy* and the smaller *Kentavros* and *Atlantis.* One week sailings include calls in Greece, Israel, Turkey, Egypt and Cyprus and I'm still trying to figure out how they manage that itinerary. It reminds me of "If it's Tuesday, it's got to be Belgium" but travelers who have little time say it's a great cruise.

LINDBLAD TRAVEL
1 Sylvan Road North
Westport, CT 06881

Lindblad isn't a cruise company, and yet it is probably much more. The World of Lindblad Travel has grown in just over 20 years to include adventures at all corners of the earth, from the warmth of the Equator to the chill of the Antarctic. It encompasses mysterious continents, little known islands, faraway kingdoms and remote nations, offering exciting, unusual and exotic tours. Many of them involve ships and cruising. With its *M.S. Lindblad Explorer,* the company developed a cruising expedition concept which added the dimension of exploration and adventure to the pure enjoyment of cruising. The *Lindblad Explorer* made wakes where other vessels feared to sail. She sailed through the Atlantic to the South Pole in 1969 and became a familiar sight in many exotic areas of the world.

In 1985, the company is offering adventures on five other vessels. On the Nile, Lindblad has its own riverboat. The 2,214 ton *Lindblad Polaris* is making explorer history with its West African safari cruises from Madeira. With a total passenger capacity of 76, the vessel is top quality in dining, ambience and experiences. Swedish crew, entertainment is highlighted by lectures, briefings and films. Average daily rate of $280 includes all shore excursions.

Lindblad's China program is receiving industry-wide attention this year. The 2,300 ton *M.S. Kun Lun* was built in 1962 and refurbished in 1984. Crew is Chinese and the experience begins on embarkation. Flights are from San Francisco to Hong Kong with boarding one week later in Guilin. Ten days of cruising the Yangtse with debarkation for five nights before the return flight to San Francisco. All shore excursions are included in the average daily rate of $215.

The 960-ton *m.s. Goddess* is priced higher at $175 a day per person and offers a few more amenities and a similar but shorter (7 nights) itinerary. *Goddess* accommodates only 60 passengers in 30 cabins. Vessel was built in 1981 specifically for this type of river cruising. The *m.v. Yao Hua* is also on similar service. She's the largest at 10,050 tons. She's stabilized, has a swimming pool, other amenities. Built in 1967, she was refurbished in 1982. In March 1985, the 90-passenger, 1,400-ton *Bashan* joins the Lindblad fleet of ships registered in the People's Republic of China. in March 1985.

Lindblad cruises are for special people who seek adventure along with creature comforts. American-style food may be ordered, all passengers eat at a single seating, all shore excursions are included in the cruise fare and there is no tipping.

TTT: Bring credit cards and cash. No travelers checks accepted for payment on board Lindblad ships operating in China..

POLISH OCEAN LINES
McLean Kennedy, Inc.
410 St. Nicholas Street
Montreal, Quebec H2Y 2P5

The Poles remain in the cruise business with their pride and joy, the *Stefan Batory*. The company is actually an old established shipping firm, formerly known as Gdynia America Line. Their 15,204-ton ship (ex Holland America's *Maasdam*) makes more transatlantic sailings than any other vessel. She also offers the cheapest crossing by sea. The *Stefan Batory* sails April through November from Montreal to Gdynia, Poland with stops at Southampton and Rotterdam. Average daily rate runs under $100 per, with minimums around $75. The *Stefan Batory* was built in 1954 and purchased from Holland America by the Polish Government in 1968. She was refitted. Most cabins do not have private facilities, so passengers should be careful booking if having to trot down the hall to a shower, etc. isn't your style of travel. She carries about 775 passengers, has two dining rooms and still has two passenger classes (first and tourist). Air conditioned and stabilized, the *Stefan Batory* is economy travel. Economy minded, budget-watching travelers report that she is a find and well worth every penny. The vessel is equipped to carry cars and pets transatlantic. She's a good riding ship, has a swimming pool and 16 public rooms.

SALEN LINDBLAD CRUISING
133 East 55 Street
New York, NY 10022

This company has no connection with Lindblad Travel or its vessels but it does market specific sailings. It has 40-some departures in 1985 and will probably have more in 1986. Most interesting is a series of six Russian river cruises aboard Soviet vessels. Also, the 11-day cruises on the Thames aboard the *Benson Bounty I,* a private cruiser that sleeps six people, provided they are child-size.

SOCIETY EXPEDITIONS CRUISES
723 Broadway East
Seattle, WA 98102

Similar in style to Lindblad cruises, Society Expeditions was founded to organize archaeological tours for special interest groups. The company has expanded beyond that purpose but still keeps all itineraries as adventures. Vessels are small enough to maneuver in shallow waters so passengers can explore remote areas of the world. The company built a fine reputation when it had the *World Discoverer* under charter. The company purchased the *Lindblad Explorer* in 1984 and will rename her the *Society Explorer* when she inaugurates ervice in mid–1985 after a $5 million refurbishing. She has 65 cabins and five suites and will cruise the Antarctica in January, the Chilean fjords in February, the Pacific in March, Indonesia in April and the Amazon River in October.

Society Expeditions has smaller vessels in other parts of the world. The *Isabela* in the Galapagos; the *Rev Vacances* in Egypt, and the *Duc de Bourgogne* barge cruises in France.

SUNDANCE CRUISES
520 Pike Street
Seattle, WA 98100

The man who started Princess Cruises, Stanley B. McDonald founded Sundance Cruises in 1984 with high hopes and a single vessel, the *Sundancer*. Unfortunately, the vessel went aground after just a couple of Alaska Cruises and was declared a total loss.

The good news is the company has found a replacement, an even larger ship and expects to be in operation by mid–1985. Sundance will retain its original schedule of sailings with "affordable rates" to Alaska and Mexico from Vancouver and Southern California. No details about the ship were available at press time other than "she will be the first in a planned fleet of three vessels" on the same kind of itineraries.

WINDJAMMER BAREFOOT CRUISES
824 S. Miami Avenue
Miami, FL 33129

This company was organized in 1947 by Captain Mike Burke, and he says "they keep alive the tradition of great sailing ships." The cruises are called "barefoot adventures." I'm told shipmates need not lend a hand, but most folks end up assisting with handling the masts. Burke buys his sailing ships from the likes of Onassis, Vanderbilt, Guinness, the Duke of Westminster, and Krupp. Sailing cruises are not for everyone. They appeal to youngish travelers looking for "barefoot" informality, a spirit of adventure, and a cruise with absolutely no regimentation. Flagship is the *Fantome*, a 282-foot barkentine originally built for the Duke of Westminster as a private floating palace. Purchased by Onassis as a wedding gift to Prince Rainer and Princess Grace, it was somehow never delivered. Tonnage: 3,000; 282 feet long; 40-foot beam. She accommodates 126 in cabins with private baths. Home port is Nassau, and she sails the second and fourth Tuesdays every month. Others in the fleet are the *Flying Cloud* (1,200 tons) positioned in British Virgin Islands; *Polynesia* (1,400 tons) positioned in St. Maarten; and the *Yankee Clipper* (800 tons) positioned in the West Indies. Incidentally, the *Yankee Clipper* was acquired from the Vanderbilt estate and had been used extensively on scientific explorations and long voyages. Originally built by the German industrialist Alfred Krupp as his personal yacht, she was confiscated by the United States as a war prize. Windjammer Cruises attract young singles. Rates run from $450 to

$800 per person. If you sailed with Windjammer before, you can take advantage of a schedule of reduced rates. Because these sailing vessels have a shallow draft, they call at small, unusual islands throughout the Caribbean.

BARGE CRUISING

This is a special form of water travel. The peaceful rivers and canals of Europe meander lazily through quiet countrysides, through tiny villages not even mentioned in guide books, past open air markets, picturesque bridges and lush green landscapes crowned with ancient chateaux. Not too many years ago, these same rivers bustled with cargo-carrying barges. Now they offer relaxation combined with attractive scenery, history, and a look at life off-the-beaten-path, sightseeing and gracious living.

Traveling on what is being described as "hotel barges" is not for everyone. It is not for anyone who is seeking excitement and the hustle, bustle, and glamour of a trip abroad. It is enjoyed by travelers who want to to relax in an informal atmosphere without structured sightseeing. Facilities on barges run the gamut from sparce to almost luxurious; from small to good sized suites. On board, you'll be served excellent food without the wide choices normally associated with cruise ships. Wine will be "on the house." Your fellow travelers will be looking for the same kind of ambience. Excitement will be a leisurely walk through a small town or village after sunset, a bicycle ride through a country path in the early morning hours, time to read, sun bathe, or just dream. One traveler described it as his time for the "soul to stretch" as the world slowly passes at about four miles an hour.

Barges cruise during summer months in England's canals and rivers which provide a wealth of charming old pubs and inns and where the air is filled with spontaneous good cheer. Colorful barges in these waters are decorated in the style they call "roses-and-castles". Holland offers more than 3400 miles of canals through areas that inspired Vermeer, Rembrandt, and Frans Hals during Holland's Golden Age. La belle France has rivers that have always been vital transport links and many of Europe's finest sights line the banks.

Barges are miniature floating hotels with a feeling of private homes, which indeed they are. Most are run by husband-wife teams and they treat passengers as though they were guests in their own homes. Boats are fitted with fine china, crystal, antiques, and a spirit of warm camaraderie.

SOME MAJOR COMPANIES *AND THEIR BARGES*

CONTINENTAL WATER WAYS

A London based company, Continental Waterways offers barge cruises through canals and waterway of France seldom seen by the visitor. 'Cruise" could be a misnomer. Floating is more like it. Barges range from small to smaller and boats are no more than seven feet wide. It takes an expert to handle them around bends and curves. Dining on board is simple and very French. Free wines with meals; frequent stops at picturesque villages allow for leisurely strolls through non-touristy France. There are lounges and dining rooms on every barge. Some accommodate passengers in 11 cabins, others in three. There are about a half dozen barges in the fleet and routes vary. Some begin in Paris, others in outlying ports depending on whether your barge will sail the Canal du Midi, Canal Lataral, Brittany, the River Marne. The company also offers barge cruises along England's Thames with a new 16-passenger boat, the *Patience.* Unlike the other barges in the fleet, the *Patience* has private facilities. Barge trips are for travelers seeking the unusual which could lead to lots of togetherness. Barge cruising has caught on, so to speak, and Continental Waterways has opened U.S. offices to service demand. Barges operate April through October. Stateside Continental Waterways' offices are at 11 Beacon Street, Boston, Massachusetts 02108.

FLOATING THROUGH EUROPE

Floating through Europe began operations in 1975 and has grown to a fleet of six barges. The boats carry as many as 24 and as few as six. Cabins are nice, small and all have private facilities. Other amenities are dining rooms, fine meals and champagne party atmosphere. Facilities are tailored to American travelers and most passengers are from the U.S. and Canada. The company also represents a number of self-drive boats in France, England and Holland. Length of trips range from one dayers to six-day canal cruises in areas like Toulouse to Carcassone to Sete on the Canal du Midi and Canal Lateral a la Garonne; also along the Canal de Bourgogne, the River Saone, River Yonne and between Sens and Tonnerre. In England a favorite is cruising the River Avon. In Holland, it's a cruise from Amsterdam to places like Delft, Gouda and Leiden. Most barges are fairly new. All are developing loyal followings. U. S. Floating Through Europe offices are at 271 Madison Avenue, New York, New York 10016.

HORIZON CRUISES

Considered the most luxurious barges operating in Europe, Horizon Cruises is based in Belleville, Illinois, undoubtedly because it was founded and is owned by a midwesterner smitten by barge cruising. Flag-boat of the fleet is the *Nenuphar* (English translation — water lily). It is well appointed and decorated with French antiques. It has seven cabins, is 126 feet by 17 feet and was converted in 1978. She has a couple of suites and seven cabins, all with nice, private facilities. She sails on one week cruises from Paris. Others are the *Horizon* — built originally in 1908 and completely refitted in 1975. She has seven cabins without facilities and sails with a crew of six from Paris. The *Dehoop* — built in 1906 for cruising the Zuider Zee, also converted in 1971, she is 65 feet long, 13 feet wide and has accommodations for six or seven passengers. Most sail from Paris on one week cruises. The company also operates some u-drive-them boats which rent for about $1,000 a week and accommodate up to eight people. Horizon Cruises is located at 215 North 75th Street, Belleville, Illinois 62223.

SHIPS OF THE NILE

From a feluca to a 185-passenger vessel — that's the choice in river navigable craft available to travelers interested in exploring the Nile, Egypt's only water source. With increase in demand for space on Nile river boats, a number of companies have entered the market. On a recent visit, I inspected a reconditioned paddlewheeler that could well have been the setting for Agatha Christie's "Death on the Nile." It was luxurious (by Egyptian standards) had a promenade area around cabins, a nice lounge and accommodated fewer than 40 passengers. Cruises ranged from three to six days. I also visited the Club Mediterrane boat and half dozen others. I sailed on Sheraton's *Aton* for 10 days, and I recommend a shorter cruise for travelers who are not Egyptologists. The two major companies operating river/resort/boats on the Nile are Sheraton and Hilton. They are geared to Americans comfort.

SHERATON NILE CRUISES

Operated by Sheraton Hotels in Egypt, the fleet consists of four identical boats that ply the Luxor-Aswan-Luxor route almost all year around. Because of lessened demand during summer months, the vessels are frequently chartered out to American and European tour operators who sell longer itineraries. The *Anni, Aton, Htop* and *Tut* each have 89 twin-bedded cabins, are 235 feet long, and have small cabins with private facilities. Boats are air conditioned, have dining rooms and lounges that double as discos at night, cocktail lounge and gathering place. There's a small swimming pool, a sun deck and two meal seatings. Breakfast and dinner are buffet style, lunch is a pre-fixed menu with no choices and is served. Shore excursions are included in the price which runs around $100 per person, per day. There is no live entertainment; in fact, no entertainment at all. See **TTT** Nile Cruising.

HILTON INTERNATIONAL

Hilton vessels in the Nile are the *Isis* and *Osiris.* They sail between Aswan and Luxor, Luxor and Aswan on four night/five day cruises year around, except for special charters. Both accommodate 124 passengers in twin-bedded cabins with private facilities. They are comfortable, and considered luxurious by Egyptian Nile standards. They are air conditioned and all cabins are small outside allowing for unobstructed views of the Nile, which is after all the reason for being here. Itinerary is exactly like Sheraton itineraries and itineraries of other Nile boats. Cruises can be purchased through travel agents in the U.S. and Canada, or as part of a package tour of Egypt. It is also possible to book last minute in Cairo. Shore excursions included in price of cruise which runs about $100 per day, per person.

TTT: Sheraton and Hilton Nile riverboats are very similar. Shore excursion price is part of the total price. Cabins are very small. Best time to cruise is when the weather cools off (late October through March, maybe early April). Food is mediocre. Ships are not spic-and-spotless, but are o.k. for up to five days on board. It is not uncommon for travelers on the Nile to suffer stomach upsets, so several notes of caution should be sounded. Come prepared with anti-diarrhea medication. The ship nurse is quick with injections ($8 charge) and it worked for most of my fellow passengers. Do not drink the water offered on board ship. That includes water in the dining room and in cabins. Ship lounge is happy to sell large sealed bottles of mineral water for $1.80 per. We discovered the same brand and size bottles sold at stands right down the gangplank at all stops along the Nile. Price on shore was equivalent to 50 U.S. cents. Consumption of fluids is a must in this hot, dry climate and we were drinking about 10 glasses of water a day, so it added up. In lounges, drink local beer. It is good, thirst quenching and a lot cheaper than other alcoholic beverages. If you are a fussy eater, food could be a problem. Morning eggs were of the powdered variety.

Noon meal offered no choice and it was usually lamb. Dinner was always the same. A buffet with rice, a noodle dish and mixed up lamb, sometimes other meats (but rarely). Desserts were pretty good. All this aside, the antiquities of Luxur, Abu Simbel, Aswan made up for inconveniences on the boat. My favorite in every port, after the monuments and tombs, was a leisurely horse and carriage ride through local markets.

CRUISING THE RHINE

Few rivers of the world claim, or deserve, as important a role in growth of a nation as does the Rhine. It has influenced the course of history, legend and wealth, even the art, of Germany and neighboring countries. Along its banks is a parade, a capsulized version of the past, present and future of Western Europe. Small wonder it attracts travelers who find the Rhine a destination within itself. The romance of the Rhine, is enhanced by tales of the likes of Lorelei and legends of warriors and castles. The Rhine entices travelers searching for alternative methods of sightseeing in Europe.

The Rhine begins in Switzerland as a trickling mountain stream and eventually passes through the Netherlands on its way to the sea. Most of its 850 miles stretch and snake through mountains and plains of West Germany. For more than 2,000 years, it was the main route of trade. Even before that, it was a well established route for cultural pursuits. Cathedrals, castles, modern industrialized cities and sleepy little towns stretch along its banks.

The most scenic route of the Rhine Valley runs from Mainz to Koblenz, the area where Lorelei supposedly lured men to their doom. The course of the Rhine also takes in the area near Bonn where Siegfried slew the dragon, and the Worms areas where Brunhilde plotted against the dragon slayer.

A wide range of boat ride possibilities is offered, from one-day outings on the Rhine to cruises from Rotterdam through Germany to Switzerland. KD Rhine Lines is the best known company in the field. It has been in the business of operating passenger carrying boats on the Rhine for more than 150 years.

Exploring the Rhine on a peaceful and fascinating cruise is an unforgettable experience. The scenery drifts slowly by and from early morning to late evening, there is a constant succession of new and unknown things to see. Travel is at a leisurely pace from city-to-city, from place-to-place. Ships make a number of stops en route, and there's plenty of time for sightseeing. Food is excellent, accommodations comfortable but not all come with private facilities. Itineraries vary with embarkation in Rotterdam, Amsterdam, Strasbourg, Basle. Length of cruises is from four-day four-country (Switzerland, France, Germany, and Holland), to seven-day special theme cruises.

The *MS Deutschland* and *MS Brittania* each accommodate 210 passengers in 105 twin-bedded, outside cabins, all with private facilities. The *MS France* accommodates 204 passengers in 102 outside cabins, but some do not have private facilities. The *MS Nederland* has accommodations for 192, and again some do not have private facilities. On the *MS Helvetia* and *MS Europa* a few cabins have facilities, but on the *MS Austria* and *MS Italia,* each of the 96 cabins has private facilities (shower, wash basin and toilet). Vessels are fully air conditioned, have dining rooms, bars, observation lounges and other amenities. The *Europa* and *Helvetia* are not air conditioned but windows open and there are lots of fans. The company calls them "fresh air ventilated."

Rates run from $130 per day to $85, depending on the boat. Travel agents are familiar with KD Rhine Line and have information. Otherwise, KD Rhine's U.S. addresses are: 170 Hamilton Avenue, White Plains, New York 10601; and 323 Geary Street, San Francisco, California 94102. Shore excursions are not included in the price.

Port Taxes

Most cruise line fares do not include departure or arrival taxes charged by the various ports. In some parts of the world, the charge is called "wharfage," but some steamship lines publish it as "port taxes."

Take Boston, for instance. The city does not have a port tax per se. What it charges is a wharfage fee for the use of the pier. Cruise lines last year were quoting the Boston "port tax" at $3.50, which doesn't really mean the passenger was being over-charged by any means, since the $3.50 is the exact total of the $1.75 fee paid by a visiting ship for each passenger entering the port and for each one leaving it.

New York confuses the situation even more. Here port taxes are based on whether the passenger is first class or tourist class, and the length of the cruise determines the charge.

When it comes time for final payment, some passengers are surprised to find $15 to $50 in port taxes tacked on to the price of the cruise.

Total port charges assessed on each voyage should appear in brochures on the same page with cruise rates. If it sounds too high, request a breakdown of port fees. But, it's like fighting City Hall. Whatever amount is quoted, it probably will breakdown to what is being charged for both port taxes and wharfage.

TTT: Most ports charge half the normal tax for children; some ports do not charge anything for children under 12. These taxes vary depending on whether the ship is delivering cargo and passengers to the port.

Fly and Cruise
Air-Sea and
Other Bargains

In the early 1960's, airlines and ship lines were engaged in a fierce marketing battle for passengers traveling the Atlantic, the Pacific, the Caribbean, and the rest of the world. Few knowledgeable industry leaders were betting on the shipping business during those days when wide-bodied Boeing 747s became the way to go transatlantic. Travel in these marvels of the air lanes was fast, more comfortable than on narrow-bodied planes, and international barriers came crumbling down.

The shipping industry suffered what could have been a mortal defeat. But, ever resilient, loss of that important battle didn't mean total defeat in an era that was to become known as the Great Transportation War. Old time shipping interests banked on cyclical trends that reflected how easily the fickle traveler is influenced by world conditions, inflation, and unstable or unfriendly governments. They counted on changing lifestyles and they were right.

During the past dozen years, economic realities teamed air and sea competitors in ways are making old-time cruising possible for new generations of travelers. With promotional packages combining air and sea at competitive package prices offering substantial savings for passengers, every inland American city has become as close to a port of embarkation as his local airport.

The formula was simple. Airlines had extra seats and ships had berths to fill. There was no population base in any port area (including New York City) that could fill the growing number of ships. So, cruise lines purchased air seats in bulk at group rates, and resold them at much less than the traveler would have to pay in the open market. In every case, the cruise line subsidized a hefty portion of the air fare. In the beginning, it was a buyer's market, and the number of offerings became mind-boggling and confusing. As berths filled, subsidies by cruise lines decreased and passengers, in some cases, paid a greater share of flight costs.

In 1983, the cyclical world of sea travel again shifted. New tonnage began making wakes faster than cruise lines could sell berths. A sluggish economy and a strong dollar that lured Americans to Europe contributed to a continuation of intense competition for passengers. As a result, fly and cruise offerings in 1985 are more attractive and far reaching than ever before in the history of sea and air travel.

Instead of just subsidizing a portion of the money it takes to bring cruise passengers to ships, many of the companies decided in 1982 to include the roundtrip air flight in the price of the cruise and, "free air" was born. With prices already announced for 1982, passengers alert to bargains cruised and flew at remarkable savings.

Response to fly-free offers was understandably great and many cruise lines in 1985–1986 no longer consider free flights as a marketing tool, but as an accepted ingredient of the total cruise package. However, they all keep their option open and expect to return to add-on rates for flights when demand catches up with berth supply. New brochures are printed every year and prices historically increase every year, so passengers flying free (or almost free) will be paying more for the total package than they did in 1982 for the total package, but a lot less than they are paying for comparable land resort packages. Cruise and fly package rates in 1985 reflect only about a five percent increase over 1984 and in some cases show substantial decreases because of special "sales" and "bargain" offers.

One of my readers sent me an old Hallmark greeting card. Charlie Brown, the pessimistic Peanuts character, is shown standing dockside wistfully saying, "Someday my ship will come in." But on the inside of the card, Charlie says, ". . . but I'll probably be at the airport."

Cruise lines bent on filling their liners seemingly try every which way to assure the Charlie Browns of the world that finding themselves at airports is the surest and cheapest way to head for their ship.

Granted, it may be more difficult to figure which offering is really the best bargain in 1985 and 1986, but there are ways to separate a realistically priced package that includes free air from a package inflated to camouflage "included free air." The wise traveler can figure almost to the dollar how much more, or less, comparable cruise packages will cost. He can even come up with how much the steamship company is willing to cut the cruise rate when it is not subsidizing the air fare.

Industry leaders view creation of the total package concept for cruising as the single element responsible for its present leadership position in the travel marketplace. They agree that it was necessary to tap markets outside ports of embarkation if ships were to fill up. And, they allow as how the concept permitted ships to be positioned in San Juan, Vancouver, Barbados, St. Croix, Jamaica or Miami and still compete with vessels sailing from New York or Las Angeles.

The original concept of including air with sea passage did not intend for the cruise line to subsidize the air portion, but merely to buy airline seats at very discounted group rates or charter flights and pass along savings to passengers through travel agents. Although the concept has changed, there is still no way a traveler can just purchase the air portion of the package for the published very low add-on price.

During the past 10 years, air-sea packages, free or for low additional prices have become an important factor in the cruise industry and it is here to stay. How to take advantage of these offerings and how to select a package is what concerns the average traveler a lot more than who is subsidizing what.

When free air was introduced by a half dozen cruise lines in mid-1982, cruise lines dug deeply into their pockets to subsidize what amounted to large cruise fare reductions disguised as "free air" offerings from 72 to 100 cities in the U.S. and Canada. Rates charged were those published, so passengers were flown to ports of embarkation without additional charges for the air portion of the vacation package.

That is not necessarily the case in 1985. Since the inception of free-air, rates have increased by 20–25 percent and there are some within the industry who claim the increases of from $100 to $250 per person are enough to cover the increased air subsidies required for those roundtrip free flights. What with reduced fuel costs and more economical engines on new cruise liners, the cruise industry is not only alive but doing very well.

To separate fact from myth in air-sea packages, look for:

Scheduled Airlines vs *Charters:* Very few charter flights are being used for transportation to ports of embarkation in the United States. There are a number of packages to the Mediterranean and European ports that still use charters from New York. In some of those cases, you pay your own fare to and from New York, or the cruise line offers an add-on lower than the lowest economy ticket.

There are different rules covering charters and schedule flights as part of air-sea packages. If your package is on a charter flight, you are obligated to return with the same group on a predetermined date. You will not be permitted (at the package rate) to arrive earlier or stay longer. You will, however, be met when the charter arrives, transferred and your baggage will be delivered to the ship. At the end of the cruise, you will be transported to the airport for your return flight home.

On scheduled air, you can usually remain in the port area for up to 30 days, stop over in another city on your way home (sometimes for a small additional charge); and, in other cases, even arrange to arrive in the embarkation city in advance of the sailing date. Every package includes transfers to and from the airport, airport security charges, baggage handling. A variable is port taxes which are rarely included in advertised package prices.

"Cruise only" rate: This rate does not include air transportation or transfers between the airport and the pier. It is lower than the air-sea rate and more accurately reflects the true "cruise-only" price once the the "transportation discount" of from $100 to $500 is deducted. Passengers making their own arrangements to get to and from the port of embarkation and debarkation are allowed this rate reduction. (cruise only, less the transportation allowance.)

Gateways: If your city is not listed as one from which the cruise line includes roundtrip air as part of the cruise price, or if it not one that offers an add-on for the flight, you are responsible for getting yourself to one of these cities or arranging for your own air to the port and paying for "cruise-only." It is almost always cheaper to take the air-sea package even if it means paying to get to the closest "free" or "add-on" point. Air-sea cities are not the same for all cruise companies. The major gateways of Los Angeles, Chicago, New York, Dallas are always included because of the large population centers served by the airports.

How Free is Free?

To find the answer to that question, passengers determined to get the best air-sea package money-wise will have to sharpen their pencils, fine tune their computers. Unfortunately, travel agents haven't fed all of the variables into their own computers and will not be able to come up with definitive answers in most cases. The variables are:

Ship Quality: Compare vessels of comparable quality and with brochure rates that do not vary more than 10 percent. In some cases, to find the real cost of a cruise use as a base the rate listed for "cruise only" which is the rate charged persons who get themselves to the gangplank without costing the cruise company an extra dollar or two.

For example: Compare offerings by ships in the same and in different price categories. When an up-scale or deluxe ship is including air when it normally offers "cruise only" rates, it may be cheaper, or at least the same price to sail a higher priced vessel.

Air offerings are called "free" by a number of companies; "almost free" and "zone policies," by others. THE TOTAL TRAVELER BY SHIP listings in this chapter should be used for guidance only. The listing includes some major gateway cities as well as a few cities considered "off-line" by cruise companies. If your city is not listed, get hold of the ship brochure. In all probabilities your city will be included as either a "free" or "add-on" city but if it isn't, getting to the nearest city listed will be the least expensive route to a ship holiday.

Shipping companies must have taken a lesson from their airline counterparts. There is very little difference in air offerings for ships leaving from the same port of embarkation for the same length cruise. Differences are greater when departures are from distant ports or from ports where competition is less than keen.

Best values are in fly-cruise packages on ships from Florida and California to Mexico and to Canada and Alaska. Few air-sea packages are available on New York to Bermuda summer sailings but this may change with more competition on those sea lanes planned in 1985. The most money can be saved on air fares when segments of world cruises require passengers to fly to Hong Kong, for example, cruise for 22 days, then fly back to the U.S. from Africa. Most companies are picking up the total air fare and subsidizing heavily. The longer the cruise, the higher the ticket price, the more money saving possibilities.

Although more than 90 percent of the passengers on any sailing have used an airplane to get them to the ship, bargains are also available in "cruise only," get-yourself-to-the-ship deals.

RULES TO FLY AND CRUISE BY

To take advantage of what seems like outstanding offers, there are a few ground rules applicable to almost all air-sea packages. The total package (cruise, flight and land where applicable) must be purchased in advance from a travel agency or from the cruise company. All cruise lines prefer passengers deal through agencies, but very few will refuse to accept a direct booking. There is little advantage in dealing directly with the line, in fact the advantage is in dealing with a travel agent. Direct dealings with cruise lines will get you no better accommodations, no discount and cruise line reservations personnel do not have the time to explain the differences in cabins. What's more, they will not discuss advantages of sailing with a competitor.

Changes in air itineraries and stopovers may not be permitted once the ticket is issued and written, so it is to the traveler's advantage to know all his options and possibilities before he makes final arrangements for the cruise package.

Cruise lines aren't the only innovative ship marketers. One travel agency in my city in 1982 offered a trans-Panama Canal Thanksgiving cruise, free air, three nights in Acapulco in a deluxe hotel, dinners and breakfasts for just $20 more than the cruise package price. Travel agents in other cities are making similar attractive offerings in newspaper, radio and television advertising. In these cases, the agent has either made a special deal with the cruise line, or is using part of his handsome commission to sweeten the package and sell more cruises.

Catch-22 on most fly and cruise programs is the cold fact that minimum and close to minimum priced cabins are usually not available. I can't say that cruise line computers block them out and use them for "cruise only" sales, or that non-availability is due to the limited number of these "loss leader" advertised rates. I do know, however, that very few air-sea passengers go aboard having paid minimum rates.

There are bargain fly and cruise combinations on ships sailing everywhere in the world; including the Mediterranean, Pacific, Greek Islands, around the world. One company, for example, offered a 14-day Midnight Sun cruise from Amsterdam for about $2,500 (minimum) and included roundtrip air from New York. Another company in 1984 offered an 18-day cruise on a nice Italian registered ship sailing from Genoa to Egypt, Israel and the Greek Islands for $2,600 and that included roundtrip air from New York and three nights in London.

Most companies have simplified air-sea programs, and that's good news for the traveler and the travel agent. It all boils down to supply and demand. The traveler who stays abreast of the ups and downs in the cruise industry catches the bargains. Judging by late booking patterns set during the past couple of years, the early booker may be paying more for his cruise than the passenger who makes up his mind 30 days before sailing. But some companies are encouraging early bookings by discounting future cruises six months in advance. Then again, the last minute decision maker may miss out on the boat, the sailing he prefers, his choice of cabin, but he does stand a good chance to save some money.

TTT: Residents of port areas get that ripped-off feeling when they board their cruise ship and find tablemates hail from 1,000 miles away and paid nothing more for the roundtrip airline ticket. Well, you too can play the air-sea game, but only when scheduled airlines are part of the package if your travel agent will cooperate and when the air-sea package has flexibility.

Here's a hypothetical situation. You live in New York and would like to cruise on a ship sailing from Miami. You either own a condo in Florida where you spend part of each year, or you want to visit a friend or relative. Here's what you can do. Buy an air-sea package from a travel agent in New York. You'll get roundtrip economy air, your cruise and transfers. You can arrange to arrive in Miami before your cruise, give up the transfers (since you are not going directly to the pier), settle in at the condo or visit the relatives, get yourself to the ship, enjoy the cruise, and you'll still have a return airline ticket to New York; all for the basic price of the cruise.

This works in most cases but make sure the airline ticket is valid for 30 or 90 days. In a very few cases, tickets are valid only on the dates marked "o.k." and then you'll have to depend on the cooperation of your travel agent to do a little maneuvering to accommodate you. In many cases, a trip to the airline ticket office and payment of an additional amount of money will get an extension of ticket validity.

This same formula can be used between any city and port of embarkation if you want to vacation or visit in the departure area. This, too, has a hooker. The greater the distance from home city to port city, the higher the add-on where it is required. Now for the good news. The better the bargain when free air is part of the package.

Scheduled airline tickets issued on air sea programs are marked "nonrefundable," which means you cannot get any money back for unused portions. But these tickets are almost always "endorsable," so you can use them on airlines other than the one on which they were written. You also can pay additional amounts (except in rare cases) to extend the time period. In some cases, the air part of the air-sea package is as good as cash as long as you spend it on air travel.

The fly-cruise game described here is legal. Cruise lines benefit because more people cruise. Airlines benefit because more people fill seats that might otherwise be empty. Most important, passengers benefit. They save money and travel with greater flexibility and convenience.

OTHER BARGAINS

Unfortunately, cruise lines frequently do not know until a month or so before sailing day that the ship may have to weigh anchor with some empty cabins. When that happens, hastily announced air-sea bargains are publicized. This is where a good relationship with a travel agent pays off. He is the first to know and a good agent will notify his clients with flexible travel schedules. When empty cabins show up on cruise line computers, companies have been known to go all the way with discounts of as much as $500 per person while still including free (or almost free) air roundtrips. When you see this type of ad, you should know the cruise company is advertising a "loss leader" much in the same manner your friendly supermarket attracts your attention with Thursday food ads. It's a marketing maneuver to bring customers looking for bargains while at the same time maintaining, or at least not permanently reducing, published or brochure rates.

Herein lies another Catch 22. Special fares may not be confirmed until close to sailing dates and in most cases, the choice of vessel is left to the discretion of the cruise line. This is an excellent way to save money if you are going to be visiting in the port of embarkation area anyway and can adjust your visit to suit your cruise plans, or the other way around.

Super Savers, Super "C" Savers and offerings by other names are for travelers with flexible time. They must be willing to get themselves to the pier. They are for travelers more concerned with the price of the cruise and the cruise experience than which ship they sail and which sea lanes they cruise.

The procedure is simple. Passengers, through travel agents, select the weekend date of their preferred sailing. They request either an inside or outside cabin. The agent then contacts the cruise line and requests the reservation. Once confirmed, full payment is forwarded and the passenger is notified of the ship and cabin to which he has been assigned. Requests are accepted within 30 days of the sailing.

While the uncertainty of ship and itinerary, to say nothing of the cabin number, may not be in line with dream vacation planning for some passengers, it's the answer to dreams for budget-minded travelers who are willing to bend and adjust plans in order to save money.

This seems to be an on-going situation and it pays to monitor advertising.

Another incentive is to be found in free (or so low cost, they qualify as almost free) land stays in combination with the air-sea package. Air-land-sea packages include stays at hotels in Mexico, Florida, the Caribbean, Hawaii, Hong Kong and Japan. Some Caribbean stays are for one week.

TTT: Many cruise lines have "past passenger clubs" in order to encourage and promote loyalty to their ships. Passengers are either automatically enrolled as members after sailing once on a company vessel, or are solicited for membership by mail on completion of the cruise. Join! You will receive newsletters, brochures, and you'll be the first to hear about "special club" cruises, sometimes at lower rates. Should you sail with the company again, you'll be invited to a past-passengers' party hosted by the captain. On board, you'll receive something like a commemorative glass in the hopes you'll sail with that Line enough times to complete a service for 12.

Here's a run-down on current offerings by some of the cruise lines. They are likely to be extended and new bargains added to air-sea packages.

FREE AIR
(And Other Special Offerings)

AMERICAN CRUISE LINES: Periodic discounts for early bookings and other incentives.

AMERICAN HAWAII CRUISES: Standby fare in California only. Standby passengers confirmed 14 days before sailing and pay $795 per person, double for inside cabins; $895 for outside. Single supplement is $99 in either category. Full payment is due within seven days. Add air-sea supplement to prices. Air-sea from 100 cities.

BAHAMA CRUISE LINE: Free air from 82 cities on all Caribbean and Bermuda cruises. Discounts for early bookings. Children under 10 sail free and 10 percent senior citizen discount on selected sailings.

CARNIVAL CRUISE LINES: Free air from more than 100 U.S. cities for full fare passengers on *Mardi Gras, Festivale, Tropicale* and *Holiday* sailings. Air add-ons for *Carnivale* three and four-day cruises. Free air and air add-ons do not apply to Super "C" Saver program.

CHANDRIS: Air add-ons from 60 cities for cruises from San Juan; from major cities for 14 day Mediterranean cruises.

CLIPPER CRUISES: Air add-ons from 15 cities for Virgin Islands cruises.

COASTWISE CRUISE LINE: Free air from Boston and New York on selected sailings.

COMMODORE CRUISE LINES: Air add-ons from 85 cities. Third and fourth cabin passenger pays $395 plus air fare.

COSTA CRUISES: Free air from 50 cities for San Juan sailings in cabins with two lower berths; passengers in upper berth cabin passengers and singles pay and $50 add-on. Free from 100 cities from Fort Lauderdale. Add-ons from 14 cities for Alaska cruises and for 10 and 14 day Mediterranean cruises. Early booking discounts.

CUNARD LINE: Free air from over 50 cities for Alaska, Caribbean and Mexico sailings. (Cunard *Countess* and *Princess*) Also limited offer to cruise second week for $99 to $299, depending on season. Free air *QE 2* World Cruise segments; also one way free air transatlantic crossings. Standby transatlantic available at good discount.

CUNARD/NAC: Free air from 68 cities for *Sagafjord* transcanal cruises; from 16 cities for transpacific and Orient cruises also for *Sagafjord* cle Pacific, some including the Corcorde. Same for *Vistafjord* sailings. $250 allowance for non-air sea passengers on transcanal voyages.

DELTA QUEEN STEAMBOAT CO.: Air add-ons and periodic seasonal special discounts

DOLPHIN CRUISE LINE: Air add-ons from 27 cities on three and four-night cruises only in upper price categories. Early booking 20 percent discount, credits toward future cruises on selected sailings. Super 1984 offer gave passengers a 1985 cruise for only $50.

EASTERN CRUISE LINES: Air add-ons from 66 cities. Third and fourth cabin passengers in upper price categories sail free.

FANTASY CRUISES: Air add-ons from 49 cities; rate reductions available almost all cruises; standby fares.

HOLLAND AMERICA CRUISES/WESTOURS: Free air from 78 cities; add-ons from selected cities for Alaska cruises; early booking discounts. Combine two 7-day cruises and receive a $250 per person discount.

HOME LINES: Free air from 75 cities for 7 to 14 day cruises from Florida; free from every Canadian and U.S. city for 16-day transcanal cruises from Florida and California. Periodic rate reductions.

NORWEGIAN CARIBBEAN LINES: Free air from 80 cities for 7-night cruises; add-ons for three and four-day cruises; Sea Saver 30 percent and more discount for bookings two to four weeks prior to sailing. (NCL selects ship and cabin)

OCEAN CRUISE LINES: Free air from selected Florida cities; add-ons from 73 other major gateways for Caribbean cruises. Add-ons Mediterranean sailings. Rate reductions selected sailings.

PAQUET CRUISES: Free air from 65 cities for all Mediterranean and Caribbean cruises; add-ons from 65 other cities for seven and 14-day Alaska cruises. Early booking discounts. Guaranteed single share rates available.

PEARL CRUISES OF SCANDINAVIA: Free air from Honolulu all cruises; add-ons from 34 cities; early booking discount of up to $800 per person.

PRINCESS CRUISES: Free air from 85 cities transcanal cruises; from 43 cities for nine and 10-day Alaska cruises and some cities for

Caribbean and Mediterranean cruises. Substantial rate reductions selected sailings (up to $800 per couple some sailings in 1984). Early booking discount and credit toward future cruise. Cruise-only discounts for transcanal $300; Caribbean $250; one way or roundtrip Mexico $100; 10-day Alaska $100; Mediterranean $550.

ROYAL CARIBBEAN CRUISE LINE: Free air from 131 cities for 10 to 14 day cruises; from 96 cities for New York-Bermuda cruises; add-on from 47 cities; eight day cruises priced same as seven days.

ROYAL CRUISE LINE: Add-ons from 30 cities; rate reductions and other incentives transcanal and Mediterranean cruises; other incentives like on board credits for bar/shops, Savings Bonds.

ROYAL VIKING LINE: Free from 48 cities all transcanal, Alaska/Canada cruises, New England cruises; add-ons from 48 cities other cruises. Rate reductions with savings up to $1,500 per person depending on itinerary and length of voyage; credit toward future cruises. Free shore excursions and land packages on Orient cruises.

SITMAR CRUISES: Free air from 140 cities all cruises; early booking discounts (up to $1,000 per couple in 1984) and rate reductions on selected cruises. Applies also to third and fourth cabin passengers.

SUN LINE CRUISES: Add-ons from 45 cities; rate reductions selected voyages.

AIR-SEA PACKAGES

(By city of origin)

(All rates quoted are per person, based on double occupancy, unless otherwise noted.)

TTT: Almost all cruise lines exempt holiday periods from air-sea offerings, or they impose an additional charge for the air and/or the sea portion of the package. Real bargains are designed to attract passengers who would not ordinarily be sailing and there is rarely a need for more passengers during the Christmas, New Year's and Easter periods. Passengers sailing during those weeks are apparently willing to pay premiums, so cruise and air rates are increased. Also, many cruise lines change rates and package prices by season of the year. Mid-summer and mid-autumn are two different seasons at sea. Least popular and lowest priced periods are May, September, October, November and early December.

Air-sea information in this chapter was furnished by cruise lines. Omissions were unintentional and unavoidable. Every effort was made to include representative package tours. Rates and itineraries are subject to change with little or no notice, so travelers are well advised to check with travel agencies or cruise lines before making final arrangements. However, once a cruise is paid for, cruise lines guarantee rates.

When flight arrangements require arrival the night before sailing, hotel overnight, dinner and breakfast are included in total package price unless otherwise indicated in brochures. Some cruise lines refer to the length of voyage by "days", others by "nights", hence the difference in listings. Either way, passengers board ships in the evening of day one and disembark during the a.m. hours on day seven of a one week cruise, for example.

ATLANTA

AMERICAN HAWAII CRUISES: Constitution, Independence from Honolulu, (7 days), add $349.

CARNIVAL CRUISE LINES: Free for *Festivale, Mardi Gras, Holiday* from Miami, *Tropicale* from Los Angeles; *Carnivale* three and four-day cruises add $125.

CUNARD LINE: Princess for Alaska, add $300; CUNARD/NAC: Free Sagafjord World Cruise.

FANTASY CRUISES: 5–7 nights, add $150.

HOLLAND AMERICA CRUISES: Free for seven-day cruises *Rotterdam, Nieuw Amsterdam, Noordam* from Florida ports and from California to Caribbean and Mexico

PAQUET CRUISES: Free *Mermoz* from San Juan, *Rhapsody* from Port Everglades. Add $390 (depending on cabin rate) *Rhapsody* seven-day from Vancouver to Alaska.

PRINCESS CRUISES: Free 14 day transcanal, 10, 11-day transcanal add $75; Caribbean sailings, free; Mexico one way, add $150; roundtrip free; 7-day Alaska add, $245; 9 and 10-day Alaska, add $200; Mediterranean, add $325.

ROYAL CRUISE LINE: Royal Odyssey, Golden Odyssey Panama Canal cruises, add $25; Caribbean, add $25; Mediterranean and Scandinavian cruises package rate includes air.

ROYAL CARIBBEAN CRUISE LINES: Song of Norway, Song of America, Sun Viking, Nordic Prince (7, 8, 10, 14 days) free. October-March, add $75; Sun Venture 7 days Miami, Barbados.

ROYAL VIKING LINE: Free for transcanal. Free or add-ons all voyages, example: Hong Kong/Kobe add $1,480.

SITMAR CRUISES: Free all cruises. Third and fourth cabin passengers free.

BOSTON

AMERICAN HAWAII CRUISES: Constitution, Independence from Honolulu, (7 days), add $495.

CARNIVAL CRUISE LINES: Free for *Festivale, Mardi Gras, Holiday* from Miami, *Tropicale* from Los Angeles; *Carnivale* three and four-day cruises add $75.

CUNARD LINE: Countess, Princess from San Juan, free; add $350 for Alaska. CUNARD/NAC: Free transcanal *Sagafjord.*

FANTASY CRUISES: 5–7 nights, add $100.

HOLLAND AMERICA CRUISES: Free for seven-day cruises *Rotterdam, Nieuw Amsterdam, Noordam* from Florida ports and from California to Caribbean and Mexico

NORWEGIAN CARIBBEAN LINES: Norway, Skyward, Starward, Southward from Miami (7 days), free. *Sunward II* three and four-day cruises, add $195.

OCEAN CRUISE LINES: Ocean Islander from Barbados, *Ocean Princess* from Montego Bay, seven days, add $100; also air-sea for Mediterranean cruises.

PAQUET CRUISES: Free *Mermoz* from San Juan, *Rhapsody* from Port Everglades. Add $390 (depending on cabin rate) for *Rhapsody* seven-day from Vancouver to Alaska.

PRINCESS CRUISES: Free 14 day transcanal, 10,11-day transcanal add $100; Caribbean sailings, add $50; Mexico one way, add $150; roundtrip add $175; 7-day Alaska add, $395; 9 and 10-day Alaska, add $200; Mediterranean, free.

ROYAL CARIBBEAN CRUISE LINES: Song of Norway, Song of America, Sun Viking, Nordic Prince (7, 8, 10, 11, 14 days) free. 7-day Sun Venture Miami, Barbados, October-March add, 95.

ROYAL VIKING LINE: Free for transcanal. Free or add-ons all voyages, example: Hong Kong/Kobe add $850.

SITMAR CRUISES: Free all cruises. Third and fourth cabin passengers free.

BUFFALO

AMERICAN HAWAII CRUISES: Constitution, Independence from Honolulu, (7 days), add $379.

CARNIVAL CRUISE LINES: Free for *Festivale, Mardi Gras, Holiday* from Miami; *Tropicale* from Los Angeles add $95; *Carnivale* three and four-day cruises add

CUNARD LINE: Countess, Princess from San Juan free; Alaska add $350.

CUNARD/NAC: Free for *Sagafjord* transcanal cruises.

HOLLAND AMERICA CRUISES: Free for seven-day cruises *Rotterdam, Nieuw Amsterdam, Noordam* from Florida ports and from California to Caribbean and Mexico

NORWEGIAN CARIBBEAN LINES: Norway, Skyward, Starward, Southward from Miami (7 days), free. *Sunward II* three and four-day cruises, add $195.

OCEAN CRUISE LINES: Ocean Islander from Barbados, *Ocean Princess* from Montego Bay, even days, add $100; also air-sea for Mediterranean cruises.

PRINCESS CRUISES: Free 14-day transcanal, 10, 11-day transcanal add $100; Caribbean sailings, add $75; Mexico one way, add $150; roundtrip add $175; 7-day Alaska add, $395; 9- and 10-day Alaska, add $200; Mediterranean, add $225.

ROYAL CARIBBEAN CRUISE LINES: Song of Norway, Song of America, Sun Viking, Nordic Prince (7, 8, 10, 11, 14 days), free. Third/fourth passenger add $195.

SITMAR CRUISES: Free all cruises. Third and fourth cabin passengers free.

CHICAGO

AMERICAN HAWAII CRUISES: Constitution, Independence from Honolulu, (7 days), add $299.

CARNIVAL CRUISE LINES: Free for *Festivale, Mardi Gras, Holiday* from Miami; *Tropicale* from Los Angeles free; *Carnivale* three and four-day cruises add $150.

CUNARD LINE: Add $350 *Princess* Alaska cruises.

CUNARD/NAC: Free for *Sagafjord* transcanal cruises.

FANTASY CRUISES: 5–7 days, add $100

HOLLAND AMERICA CRUISES: Free for seven-day cruises *Rotterdam, Nieuw Amsterdam, Noordam* from Florida ports and from California to Caribbean and Mexico

NORWEGIAN CARIBBEAN LINES: Norway, Skyward, Starward, Southward from Miami (7 days), free. *Sunward II* three and four-day cruises, add $195.

OCEAN CRUISE LINES: Ocean Islander from Barbados, *Ocean Princess* from Montego Bay, even days, add $125; also air-sea for Mediterranean cruises.

PAQUET CRUISES: Free Mermoz from San Juan, *Rhapsody* from Port Everglades. Add $390 (depending on cabin rate) Rhapsody seven-day from Vancouver to Alaska.

PRINCESS CRUISES: Free 14 day transcanal, 10, 11-day transcanal add $75; Caribbean sailings, add $75; Mexico one way, add $100; roundtrip add $125; 7-day Alaska add, $395; 9- and 10-day Alaska, add $175; Mediterranean, add $175.

ROYAL CARIBBEAN CRUISE LINES: Song of Norway, Song of America, Sun Viking, Nordic Prince (7, 8, 10, 11, 14 days) free. Third/fourth passenger, add $195.

ROYAL VIKING LINE: Free for transcanal. Free or add-ons all voyages, example: Hong Kong/Kobe add $850.

SITMAR CRUISES: Free all cruises. Third and fourth cabin passengers free.

DALLAS/FT. WORTH—HOUSTON

AMERICAN HAWAII CRUISES: Constitution, Independence from Honolulu, (7 days), add $339.

CARNIVAL CRUISE LINES: Free for *Festivale, Mardi Gras, Holiday* from Miami; *Tropicale* from Los Angeles free; *Carnivale* three and four-day cruises add $175.

CUNARD LINE: Add $250 *Princess Alaska* cruises.

CUNARD/NAC: Free for *Sagafjord* transcanal cruises.

FANTASY CRUISES: 5–7 days, add $200

HOLLAND AMERICA CRUISES: Free for seven-day cruises Rotterdam, Nieuw Amsterdam, Noordam from Florida ports and from California to Caribbean and Mexico

NORWEGIAN CARIBBEAN LINES: Norway, Skyward, Starward, Southward from Miami (7 days), free. *Sunward II* three and four-day cruises, add $195.

OCEAN CRUISE LINES: Ocean Islander from Barbados, *Ocean Princess* from Montego Bay, seven days, add $150; also air-sea for Mediterranean cruises.

PAQUET CRUISES: Free Mermoz from San Juan, *Rhapsody* from Port Everglades. Add $360 (depending on cabin rate) *Rhapsody* seven-day from Vancouver to Alaska.

PRINCESS CRUISES: Free 14-day transcanal, 10-, 11-day transcanal add $75; Caribbean sailings, add $75; Mexico one way, add $75; roundtrip add $100; 7-day Alaska add, $395; 9- and 10-day Alaska, add $150; Mediterranean, add $325.

ROYAL CARIBBEAN CRUISE LINE: Song of Norway, Song of America, Sun Viking, Nordic Prince (7, 10, 11, 14 days) free.

ROYAL VIKING LINE: Free for transcanal. Free or add-ons all voyages, example: Hong Kong/Kobe add $800.

SITMAR CRUISES: Free all cruises. Third and fourth cabin passengers free.

DAYTON

AMERICAN HAWAII CRUISES: Constitution, Independence from Honolulu, (7 days), add $379.

CARNIVAL CRUISE LINES: Free for *Festivale, Mardi Gras, Holiday* from Miami; *Tropicale* from Los Angeles free; *Carnivale* three and four-day cruises add $175.

HOLLAND AMERICA CRUISES: Free for seven-day cruises *Rotterdam, Nieuw Amsterdam,* from Florida ports to Caribbean; add $100 for *Nieuw Amsterdam* and *Noordam* cruises to Mexico.

NORWEGIAN CARIBBEAN LINES: Norway, Skyward, Starward, Southward from Miami (7 days), free. *Sunward II* three and four-day cruises, add $195.

OCEAN CRUISE LINES: Ocean Islander from Barbados, *Ocean Princess* from Montego Bay, even days, add $150; also air-sea for Mediterranean cruises.

PAQUET CRUISES: Free Mermoz from San Juan, *Rhapsody* from Port Everglades. Add $340 (depending on cabin rate) *Rhapsody* seven-day from Vancouver to Alaska.

ROYAL CARIBBEAN CRUISE LINES: Song of Norway, Song of America, Sun Viking, Nordic Prince (7, 8, 10, 11, 14 days) free.

SITMAR CRUISES: Free all cruises. Third and fourth cabin passengers free.

DENVER

AMERICAN HAWAII CRUISES: Constitution, Independence from Honolulu, (7 days), add $349.

CARNIVAL CRUISE LINES: Free for *Festivale, Mardi Gras, Holiday* from Miami; *Tropicale* from Los Angeles free; *Carnivale* three and four-day cruises add $175. (no overnight)

CUNARD LINE: Princess Mexico cruises from Los Angeles and Acapulco, add $200; Alaska from Vancouver add $250.

FANTASY CRUISES: 5-7 days, add $200

HOLLAND AMERICA CRUISES: Free for seven-day cruises *Rotterdam, Nieuw Amsterdam, Noordam* from Florida ports to Caribbean and from California to Mexico.

NORWEGIAN CARIBBEAN LINES: Norway, Skyward, Starward, Southward from Miami (7 days), free. *Sunward II* three and four-day cruises, add $225.

OCEAN CRUISE LINES: Ocean Islander from Barbados, *Ocean Princess* from Montego Bay, seven days, add $100; also air-sea for Mediterranean cruises.

PAQUET CRUISES: Free *Mermoz* from San Juan, *Rhapsody* from Port Everglades. Add $390 (depending on cabin rate) *Rhapsody* seven-day from Vancouver to Alaska.

PRINCESS CRUISES: Free 14-day transcanal, 10, 11-day transcanal add $75; Caribbean sailings, add $100; Mexico one way, add $75; roundtrip add $100; 7-day Alaska add, $245; 9- and 10-day Alaska, add $125; Mediterranean, add $425.

ROYAL CARIBBEAN CRUISE LINES: Song of Norway, Song of America, Sun Viking, Nordic Prince (7, 8, 10, 11, 14 days) free. 7-day Sun Venture Miami, Barbados, October-March add, $95.

ROYAL VIKING LINE: Free for transcanal. Free or add-ons all voyages, example: Hong Kong/Kobe add $1,270.

HARTFORD

CARNIVAL CRUISE LINES: Free for *Festivale, Mardi Gras, Holiday* from Miami; *Tropicale* from Los Angeles free; *Carnivale* three and four-day cruises add $175.

CUNARD LINE: Countess, Princess from San Juan add $100; Alaska cruises add $350.

HOLLAND AMERICA CRUISES: Free for seven-day cruises *Rotterdam, Nieuw Amsterdam, Noordam* from Florida ports to Caribbean and from California to Mexico.

NORWEGIAN CARIBBEAN LINES: Norway, Skyward, Starward, Southward from Miami (7 days), free. *Sunward II* three and four-day cruises, add $195.

OCEAN CRUISE LINES: Ocean Islander from Barbados, *Ocean Princess* from Montego Bay, seven days, add $125; also air-sea for Mediterranean cruises.

PAQUET CRUISES: Free *Mermoz* from San Juan, *Rhapsody* from Port Everglades. Add $240 (depending on cabin rate) *Rhapsody* seven-day from Vancouver to Alaska.

ROYAL CARIBBEAN CRUISE LINES: Song of Norway, Song of America, Sun Viking, Nordic Prince (7, 8, 10, 11, 14 days) free.
SITMAR CRUISES: Free all cruises. Third and fourth cabin passengers free.

KANSAS CITY

AMERICAN HAWAII CRUISES: Constitution, Independence from Honolulu, (7 days), add $379.
CARNIVAL CRUISE LINES: Free for *Festivale, Mardi Gras, Holiday* from Miami; *Tropicale* from Los Angeles free; *Carnivale* three and four-day cruises add $185.
CUNARD LINE: Princess from Vancouver to Alaska add $300.
HOLLAND AMERICA CRUISES: Free for seven-day cruises *Rotterdam, Nieuw Amsterdam, Noordam* from Florida ports to Caribbean and from California to Mexico.
NORWEGIAN CARIBBEAN LINES: Norway, Skyward, Starward, Southward from Miami (7 days), free. Sunward II three and four-day cruises, add $195.
OCEAN CRUISE LINES: Ocean Islander from Barbados, *Ocean Princess* from Montego Bay, seven days, add $150; also air-sea for Mediterranean cruises.
PAQUET CRUISES: Free *Mermoz* from San Juan, *Rhapsody* from Port Everglades. Add $390. (depending on cabin rate) *Rhapsody* seven-day from Vancouver to Alaska.
PRINCESS CRUISES: Free 14-day transcanal, 10-, 11-day transcanal add $75; Caribbean sailings, add $75; Mexico one way, add $75; roundtrip add $100; 7-day Alaska add, $395; 9- and 10-day Alaska, add $150; Mediterranean, add $350.
ROYAL CARIBBEAN CRUISE LINES: Song of Norway, Song of America, Sun Viking, Nordic Prince (7, 8, 10, 11, 14 days) free. 7-day Sun Venture Miami, Barbados, October-March add, 95.
ROYAL VIKING LINE: Free for transcanal. Free or add-ons all voyages, example: Hong Kong/Kobe add $1,310.
SITMAR CRUISES: Free all cruises. Third and fourth cabin passengers free.

LOS ANGELES/SAN DIEGO/SAN FRANCISCO

AMERICAN HAWAII CRUISES: Constitution, Independence from Honolulu, (7 days), add $179.

CARNIVAL CRUISE LINES: Free for *Festivale, Mardi Gras, Holiday* from Miami; *Tropicale* from Los Angeles deduct $100.

CUNARD LINE: Princess from Acapulco free; from Vancouver to Alaska add $100.

FANTASY CRUISES: 5–7 days, add $200

HOLLAND AMERICA CRUISES: Free for seven-day cruises *Rotterdam, Nieuw Amsterdam, Noordam* from Florida ports to Caribbean; from California to Mexico deduct $100.

NORWEGIAN CARIBBEAN LINES: Norway, Skyward, Starward, Southward from Miami (7 days), free.

OCEAN CRUISE LINES: Ocean Islander from Barbados, *Ocean Princess* from Montego Bay, seven days, add $200; also air-sea for Mediterranean cruises.

PAQUET CRUISES: Free *Mermoz* from San Juan; *Rhapsody* from Port Everglades. Add $360 (depending on cabin rate) for *Rhapsody* seven-day from Vancouver to Alaska.

PRINCESS CRUISES: Free 14-day transcanal, 10-, 11-day transcanal add $50; Caribbean sailings, add $100; Mexico one way, free; roundtrip free; 7-day Alaska add, $245; 9- and 10-day Alaska, free; Mediterranean, add $325.

ROYAL CRUISE LINE: Royal Odyssey, Golden Odyssey Panama Canal cruises, Caribbean, Mediterranean and Scandinavian cruises, brochure rate includes air.

ROYAL CARIBBEAN CRUISE LINES: Song of Norway, Song of America, Sun Viking, Nordic Prince (7, 8, 10, 11, 14 days) free. 7-day Sun Venture Miami, Barbados, October-March add, $175.

ROYAL VIKING LINE: Free for transcanal. Free or add-ons all voyages, example: Hong Kong/Kobe add $750.

SITMAR CRUISES: Free all cruises. Third and fourth cabin passengers free.

MIAMI/FORT LAUDERDALE

AMERICAN HAWAII CRUISES: Constitution, Independence from Honolulu, (7 days), add $349.

CARNIVAL CRUISE LINES: Carnivale, Festivale, Mardi Gras from Miami (7-days), deduct $100; *Tropicale* from Los Angeles free.

CUNARD LINE: Countess, Princess from San Juan free; *Princess* from Vancouver to Alaska add $300.

HOLLAND AMERICA CRUISES: Deduct $100 for cruises from Florida when no air transportation involved; free from California to Mexico.

NORWEGIAN CARIBBEAN LINES: Deduct $100 for seven day sailings *Norway, Skyward, Starward, Southward* from Miami.

OCEAN CRUISE LINES: Ocean Islander from Barbados, *Ocean Princess* from Montego Bay, seven days, free; also air-sea for Mediterranean cruises.

PAQUET CRUISES: Free *Mermoz* from San Juan. Add $240, (depending on cabin rate) *Rhapsody* seven-day from Vancouver to Alaska.

PRINCESS CRUISES: Free 14-day transcanal, 10-, 11-day transcanal add $50; Caribbean sailings, free; Mexico one way, add $150; roundtrip add $175; 7-day Alaska add, $395; 9- and 10-day Alaska add $200; Mediterranean, add $175.

ROYAL VIKING LINE: Free for transcanal. Free or add-ons all voyages, example: Hong Kong/Kobe add $850.

SITMAR CRUISES: Free all cruises. Third and fourth cabin passengers free. Deduct $100 for cruises from Port Everglades.

MILWAUKEE

AMERICAN HAWAII CRUISES: Constitution, Independence from Honolulu, (7 days), add $349.

CARNIVAL CRUISE LINES: Free for *Festivale, Mardi Gras, Holiday* from Miami; *Tropicale* from Los Angeles free; *Carnivale* three and four-day cruises add $150.

HOLLAND AMERICA CRUISES: Free from Florida to Caribbean seven day cruises *Rotterdam, Nieuw Amsterdam* and *Noordam* from California to Mexico.

NORWEGIAN CARIBBEAN LINES: Norway, Skyward, Starward, Southward from Miami (7 days), free; Sunward II three and four-day sailings add $175.

OCEAN CRUISE LINES: Ocean Islander from Barbados, *Ocean Princess* from Montego Bay, seven days, add $150; also air-sea for Mediterranean cruises.

PAQUET CRUISES: Free *Mermoz* from San Juan; *Rhapsody* from Port Everglades. Add $390, (depending on cabin rate) *Rhapsody* seven-day from Vancouver to Alaska.

ROYAL CARIBBEAN CRUISE LINES: Song of Norway, Song of America, Sun Viking, Nordic Prince (7, 8, 10, 11, 14 days) free. 7-day Sun Venture Miami, Barbados, October-March add, $95.

ROYAL VIKING LINE: Free for transcanal. Free or add-ons all voyages, example: Hong Kong/Kobe add $1,410.

SITMAR CRUISES: Free all cruises. Third and fourth cabin passengers free.

MINNEAPOLIS

AMERICAN HAWAII CRUISES: Constitution, Independence from Honolulu, (7 days), add $379.

CARNIVAL CRUISE LINES: Free for *Festivale, Mardi Gras, Holiday* from Miami; *Tropicale* from Los Angeles free; *Carnivale* three and four-day cruises add $175.

HOLLAND AMERICA CRUISES: Free from Florida to Caribbean seven day cruises *Rotterdam, Nieuw Amsterdam* and *Noordam* from California to Mexico.

NORWEGIAN CARIBBEAN LINES: Norway, Skyward, Starward, Southward from Miami (7 days), free; *Sunward II* three and four-day sailings add $195.

OCEAN CRUISE LINES: *Ocean Islander* from Barbados, *Ocean Princess* from Montego Bay, seven days, add $150; also air-sea for Mediterranean cruises.

PAQUET CRUISES: Free *Mermoz* from San Juan; *Rhapsody* from Port Everglades. Add $390, (depending on cabin rate) *Rhapsody* seven-day from Vancouver to Alaska.

PRINCESS CRUISES: Free 14-day transcanal, 10-, 11-day transcanal add $100; Caribbean sailings, add $100; Mexico one way, add $100; roundtrip add $125; 7-day Alaska add, $395; 9- and 10-day Alaska add $175; Mediterranean, add $275.

ROYAL VIKING LINE: Free for transcanal. Free or add-ons all voyages, example: Hong Kong/Kobe add $1,370.

SITMAR CRUISES: Free all cruises. Third and fourth cabin passengers free.

NEW YORK

AMERICAN HAWAII CRUISES: Constitution, Independence from Honolulu, (7 days), add $299.

CARNIVAL CRUISE LINES: Free for *Festivale, Mardi Gras, Holiday* from Miami and *Tropicale* from Los Angeles; *Carnivale* three and four-day cruises add $125.

CUNARD LINE: Countess, Princess from San Juan free; from Vancouver to Alaska add $300.

FANTASY CRUISES: 5–7 days, add $100

HOLLAND AMERICA CRUISES: Free from Florida to Caribbean seven day cruises *Rotterdam, Nieuw Amsterdam* and *Noordam* from California to Mexico.

NORWEGIAN CARIBBEAN LINES: Norway, Skyward, Starward, South-ward from Miami (7 days), free; Sunward II three and four-day sailings add $150.

OCEAN CRUISE LINES: Ocean Islander from Barbados, *Ocean Princess* from Montego Bay, seven days, add $100; also air-sea for Mediterranean cruises.

PAQUET CRUISES: Free Mermoz from San Juan, *Rhapsody* from Port Everglades. Add $360, (depending on cabin rate) *Rhapsody* seven-day from Vancouver to Alaska.

PRINCESS CRUISES: Free 14-day transcanal, 10-, 11-day transcanal add $100; Caribbean sailings, add $100; Mexico one way, add $100; roundtrip add $125; 7-day Alaska add, $395; 9- and 10-day Alaska add $175; Mediterranean, add $350.

ROYAL CRUISE LINE: Use published rate as base and add or subtract depending on itinerary. Example: *Royal Odyssey* Panama Canal from Miami to Acapulco, subtract $50; transcanal from Acapulco to Curacao, subtract $20; Mediterranean , subtract $285.

ROYAL CARIBBEAN CRUISE LINES: Song of Norway, Song of America, Sun Viking, Nordic Prince (7, 10, 11, 14 days) free. Bermuda cruises, deduct $50.

ROYAL VIKING LINE: Free for transcanal. Free or add-ons all voyages, example: Hong Kong/Kobe add $850.

SITMAR CRUISES: Free all cruises. Third and fourth cabin passengers free.

PHOENIX

AMERICAN HAWAII CRUISES: Constitution, Independence from Honolulu, (7 days), add $239.

CARNIVAL CRUISE LINES: Free for *Festivale, Mardi Gras, Holiday* from Miami and *Tropicale* from Los Angeles.

CUNARD LINE: Princess from Los Angeles/Acapulco add $100; from Vancouver to Alaska add $250.

HOLLAND AMERICA CRUISES: Free from Florida to Caribbean seven day cruises *Rotterdam, Nieuw Amsterdam* and *Noordam* from California to Mexico.

NORWEGIAN CARIBBEAN LINES: Norway, Skyward, Starward, South-ward from Miami (7 days), free,

OCEAN CRUISE LINES: Ocean Islander from Barbados, *Ocean Princess* from Montego Bay, seven days, add $200; also air-sea for Mediterranean cruises.

PAQUET CRUISES: Mermoz from San Juan, add $95; *Rhapsody* from Port Everglades, free. Add $390, (depending on cabin rate) *Rhapsody* seven-day from Vancouver to Alaska.

PRINCESS CRUISES: Free 14-day transcanal, 10-, 11-day transcanal add $100; Caribbean sailings, add $50; Mexico one way, add $150; roundtrip add $175; 7-day Alaska add, $395; 9- and 10-day Alaska add $200; Mediterranean, free.

ROYAL CRUISE LINE: Use published rate as base and add or subtract depending on itinerary. Example: *Royal Odyssey* Panama Canal from Miami to Acapulco, subtract $50; transcanal from Acapulco to Curacao, published fare; Mediterranean, subtract $25.

ROYAL CARIBBEAN CRUISE LINES: Song of Norway, Song of America, Sun Viking, Nordic Prince (7, 8, 10, 11, 14 days) free.

ROYAL VIKING LINE: Free for transcanal. Free or add-ons all voyages, example: Hong Kong/Kobe add $750.

SITMAR CRUISES: Free all cruises. Third and fourth cabin passengers free.

SALT LAKE CITY

CARNIVAL CRUISE LINES: Add $95 for *Festivale, Mardi Gras, Holiday* from Miami; free for *Tropicale* from Los Angeles.

CUNARD LINE: Princess from Los Angeles/Acapulco add $200; from Vancouver to Alaska add $250.

HOLLAND AMERICA CRUISES: Add $100 from Florida to Caribbean seven day cruises *Rotterdam, Nieuw Amsterdam; Noordam* from California to Mexico, free.

NORWEGIAN CARIBBEAN LINES: Norway, Skyward, Starward, Southward from Miami (7 days), free,

OCEAN CRUISE LINES: Ocean Islander from Barbados, *Ocean Princess* from Montego Bay, seven days, add $200; also air-sea for Mediterranean cruises.

PAQUET CRUISES: Mermoz from San Juan, add $95; free *Rhapsody* from Port Everglades. Add $240, (depending on cabin rate) *Rhapsody* seven-day from Vancouver to Alaska.

PRINCESS CRUISES: Free 14-day transcanal, 10-, 11-day transcanal add $75; Caribbean sailings, add $100; Mexico one way, free; roundtrip, free; 7-day Alaska add, $245; 9- and 10-day Alaska, free; Mediterranean, add $425.

ROYAL CARIBBEAN CRUISE LINES: Song of Norway, Song of America, Sun Viking, Nordic Prince 7, 8 days, add $75. Longer voyages free.

SITMAR CRUISES: Free all cruises. Third and fourth cabin passengers free.

SEATTLE

AMERICAN HAWAII CRUISES: Constitution, Independence from Honolulu, 7 days, add $249.

CARNIVAL CRUISE LINES: Free for *Festivale, Mardi Gras, Holiday* from Miami and *Tropicale* from Los Angeles.

CUNARD LINE: Princess from Los Angeles/Acapulco add $200; from Vancouver to Alaska free.

HOLLAND AMERICA CRUISES: Free from Florida to Caribbean and California to Mexico seven day cruises *Rotterdam, Nieuw Amsterdam, Noordam.*

NORWEGIAN CARIBBEAN LINES: Norway, Skyward, Starward, Southward from Miami (7 days), free.

OCEAN CRUISE LINES: Ocean Islander from Barbados, *Ocean Princess* from Montego Bay, seven days, add $200; also air-sea for Mediterranean cruises.

PAQUET CRUISES: Free *Mermoz* from San Juan, *Rhapsody* from Port Everglades. Add $240, (depending on cabin rate) *Rhapsody* seven-days from Vancouver to Alaska.

PRINCESS CRUISES: Free 14-day transcanal, 10-, 11-day transcanal add $75; Caribbean sailings, add $100; Mexico one way, add $100; roundtrip, add $75; 7-day Alaska add, $245; 9- and 10-day Alaska, add $100; Mediterranean, add $475.

ROYAL CARIBBEAN CRUISE LINES: Song of Norway, Song of America, Sun Viking, Nordic Prince (7, 8, 10, 24 days), free.

SITMAR CRUISES: Free all cruises. Third and fourth cabin passengers free.

ST. LOUIS

AMERICAN HAWAII CRUISES: Constitution, Independence from Honolulu, (7 days), add $349.

CARNIVAL CRUISE LINES: Free for *Festivale, Mardi Gras, Holiday* from Miami and *Tropicale* from Los Angeles; *Carnival* three and four-day cruises add $175.

HOLLAND AMERICA CRUISES: Free from Florida to Caribbean and California to Mexico seven day cruises *Rotterdam, Nieuw Amsterdam, Noordam.*

NORWEGIAN CARIBBEAN LINES: Norway, Skyward, Starward, South-ward from Miami (7-days), free; Sunward II three- and four-day cruises, add $175.

OCEAN CRUISE LINES: Ocean Islander from Barbados, *Ocean Princess* from Montego Bay, seven days, add $150; also air-sea for Mediterranean cruises.

PAQUET CRUISES: Free all cruises from Florida and San Juan. Add $390, (depending on cabin rate) *Rhapsody* seven-days from Vancouver to Alaska.

PRINCESS CRUISES: Free 14-day transcanal, 10-, 11-day transcanal add $100; Caribbean sailings, add $125; Mexico one way, add $100; roundtrip, add $75; 7-day Alaska add, $65; 9- and 10-day Alaska, add $125; Mediterranean, add $325.

ROYAL CARIBBEAN CRUISE LINES: 7-day *Sun Viking* Sun Venture from Miami or Barbados, add $95; other times free.

ROYAL VIKING LINE: Free for transcanal. Free or add-ons all voyages, example: Hong Kong/Kobe add $1,270.

SITMAR CRUISES: Free all cruises. Third and fourth cabin passengers free.

Ports of Call

PICK A PATCH of blue ocean in any part of the world, and there's a better than even chance you'll find cruise ships plying the waters. Passenger-carrying vessels cruise within sight of each other in the Caribbean, meet in West Indies and Mexican ports, cruise the islands in the South Pacific, sail up and down North America's inland waterways, visit the exotic Mediterranean, dodge icebergs in the Land of the Midnight Sun and call at exotic Far East ports. Almost every country in the world is in the passenger cruise business.

All cruise ships offer "shore excursions," inclusive sightseeing packages. Buses or taxis pick up passengers dockside, a guide explains the sights, usually some shopping time is allowed, and passengers are returned to their ship or dropped off in town to browse on their own.

While a small number of cruise travelers prefer to stay on board when the ship visits a port, most passengers go ashore for sightseeing, shopping, beaches, and night life. Ship activities are restricted during time in port, so passengers who do not disembark are opting for a quiet day. Meals on board are served on a schedule to fit the ship's time in port.

There's no question it is advantageous to make the most of hours on shore, be it a day, an evening, or a few hours. Trial-and-error sightseeing on your own is logical if you have several days or a week on an island, but it is an extravagant waste of time when your visit is by cruise ship and your time ashore is measured in hours. So, should you take the ship's prearranged shore excursion or do it on your own?

In the Caribbean, shore excursions arranged by ships cost about $15 for four hours of sightseeing. Excursions in Mediterranean ports can run as high as $75 for a full day in Israel, for instance, and as low as $7 for a tour by donkey in Santorini. Excursions in Baltic countries average out at about $20 for half-day tours. There are longer trips where air travel is involved, and these can run into hundreds of dollars and sometimes include hotels and meals. The usual shore excursion is either half day, full day, or an evening outing. Nightclub tours cost about $30 in San Juan and about $20 in Mexico. The advantages of purchasing the ship's shore excursion are obvious. The tour is fully escorted (usually a ship cruise staff member accompanies the tour), the guide speaks English, and there is some degree of responsibility and supervision exercised by the ship. In almost all cases, the ship acts as an agent for a land-based tour operator and adds several dollars to the price at which the tour is sold to passengers. The ship makes it very clear that it assumes no legal liability for shore excursions, but the good news is that cruise lines know a bad shore excursion can spoil an entire cruise experience so everything possible is done to make sure passengers are satisfied.

Doing the port on your own is possible almost everywhere. If there are four of you, a day outing will probably cost less than the total of four individually purchased shore excursions. However, in non-English speaking countries or islands, there's no assurance your guide will speak English or show you the most interesting places. His "yes" to your question "Do you speak English?" may be the only English word he knows. There is always the possibility of disputes arising at the end of the tour as to price and original agreement.

Taxi drivers on some islands are famous for the "sightseeing" tour of shops where they receive a commission for bringing passengers. Rental cars are available in most ports if you like seeing a place on your own, and limousines with drivers and rental motor-scooters take up the slack for preferences at opposite ends of the spectrum.

For women traveling alone, nightclub tours provide a sense of security. Shore excursions relieve them of the annoyance of thinking about taxi fares, checks, and gratuities.

It is not a good idea to depend entirely on taxi drivers and local tour operators. If you have ever seen the mob of eager cab drivers waiting for ships to dock in some ports, you'll agree with that advice. Many of the drivers are competent, but others lack proper training as guides; still others succumb to the temptation to overcharge.

How you should divide your time on an island or in a city follows no set formula. There's no rule that fits every port. Some are scenic and tempt exploration; others have idyllic beaches hard to resist. Snorkeling, sailing, fishing, cultural monuments, and museums — every port has a little of one attraction, more of another. A good tour combines the best of everything.

This chapter was not written as a guide for travelers spending days or weeks in the port city or ports of call. Visitors arriving by plane have more time to explore and should have more details at hand for complete enjoyment. Information on sightseeing in ports of call is predicated on spending about six hours in the port. Every effort has been made to inform readers of the most interesting sights. For Mediterranean and North Sea ports, the average time spent in port by cruise ships was used as a basis for recommended sightseeing.

It is impossible to list every port in the Bahamas, Caribbean, West Indies, Mexico, Alaska, Canada, Greece, Israel, Turkey, North Africa, Italy, England, Holland, Denmark, Sweden, Norway, Russia, and about fifty others, so only those most frequently visited by major cruise lines have been included. For the first time, THE TOTAL TRAVELER BY SHIP is including China visits by ship. Average shore excursion prices (per person) are listed for every port. This information was obtained from ships visiting these ports and from shore tour operators. However, these prices are subject to change with very little or no notice but should not vary more than 10 –20 percent in an upward direction. Shore excursion prices never seem to go down, but some cruise lines are including shore excursions in the cruise package. I commend them and would like to see this trend extended so cruise packages become all-inclusive.

Exchange rates of foreign currency vs the U.S. dollar are not listed because they are so volatile and what is accurate at press time could be completely out of date by the time this book reaches the book stores. We have listed names of currency and existing money exchange restrictions along with tips on how to get the most for your money in each country. You can get current exchange rates on board ship from the purser's office. The information is usually available at port briefing talks held regularly on board all ships. Don't worry about converting your money for short stays on shore. Shopkeepers are happy to accept U.S. dollars, travelers' checks, and major credit cards. Even Russian ports take dollars or travelers' checks, but they stop short of accepting our plastic money. Friendship Stores in the People's Republic of China even accept the credit cards but require the amount of purchase be charged to your account in dollars. The money is then converted to Yuan and given to you to pay for your purchase.

Alaska and Canada

Cruising the inside passage to Alaska and Canada proved to be a summer sleeper for the cruise industry. As popularity increased and vessels posted "sold out" signs, more ships headed for the northern route for the months May through September. With a dozen ships plying the waterways, supply has caught up with demands, and it is possible to book space on almost every ship for every voyage. It is possible to buy space within a few weeks of sailings, but you may not get the price range your budget calls for or the ship you prefer. There are price advantages for early bookings and some are balanced out with "last-minute sales." (See Air-Sea and Other Bargains Chapter)

ALASKA

Cruise Season: May through September.

Climate: Temperatures range from the mid–40s (May and September) to a high of 70. June, July, August temperatures go from mid–50s to mid 70s. Most popular cruise months: July, early August.

Currency: U. S.

Language: English.

Time: Four hours behind EST.

Tipping Ashore: Similar to the United States.

More Information: State Division of Tourism, Juneau, AK 99811

What to Wear Ashore: Let the weather be your guide. Anything comfortable is acceptable. Lightweight woolens, slacks, sweaters, water-repellent coats are suggested. Shipboard clothing ranges from swim suits for sunny days on deck to fur coats and parkas for chilly evenings.

Shopping: Similar in all ports. Fur parkas are priced higher than in your home town, but Alaskan Indian carvings and native artifacts are excellent souvenirs. Alaskan jade (not as valuable as Oriental) varies in form from trinkets priced at a couple of dollars to carvings priced at a couple of hundred dollars. Everything purchased in Alaska is duty-free for returning U.S. residents and should not be included in your customs declaration.

TTT: Swingers will find life in these small communities dull and boring, but visiting the 49th U.S. state is visiting rural towns adjusting to accommodate tourists during summer months. Nothing in these communities (except for a couple of dance recitals) is a "put on" for visitors. You will see life as it is. Prices for food and housing are high, fishing is excellent, and the family boat is more important than the family car. School buses are used for shore excursions in some places. The same school buses transport the kids during winter months. Guides are local residents, proud of their communities and happy to talk about life in Alaska.

Don't expect to find sophisticated entertainment, trendy boutiques, Eskimo camps, gold mines, or the Alaska pipeline. That comes with flying around the state and spending more time than is allowed on cruise ship visits.

GLACIER BAY

Glacier Bay is not only a port of call but also the highlight of all Canada-Alaska cruise experiences. It is a day spent with nature. Cruise ships slip through Icy Strait into the awesome and glacial 50-mile-long Glacier Bay. It is rimmed with a score of active glaciers, and hunks of ice frequently tumble off 250-foot heights.

A ranger from the National Park Service boards every ship gliding through this natural phenomena. A knowledgeable guide, he explains the sights over the ship's public-address system.

Glacier Bay's advancing and retreating glaciers record a history of rhythmic changes in the climate of the planet. Centuries of mild climate in the far north have alternated with long, cold periods of successive ice ages. Since life everywhere presses against its frontiers, this area records an extension of moss-carpeted primeval forests and their inhabitants in the wake of retreating ice, then extinction or withdrawal when overwhelmed by advancing glaciers—and again the forests' recovery, as in our time.

Glaciers form because heavy snowfall every year in the high mountains does not all melt but accumulates and is transformed into ice. New-fallen snow changes first into granular snow consisting of round grains of ice. As the depth increases, the ice grains become more closely packed and in time fuse into solid ice, which, when of sufficient thickness, volume, and weight, flows down-slope into lower regions to a point where the rate of melting equals the rate of accumulation. That point is the terminus, or snout, of a glacier. The advance or retreat of a glacier terminus reflects the rate of snowfall, the topography, and trends in climate.

When Captain George Vancouver sailed through the ice-choked waters of Icy Strait in 1797, Glacier Bay was little more than a dent in the shoreline. Across the head of this minor inlet stood a towering wall of ice—a wall that marked the seaward outlet of an immense glacier completely filling the broad, deep basin of what is now Glacier Bay. To the north, ice extended more than 100 miles covering widths of about 20 miles. In places the ice was 4,000 feet deep. By 1879, the ice front had retreated 48 miles, inlet was free of ice, and the terminus of Grand Pacific Glacier was 65 miles from the mouth of Glacier Bay. The speed at which Glacier Bay's ice sheet is shrinking has attracted much interest. By contrast, the glacier termini on the west side have been almost stable since 1929.

The glaciers seen today are remnants of a general ice-advance that began some 4,000 years ago. This period is sometimes called the "little ice age." Few of the many glaciers that once supplied the huge ice sheet still extend to the sea, but there are 11,400 square miles in Glacier Bay National Monument enclosing 16 active tidewater glaciers. Icebergs, which have cracked off from near-vertical ice cliffs, dot the waters of the bay.

This is the day everyone spends on deck, and cameras click throughout the ship. During the summer months, daylight extends to past midnight; on the longest day of the year, there are about two hours of near darkness.

TTT: In response to pleas by ecologists, the number of ships cruising Glacier Bay is being limited. If Glacier Bay is important to you, check brochures and sailing dates carefully. Not all ships listing Glacier Bay cruising actually cruise Glacier Bay on every sailing. Many ships alternate cruising of Glacier Bay with Alert Bay, also beautiful, but not quite the same as Glacier Bay.

ALERT BAY

When Captain Cook first visited Cormorant Island, off the coast of Vancouver Island, he found a native population with a lot of leisure time. Timber, fish and game were plentiful. In Alert Bay today, the vestiges of the Indian culture is still visible in wood carving and weaving. The area is so small, shore excursions are not offered. Scenery is worth the trip.

JUNEAU

Alaska's capital city contains many buildings of interest, among them the state museum and governor's mansion. There is a 13-mile bus trip on Glacier Highway to Mendenhall Glacier, a vast receding river of ice. Driving through the Mendenhall Valley, one goes through the Tongass National Forest, largest national forest in the United States. The river of compressed blue ice, hundreds of years old, is one of the most rugged glaciers accessible by road. Another interesting site is the Chapel, from which a spectacular view of the Mendenhall Glacier is reflected on Aule Lake.

Shore Excursions: Juneau City and Mendenhall Glacier Tour (3 hours), $20; Juneau Flightseeing Tour (45 minutes) is a fly-over the massive Taku Glacier and weather permitting, a climb over the top of the Mendenhall Ice Fields, $65. Mendenhall Glacier Float Trip is whitewater rafting for people of all ages. Passengers don ponchos, life jackets and waterproof boots (all provided) and float by raft through the magnificent lakes, (4 hours), $60. The Gold Panning and Gold Mine Tour is a favorite. Passengers travel by van up Gold Creek, following the same route taken by prospectors more than 100 years ago less than 2 hours), $17. Alaska Salmon Bake is an opportunity to sample one of Alaska's taste treats—Alaskan salmon barbecued over an alderwood fire in a sheltered picnic area by the side of a mountain stream (2 hours), $15. The Wilderness Lodge Adventure is an all-day tour to a remote wilderness lodge nestled amid glaciers, mountains and forest. Freshly baked salmon is served at lunch, $97.

KETCHIKAN

Ketchikan owes it beginnings to the gold rush of the 1890s, when it became the chief center for Alaska's fishing industry. But it's not the fishing that brings cruise ships into the harbor. Ketchikan is the most southern important town on the Inside Passage, just 230 miles southeast of Juneau. It is Alaska's fourth largest city with a population of 14,000. The city is wedged between mountains and waterfront in Alaska's panhandle and is best known by visitors for totem poles. Indians used them to record business transactions, social standing and illustrate stories.

The Indian totems at Saxman Park, two miles from town, are a camera buff's delight. There are more totems in Totem Bight, about 11 miles from the city. Ketchikan considers itself the salmon capital of the world, and great schools of migrating salmon pass through the narrow straits. The waterfront is always a busy place, and a walking tour affords an interesting contrast of old and new—sawdust-floored saloons side by side with modern department stores.

Shore Excursions: Totem Bight State Park and Rain Forest (3 hours), $15; Waterfront Cruise (2 hours), $32; Totem Heritage and Rain Forest (3 hours) combines a look at the salmon industry and the rest of Ketchikan and its totems, $18; Tlingit Indian Canoe Trip (4 hours) offers a glimpse of small animals that live around Connell Lake perched beneath Diana Mountain, $60.

SITKA

For more than 126 years, Alaska was explored and ruled by Russia. Although the United States took over in 1867, the charm of the old city, capital of the Russian Territory, is still alive in Sitka. Alaska's oldest town, it has also been called the most beautiful.

Sitka is on Baranof Island, 100 miles southwest of Juneau. Snow-covered mountains tower over it and surround it. Founded by Branov in 1799, it was first called Novo-Arkhangelsk (New Archangel). The name was later changed to Sitka when it became headquarters of all Russian activities in Alaska.

Most tours include a visit to the national monument where the great battle of Alaska was fought in 1804. Other highlights include visits to the Alaska Museum, the site of St. Michael's Cathedral with its strong Russian motif, rich oil paintings, and large icon collections-collections. The cathedral has been restored, and all of the treasures are on display. The small city of Sitka is surrounded by intensely blue waters, and many of the residents are descendants of the Tlingit Indians.

Several tours are offered by most ships. Unforgettable is a scenic seaside drive in Sitka. The best view is experienced by passengers on a helicopter tour. Highlights include views of Sitka Sound, filled with evergreen-covered islands, some of which still have abandoned World War II fortifications. Another view is of St. Lazari Island National Bird Reserve, home of the eagles. The helicopter tour lands in such inaccessible areas as the crater of Mount Edgecumbe and deserted beaches. Don't book the helicopter tour until the very last minute. Sights and landings depend on weather.

If aerial views don't interest visitors, there's an 18-mile cruise through virgin wilderness aboard a 62-foot covered yacht. The river route passes one of the first hard-rock gold mines in Alaska, and a highlight is a closeup of Green Lake Falls. Don't expect to pan any gold, though. The mines were abandoned years ago and tours including panning offer a tourist version of what it's really like. A fun tour, however, so don't be turned off by the obvious put-on.

Should you see Sitka on your own, "musts" include the cathedral and the large collection of restored totems dominating Sitka National Monument.

Shore Excursions: Sitka area (3 hours), $17.50; Green Lake Falls scenic tour (3 hours), $18; helicopter scenic tour, $75.00 to $100; Nature cruises (2 hours), $20.

SKAGWAY

Once a boomtown with a floating population of more than 20,000, Skagway retains the flavor of its historic past as the gateway to the Klondike gold fields. Gold Rush memories linger on in the town's wooden sidewalks, unpaved streets, and turn-of-the-century frame buildings. Guides tell colorful stories of Skagway's history. Visit beautiful Reid Falls, the famed White Pass and Yukon narrow-gauge railroad headquarters, the Trail of '98 Museum with its many authentic artifacts of the Gold Rush era, and the Gold Rush cemetery that holds the remains of villains and good guys.

Shore Excursions: City tour (2 hours), $13; railway tour (6 hours, including "miner's-style luncheon"), $25 to $40; Flightseeing $75.00.

CANADA

(Statistics do not cover all of Canada, just the cruise-port areas in British Columbia).

Cruise Season: Late May through early October. Most popular months: July and August.
Climate: Temperatures range from the low 50s in May and October to a high in the mid–80s. July and August lows run in the 60s.
Currency: Canadian dollar (fluctuates greatly)
Language: English. French is also an official language but is used more in eastern Canada.
Shopping: All made-in-England items are available at good prices; woolens, china, and Alaska Eskimo artifacts and art works are popular purchases.

Time: Four hours behind EST.

Tipping Ashore: Similar to the United States. Tip about 15 percent for all services; taxi drivers expect a little more; cloakroom attendants receive 50 cents U.S.

Transportation: See shore excursions and transportation information under each port.

What to Wear Ashore: Comfortable, city-type clothing. Jackets are required for dinner in more expensive hotel dining rooms and in restaurants. Have a sweater or lightweight jacket handy as temperatures change quickly.

More Information: Canadian Government Office of Tourism, 1251 Avenue of the Americas, New York, NY 10020; or Vancouver Visitors Bureau, 650 Burrard Street, Vancouver, British Columbia; or British Columbia Department of Travel Industry, 1019 Wharf Street, Victoria, British Columbia.

TTT: It doesn't happen very often, but often enough to put American travelers on the alert for merchants who quote prices in dollars (Canadian) and take payment in U.S. The Canadian dollar is worth less (sometimes as much as 30 percent) and payment in U.S. currency should be based on current exchange rate.

PRINCE RUPERT

Known as the "halibut capital of the world," Prince Rupert is the largest Canadian seaport and fishing center in the Northwest. Things to see include the city itself, the Museum of Northern British Columbia, local handicrafts, rare Haida argillite poles and Tsimshian Indian crafts, and the art gallery — and click your cameras. If you like spectacular views and sky-lifts, take the 4,000-foot gondola lift straight up from the base of Hays Mountain to a newly constructed lodge.

Shore Excursions: City tour (3 hours), $20; city tour and sky ride (4 hours), $20.

VANCOUVER

Vancouver reminds some people of San Francisco, others of Los Angeles or Toronto. For the most part, it is a city full of surprises.

Americans on a first-time visit expect Vancouver to be colder, smaller, duller, and not quite as overpowering scenically.

The city is located in the gap between the snowcapped peaks of the Cascade and Coastal ranges. To the west is the sea, the strait of Georgian, separating the city on the mainland from Vancouver Island and the Pacific. The geographic configuration explains the direction the city has taken. Land is at a premium, and construction on mountainside properties has reached the point where developers advertise "below the snow line". Downtown is hemmed in by water on two sides and park land on a third, so it is growing straight up.

Vancouver has an impressive skyline. Viewed from the city marina, from Stanley Park, or from nature's own highrise, Grouse Mountain, the city at night looks like a multi-masted schooner steaming out to sea. The streets that run along English Bay are lined with high-rise apartments. Office buildings are closer to downtown, at the intersection of Georgia and Burrard streets.

Glitter has been added on nearby Robson Street (also called Robsonstrasse), a three-block-long collection of Middle European shops, cafes, and restaurants. There are cafes specializing in strudel, Sachertorte, and a butter horn, the Pacific Northwest's equivalent of a sweet roll, mit Kaffee. Gastown, formerly a no man's land of warehouses and railroad yards, has been restored to a turn-of-the-Century corner of the city, with cobblestone streets, squares, and alleys. Gastown was named for a gent called Gassy Jack Deighton, who built a saloon and hotel in 1867. The origin of his nickname has been lost in time, but there is a theory it had something to do with monks and Australian wine.

The crest of all residential areas is Queen Elizabeth Park on Little Mountain, the highest point in the city.

The Capilano Suspension Bridge with its collection of totem poles is an unusual sight, and the Grouse Mountain Skyride transports you via aerial tramway to the highest point in the area. If you're lunching in town, sample any of the dozens of authentic Chinese restaurants in Chinatown. Vancouver's Oriental population is supposed to be the largest of any city in the Western Hemisphere.

There are numerous department stores, specialty shops, and English import stores. Prices are comparable to the United States. An outstanding shopping center is the Royal Centre Mall adjacent to the new Hyatt Hotel. There are seventy stores under one roof. English woolens are interesting because of the large selection of sweaters, jackets, and so on. Canadian vs U.S. dollar exchange rates make price savings worthwhile.

TTT: Vancouver is the port of embarkation for about six Alaska-bound, one-week cruise ships. All combine air and sea; some include land packages.

Shore Excursions: City tour (3 hours), $20. Metered taxis, city buses, and rental cars available. Free roundtrip transportation from pier to Royal Centre Mall in the center of town.

VICTORIA

Capital city of the Province of British Columbia, Victoria is usually the first or last stop on Alaska-Canada cruises and is the port of embarkation for cruises to Alaska. Located on Canada's west coast, Victoria with its quarter of a million residents retains a sharply British attitude, which blends successfully with Canadian conveniences. Victoria is a mixture of old and new, a city of picturesque old buildings containing shops selling English china and glass, woolens, sweets, and biscuits, and colorful hanging flower baskets forming unique street lamps. It maintains a calm, quiet pace, far removed from the hectic world.

The city was chosen in 1842 as a Hudson Bay trading post and fort. With the discovery of gold on the Fraser River in 1858, Victoria became the outfitting center for adventurers and miners. In 1859, Victoria became a free port, and when British Columbia joined the Dominion of Canada in 1871, Victoria became the capital city of the most westerly province.

There is much to see in Victoria: Bastion Square with its fine old buildings; the Empress Hotel with its gleaming crystal and castle-like architecture; Beacon Hill Park; Craigdarroch Castle (named for Annie Laurie's home in Scotland, it was built in 1888 and was eventually raffled for a dollar a ticket. The winner could not afford the heating bills, and the castle was turned over to the city); the Maritime Museum, devoted to artifacts connected with maritime history; Anne Hathaway's Cottage; life-size replica of the thatched cottage in which William Shakespeare's wife was born; Buchart Gardens, acres and acres of manicured and pampered gardens famous throughout the world for their incredible beauty.

Shore Excursions: City and Buchart Gardens (3 hours), $20; Buchart Gardens at night (4 hours), $20; Chaucer Lane and Anne Hathaway's Cottage (2 hours), $15; Metered taxis and city buses available dockside for transportation and sightseeing. Rental cars offer half and full-day rates.

TTT: Victoria is a good place to shop. Eskimo-carved soapstone; Alaska and Canadian jade; Indian artifacts; and antique shops specializing in English china and jewelry.

MEXICO

No other country enjoys so many popular cruise ports. Mexico has two long coastlines with deep blue harbors and beautiful small cities that have learned to accommodate visitors. Twice in 400 years the country was destroyed and a new culture imposed on its people: when Hernando Cortes conquered the ancient empire with only 400 men and forced on it the Spanish language and a Christian God; and during the repeated revolutions of the last century. Each upheaval left contrasts. Great pyramids sit in the middle of jungles, and Christian fiestas take over the cities during holiday times. Mexico City used to float on a lake and now has a subway system famous for its speed, efficiency, and modern art. Mexico offers long beaches, air conditioned hotels, a beautiful countryside, and warm, friendly people. The temperature in all port cities in semitropical, but because of its altitude Mexico City is much cooler.

Cruise Season: Most popular months are from October through May, but ships call at Mexican ports all year.

Climate: Temperature is fairly constant all year. During February, it can go from a low of 43 in northern sectors to a high of 85 in Acapulco, the southernmost port of call. Reported average temperatures in central-western ports of call are closer to the mid- and high 70s.

Currency: Mexican peso (exchange rate varies greatly almost from day-to-day)

TTT: A couple of years ago, when the peso was devalued, Mexico was a bargain for Americans. It is no longer the same kind of bargain but is a good travel buy. It's one country where the American gets his money's worth and then some. Cruise passengers are taking advantage of shopping opportunities, While last reports indicate prices are creeping up they still fall short of what they were when the peso was selling at 12.50 or 23 pesos to U.S. $1. At around 100 pesos for the U.S. dollar, Mexican-made products are still a bargain.

Language: Spanish, but English is spoken in all tourist centers and in restaurants, shops, and hotels.

Shopping: For less than $25 you can buy hand-made shirts, dolls, and sometimes full-sized guitars. There are also basket works, pottery and tiles, carved onyx, tin and copper work, hand-blown glass, and other handicrafts in local markets and stores. Check the beautiful hand-finished and embroidered patio dresses. Original models in specialty shops sell for about U.S. $65, and stateside boutiques have them priced at more than $200. There are less expensive models that can be bought for under $20 and are worth at least three times the price. They are available throughout Mexico, but I found the prices and selection best in Mazatlan. Acapulco is trendier and also more expensive. Men's hand-embroidered shorts are excellent buys and sell for about $18.

TTT: Don't hesitate to bargain everywhere except in department stores. Mexicans do not take offense. If the price is set, they will say so. If not, you will both enjoy the bargaining. Only problem is, "How low is the lowest?" You'll never know until you compare purchases and prices with shipmates after you leave port.

Time: One hour ahead of EST.

Tipping Ashore: Taxi drivers do not expect a tip, but sightseeing guides expect about 50 pesos per person; museum guides, five pesos; and waiters are usually tipped 15 to 20 percent of the bill, depending on the type or restaurant and service rendered.

Transportation: (See "Shore Excursions" for each port.) Taxis, tour buses, and railroad, as well as rental cars, mopeds, and cycles in most ports.

What to Wear Ashore: Comfortable, resort-type clothing. Sandals, jeans, and shorts are acceptable. All Mexican ports of call are resort areas, and informality in dress is one of the Mexican Riviera's choice attractions. Bring swimwear for Acapulco's beaches and for use in Puerto Vallarta and Mazatlan. Jackets are required only in very exclusive clubs and restaurants in Acapulco.

TTT: The water in Mexico is fine for Mexicans, but visitors frequently can't tolerate it. We suggest bottled drinks with no ice (which is made from tap water). Tequila and Margarita are popular and inexpensive. Bars are "for men only" in Mexico. Whiskey is very expensive, and a Scotch and soda costs more than $4 at an ordinary bar. Mexican beer is good and very inexpensive.

More Information: Mexican National Tourist Council, 405 Park Avenue, New York, NY 10022.

POPULAR PORTS OF CALL

ACAPULCO

This is one city where visitors never have to dress, and some never do. No one is a clock watcher. Breakfast is any time after waking up; lunch is from one to four; cocktails follow a siesta, and swimsuits are the uniform of the day. Dinner is served after 9 P.M. Cruise ships enter a sparkling bay and ocean backdropped by mountains accented with rows of palms and masses of purple flowers. There are miles of public and hotel beaches offering every type of water-sport facility. Don't miss Puerto Marques Beach during the day, Pie de la Cuesta at sunset, and take a glass-bottomed boat ride around the bay. Watch the high divers and the parachute skiing, or rent a boat and fish for the big ones. Shops are filled with handicrafts and chic clothes. There are elegant restaurants and a busy night life.

Shore Excursions: City tour (4 hours), $15; all-day tour, $25; Acapulco night tour, including Aztec Flyers, $30; overnight tour to Tasco (for ships that spend 48 hours in port), including hotel and meals, $120.

TTT: If you like flea markets, you'll love the one in Acapulco. The area is not dangerous, but visitors should be alert for pickpockets and thieves while shopping.

CABO SAN LUCAS

Cabo San Lucas is in Baja California, Mexico, that 800-mile sliver of Mexican territory extending south of the California border between the Pacific and the Gulf of California. Cabo San Lucas is the tip of the peninsula where the Pacific and the Gulf meet. The waters are cool, and sand and air warm, and the area unspoiled by masses of tourists. The ground is sandy and has been called "Mexico's desert." Fishing is the main sport as well as the most important industry. Picturesque, quiet and relaxing. Cruise stops depend on tide and weather conditions.

New hotels have been built, and the footsteps in the sand are being made by visitors bent on finding a "new" destination. Most impressive sight is the Cabo San Lucas Arch, a huge, natural stone formation made by the waters of the Pacific and the Sea of Cortes. Best seen on short boat trips.

Shore Excursions: Limited; a walk around the island satisfies most visitors. Some cruise lines offer a combination land and boat ride around the island for about $17.50.

ENSENADA

A picturesque port located on the north end of Todos Santos Bay, less than 100 miles south of the California-Baja border. No shore excursions are offered, so enjoy a stroll around the town and shop for Mexican arts and crafts at duty-free prices. Better still, since your ship will be visiting larger Mexican cities, stop at a native cantina and sip a cool Margarita.

MANZANILLO

This quiet, remote Mexican port really puts out a warm welcome mat when cruise ships arrive. They even ring the giant church bells. Manzanillo has a series of bays and coves, narrow streets, so-so shops, coconut and banana plantations, and Mexico's plushest, lushest resort — Las Hadas.

Shore Excursions: (3 hours) run around $15 and include a visit and drink at Las Hadas, where daily rates run up around $200 per person. Its guest list includes the famous and infamous, the great, and the traveler who likes to rub elbows with names-in-the-news.

MAZATLAN

Mazatlan, 20 miles below the Tropic of Cancer, sits on a peninsula surrounded by seemingly endless miles of beaches and rocky cliffs. It is typical of Mexico's best-known cities in the sun. It's modern port facilities are among Mexico's busiest, and both sport and commercial fishing contribute heavily to the local economy. The long, dazzling beaches attract visitors to luxury hotels.

The colonial area in the heart of downtown is 18th and 19th century, obviously untouched by the 20th century except for power lines and neon signs. Outdoor activities range from exploring coral pools to bird watching on small islands to shrimp feasting from vendors' carts and rides in two-wheeled carriages called "spiders."

Mazatlan is affectionately called "the fish trap", and they say marlin run up to 750 pounds. To prove the fish tales, scores of billfish are strung across arches on the dock. Most cruise ships arrange fishing parties on local yachts for passengers who just can't resist the temptation of marlin, dolphin, and shark at the end of their lines.

Pacifico is the local beer recommended as a thirst-quencher and the Shrimp Bucket is a good place for lunch or a snack.

Mariachi bands and high-spirited diners and drinkers are part of Mazatlan. Mexico at its leisurely best. For shopping passengers have a choice of street vendors who set up stalls pier-side, trendy shops, and city markets. Merchandise runs the gamut from an assortment of rebozos and rugs to fine jewelry and excellent shoes.

The main town square is where everyone in Mazatlan meets everyone else in Mazatlan. It's a labyrinth of narrow streets and small souvenir shops. The Golden Zone is the main tourist development area with hotels, restaurants and shops.

Shore Excursions: City tour (3 hours), $15; all day-tour, city and surrounding countryside, including lunch (7 hours), $35; fiesta evening party, $25, deep-sea fishing, private yacht with ship group, including lunch (7 to 8 hours), $75. City center is a 20-minute walk from the pier; a $4 taxi ride.

PUERTO VALLARTA

The classic vision of Old Mexico, of red tiled roofs and cobblestone streets, is a reality in Puerto Vallarta. Success hasn't spoiled this city perched on horseshoe-shaped Banderas Bay, and census takers can't keep up with growing numbers of residents and visitors. But there is still just one traffic light here, with 30,000 permanent residents determined to resist change. Donkey carts rattle over cobblestones and flaming bougainvillea hug pastel stucco walls. Houses are colorfully tiled. The Sierra Madre jungle rises above and beyond sandy beaches and plush resorts. Lovers Lane is the malecon (sea wall), and the Guadalupe Church with its lighted, crown-shaped tower adds fairyland atmosphere on moonlit nights. Puerto Vallarta is divided by the Cualo River where native women wash their clothes by pounding them on rocks and fishermen hawk their wares in early morning hours.

One side of Puerto Vallarta is complete with shops, restaurants, and nightclubs. The other side consists of wide stretches of uncrowded, uncluttered beaches, luxury hotels, and American homes. Richard Burton (and Elizabeth) and Ava Gardner almost literally put Puerto Vallarta on the map when they filmed the "Night of the Iguana" here. Shopping is convenient and within walking distance. Nearby is the picturesque village of Yelapa, preserving from the past its almost vanished Indian culture.

In the shops around the Zocalo, practice that time-honored art of bargaining for hand-crafted articles and embroidered goods. Sharpen your bargaining skills when you deal with street vendors. Shopping is convenient, and if your ship docks at the old pier, the center of town is in walking distance. From the new pier it's a 10-minute, $4 taxi ride. Siesta is between 1 and 4 P.M., and shops remain open until 7 P.M.

Shore Excursions: City tour (3 hours), $9.12; fiesta dinner and show (evening) $25; cruise around the island and beach party, $13.

TTT: If you're into crafts, check La Fuente, a local crafts-center with interesting made-in-Mexico items.

ZIHUATANEJO

An idyllic village with a different name (see-wah-tan-NEH-hoh), Zihuatanejo slumbers like a South Sea paradise waiting to be discovered. North of Acapulco, it offers a Polynesian-type vacationland, complete with coral reefs, coconut plantations, and a glistening beach where outrigger canoes are drawn right up on the sand. A comparison to the South Seas is not far fetched. Inhabitants of the region are descendants of Polynesians brought to Mexico by the Spanish in their conquest of the Pacific. These dislocated islanders continue to live on a tropical coast very much like their homeland. This rustic village is so remote that the last 30 miles of road from Acapulco were paved just a few years ago, but cruise ships have provided easy access for about 15 years. The village has become a popular one day stop for passengers on longer cruises to the more cosmopolitan ports of Mazatlan, Puerto Vallarta and Acapulco. The origin of the village's name is Tarascan, meaning "dirty women." And, while it is known that the town was founded by a Tarascan chief, the relationship of the name to the village continues to be a mystery. Water-related activities and superb beaches head the visitor's list of things to do and see. To see, there's central market square, the Potosi lighthouse at the southern tip, Las Gatas lined with thatched shelters, and miles of colorful tropical foliage and exotic birds. Pigs, dogs and stately Brahma cattle wander the streets between the buildings.

Shore Excursions: City and surrounding area (3 hours), $15.

THE YUCATAN PENINSULA

COZUMEL

The sun-drenched, easternmost tip of Mexico has recently been "discovered" by cruise ships and is on its way to becoming an "in" destination. Acapulco-type accommodations have not been completed, but the huge stretches of beach and the many inland Mayan attractions make popularity of the peninsula inevitable. Cozumel is an off-beat, tranquil vacation isle, 30 miles long, eight miles wide, and 12 miles east of the Yucatan Peninsula. Pronounced "coo-zoo-MEHL," it is definitely an area where the action isn't, but where swimming, diving, boating, and sightseeing are primary. Dress is completely informal, waters are temperate, crystal clear, and grade from the deepest indigo to sparkling topaz and aquamarine. Tropical blooms scent the air, and the only things lacking are miles of walkable beaches adjacent to the hotels.

Shore Excursions: Tour (3 hours) or beach party, $15.

MERIDA

One of the most remote and isolated of Mexico's larger cities, Merida is the capital of the state of Yucatan and the chief city on the peninsula. Overnight shore excursions are available (time permitting) from Cozumel for $75. Merida's chief interest for the visitor is as a base from which to explore the unusual Mayan ruins to the south and east of the city. Of these, the most famous is the archaeological zone of Chichen Itza, 70 miles to the east, where two groups of ancient buildings have been excavated. Several are well restored and are regarded as among the most remarkable ancient ruins in the world. Equally remarkable is another group of Mayan ruins, called Uxmal, 50 miles to the south of Merida, believed to have been an aristocratic center of Mayan rule. Most buildings date between the 7th and 11th centuries, known as the "great classic period."

PLAYA DEL CARMEN

Gateway to the Yucatan, Playa del Carmen has beautiful beaches, and a delightful small-town atmosphere. This is the most convenient point from which to see some of North America's most significant archaeological finds.

319

TULUM: A 45-minute drive to the magnificently-restored ruins of
great Mayan temples overlooking the sea.

COBA: The newest dig in the Yucatan, it is the site of a major restoration project which may turn out to be the largest Mayan city ever
discovered.

CHICHEN ITZA: The most famous Mayan/Toltec ruins about three
hours by tour bus or taxi from the port of Playa del Carmen. This is
an all-day excursion sold on board ship and includes lunch and in-
depth sightseeing. Returns to the ship about 5 p.m. and well worth
the price (varies from ship to-ship, but usually about $50).

CANCUN: Sun lover, water sports enthusiasts and beach baskers say
Cancun is as near perfect a resort as can be found anywhere in the
world. About a 45 minute drive from Playa del Carmen, it's a one-
day optional tour on most ships. There are outdoor cafes and good
shopping opportunities for Mexican silver and handicrafts.

The Mediterranean and the Black Sea

For generations, people have been fascinated by the timeless beauty of the Mare Nostrum and the wine-dark sea of Homer, by the age-old charm of their countries and the mystery of their ancient civilizations. No cruise itinerary covers all of the ports, but many ships offer a multi-faceted combination of cultures in these sun-drenched islands. For those who know the Mediterranean, cruise travel to the area is a return to familiar scenes that change so subtly it's hard to define progress. For new travelers to the area, it is a fascinating journey to discovery — minarets and winding alleyways in Cairo; Delos and Mykonos, two unspoiled gems of the Cyclades Islands; the Bay of Naples and Vesuvius; and much more.

For reasons of space, we are including only the ports most frequently visited by major cruise ships. Again, the information is geared to a short visit, during which the traveler wants to see the highlights, get a feel of the atmosphere, and check the shopping. shore excursion prices are based on current average charges by cruise lines and are subject to change. These rates will vary as much as 25 percent, depending on the ship and the quality of the tour. Don't expect air conditioned comfort on buses or in taxis in some of the Greek Islands. You can, however, expect a warm welcome.

Passports are required but inoculations are no longer necessary in most countries. Shore excursion prices vary from ship-to-ship but average out at about $25 for a half day without lunch.

CANARY ISLANDS

Legend puts these seven islands into the legendary lost continent of Atlantis, supposedly its highest peaks. The islands are Spanish provinces and retain much of the mother country's culture and traditions. The Canaries are 72 miles from the northwest coast of Africa and about 650 miles from the southern tip of Europe.

Cruise Season: From April through October. Most popular months are June, July, August. World cruises call during winter months.

Climate: Temperature averages 76 degrees in August, 64 degrees in January. Spring-like all year.

Currency: Spanish pesetas

Shopping: Stores closed between 1 and 4 P.M. Saturday and all day Sunday.

Time: Seven hours ahead of EST.

Tipping Ashore: Restaurants, bars, and hotel service personnel expect 10 to 15 percent when no service charge has been added. Same to taxi drivers, but never less than 20 pesetas.

Transportation: Rental cars, taxis, local buses, tours are available.

What to Wear Ashore: Casual, resort-type lightweight clothing. Swimwear to use on the beautiful beaches; jackets for men and more dressy resort clothes for dinner in better restaurants and hotel dining rooms.

More Information: Spanish National Tourist Office, 665 Fifth Avenue, New York, NY 10017.

EGYPT

Cruise Season: Late March through mid-November. Most popular months: May through mid-October, but world cruises call all year.

Climate: Relatively mild in port areas, but dips to a windy low in the mid–40s in Alexandria in mid-January.

Currency: Egyptian pound

Language: Arabic, but English is spoken in large cities and in hotels catering to Western visitors.

Time: Seven hours ahead of EST.

Tipping Ashore: A service charge of 10 to 15 percent is added in restaurants and hotels, and it is not necessary to tip in addition. However, 5 to 10 percent is usual. Taxi drivers expect at least 10 percent.

Transportation: Taxis are metered and inexpensive. Rental cars are available, but traffic is fierce and competitive, especially in Cairo. Short-term visitors do better using cabs. Outside of Cairo, horse and carriages are available in most cities for $4 to $7 per hour, depending on the size of the city and demand of the moment.

Shopping: Bazaars are visitors' delights, but sharpen your best bargaining skills. Everything is negotiable. Good buys in gold cartouches (pendants to wear on neck chains) made to order with your name in heiroglyphics; available in 10 to 24-carat gold and priced accordingly. Also, handicrafts, cotton, carpets, jewelry.

What to Wear Ashore: Casual, lightweight cottons and drip-dry clothing. Summer months are very, very hot, so bring a hat. (See additional tips under "Cruising the Nile"). No shorts, ladies. That is, unless you don't mind attracting attention, snickers and sneers; not to mention a lot of touching by native men.
More Information: Egyptian Tourist Office, 630 Fifth Avenue, New York, N.Y. 10020.

ALEXANDRIA

Most ships call at Alexandria and allow one or two days in port. This is a seaside resort with modern facilities and ancient sites. Shore excursion options include sightseeing in and around Alexandria; also one-day and overnight tours to Cairo, depending on how long the vessel remains in port. In Alexandria, you'll see the Graeco-Roman Museum with a collection of items dating back to the 3rd century B.C.; the Serapium Temple with Pompey's Pillar about its ruins; the Catacombs of Kom El Shugaffa; the residence of the former royal family; the Amphitheater with its famed marble terraces.

CAIRO

A one-day visit to Cairo allows for merely a sampler of what this city and its surroundings have to offer. If this is your first visit, your "must list" is headed by the three great Pyramids of Giza and the Sphinx. You'll probably opt for the camel ride around the Pyramids and be photographed. Time permitting, you should see the Step Pyramid, about an hour's drive to Sakkara. In Cairo, highlight of any visit must be a few hours at the Egyptian Museum with its treasures dating back as far as 5,000 years. There's the Citadel of Cairo built in 1183, the Al Azhar Mosque, the cities of the dead, the old synagogue, the Coptic church and a lot more. Evening entertainment ranges from a romantic felucca (native boat) ride on the Nile to Las Vegas-type revues, belly dancers and casinos in Western-style hotels.

TTT: For guidance on bargaining techniques in Egypt, I pass along a personal experience. The first asking price for a galabea (long, native-type dress comparable to a patio-type dress) was $85. I didn't respond quickly, and before I could counter-offer, the asking price dropped to $60. I hesitated again. While evaluating how much the fancy I had taken to the dress was worth, the price dropped to $50. As a starting point of the negotiations, I offered $20. When the vendor countered with $50, I stuck to my $20, rapidly developing more interest in the game of haggling than I had in the dress. Within a couple of minutes the galabea was mine for the $20. Can't promise the same kind of success in all Egyptian markets or stores, but it is worth the effort if you don't want to overpay and want the fun of trying for the lowest price. Bargaining is expected in all stores and markets, except in five-star hotel, but it's worth a try even here. I heard of good "discounts" in even the most exclusive places.

FRANCE

Cruise Season: April through October. Most popular months: June, July, and August.

Climate: Summer temperature in northern France averages 76 degrees; the Riviera is sunny and warmer in summer, with an average January temperature of 48 degrees.

Currency: French franc

Language: French

Shopping: Many shops still close between noon and 2 P.M. Ready-to-wear, perfumes, gloves, and crystal are favorites with visitors. Department stores are good places to shop.

Time: Six hours ahead of EST.

Tipping Ashore: This is part of the French way of life. The usual 15 to 20 percent service charge is added to restaurant and hotel bills, but waiters and other service personnel expect an additional 5 to 10 percent. Taxi drivers expect 15 percent; cloakroom attendants, two francs.

Transportation: Local buses, metered taxis, rental cars are available.

What to Wear Ashore: City-type clothing, if the tour takes you to major urban areas; dressy, casual resort-wear on the Riviera; jackets for dinner in nicer restaurants and hotels.

More Information: French Government Tourist Office, 610 Fifth Avenue, New York, NY 10020.

CANNES

The city may owe its name to the abundance of reeds (cannes) in marshes long drained, but Cannes owes its rise to fame to the outbreak of an epidemic in the better-known resort of Nice in 1834, just as an important English lord was getting ready for his holiday there. He sojourned in Cannes instead and returned to London with nothing but praise. From then on, progress advanced rapidly — including casinos, the film festival, resort-hotel complexes. The seaside setting, sandy beaches, and ritzy tone helped boost real estate values. If time allows, be sure to wander outside Cannes to visit Provence, Grasse, Vence, St. Paul de Vence, Antibes, and Juan-les-Pins. The best time of year is early spring. Cannes is hardly the place to do your bargain shopping. World-famous jewelers and dress designers usually offer the same merchandise everywhere else at lower prices except during this strong U.S. dollar period. High fashion clothes carrying big ticket numbers are good buys if you wear the labels.

Shore Excursion: To Nice (4 hours), $45; to Cap d'Antibes (9 hours), $80, including lunch.

GIBRALTAR

A self-governing British colony since 1704, Gibraltar is strategically placed opposite Ceuta. Together, they form the legendary Pillars of Hercules. Within this tiny British enclave is a wealth of scenery, history, and even wildlife, in the form of the mischievous Barbary apes you can see during your trip to the famous Rock. Gibraltar is 1,400 feet above the sea, and though it is part of the Iberian Peninsula geographically, its geology is African. The town is noisy and very busy.

Cruise Season: April through October.
Climate: Mild winters; hot summers average 88.
Currency: Gibraltar pound
Language: English and Spanish.
Shopping: Not much. However, imported pharmaceuticals and toiletries are relatively inexpensive.
Time: Six hours ahead of EST.
Tipping Ashore: A service charge of 10 to 15 percent is added to restaurant bills; otherwise, tip 10 percent. Taxi drivers expect 10 percent.
Shore Excursion: Scenic tour (4 hours), $16.00.
Transportation: Fixed rate taxis for point-to-point or by the hour (about $7 for the first hour). Car ferry and passenger boats to Tangiers take almost 3 hours for day excursions and cost about $35.
What to Wear Ashore: Comfortable, informal lightweight clothing.
More Information: Gibraltar Tourist Office, 2 Grand Building, Trafalgar Square, London, WC 2, England.

GREECE

Cruise Season: April through late October. High-season months: June, July, August.

Climate: Athens temperatures range from low of 52 in April to high of 90 in July and August. Islands to the south of Athens average 10 to 15 degrees warmer.

Currency: Drachma

Language: Greek but English and French are widely spoken and understood.

Shopping: Original designs in 18-carat gold jewelry, but prices are not cheap. Good buys in locally woven fabrics, handmade silver jewelry, icons, and ornaments. Shops usually closed Monday, Wednesday and Saturday afternoons; all day Sunday.

Time: Seven hours ahead of EST.

Tipping Ashore: A service charge of 8 to 10 percent is included in restaurant and hotel checks, but waiters expect an additional 10 percent in restaurants, 5 percent in cafes and bars, taxi drivers are happy with 5 to 10 percent, but it is not obligatory; tour bus guides and drivers should be tipped about 20 drachmas.

Transportation: To Athens from Piraeus: buses and taxis. On islands: shore excursions; taxis, some buses, car rentals; and on foot or by donkey. Depending on the ship's time in port, a variety of tours are offered. Athens and the Acropolis (3 hours), $25; evening ashore (includes show and dinner at deluxe hotel), $70; all-day tours to surrounding areas and cities, $40 (including lunch). Public transport is good and reasonable. Taxi from port to Athens, about $25.

What to Wear Ashore: City clothing in Athens; comfortable shoes for the Acropolis and other sightseeing walks. Comfortable, resort-type clothing for island ports of call.

More Information: Greek National Tourist Office, 150 East 58th Street, New York, NY 10022.

ATHENS AND PIRAEUS

Nothing rivals the ancient classical perfection of the Acropolis in Athens. The Parthenon, the Temple of the Winged Victory, the Erechtheum with the Caryatids supporting the porch, and the Acropolis Museum are ageless in their beauty. Spreading out below these memorials to the past is a modern European capital, gay and animated; a city of striking contrasts. Other scenes of classic fame lie nearby: Corinth, the Temple of Poseidon at Sounion, Delphi, and Mycenae.

All ships bound for Athens arrive in its port, Piraeus, about 14 miles away. Whether you opt for the ship tour, the local bus or trolley car, or a taxi, the ride from the port takes you through smaller fishing villages and ports. You'll travel to Constitution Square, the Tomb of the Unknown Soldier, the Old Palace. On the way to the Acropolis (a must for both first-timers and repeat visitors), pass the Temple of Zeus, Hadrian's Arch, and the National Library, and mix with the natives at sidewalk cafes, shops, and on the streets.

Athens is truly an inspiring city, ideal for tourists and an ideal starting point for any Greek adventure. It is a pastel-toned city, offset by greenery that surprises many visitors. Built as an outdoor city, every house has a or garden. Coffee shops, bars and taverns are everywhere. Athens is a walking city, and a comfortable pair of shoes is essential here and throughout Greece. Few visitors leave without climbing the Acropolis for a view of modern Athens and a feel for ancient Athens. From ancient relics to encounters with Lady Luck in 20th-century casinos, Greece accommodates the visitor. There are casinos as active as any in Europe, situated atop Mt. Parnes (about an hour's drive from Athens) and on Rhodes and Corfu.

My best encounter with Greek history was my first "Sound and Light" performance at the Acropolis. My second encounter was the same type of show in Rhodes. Both are inspiring, educational and entertaining which is about all one can expect from a day or two in any port of call.

THE GREEK ISLANDS

Don't expect great sights on the Greek Islands. They are peaceful retreats where history happened. Some offer more tourist pleasures than others that merely afford a chance to visit a small unspoiled village. Most are too small for group excursions, and you can walk the island in an hour or so. Where excursions are offered, they cost between $10 and $18.00 for three or four hours. Taxis are available. Wear very comfortable, low-heel shoes.

YACHT CHARTERS

Adventurous travelers searching for the unusual, but addicted to the sea, are opting for private yacht charters. They are finding these yachts in the Greek Islands and in Caribbean ports. When three couples get together and share the experience and expenses, it becomes affordable. Calculating costs on that basis (six persons), for $150 per, they can charter a good-sized sailing yacht or motor sailor staffed and crewed, including a cook. Prices run higher in the Caribbean.

Chartering is the best way to explore less-frequently visited islands, and in Greece there are about 1,000 yachts to choose from, ranging from a be-your-own-crew, 24-foot sailboat sleeping four (about $80 per day, per person), to the Belle Simone, the 250-foot, 436-ton, ocean-going yacht used in the motion picture "The Greek Tycoon", suitable for tycoons who can afford the $10,000-a-day tab. All Greek cruisers are government registered and inspected annually by the Ministry of Merchant Marine.

For details, contact the Greek Yacht Brokers & Consultants Association, 36 Alkyonis St., Palaio Phaleron (Athens), Greece, or the Yacht Owners Association, 43 Freatidos St., Piraeus, Greece.

THE ISLANDS

CORFU — An Ionian island with not much more than great scenery and sandy beaches. There is a resort center and the 16th-century Church of St. Spyridon, patron saint of the island.

CRETE — Heraklion is the main city of Crete, the largest of the Greek islands. It was founded by the Saracens about 1,000 B.C. They were followed by the Venetians, then the Turks, who held on for a couple of centuries. In 1913, Crete became part of Greece. Since most cruise ships stop here, the natives are ready for the tourists, and street shops beckon with homemade goods. Tours and sightseeing take the visitor to see the El Greco icons at the church of St. Menas, and two museums.

DELOS AND THE CYCLADES — Delos, birthplace of Apollo and Artemis, is the smallest of the Cyclades islands. It became the religious center of the Ionians and the site of annual festivities during the Golden Age. Excavations have revealed remains of temples, commercial houses, theaters, sanctuaries, and quantities of fine mosaics from those long-ago times.

Center of the Cyclades, this three-mile square rocky island, now deserted, was once the wealthiest of the Aegean, with a population of over 20,000. Officially an archaeological site, Delos served as the center of the civilized world in its days of glory. Most interesting is the Alley of the Lions. Tours are offered by ships calling at Delos and at Mykonos.

MYKONOS — Mountainous and rocky Mykonos rises up from the dark Aegean Sea to a height of almost 1,200 feet. A beautiful island famous for its gleaming white windmills and neat, cube-like houses, Mykonos is considered the gem of the Cyclades. The life-style for visitors and residents is tranquil and unhurried, which probably accounts for the influx of artists and jetsetters from all over Europe during the summer months. A "swinging island", it has a number of bars, clubs and discos (as well as an inordinate number of beautiful people). Mykonos also is noted for its nudist beaches and boutiques lining narrow and quaint cobblestone alleyways. Favorite snack is octopus with ouzo and fresh lobster meat. (No shore excursions are offered.)

RHODES and the DODECANESE — The 600-square mile island has over 26,000 hotel beds, but can hardly be called over developed, since the concentration of the accommodations is in the "new" city of Rhodes, and stretched along the two coasts out of the city of Rhodes for about 20 miles.

Situated on the pointed tip of the island's north, the town of Rhodes with its full-time population of 35,000 is divided into two sections: one is the colorful and interesting Old Town or medieval city "Protected" by 30-foot-high, five-mile-long sandstone walls. This is home to some 8,000 people who live in arched, high-ceilinged apartments. Exteriors of buildings have not been altered, and many have been discreetly restored. One walks the cobblestone streets and alleyways much as the knights of St. John of Jerusalem did centuries earlier.

Among the offerings are antiques, copper, modern jewelry fashioned in a workshop adjoining the store, ceramics, donkey saddles, freshly-ground coffee, fine worsted and other cloth, shoes, sandals, handbags, old goldsmiths' balances, pistols, swords, daggers, muskets, blunderbusses, hand-cranked coffee mills, brass candlesticks, replica icons, scarves, T-shirts, carpets, flokati rugs, marble tables, chess sets with table of onyx and metal, mink coats, fur jackets, votive offerings, hand-made candles, a birthday cake, a seafood meal, Greco-Turkish sweets and 72-hour made-to-measure suit, among other items.

The other section of town is called the "new" town, and includes the octagonal marketplace and the bustling yacht harbor of Mandraki in front of it. The latter is "guarded" by two friendly deer, the symbol of the island.

Rhodes is the largest and most beautiful of the Dodecanese Islands. The popular port of call contrasts neat, blue-trimmed and white-washed houses, tidy parks, and the walled medieval city. There are excursions to the nearby ancient town of Lindos to see the Sanctuary of Athene in its acropolis overlooking the sea. Another excursion goes to the northern coast to the city of Kamiros, built in the shape of an amphitheater, on the slopes of a wooded hill.

SANTORINI—Known as Kalliste (or most beautiful) and Strongyli (round) in ancient times. Santorini is rich in history. It was thought by many scientists to have been the lost continent of Atlantis. There is an exciting donkey-back climb up a zig-zag steep trail to reach the village of Thera atop the precipice, from which you can sip local wine and stare at the cone of Greece's last active volcano.

At the village of Akrotiri a museum is being built on the site where the sensational discoveries of a buried city were unearthed in 1967.

TTT: There is a newly-completed, paved road up to the mountain to Thera, but the donkey ride is Santorini the way it used to be. Tours by taxi are available, but the donkey ride is more fun. Bargain for either one way or roundtrip. And, don't pay the until you are safely down the mountain.

If you are an animal lover and will be offended because the donkey master hits the animal to get him moving, take the taxi ride up. I didn't mind and neither did the donkey. There is great camaraderie between the animal and the man who feeds it.

ISRAEL

Cruise Season: March through mid-November. Most popular months: May through September, but world cruises call all year.

Climate: Mild in port areas, with a low of 46 in March, high of 87 in August in Haifa and Tel Aviv, cooler in mountain areas.

Currency: Israeli Shekel

Language: Hebrew; signs are also in English, which is widely spoken. Yiddish, German, Arabic and French are also spoken.

Shopping: All major stores are closed from sundown on Friday to Sunday morning. Good buys in locally made jewelry, beachwear, copper, knitwear, religious ornaments, and diamonds of less than one carat (but shop carefully).

Time: Seven hours ahead of EST.

Tipping Ashore: A service charge of 10 to 15 percent is usually included in restaurant and hotel bills, but it is customary to add additional 5 to 10 percent; taxi drivers expect 10 percent. It is customary to tip as much as 25 percent in nightclubs.

Transportation: Local and inter-city buses, metered taxis, sheruts (shared taxis, or jitneys, with fixed rates), rental cars are available.

What to Wear Ashore: Casual, lightweight cottons and drip-dry clothing. Take a raincoat and light woolens during late fall and winter months for touring; sturdy shoes are a necessity for exploring outside major cities.

More Information: Ministry of Tourism, Israeli Government, 488 Madison Avenue, New York, NY 10022.

HAIFA

Unfortunately, most cruise ships only spend two days in Israel, a country where one can spend a lifetime and still not see or understand it all. So what can you do with a single day in Israel, or with two days. With 24 hours in the Holy Land, you can see the port city of Haifa, travel by motorcoach to Nazareth to see the Church of St. Joseph, Mary's Well, and other historical sites before continuing past the village of Cana to Tiberias on the shore of the Sea of Galilee. From there to Capernaum to visit the ruins of the ancient synagogue and to the Mount of Beatitudes (scene of the Sermon on the Mount). Return to Haifa along the shores of the Galilee to visit a kibbutz and take in a final panoramic view from Mount Carmel. With an extra day in port, Jerusalem, Bethlehem, and Tel Aviv can be added to your bird's eye view of Israel.

Shore Excursion: Full days (without lunch), $50; half-day city tours, $35. Car rentals, limos with guides are available. Inter-city bus service is excellent. Some ships offer overnight tours to Jerusalem, about $250 per person, double.

TTT: If this is your first visit to Israel, don't try to see it all in 24 hours. Choose the highlights and plan to return. If Israel is a highlight of your cruise, select a ship that spends more time in port. Occasionally ships have special itineraries. I found one a couple of years ago that spent eight days of a 14-day cruise in Israel. Ship was my hotel, and Israel was a gangplank away. Some ships call at Ashdod instead of Haifa, which is more convenient for sightseeing but more isolated for just walking around. Wear comfortable shoes for a fast day of sightseeing.

ITALY

Cruise Season: March through November. Most popular months: May through September.

Climate: Temperatures range from a low of 46 in April to a high of 90 in August. Generally mild in port areas all year.

Currency: Lire

Language: Italian.

Shopping: The strong dollar has made Italy a delightful "bargain" for Americans. There are excellent good buys in shoes, handbags, all leather goods, jewelry, gloves, and glassware. Best buys are in designer wear. The more expensive the item, the larger the differential between what the item sells for in Fifth Avenue shops. Stores in major cities remain open during lunch hours.

Time: Six hours ahead of EST.

Tipping Ashore: When a service charge is included in the bill, tip an additional 10 percent; otherwise, tip 15 to 20 percent. Taxi drivers expect 15 percent; same in bars, more in nightclubs. Tip guides the equivalent of U.S. $1.

Transportation: Good local bus system, subway in Rome, plenty of metered taxis, and rental cars (but watch out for wild and reckless drivers, who treat highways like the Grand Prix).

What to Wear Ashore: Depends on tour area, but "comfort" and "casual" are key words. Remember: head, shoulders, and arms should be covered on visits to churches. More formal for dinner in posh restaurants.

More Information: Italian State Tourist Department, 630 Fifth Avenue, New York, NY 10020.

GENOA

The harbor entrance to Genoa is spectacular. The fifth largest city in Italy and the major port, Genoa has been the birthplace and home of such world-famous men as Christopher Columbus, the Italian patriot Guiseppe Mazzini, and the violinist Paganini.

Genoa has become a popular passenger port of embarkation for Mediterraneanbound cruise ships and for other vessels. Most air-sea programs allow for time to sightsee in and around the city.

It's easy to get around Genoa by taxi, bus, or private car, and all ships offer shore excursions to Columbus' home outside the old city gates, the San Lorenzo Cathedral, the ducal palace, the Bianco Palace, and the Staglieno Cemetery. Some tours go beyond Genoa along the coastline through the Maritime Alps. It's a particularly scenic highway linking small fishing villages, old towns, and the French border.

It time permits, include a visit to Savona, 20 miles to the southwest of Genoa. Savona has an old cathedral and an excellent museum.

NAPLES

The ship's arrival at Naples is worth a 6 A.M. call. You'll glide past the craggy islands into the great bay, past the Castel del'Ovo, once the home of Lucullus, on its mini island. The city, stacked up like a great amphitheater constructed of boxes, is guarded by castles. Naples is a glorious mixture. Italy's third largest city, it is divided into districts that have their own dialects. The great harbor of Naples can be seen on hydrofoil or steamer trips to the nearby islands of Capri, Ischia, and Procida. Naples is a delight in springtime. The weather is mild all year, but a summer walk around the curving sea promenade, a stop for Campari soda or coffee in cafes, or lunch at a waterside restaurant before the summer crowds arrive is rewarding. There is much to see here — the cathedral, 13 museums, the architecture. Though Naples seems like a constant whirl of traffic, there are quiet areas, such as the Catacombs of San Gennaro or the park around Villa Floridiana. The main shopping area is the Via Roma, but bargains are more likely to be found in the small shops anywhere in the city. Silk scarves, luggage, handbags, and accessories by well-known Italian designers cost a lot less than they do back home.

Shore Excursion: City tour and Pompeii (9 hours), $50.00 including lunch; half-day city tour, $20.00.

VENICE

This must be the most beautiful and romantic city in the world. It is justly renowned as Queen of the Adriatic and befittingly adorned with fabulous treasures. All tours start with the Palace of the Doges, the Basilica of St. Mark with its wonderful mosaics, St. Mark's Square, where everyone feeds the pigeons that obligingly pose for photographs, the Bridge of Sighs, the magnificent Palazza Rezzonico, and the Ca' d'Oro, one of the city's oldest houses. Venice also means the silent gliding of gondolas along the Grand Canal, exquisite glassware, and great shopping opportunities. Visitors long remember their stay in this city of lagoons.

Shore Excursion: By gondola and on foot (4 hours), $25.

MADEIRA

Truly an enchanted island, Madeira rises green and steep from the depths of the Atlantic, its contours visibly volcanic. The island as it is

333

today was created by man from sheer wilderness. Goncalves Zarco and his company landed in 1419, Madeira was uninhabited and so densely wooded that immense forests had to be cleared before it could be settled. Legend has it that, almost a century before, a young Englishman and his lady friend were eloping. Their ship foundered, and they were cast ashore at Madeira. The soldiers accompanying them escaped to the north coast of Africa and were sold into slavery. When the story eventually reached Prince Henry the Navigator, Zarco was dispatched to find the island. Whatever the truth, visitors now find it one of the nicest islands on earth, probably best known for its Madeira wine. Funchal and Machico, the principal towns, both lie on charming bays. Funchal has a leisurely Old World atmosphere with cobbled streets, marble pavings, and elegant balconies. The cathedral has arcades of painted lava rock and a remarkable ceiling of ivory inlaid in cedar wood. Inland lie dramatic valleys and sharp, high mountain peaks.

Shore Excursion: Scenic tour (4 hours), $25.

MALTA

Cruise Season: April through mid-November.
Climate: Winters are mild; summers can be very hot, with temperatures from a low of 72 to a high of 90 in August.
Currency: Maltese pound
Language: English, Maltese, and Italian.
Shopping: Good buys in heavy lace and cloth, pottery, ceramics, wall plates, and replicas of antique jewelry in gold and silver. Be sure to see some of the famous filigree and the dolls. Check the prices of French perfume.
Time: Six hours ahead of EST.
Tipping Ashore: About 10 percent of bill in restaurants, in bars, and to taxi drivers.
Transportation: Colorful local buses, metered taxis, rental cars, water taxis are available.
What to Wear Ashore: Lightweight, informal, easy-to-wash clothing.
More Information: Malta Mission to the United National, 249 East 35 Street, New York, NY 10016.

MOROCCO

Cruise Season: April through November.
Climate: Sunny and warm all year. Temperatures average from a low of 60 to a high of 95 in summer months.

Currency: Dirham
Language: Arabic and French. English understood widely.
Shopping: Good buys are copperware, caftans, silver and gold jewelry, and handcrafted items. Shop in the souks (markets), but bargain, bargain, bargain.
Time: Six hours ahead of EST.
Tipping Ashore: A service charge of 10 to 15 percent is usually added to restaurant and hotel bills; additional tips not required. Taxi drivers ex pect 15 percent.
Transportation: Local buses are not recommended. Plenty of metered taxis and chauffeur-driven limousines. Special gas coupons for reduced price fuel for rental cars.
What to Wear Ashore: Casual, lightweight clothing; sandals and comfortable shoes; but no shorts for women.
More Information: Moroccan National Tourist Office, 521 Fifth Avenue, Suite 280, New York, NY 10017.

TANGIER

Standing at the entrance to the Strait of Gibraltar, Tangier presents a fascinating picture of East and West. The old casbah of narrow souks huddled around the Sultan's Palace is worthy of an illustrated Arabian Nights, but modern Tangier is a sophisticated European-style city with smart shops and good hotels. Most visitors enjoy bargaining in the bazaars. Favorite items are leatherworks, Moroccan rugs, and Oriental-styled jewelry.

Shore Excursion: City and surrounding area (4 hours) $20.

PORTUGAL

Cruise Season: From late March through early November. Most popular months: April through September.
Climate: Generally mild with summer temperatures reaching highs in the 90s, lows in the 60s. Lisbon is much cooler during winter months.
Currency: Portuguese Escudo (The written sign for escudo is similar to the U.S. dollar sign ($), so be careful when shopping.)
Language: Portuguese, English is spoken widely.
Shopping: Good buys are wines, handicrafts, baskets, some jewelry, and, of course, Madeira lace.
Time: Seven hours ahead of EST.

Tipping Ashore: A tax of about 5 percent is added automatically to all restaurant and hotel charges, as is a 10 percent service charge, but waiters still expect at least 10 percent more. Tip taxi drivers between 15 and 20 percent of the meter or agreed-upon price.

Transportation: In Lisbon: buses, taxis, and rental cars. In other ports: local buses are slow, but taxis are plentiful (some are without meters, so prices should be agreed upon in advance.)

What to Wear Ashore: If your port of call is Lisbon, count on seasonal, city-type clothing. In resort areas, dress casually. The islands are less formal than the capital city.

More Information: Portuguese National Tourist Office, 548 Fifth Avenue, New York, NY 10036.

LISBON

Whether Lisbon is a port of embarkation or a port of call, you should take time to see some of the great places. Even the churches are rated as museums. Your tour should include the old riding school of the royal palace, the Naval Museum, which houses an impressive collection of artifacts, the wide avenues, the beautiful shops, and the nearby famous resort of Estoril, where deposed royalty spends much of its time.

Lisbon is a city with much to offer, and a cruise ship visit only encourages travelers to return for further exploration. This is one port where dinner or lunch in a fabulous seafood restaurant is worthwhile, and where a passenger will enjoy just walking the streets, sipping native wine at one of the many cafes, and mingling with the friendly Portuguese people.

MADEIRA

Some 600 miles southwest of the mainland, Madeira is mountainous and cultivated with tropical fruits, a profusion of flowers and those famous grapes used in Madeira wines. It is often described as a floating garden in the Atlantic.

Funchal is the port city and has about 100,000 residents, or about one-third the island's population. Flower vendors are a few steps down the gangplank, and wineries are generous with their free samples. The island has one beach at Prainha, but all major hotels have swimming pools and usually welcome cruise ship passengers. Among things to see and do are visits to the village of Monte or Terreiro de Luta. A memorable return is by non-conventional toboggan slide downhill over cobblestones worn smooth from the days when hill villagers sent produce to market this way. Ride is in a large basket on wooden runners, with two men keeping pace alongside to control the trip with ropes. Not recommended for the faint of heart. In Funchal, see the Mercado do Lavradores near the port. The stalls are manned by costumed flower vendors. Also see the Museum of Sacred Art, the Cathedral and the Casa do Turista for local handicrafts.

SPAIN

Cruise Season: April through October. Most popular months: June–August.

Climate: Temperatures range from a low of 50 in April to a high of 86 in August. Average temperature is 80 during June, July, and August.

Currency: Spanish peseta

Language: Spanish

Shopping: Best buys include leather items (shoes, handbags, luggage), suede, ceramic (Lladro) figures, Mallorca pearls. Some shops closed 1–4 p.m.; all closed on Sundays, and Saturday afternoon. Department stores remain open through siesta hours and on Saturdays.

Time: Six hours ahead of EST.

Tipping Ashore: In restaurants, tip 10 percent above the 15 percent service charge added to bills; a minimum of 10 pesetas to taxi drivers; tip tour bus drivers and guides 25 to 50 pesetas, depending on services.

Transportation: In cities, buses, metered taxis, and rental cars; a subway in Madrid.

What to Wear Ashore: City clothes in Barcelona; resort-type clothing on other ports of call. Conservative is Spanish style.

More Information: Spanish National Tourist Office, 665 Fifth Avenue, New York, NY 10017.

BARCELONA

Christopher Columbus' statue gazes from its pillar in Plaza Puerta de la Paz across the large, bustling port of Barcelona, observing the spectrum of liners, cargo and fishing boats, pleasure craft, and the full-size replica of Columbus's Santa Maria. Barcelona was an important center of civilization long before Roman times, and ancient remnants are visible in Barcelona square, in mosaics on houses, and in the museums. Barcelona is a beautiful city combining the old with the new in a mellow way. The spectacular spires of Gaudi's unfinished Sagrada Familia church, his Parque Guell, Picasso's works in the Cofradia Street Museum, and the fountains of Carlos Buigas bear witness to the artistic genius of the past. The circular Plaza Rambla de Cataluna is circled with antique shops and is the center of life in Barcelona. The ramblas radiating from it have wide central pavements famous for morning flower markets that also sell birds, tortoises, and kittens. Top couturier boutiques are on the Paseo de Gracia, and excellent shops featuring mens' and women's clothing, leather, and jewelry are well located throughout the city. A visit to Barcelona without a taste of zarzuela (a rich shellfish dish) would be a pity.

Shore Excursions: City tour (4 hours), $25; tour of countryside (4 hours), $30.00.

MALAGA

One of Spain's leading resort cities, Malaga has fine hotels, excellent shops, and parks, as well as interesting reminders of the past in the cathedral and the Moorish Palace of the Alcazar. It boasts a splendid bullring, and from the vantage point of Gibralfaro, there is a magnificent view of the city. A few miles away is the smart resort of Torremolinos.

Shore Excursions: City tour (3 hours), $25; Grenada (10 hours), $65, including lunch.

PALMA DE MALLORCA
(Balearic Islands)

This fashionable resort-island city is another blend of old and new. Modern holiday hotels are door-to-door with a magnificent 13th-century cathedral, winding lanes, and medieval palaces. Of interest is a scenic drive to the Carthusian Monastery at Validemosa, where George Sand and Chopin set up housekeeping, thus causing more than a casual ripple of scandal in polite Victorian households. Known for its beaches .paand thousands of European visitors, Palma de Mallorca has been replaced on the jet-setters' list of favorite places.

Shore Excursion: City and surrounding (4 hours), $20.

TURKEY

Cruise Season: All year. Most popular months: April through mid-November.

Climate: The Black Sea coast is damp and mild; the Mediterranean is sunny and warm. Temperatures in Istanbul range from 58, to 85 in July.

Currency: Turkish lire

Language: Turkish, Greek, and Arabic.

Shopping: Head for the bazaar and look for jewelry, Meerschaum pipes, daggers, ceramics, rugs, and carpets, and don't hesitate to bargain for the last lire. That's part of the sport! But buyer beware when it comes to expensive items, particularly jewelry and antiques.

Time: Seven hours ahead of EST.

Tipping Ashore: A service charge of 10 to 15 percent is added to restaurant and bar bills, but tip an additional 5 percent; taxi drivers do not expect a tip.

Transportation: Avoid public transportation. There are plenty of taxis, but determine price in advance.

What to Wear Ashore: Light, casual clothing; comfortable shoes; head and arms should be covered for visits to Mosques. Avoid shorts and mini-skirts.

More Information: Turkish Government Tourism and Information Office, 821 United Nations Plaza, New York, NY 10017.

ISTANBUL

The approach to Istanbul by ship is a spectacular introduction to a city where 2,500 years of history are so closely woven together it is hard to separate the threads. Most ships spend a complete day and evening in Istanbul, and it is possible to see the city on your own or with the ship tour, which returns passengers to the vessel for lunch, then picks them up for the afternoon tour. Highlight of any visit to Istanbul must be the Blue Mosque, the Aqueduct of Valens, the Old Seraglio, and, of course, the covered bazaar. The size of this Middle Eastern supermarket is overwhelming to first-time visitors. From harem clothes to antiques and precious gems—it's all available at a price. The price. That's between the buyer and seller, and no two passengers ever end up paying the same amount of money for the identical item. Bargain, bargain, bargain! They take U. S. dollars, traveler's checks, personal checks, or what have you, and merchants will do anything, or almost anything, within their power to close a sale.

Shore Excursions: City tour, including the bazaar (8 hours), $30; nightclub tour with typical entertainment (4 hours), $45.

YUGOSLAVIA

Cruise Season: Mid-April through mid-October.
Climate: Warm and dry along the coast. Temperatures in Belgrade range from 55 to 85 in summer months.
Currency: Dinar
Language: Serbo-Croatian, Slovenian; also German and some English.
Shopping: Good buys in native handicrafts, dolls, gold and silver filigree jewelry, carpets, leather goods, crystal, and pottery.
Time: Six hours ahead of EST.
Tipping Ashore: Not required, but 10 percent is considered a fair tip in restaurants, bars, and to taxi drivers.
Transportation: Local buses are good, plenty of taxis, rental cars.
What to Wear Ashore: Casual, lightweight clothing and swimwear; dressier for dinner in better restaurants, hotels and casinos.
More Information: Yugoslav National Tourist Office, 630 Fifth Avenue, New York, NY 10020.

DUBROVNIK AND KOTOR BAY

Sail along the coastline of Yugoslavia to Dubrovnik, the quaint old seaport of Dalmatia. Within its ancient walls and narrow streets are 15th century Rector's Palace, now a magnificent museum. A wealth of medieval buildings includes Franciscan and Dominican monasteries, old churches, towers, and city gates. Most shore excursions will include a drive to the heights above the town, which afford spectacular panoramic views, including the tiny island of Lokrum, where Richard the Lion-hearted was allegedly shipwrecked in 1190.

The North Cape,
Northern Europe, and
the Soviet Union

A thousand years ago, the Norsemen left their homeland in dragon-bowed wooden vessels. Today they're back, bringing with them thousands of passengers on board sleek and not-so-sleek ships. They sail up the rugged, jagged fjord-laced coast of Norway, across the Artic Circle, and on to Europe's northernmost point, the magnificent North Cape.

Other ships sail into the Baltic and to the sophisticated cosmopolitan cities in Scandinavia and on the Continent, where once the sight of a foreign ship meant trouble. Today it means scores of eager visitors anxious to explore. Other ships combine the North Cape with the Baltic, then sail on to visit the contemporary life and cultural richness of Europe and Russia.

While the isolated master works of nature are the essence of North Cape cruises, on Soviet Union-Europe sailings the emphasis is on man's creative masterpieces. Typical is the Hermitage Museum in Leningrad with its collection of art treasures. If you are frustrated after an afternoon at the Hermitage, remember that experts estimate it would take six years to see everything housed in this magnificent museum.

Other examples of man's accomplishments are evidenced throughout these cruise visits. You see it in the clean, carefully planned capitals of Scandinavia where ancient palaces, squares, and monuments stand in contrast to striking triumphs of modern architecture; in canals of Amsterdam and the Kiel Canal, one of the great engineering feats of the last century. Much of what a cruise passenger sees in these ports is unforgettable. There's the lighthearted magic of Tivoli Gardens in Copenhagen; the rollicking, frolicking beer halls of Hamburg; the warm beaches around Visby, Sweden's vacation paradise.

Included in this chapter are ports most frequently visited by major cruise companies. Most of these European cities are worthy of two or three-week visits, and the wise cruise passenger doesn't expect to see Germany because his or her ship stopped in Hamburg for six hours. In fact, you would be wiser still if you didn't expect to see much of Hamburg during that short time either. If you use your time wisely, you'll leave Hamburg knowing what the city looks like, will have tasted the foods and experienced a sample of the life-style.

TRANSPORTATION

The cost of living in this part of the world is high. In fact, Sweden tops the list. So expect to pay more for sightseeing than you would in the Caribbean or Mediterranean. On average, tours run upwards of $25 for four hours. Most ships cruising the North Cape offer optional three or four-day land packages with hotel over nights and prices are available from cruise lines. Taxis are available in all ports, and when you reach metropolitan cities, self-drive rental cars and chauffeur-driven cars can be reserved. Public transportation is very good in cities like Copenhagen, Oslo, or Stockholm.

PASSPORTS AND VISAS

Passports are required, but all of the countries have now lifted visa requirements for cruise ship passengers who use the ship as their hotel. This includes the Soviet Union, but they have tacked a restriction on to the lifting of a restriction. If your ship is in Leningrad and you want to see the sights, you must purchase the excursion from the ship if you do not have an individual visa. You will not be permitted to leave the ship at will and wander. Your tours must also be reserved and paid in advance of your sailing from the United States. The Soviet immigration people clear all passengers as a group. Some ships spend a few days docked in Leningrad and offer optional tours to Moscow. A visa is required for hotel stays overnight, and your travel agent or the cruise company will assist you with the necessary papers.

TTT: The Soviet Union may be a "people's republic," but the Russians charge high rates for tours of their country. Half-day sightseeing costs $45 to $60 depending on the ship. You are picked up dockside for the morning tour; returned to the ship for lunch; picked up for the afternoon tour; returned for dinner; then picked up for the evening theater tour and returned by midnight. There's no getting away and tasting the borscht on your own. They count heads, and we waited about 45 minutes for a photographer who wandered off. Our guide refused to leave without him. My advice is: Get an individual visa if you're heading for the Soviet Union. With that visa you'll be cleared separately, but you'll be allowed to arrange for a private car to tour the city and surrounding area more or less on your own if you made the arrangements through your travel agent before you left home. Weather is best in North Sea, June, July, and early August for North Cape. Weather is unpredictable, so expect chilly nights and coolish days; but be prepared for warmer weather in European capital cities.

BELGIUM

Cruise Season: Early April through early October. Most popular months: July and August.

Climate: Unreliable and frequently damp. August temperatures average from a low of 54 to a high of 73, but be prepared for a variance of 10 degrees in either direction.

Currency: Belgian franc

Language: Flemish and French; English is widely spoken and understood.

Shopping: Best buys are in chocolates (pralines); Bruges lace, brassware, copper; and linen. Diamonds are also touted as a good buy, but it's best to know before you invest in a big-ticket item, although Belgian merchants are known for reliability.

Time: Six hours ahead of EST.

Tipping Ashore: When service charge has not been added to restaurant or bar bills, tip 15 percent; otherwise round out the bill with leftover change. Taxi-meter price includes tip, so an additional gratuity is not required.

Transportation: Excellent bus service from port cities to Brussels. Within Brussels, subway, bus, streetcars, and metered taxis. Rental cars are available in all cities.

What to Wear Ashore: Casual city clothing suitable for sightseeing in spring-like weather. Rain coats and umbrella will come in handy on all-day excursions. Jackets are required in better restaurants and hotel dining rooms for dinner meals.

More Information: Belgium Tourist Bureau, 720 Fifth Avenue, New York, NY 10019.

TTT: Cruise ships usually call at Antwerp, Ostend and Zeebrugge. Since Belgium is a small country geographically, it is easy to get around, and in a single day much of the country can be seen. Most ships offer all-day excursions for about $45. It is usually the best way to tour when time is limited. Information given on Zeebrugge covers the other areas.

ZEEBRUGGE

From the seaport of Zeebrugge you can easily visit the lovely Belgian capital, Brussels, a worthy rival to Paris with its magnificent monuments, squares, parks, as well as its luxurious boutiques and stores. Nearby Ghent and Bruges contain beautiful historic buildings, museums, and magnificent old churches that reflect the genius of the Flemish artists who contributed so much to these cities of art.

DENMARK

Cruise Season: May through early October. Most popular months: July and August.

Climate: Temperatures range from 48 to 72 degrees in summer months; cooler in May and September.

Currency: Danish Kroner

Language: Danish, most people speak some English.

Shopping: Stores are open from 9:00 a.m. to 5:30 p.m.; open later on Fridays, closed on Sundays. Well known for silver, flatware, and jewelry, modern furniture and accessories. Sweaters are a good buy.

Time: Six hours ahead of EST.

Tipping Ashore: Included in 15 percent service charge; automatically added to restaurant and hotel bills; taxi fares also include tips; cloakroom attendants expect 2 kroner.

Transportation: Excellent "S-train" system in Copenhagen. Local buses and trains charge per hour of travel. Metered taxis and rental cars are also available.

What to Wear Ashore: Be prepared with lightweight knit clothing, even during summer months. Weather is unpredictable, so take layered outfits that lend themselves to wear without jackets for warm days, with jackets when the temperature drops. Rainwear is an all-year requirement.

More Information: Danish Tourist Board, 505 Fifth Avenue, New York, NY 10017.

COPENHAGEN

One of the world's best-loved cities, not only is Copenhagen a gracious and comfortable place, but the natives are hospitable and fun-loving. The city is dominated by green towers and spires rising above a jumble of old houses, with an occasional skyscraper mixed in. From the lingering memory of the gentle tales of Hans Christian Andersen to the soft colored lights of Tivoli Gardens, Copenhagen enchants the visitor. Museums, the Royal Theater, the castle, and, of course, the famous Little Mermaid are some of the highlights of most tours. A good place to shop is the "Walking Street," where Danish china is beautifully displayed. Prices are high.

ENGLAND

Cruise Season: April through mid-November. Most popular months: June, July, and August.

Climate: Unpredictable, with rainfall heaviest on west coast. Mild summers, with temperatures in London at a low of 50 to a high 70.

Currency: Pound

Language: English.

Shopping: Best in specialty and department stores. Good buys in woolens, raincoats, high-quality porcelain, crystal, and pewter. Some antiques still available. Sheffield cutlery and old books are good purchases.

Time: Five hours ahead of EST.

Tipping Ashore: Expected everywhere. Add 5 percent where service charge is included; 15 to 20 percent otherwise. Taxi drivers expect 10 to 15 percent; give theater ushers about 50 pence; the same to guides.

Transportation: Excellent bus service between Tilbury and London. Subway, buses, metered taxis, and rental cars available in London.

What to Wear Ashore: Casual, medium-weight clothing, city-type; no shorts. Comfortable shoes and rain gear are essential.

More Information: British Tourist Authority, 680 Fifth Avenue, New York, NY 10019.

TTT: At press time the British pound was at its lowest value against the U.S. dollar and Americans were heading across the Atlantic in record numbers to take advantage of outstanding bargains.

TILBURY

Tilbury, on the River Thames, is your port for London. You usually have a day or so there, time enough to visit the great city, see the Tower of London, St. Paul's Cathedral, Westminster Abbey, the National Gallery, and many other historic places. You can stroll along Piccadilly and Regent Street for a shopping tour and, time permitting, take an evening at the theater.

FINLAND

Cruise Season: Late May through September. Most popular months: July and August.

Climate: Temperatures during the short summer range from 60 to 75 degrees. Midnight Sun from mid-July to end of July.

Currency: Finmarks

Language: Finnish is the official language, Swedish the second language, English is taught in schools.

Shopping: Shops are open late on Mondays and Fridays, but other days vary; stores close at 2 p.m. on Saturdays. China, jewelry, and furs appeal to tourists.

Time: Seven hours ahead of EST.

Tipping Ashore: A service charge of 15 percent is included in restaurant and hotel bills, so little tipping is expected; no tip to taxi drivers or guides.

Transportation: Local streetcars, buses, metered taxis, rental cars are available.

What to Wear Ashore: Heavy springtime clothing and rainwear recommended.

More Information: Finland National Tourist office, 75 Rockefeller Plaza, New York, NY 10019.

HELSINKI

The "White City of the North" was founded in 1550 by royal order of King Vasa when Sweden held Finland. Helsinki became the capital in 1812 when Tsar Alexander I decided the old capital was not close enough to Russia. Today's city owes much of its good planning to a disastrous fire in the early nineteenth century, after which almost the entire city was rebuilt. Finland has produced astonishing artists, sculptors, and designers whose works are displayed throughout the city and suburbs. Sightseeing should include the unique Rock Church, the Olympic Stadium, residential districts, Finnish craftsmanship, the Lutheran Cathedral, and the Uspenski Cathedral topped with a mass of gilded onion-shaped domes.

FRANCE

(For specifics on France, see "France" under "The Mediterranean and the Black Sea.")

LE HAVRE

Le Havre is the leading port of the French Channel province of Normandy and scene of the Allied invasion landings in 1944. Since then the city has been completely rebuilt, with wide, handsome avenues and a modern shopping center. Le Havre is an excellent starting point for tours to many varied and interesting places: to Rouen, with its magnificent Gothic cathedral and countless examples of 14th and 15th-century architecture; to the quaint fishing village of Honfleur and the fashionable seaside resort of Deauville. And, of course, to Paris, the incomparable capital of France.

GERMANY

Cruise Season: Late May through September.
Climate: Temperatures range from 48 to 78 degrees during cruise season.
Currency: Deutsche mark
Language: German.
Shopping: Prices are comparable to the U.S. in spite of the favorable exchange rate. But thee are good buys in quality items like cameras, Dresden, Meissen, wood carvings, clocks and toys.
Time: Six hours ahead of EST.
Tipping Ashore: A service charge from 10 to 15 percent is added to all restaurant and hotel checks, but service personnel expect an additional 5 percent; taxi drivers also expect 5 percent.
Transportation: Excellent local buses and trains; also metered taxis and rental cars.
What to Wear Ashore: City clothing similar to that suitable in New York or Chicago during the same season.
More Information: German National Tourist Office, 630 Fifth Avenue, New York, NY 10020.

HAMBURG

The residents of Hamburg, historically a "free city," still retain their independence of spirit. The city has long been Germany's principal port, and its dock areas are enormous. The gaudy, licentious Reeperbahn ("Anchorage of Joy") is fully prepared to offer every form of entertainment to the world's sailors. For visitors preferring more subdued entertainment, there's a nightly Dancing Waters Show, the

Kunsthalle with its outstanding collection of 15th to 20th-century master works, and the former Renaissance Rathaus (city hall) sitting atop some 4,000 piles driven into marshy ground, proving the centuries-old skill and imagination of Hamburg's engineers. Some ships stay in port long enough to offer an optional tour to Berlin, East and West, with an overnight stay.

IRELAND

Cruise Season: Late April through mid-October.
Climate: Temperature averages range from low of 40 in April to a high of 70 in July; on the damp side.
Currency: Irish pound (also called "pund")
Language: English and Gaelic.
Shopping: Ireland is a Common Market country, so prices of domestically manufactured items are similar to those in other European countries. I found good buys in handknit sweaters, walking sticks, pipes, Waterford glassware, Belleek china, and old books.
Time: Five hours ahead of EST.
Tipping Ashore: The Irish do not expect lavish tips; 10 to 15 percent service charge is added to restaurant, pub, and hotel bills. Patrons leave less than 5 percent more. Taxi drivers are happy with 10 percent over the meter, guides with about 25 percent.
Transportation: Local buses, metered taxis, rental cars available.
What to Wear Ashore: Country-type, casual clothing. Jackets and ties are not required, except in the most elegant restaurants and clubs.
More Information: Irish Tourist Board, 590 Fifth Avenue, New York, NY 10036.

DUBLIN

Dublin, Ireland's capital, is a city steeped in history, tragic and glorious, with haunting memories of great patriots, statesmen, scientists, and scholars. It is a city of spacious streets, fine buildings, and friendly people; one that combines the beauty of past centuries with modern progressiveness. Dublin rose to fame and wealth in the 18th century, when its fine streets and squares were laid out. Leinster House, home of the Irish Parliament, inspired the architecture of our White House in Washington. Dublin's name in modern Irish is Baile Atha Cliath, or "town of the ford of the hurdles." Don't leave without a bottle of Irish Mist, a stop at any pub, and an Irish coffee, or two.

THE NETHERLANDS

Cruise Season: From April to late October. Most popular months: July and August.

Climate: Warm summers, mild winters. Tends to be damp most of the year. Summer low of 52, up to 75 in July.

Currency: Guilder (or florin)

Language: Dutch, English, French, and German widely spoken.

Shopping: Good buys include Delftware, porcelain, Indonesian batiks, figurines, and pewterware.

Time: Six hours ahead of EST.

Tipping Ashore: Appreciated, but not required. All restaurants and cafes add a 15 percent service charge to the bills; taxi drivers are happy with 5 to 10 percent.

Transportation: Local streetcars, buses, metered taxis, rental cars available.

What to Wear Ashore: Comfortable city-type clothing; especially shoes for walking.

More Information: Netherlands National Tourist Office, 576 Fifth Avenue, New York, NY 10036.

AMSTERDAM

Amsterdam, a city built on the water, has an extraordinary network of canals lined with elegant hotels, quaint shops, old burgher mansions, and exquisite facades. Don't fail to take a trip in one of the glass-topped launches. Most city tours include a visit to Delft, home of the famous blue pottery, and Marken, overlooking the Zuider Zee, where practically everyone still wears traditional costumes and wooden shoes.

Unfortunately, most cruise ships do not allow enough time to see either Rotterdam or The Hague. Rotterdam, is well worth a visit and when time allows visitors marvel at this city literally built into an ultra-modern metropolis as a result of its almost total destruction during the Second World War. Rotterdam is rated as the busiest port in the world and many European steamers begin spring to fall voyages from here.

NORWAY

Cruise Season: Late May through mid-October.

Climate: Summer days have daylight for as long as nineteen hours. Temperatures in July range from a low of 56 to a high of 73.

Currency: Norwegian Krone

Language: Norwegian; English also widely spoken.

Shopping: Best buys are Norwegian-made sweaters, glass, and pewter, but prices are high.

Time: Six hours ahead of EST.

Tipping Ashore: A service charge of about 15 percent is added to restaurant and cafe bills, but round this out to the nearest krone; no tip to taxi drivers, but round the fare out to the nearest krone.

Transportation: Buses, subways in Oslo, metered taxis, rental cars, and by foot.

What to Wear Ashore: Fall-type country clothes; sweaters, slacks, skirts. Jackets and ties in better restaurants for dinner.

More Information: Norwegian National Tourist Office, 75 Rockefeller Plaza, New York, NY 10019.

BERGEN—Norway's second capital and capital of western Norway, Bergen is a city where fishing and sailing boats crowd the picturesque harbor. The Floeyen, the steep, 1,000-foot mountain overlooking the town, is easily reached by cable car, and from it you can pick out Haakon's Hall and the medieval buildings of the Hanseatic era. The town's fur and silver shops will tempt you. Specially recommended are a visit to the aquarium and to nearby Trollhaugen, home of Edvard Grieg.

NORTH CAPE—From Skarsvaag, the road traverses the wild and bleak tundra to the North Cape rising 1,007 feet sheer from the Barents Sea of the Artic Ocean. The panorama from the Cape, considered the northernmost point of Europe, offers a rare experience as one stands on an endless summer's day and gazes over the vast ocean stretching to the distant polar ice pack.

OSLO—Visitors find a variety of things to see in Oslo, particularly the unique Vigeland sculptures in Frogner Park, the open-air Folk Museum, the Viking Museum, and the Kon Tiki raft. The splendid City Hall in downtown Oslo was lavishly decorated by many of Norway's leading artists.

THE SOVIET UNION

Cruise Season: Mid-May through September.

Climate: There is a wide temperature range, even in summer months, from a low of 48 to a high of 78 in July, in the coastal area.

Currency: Ruble (Rate is set monthly by the Soviet Government).

Language: Russian; some English spoken by younger people and all official guides.

Shopping: Difficult at best, and nearly impossible during a short cruise stop. I shopped hotel stores and the Beriozka (tourist shops) and found nice embroidery, dolls, caviar at a good price, and vodka.

Time: Eight hours ahead of EST.

Tipping Ashore: Officially frowned upon but generally accepted. Ten to 15 percent of any check (and in taxis) will be gratefully received. Guides prefer small Western gifts, such as ballpoint pens, but rubles are also accepted.

Transportation: Leningrad has an excellent subway, bus, and tram system and taxis.

What to Wear Ashore: Conservative, city-type clothing; pants acceptable for women. Most men wear jackets. Comfortable shoes and rain gear are necessities.

More Information: Intourist, 45 East 49 Street, New York, NY 10017.

LENINGRAD

Founded in 1703 by Peter the Great to serve as his "window on the west," St. Petersburg gradually emerged following the patterns of Western European cities. From 1712 to 1914, it was designated capital of imperial Russia. Immediately following the revolution it was renamed Petrograd and in 1924 was renamed again, in honor of Lenin. Today, this gray-brown city is the second largest in the Soviet Union and the country's major cultural center as well as its principal Baltic port. The famous Hermitage Museum holds one of the world's most extensive collections of art treasures, and several great palaces are nearby. Petrodvorets and Pushkin, which have been classified as "important to the Russian historical heritage," are being carefully restored. Tour guides speak excellent English and, though polite, stop just short of being friendly.

SWEDEN

Cruise Season: Late May through September. Most popular months: July and August.

Climate: Dry, sunny summers. Temperatures range from a low of 45 to 75, in July in Stockholm.

Currency: Krona

Language: Swedish; some English spoken.

Shopping: There are still good buys in glassware, ceramics, textiles, and high-quality stainless steel flatware.

Time: Six hours ahead of EST.

Tipping Ashore: Service charges included in all bills, additional tips expected for special services, tip taxi drivers 15 percent.

Transportation: from ports to Stockholm, ferries; trains buses, taxis. In Stockholm: buses, subway, ferries, taxis.

What to Wear Ashore: Medium-weight clothing with an all-weather coat for topper. Comfortable shoes are essential. Swedes dress conservatively. Jackets and ties for dinner in most restaurants.

More Information: Swedish National Tourist Office, 75 Rockefeller Plaza, New York, NY 10019.

STOCKHOLM

Capital of Scandinavia's largest country, Stockholm is one of Europe's most prosperous cities, with a population of more than a million people. Amid the modern buildings and the bustle, you'll find fine examples of architecture from much earlier periods. A city of islands, canals, and bridges, Stockholm is blessed with spacious park areas that give the metropolis a feeling of openness and freedom. Most tours include visits to the medieval quarter known as "the city between the bridges," the distinctive City Hall. Royal Palace, the famous seventeenth-century man-of-war *Wasa,* and nearby Millesgarden, home of the famous sculptor Carl Milles.

SOUTHEAST ASIA
and
PACIFIC PORTS

It is impossible to cover all of this vast area in a guide to travel by ship. Again, the information is intended to help make a six hour visit pleasurable in some of the popular ports, with special emphasis on countries and itineraries emerging as "routes of the future."

SRI LANKA (CEYLON)

The country is once again called by its ancient name of Sri Lanka and visitors are fascinated by its ancient history. First recorded visitors were the Aryan Indians in 483 B.C. From the time of the prince's marriage to a local princess, the major ethnic group of Ceylon, the Sinhales claim descent from Aryan stock. Many cultures came to Ceylon and today it is a mix of Buddhism (from 307 B.C.), Portuguese who arrived in 1505 and settled in costal areas; and the Dutch, who converted many locals to Catholicism. Ceylon was annexed by the British in 1796 and they kept control until 1948. More than 14 million people live in Sri Lanka. The first great cities were built during the Buddhist period. Terrain blends from tropical forest, mountains and flat sandy plains. There are over 1,000 miles of beaches.

Cruise Season: December through March
Climate: Sunny for months on end with an average annual temperature in the low 80s. Rainy season from November to January and from May to July.
Language: Sinhalese, Tamil and English
Currency: Rupee
Shopping: Handicrafts, semi-precious stones, sapphires, topazes, zircons and garnets. Fair prices at government operated handicraft shops in Colombo.

353

Time: 10 hours and 30 minutes ahead of EST

Tipping ashore: About 10 percent as a general rule. Taxi drivers are happy with the leftover change and porters at airports and piers have fixed rates posted.

Transportation: Taxis, buses, rental cars. Good intra-city public transportation

What to Wear Ashore: Informal except for a few elegant restaurants in top hotels. Lightweight clothing recommended but evening can be cool.

More information: Sri Lanka Tourist Board, 609 Fifth AVenue, New York, NY 10017

TTT: The State Gem Corporation operates show rooms at 24 York Street, Colombo, at the Hotel Sri Lanka Inter Continental, and at the airport. The corporation sells gems (rubies are fantastic buys) and will certify whether the gems you have bought anywhere in the country are genuine. Don't leave Ceylon without a package of the famous tea.

COLOMBO

Time in port usually only allows for sightseeing in Colombo, the country's capital. Streets are lined with Victorian houses and crowded with ox carts, buses, pedestrians, barefoot children, Englishmen in tweeds, market stalls and markets. It's an exciting city for walking. Tours include the National Museum, Zoological Gardens and the Raja Maha Vihare temple. The countryside is beautiful and well worth the time. So is the 72 mile ride to Kandy with its Buddhist temples, some dating back 1,500 years.

JAPAN

Cruise Season: March through November

Climate: Differs by region, warmer in the south, cooler in mountain areas. Tokyo temperature from high of 83 degrees in July to low of 46 in April.

Language: Japanese. English spoken in tourist hotels

Currency: Yen

Shopping: Japanese items sold in the U.S. are generally available on the Japanese market at prices about 25 to 30 percent less. Good buys in electronics, silks and jewelry.

Time: 14 hours ahead of EST

Tipping ashore: Tipping is not customary in Japan by Japanese; however, while there is no solicitation of gratuities, there are exceptions for outstanding service in hotels, etc. Rather than tips, there are fixed charges for baggage handling at piers, airports and railroad stations. Not necessary to tip taxi drivers and 10 percent is added to restaurant bills.

Transportation: Taxis, rental cars, limos, excellent trains and subway system.

What to Wear Ashore: Dress for the city in Tokyo, comfortably for touring.

More information: Japan National Tourist Office, 45 Rockefeller Plaza, New York, NY 10020.

KOBE — A beautifully sheltered port on the Inland Sea, its Port Tower affords the best view of the city and the backdrop of the Rokko Mountain Range. Sightseeing is limited to Kobe's Ikuta Shrine. It is a bustling city with an excellent harbor.

TOKYO — It's the largest city in the world and the fastest paced. Tokyo's port is Yokohama, an hour's bus ride away. No matter whether your ship docks in Kobe or Nagasaki, all shore excursions should include a few days in Tokyo. The city is the hub of the Far East and could easily overwhelm a visitor. Situated on the island of Honshu, the largest of four islands that make up Japan and considered its mainland. The area is a little larger than Great Britain and within its borders are 34 of the country's 46 prefectures. There are shrines, palaces and gardens; museums, universities and elegant hotels. Shopping districts are everywhere and prices are just about the same throughout the city, cheaper on the outskirts.

NAGASAKI — The city has become a popular cruise ship port of call. Nagasaki was rebuilt after the Second World War and is now one of the most orderly cities in the world. Neat and well planned, the city's most important site is the memorial park dedicated to world peace.

NIKKO — There's an old Japanese saying that translates into, "Never say splendid until you have seen Nikko." Situated 93 miles north of Tokyo, it is indeed "splendid". Within its confines are the most magnificent religious architecture in Japan. Visits to the Toshagu Shrine in Nikko National Park, the Rinnoji Temple, the Futaarasan Shrine are highlights.

OSAKA—Second largest city in Japan, Osaka is built on a bay and is crisscrossed by canals. It is well known for its 16th century Osaka Castle, numerous shrines and proximity to other attractions like Nara. Many ship tours overnight in Osaka. It's an excellent city for shopping.

TTT: Japan's bullet trains deserve their world-wide reputation of excellence. However, you should know a little about them if you decide to travel within Japan on your own before or after you disembark. If this is your first trip to Japan, I urge you to take advantage of land packages offered by cruise lines. If you are comfortable seeing Japan for the second or third or more time and doing so on your own, travel by rail is your best bet. First class tickets are not expensive and are available without reservations at every station. However, you cannot check your luggage through to your final destination at every station. For example, we disembarked in Kobe with five bags which we could not check at the station and we could not handle the bags. There are no porters to help passengers on and off trains with luggage. Trains are primarily for commuters who carry their own small bags. We persisted and found if we went to the cargo office at the Main Station, we could ship the bags to Tokyo for a nominal fee. For a slight additional charge, the bags were delivered to our hotel. Bags arrived two days after we did. Fortunately, we had packed for such an eventuality. We were on Royal Viking Line and the company's port agent was arranging to transfer bags to Tokyo hotels for about $20 per bag. These bags were going to Tokyo by truck and would take about 35 hours to arrive. Passengers who were on the ship tour were the least concerned. Their bags were also going to Tokyo by truck and would be waiting for them in their hotel rooms when they arrived.

THAILAND

Visitors have pre-conceived exotic images of Thailand and most are not disappointed. It is a diverse country where Bangkok seems worlds away from the less populated inland regions or border communities. There are marvelous temples, ancient cities, elephants, dense jungles and a capital city laced with watery thoroughfares and a disappearing way of life.

Cruise Season: Almost year around for South Pacific itineraries with two
   high season—November to March and from May through October.
Climate: Hot all year with hottest months May through June

Language: Chinese languages spoken widely with English almost a second language.

Currency: Baht

Shopping: Excellent. Best buys in semi-precious gems and handicraft. Good tailors deliver made-to-measure clothing within a few days. Prices are very low and competitive with Hong Kong, Korea and the Philippines.

Time: 12 hours ahead of EST

Tipping ashore: Optional in native restaurants but expected from foreign visitors. Some restaurants add 10 percent service charge but it is acceptable to leave loose change.

Transportation: Difficult because of the huge crowds everywhere in Bangkok. Taxis come in two sizes and are very cheap. Where there is a choice, opt for water taxis. Three-wheeled taxis are very plentiful and very cheap. Also cheaper than taxis and a lot more fun.

What to Wear Ashore: Very lightweight clothing and comfortable shoes. Everything is informal and jackets for men are not required.

More information: Tourism Authority of Thailand, 5 World Trade Center, Suite 2449, New York, NY 10048.

BANGKOK: Best way to see a sampling of Bangkok's 300 temples is by conducted bus tour. You'll want to visit the floating market for a glimpse of life along the klongs (canals). Most ship tours will include a sampan ride and the most important temples—Temple of the Reclining Buddha, Temple of the Emerald Buddha, Temple of the Golden Buddha, Temple of the Dawn and the Marble Temple. All allow time for shopping and browsing. Bangkok is one of the noisiest, most polluted cities in the world but well worth a visit.

HONG KONG

My absolute favorite port of call and one that should not be timed for a one day visit or you'll feel cheated. Almost all cruise lines allow for at least two days in port with the ship as your hotel, or offer pre and post-cruise land packages so passengers can explore Hong Kong in more than just a few hours. Hong Kong is a city of modern offices, apartment buildings and factories in the middle of walled villages and ancient temples. It's a world trade center and a lot more.

The Portuguese were the first Europeans to sail into Hong Kong Harbor, The British arrived in the late 1600s and set up the East India Company which dominated trade in the area for centuries. It was the Treaty of Nanking in 1842 which ceded Hong Kong to the British. In

1860 Kowloon was added and the New Territories and adjacent islands were leased from China in 1898.

Cruise Season: March through November
Climate: Mild with highs near 90 degrees in July and August and lows of 55 degrees in January.
Language: Chinese and English
Currency: Hong Kong dollar
Shopping: Best in the world for jewelry, clothing, high fashion items, accessories, rugs and anything made in China.
Time: 13 hours ahead of EST
Tipping ashore: Customary. When restaurants add 10 percent to the bill, customers are expected to up the tip by five percent. Ten percent to taxi drivers.
Transportation: Taxis, rental cars, limos, buses and ferries.
What to Wear Ashore: Casual wear is acceptable except in some of the fashionable restaurants where jacket and tie are required.
More information: Hong Kong Tourist Association, 548 Fifth Avenue, New York, NY 10036.

TTT: Hong Kong is a shopper's and diner's delight. For the latter, there are restaurants to suit every palate and pocketbook. Chinese delicacies are outstanding. As for shopping, it's hard to avoid. Temptation lies at every turn of the sidewalk. Visitors to Hong Kong spend more money here on shopping than in any other comparable tourist destination. There are elegant "name" shops from all over the world and there are flea markets that astound. Stop at one of the Hong Kong Visitor Information Centers and ask for booklets listing specialty shops for anything that might interest you and be sure to pick up a copy of their factory outlet list. It will head bargain hunters in the right direction for items manufactured in Hong Kong for export to the U.S. and Europe.

PEOPLE'S REPUBLIC OF CHINA

Other countries visited in this part of the world reflect Chinese culture and style, history and its peoples. So, it is no wonder that once the curtains parted, Americans are traveling to China in ever increasing numbers. They come by air and by land through Hong Kong. And, they are coming by sea. China's population is more than 25 percent of the world population and its territory covers more than continental Europe. Its civilization was more advanced than Europe's at the time of Marco Polo's visit. Wars and periods of isolation have left China a country apart and a country of mystery.

China is catching up and is the process of "democratizing" its communist-socialist form of government. It is also refurbishing and building a new network of tourist facilities, among which are some of the finest in the world.

Because it is such a tremendous country, customs, languages and climate differ greatly. Terrain is moutainous and arrid in some places.

China is not a six-hour port visit and almost all ships that call at some of its famous ports allow for three ports of call and from one to three days in each. It is impossible in very limited space to describe the experience awaiting visitors to China. All we can do in THE TOTAL TRAVELER BY SHIP is highlight the most important points and offer a few suggestions for maximum enjoyment of the experience.

Cruise Season: late March through mid-November

Climate: varies by region, but comfortable during spring to fall months

Language: Official language is Beijing dialect of Mandarin, but Cantonese is also spoken widely. Limited English, except by trained guides and at tourist hotels.

Currency: yuan (renminbi)

Shopping: Best buys are jade, works of art, silk, carpets, porcelain, and antiques. Friendship Stores and Arts and Craft Stores are operated by the government and easiest to shop in. Shanghai Friendship Stores is supposed to be the best. My experience was that special items are not necessarily carried in the next Friendship store you come upon, so buy it when you see it. (See **TTT**)

Time: 13 hours ahead of EST

Tipping ashore: Not permitted or required

Transportation: Taxis and trains. It is not possible to hail a taxi on the street. Taxis must be ordered from tourist hotels and rate is pre determined. Special arrangements may be made for chauffeur driven cars.

What to Wear Ashore: Comfortable clothes and shoes

More information: China Touring Center, 200 West 57th Street, New York, NY 10019

BEIJING (Peking)—On *Royal Viking, Pearl of Scandinavia* and other vessels, passengers disembark at a port some distance from Beijing and a five hour bus ride away. There are limited toilet facilities along the route, but buses are comfortable and the ship provides snacks, lunch and drinks. Royal Viking passengers spend two nights at The Great

Wall Hotel, an experience in itself. But the highlight is a visit to The Great Wall. Other highlights are the Temple of Heaven and the Summer Palace and walking the streets of Beijing where foreigners don't even warrant a second glance.

DALIAN — China's third largest port, Dalian is a delightful city. It sees few foreign visitors and the hospitality is warm. To find it on a map, look for Darien as it was known during the Japanese occupation, or Luda, or look in the area of Port Arthur, the nearby naval base. The city was occupied by Russia as well as Japan (at different times) and has a very un-Chinese look. Dalian is a medley of architectural styles with a dash of Japan, a touch of old Russia and a lot of realism graced by Oriental customs and styles. Streets are very wide with open squares typical of Tsarist Russia. Dalian seems far less crowded than most Chinese cities probably because of its design which resembles a modern European metropolis hemmed in by hills.

Ships dock walking distance from the center of Dalian and free shuttle buses transport passengers to the Friendship Store and Seaman's Club.

SHANGHAI — One of the few major Chinese cities that didn't undergo a name change, it has become a mere shadow of its former self. Once the center of social activities for embassies and diplomats, Shanghai is now a factory city, heavy with pollution. Ships are lucky enough to dock almost mid-city give their passengers a lot of extra time in port. Others are forced to dock about an hour's ride away and much of the time is spent shuttling between city and dock. Most ships spend one night and two days in Shanghai. The first day is spent touring the city, the second a day in the outskirts. The success of the second day depends on the luck of the draw. Half the passengers go to Suzhou, the other half to Wuxi. Both groups use bus and train transportation and start out together. Wuxi is the better tour, if you have a choice.

A few words about Chinese trains are in order. They are immaculate, comfortable with upholstered sofa-like seating. Tea is served and vendors come through selling small gift items and other snacks.

In Shanghai, tours visit the carpet factory, see a theatrical performance, spend time shopping and spend almost half a day at the Childrens' Palace.

TTT: An awful lot of time is wasted for lunches and dinners on these tours and if you would rather go off on your own, you are allowed to do so. You can arrange for a taxi to stay with you, but don't count on having a conversation with the driver. Have the places you want him to take you written down for you in Chinese, including the location of your ship.

Some things you can count on when visiting China. You will see at least one factory every day and every factory will have a shop which has an exchange booth to change dollars into yuan. There are toilet facilities at every tourist stop, but don't count on Western-style toilets, so bring tissues and a sense of humor. You will shop and you will spend a lot more money than you intended. After all, who can resist cashmere sweaters for under $35. Although rules say no bargaining, it pays to haggle on big ticket items. I saved $50 on shipping charges by saying the cost was too high. Don't be concerned about shipping bulky items back home. They arrive when promised and Customs is very easy on taxes. Bring credit cards. Dollars are exchanged at the official rate, plus a minimal commission. Travelers checks are charged a slightly higher commission and credit cards are charged a commission for use, then the dollars are converted to yuan at a still higher commission.

South America, the Caribbean, Bahamas, Bermuda and the West Indies

ANTIGUA

(Population 70,000)

Christopher Columbus discovered Antigua (largest of the Leeward Islands) and its dependent islands of Barbuda and Redonda in 1493 during his second voyage to the New World. Columbus named Antigua for the church of Santa Maria la Antigua in Seville, Spain. Unsuccessful attempts to settle the island were made by the Spanish and French before English planters from St. Christopher gained a foothold in 1632. A formal grant of the island was made to Lord Willoughby in 1633 by King Charles II of England. In 1633 the French occupied Antigua, but the island was ceded to England in 1667 by the Treaty of Breda and remained British. During the 18th and 19th centuries the island served as a British naval base; it was Lord Nelson's station from 1786 to 1788. Abandoned in 1889, the base was recently restored as a major tourist attraction. In the late 17th century, the governor of the Leeward Islands was granted a lease on Barbuda (formerly Dulcina) by the British government, and Barbuda is now part of the State of Antigua. An independent state in the British Commonwealth, Antigua retains much of the charm and culture of its first mother country. St. Johns is the capital city.

Size: 16 miles across at almost any point, the island covers 108 square miles.
Climate: Sunny all year, temperature from 76 degrees in January to 81 in August.
Currency: Eastern Caribbean dollar (ECD)

Language: English.

Shopping: Shops close between noon and 1 p.m. and are closed Thursday afternoons. Antigua rum sells for $1.50 a bottle, and hand-screened print fabric locally made into patio-type dresses selling for under $40. Other good buys are English imports, local handicraft, garments made in Hong Kong, Swiss watches, pottery, and Cuban cigars. Local handicrafts also of interest to tourists: tortoise items, ceramics, and the Mary hat of Madras-lined linen that folds flat for packing.

Time: One hour ahead of EST.

Tipping Ashore: 10 to 15 percent service surcharge is added automatically; no additional tip necessary in restaurants and hotels. Cab drivers are generally satisfied with 10 percent.

Transportation: Shore excursions (3 hours), $18; Taxis cost $1. U.S. per mile. Car rentals available.

What to See: English Harbor, site of Admiral Nelson's dockyard, is the most important non-beach attraction. The historical harbor is now used as a yacht center; its restored buildings contain restaurants and small hotels. Also worth visiting: Clarence House, the governor's country house, built in 1787; Fig Tree Drive in the mountainous tropical sector of the island; the hundreds of beautiful beaches and coves protected by off-shore reefs; the Angelican Cathedral, Court House and Marlet in St. Johns; a sugar factory; and several old forts.

What to Wear Ashore: Lightweight summer clothing all year.

More Information: Antigua Tourist Board, 610 Fifth Avenue, Suite 311, New York, NY 10020.

ARUBA

(Population 66,000)

A small island 15 miles off the coast of Venezuela, Aruba is a bit of Holland transplanted into the West Indies. Although the Spanish discovered the island in 1500, it is the Dutch whose influence dates from Peter Stuyvesant's arrival in 1624. Since those days and the days of the Arawak Indians, people from more than 40 nations have settled on this coral-rock island. The architecture is a blend of Holland and the West Indies; homes are painted vivid colors of the rainbow. There is no written historical record of how Aruba was discovered, but early Spanish sailors landed here in 1499 and named it Ora Uba, "island of gold". They were not the first inhabitants of Aruba. Hatchets, hammers, and hieroglyphics found in chalk caves indicate it was inhabited for centuries by Arawaks. Gold was discovered in 1825, and although the mine's yield was good, the industry was abandoned in 1916. Prosperity came to Aruba with the importation of "black gold" by Standard Oil of New Jersey. The oil refinery it built on the island employs 8,000. Aruba has one of the highest standards of living in the West Indies. Unfortunately, Standard Oil is talking about closing or drastically reducing this operation so the economic future of Aruba is bound to become even more dependent on tourism.

Today, the most important source of gold is tourists who come in search of gold in the plush island casinos in all of the major hotels. Growth of tourism is relatively new. Just a couple of decades ago, there was almost nothing here except relics of sunken ships just outside the harbor, caves with petroglyphs made by the Arawaks and enormous rock formations which continue to puzzle geologists. Aruba is just 15 miles from Venezuela and is a popular weekend retreat for South Americans.

Size: 19 miles long and 6 miles wide.

Climate: Naturally air conditioned by trade winds; temperature averages 82 degrees the year round, with less than 20 inches of rain annually.

Currency: Florin or guilder (NAG)

Languages: Papiamento (a patois that is both spoken and written), Dutch, Spanish, and English.

Time: One hour ahead of EST.

Transportation: Shore excursions (2 to 3 hours) $15.00; Metered taxis, cars, scooters, motorbikes available for rentals.

What to See: Natural bridge on the north coast, carved out of solid coral rock by the sea; William III Tower, which dates back to 1867, once served as a prison, and is now a colorful "timepiece"; Mount Hooiberg for an interesting view; Ranchostraat's Lime Kiln, a gigantic oven used in the early 1900s to make lime. Aside from the miles of snow-white beaches, the most photographed sight on the island is the divi divi tree, a scraggly little tree that caught the tourist's fancy and has become the unofficial symbol of the island. Constant trade winds blow in a southwesterly direction, and divi divi trees stand about 20 feet high, with their top branches taking off at a right angle to their trunks.

Tipping Ashore: 10 percent to the taxi driver; 10 to 15 percent service charge added in all restaurants and hotels.

What to Wear Ashore: Lightweight summer clothing all year. Dressier toward evening if you are going to one of the hotel casinos.

Shopping: Nassau Street is the shopping street on this duty-free island. Good buys are Swiss watches, perfume, cameras, cashmeres, china. Many of the well known shops have branch stores on other islands. Some stores closed noon to 2 p.m. All stores closed Sundays.

More Information: Aruba Information Center, 1270 Avenue of the Americas, New York, NY 10020.

TTT: Most ships spend a day and an evening so you might want to taste Indonesian rijsttafel dishes in specialty restaurants and hotels. After dinner, casinos in major hotels offer the usual games of chance.

THE BAHAMAS

(Population 235,000)

Christopher Columbus arrived in the Bahamas on October 12, 1492, and called the original inhabitants "Indians," thinking he had arrived in India, although they were actually Arawaks or Lucayans. Today's population consists chiefly of descendants of English settlers, American Loyalists and Confederates, who came here in the late 17th and 18th centuries, and slaves from Africa, whose descendants now account for about 80 percent of the population. They like to call Columbus their first tourist.

Size: The 700 limestone islands and more than 2,400 cays that make up the Bahama group form a 760-mile arc about 50 miles from Florida's coast.

Climate: Similar to south Florida; temperatures range from 60 to 85 degrees all year.

Currency: Bahamas dollar

Language: English.

Time: EST.

Tipping Ashore: 15 percent is expected in restaurants and hotels, usually added or included in bills. When it is, menu should say so. Same to taxi drivers.

What to Wear Ashore: Lightweight, casual clothing. More dressy for evenings at nightclubs, restaurants, hotels, and casinos.

More Information: Bahama Islands Tourist Office, 10 Columbus Circle, New York, NY 10019.

TTT: Make sure the taxi driver uses his meter, or establish your rate in advance to avoid unpleasant discussion. At the pier in Nassau, taxi drivers have a way of piling passengers in and charging on a per person basis, rather by the meter.

FREEPORT
(Grand Bahama Island)

This coral rock island is a relative newcomer to the tourist scene and is a result of an American financier's imagination. Unlike other islands of the Bahamas, Freeport stresses the new as opposed to the quaint and traditional, all with a Bahamian touch.

Shopping: Prices are the same as in Nassau, but the atmosphere is international in the bazaar, which changes sidewalks and street lights in each country's area. Of interest to tourists are English imports, straw and other native work, baskets, jewelry, and some art.

Transportation: Taxis, car, and motor-scooter rentals available.

What to See: Nearby fishing village for a look at the way the island was before 1955; the international bazaar; Lucaya; downtown Freeport; the many golf courses, El Casino, and Garden of The Groves, a beautiful botanical garden.

TTT: The Freeport area, with its hotels and casinos, is an $8.00 taxi ride from the pier. As Islands go, Freeport cannot be called "beautiful". It was intended to offer the visitor and vacationer everything he might want. Much of the construction went up too quickly, and the Lucayan area is now being rebuilt and should be open with a newly-renovated hotel and casino in mid-1985. The big casino, El Casino, is supposed to be one of the largest in the world. And, it is big. Plan on sticking to the slots, unless you are the $10 minimum blackjack player. A few $5 tables are open during the afternoon. The International Bazaar is interesting, and every visitor should spend an hour going through. Food in the Bazaar-casino is varied.

NASSAU

Nassau has native charm. It is where everything in the Bahamas happens. It is a busy, bustling, capital city in the sunshine, a charming laid back resort center on New Providence Island. Beaches are outstanding, particularly on Paradise Island and at Cable Beach. Climate is ideal year around. One day in the Port of Nassau could be a very busy day and a tour is recommended for first time visitors. Take either the ship excursion or hire a cab at dock. They all speak English and know their island better than some of us know our own home towns. I like the one hour horse-and-buggy tour (about $8 for two). Drivers are old timers who take you over back roads and come up with the best stories about the good-old-days. Harbor cruise transportation between the dock and beaches on Paradise Island runs regularly (one dollar per person). Taxi cost about $3 per person to Club Med and the main hotel and casino district. Harbor cruises to nowhere also available for a seaside look at Paradise Island and Nassau.

Shopping: English imports, crystal, china, woolens, jewelry are of interest. Bay Street shops stock everything, and a leisurely stroll will put you in front of the most reputable stores. Several have annexes in hotels.

Transportation: Shore excursions (2 to 3 hours), city and Ardastra Gardens, about $15 on board ship. In town, anywhere from $8 to $28, so shop the waiting taxi drivers. Harbor cruise (3 hours), $20. Taxis, car, and motor- scooter rentals available. Driving is on the left side of the road.

What to See: Fort Charlotte; historic old churches; Blackbeard's Tower; the Queen's Staircase, Ardastra Gardens, Paradise Island. Stroll the waterfront area for local color; or rent a small power-boat and get yourself over the narrow waterway to Paradise Island or take the ferry to Paradise Island for $1.00 per person. It leaves from the pier area.

TTT: Two of the busiest casinos in the world are in Nassau. The oldest is on Paradise Island; the newest is the Cable Beach Casino, adjacent to the newest luxury hotel on the island, the Cable Beach Hotel. Casinos open at 1 p.m. and has craps, roulette, slots, blackjack, and a few other games unfamiliar but interesting to most of us. Slot-machine play is open 24 hours. There are fine beaches in both areas but the newest "in" touristic area in Nassau is Cable Beach. In addition to the new Cable Beach Hotel, the Casino is huge and still has $2 blackjack tables. While not the most beautiful in the world, it has a lot going for it. Croupiers are mostly female and friendly. Every conceivable game of chance has been included. There's also a fantastic show in the Casino theater. Both the Cable Beach and Paradise Island nightclub shows are sold on all ships or you can make arrangements to see them on your own. Taxis charge per person in both directions and admission to shows, including drinks, runs around $18 to $20. If you have seen Paradise Island, try Cable Beach on your next visit.

OUT ISLANDS

The Bahamas has a thousand or so Out Islands which they call Neighbor Islands, but up until the last few years, cruise ships headed for Nassau and Freeport and by-passed the islands. They have been "discovered" by cruise lines looking for "new" destinations and now have "beach parties" on uninhabited, or sparsely inhabited Bahamas islands. Ships stop for about four or five hours. There are no shore excursions sold and passengers disembark by tender. There are no changing facilities on most, so wear your bathing suit, sandals and a cover-up. Buffet picnic-type lunch is served on the island. Some ships recommend you bring ship towels ashore, then return them to your cabin steward, others furnish towels on the island. Some ships offer water sports activities on the island, others provide only a day at the beach and lunch. There are umbrellas on the islands for passengers who are trying to stay out of the sun, but not enough. Bring head covers. It's an enjoyable day on islands that are unspoiled and the way the Bahamas were not too many years ago.

BARBADOS

(Population 254,000)

Captain John Powell led the first British settlers when they landed in Barbados in 1625. He claimed the island in the name of King James I of England; it remained an English colony until 1966, when it became an independent nation. The Parliament of Barbados dates back to 1639 and is the third oldest government in the Commonwealth. A mark of the island's stability is its democratic government, which has continued without interruption since that time. Bridgetown is the island's capital, port, and commercial center, and its bustling harbor is the focus of all sights and sounds of a West Indian seaport. Harbor police wear uniforms alike those worn in Admiral Nelson's navy; his statue decorates Trafalgar Square and St. Michael's Cathedral, where George Washington supposedly worshipped. The Barbadians are chiefly of British (5 percent) and African (95 percent) descent and speak with a soft, eighteenth-century inflection. Donkey carts, bicycles, and pushcarts share the roads with buses and motorcars while Barbadians sip afternoon tea on verandah and share tidbits with the native sugar-birds. Small wonder Barbados is so very British. Although the Portuguese first laid claim to the island in 1536, it was the British who came in 1625 and stayed until independence in 1966. Barbados is one of the most stable countries in the Caribbean and is the third oldest democracy in the Commonwealth. British traditions and customs carry over in spite of independence. The police band gives outdoor concerts, everyone stops for afternoon tea, sailors still dress in the style of Lord Nelson and judges still wear wigs in courtrooms. Cricket and polo, croquet and parishes with names like St. James and St. Michael make most Americans think they have landed in the British Isles.

Size: This easternmost West Indies island is 14 miles wide, 21 miles long; total area is 66 square miles.

Climate: Temperatures range from 70 to 86 degrees. The island is cooled all year by northeast trade winds.

Currency: Barbados dollar

Language: English.

Shopping: Barbados rum is sold for about $3.25 a bottle at the port shops; there are also china, crystal, cameras, watches, cashmere, and linens, as well as native handicrafts of straw, mahogany, shell, and coral. Stores open 8 a.m. to 4 p.m. Monday through Friday; closed Saturday afternoon and Sunday.

Time: One hour ahead of EST.

Tipping Ashore: Restaurants and hotels add 10 percent to bills for gratuities; taxi drivers expect 10 to 15 percent.

Transportation: Shore excursions (4 hours), $19. Public buses, 50 cents U.S. for a full route; official taxi fares set by government. (See TTT:) Official rate between pier is U.S. $2.00 per car; motor-scooters, bikes, cars, available for rental. Driving is on the left side of the road.

TTT: Island taxi and bus rates are posted in Barbados dollars on a billboard at the port exit and clearly marked either per vehicle or per person. Avoid problems by repeating the price agreed upon with the driver. Unfortunately, drivers do not honor posted prices and disagreements are common. Local police pay no attention to complaints, so don't bother going to them for assistance. At the Barbados port, you are at the mercy of taxi drivers if you want to go into Bridgetown unless you have purchased a shore excursion sold on board ship. I have given up fighting the system and I pay whatever the driver asks. I do refuse to pay per person rates and once we have agreed, I insist taxi drivers adhere to the agreed upon rate. As of a few months ago, the same signs were still posted and the same arguments were heard at the port. It's the only ripoff I found in Barbados but it sure gets blood pressures soaring.

Shopping **TTT:** There are a few out-of-the-way antique shops with old English furniture and bric-a-brac from 18th century manor homes that are being torn down.

What to See: Magazine Lane, where the Montefiore Fountain was presented to the island's people by a prominent Jewish family; the 18th century Town Hall, former meeting place of the House of Assembly; Trafalgar Square with Lord Nelson's statue; the Barbados Museum with relics of the island's history; St. Michael's Cathedral, rebuilt on coral rock in 1780. If time permits, take the spectacular drive across the island from Bridgetown to Bathsheba on the Atlantic coast.

What to Wear Ashore: Summer clothing all year, but shorts are not seen on Bridgetown streets.

More Information: Barbados Board of Tourism, 800 Second Avenue,New York, NY 10017.

BERMUDA

(Population 56,000)

A tiny speck in the Atlantic, Bermuda is about 1,000 miles north of the Caribbean and 70 miles southeast of New York. It's an informal island with an occasional swing to extreme and very British pageantry. An ancient ceremony in the old town of St. George's, a Queen's birthday parade in Hamilton, and the opening of the island's parliament and supreme court are examples. Bermuda is actually seven large islands linked by bridges and causeways and 143 smaller ones. There are four formal settlements, and Hamilton, near the center, is the only city and serves as the capital. At the east end is Saint George's Town, first settlement on the islands, founded in 1612 by the Bermuda Company of Adventurers.

Size: The 150 islands of Bermuda cover 21 square miles. The mainland is 22 miles long and a maximum of one mile in width.

Climate: Two seasons—summer temperature (from May to Mid-November) from 75 to 85 degrees; winter temperature (from mid-December to March) from 60 to 70 degrees.

Currency: Bermuda dollar

Language: English

Shopping: English leather goods, china, silver, some antiques, gloves, cashmere, and Scottish woolens. Shops open 8 a.m. to 4 p.m. weekdays; closed Saturday afternoon and Sunday.

Time: One hour ahead of EST.

Tipping Ashore: About the same as in the United States; 15 percent for most services.

Transportation: Shore Excursions (3 hours), $20 (in cars); boat tour, $25. No rental cars available, but there are plenty of taxis, buses, ferries, and bicycles. Driving is on the left side of the road, and speed limits are posted at 15 miles per hour in town and 20 elsewhere.

What to See: Gibb's Hill Lighthouse; Fort Scaur; Somerset Bridge; Saint George's area; Carriage Museum; Ducking Stool; Old Rectory; Hamilton; Bermuda Cathedral; City Hall. Bermuda's chief attractions are natural rather than man-made, and the superb beaches, tinted pink from powdered coral, look exactly like the picture postcards.

What to Wear Ashore: Bathing suits, bikinis and/or bare feet are not acceptable for street wear. Lightweight clothing for daytime and dressier evenings. Ties and jackets required for dinner and evening activities in hotels.

More Information: Bermuda Department of Tourism, 630 Fifth Avenue, New York, NY 10020.

TTT: Go Bermudian. See the island by motor-scooter. Even if you have tried those two-wheelers before, you'll enjoy Bermuda more if you go native. It's the best way to get around. St. George's is the most charming part of the island. Founded in 1612, it's old world look has been very well preserved. At Paget, visit the lovely Botanical Gardens, Camden Museum and 17th century Verdmont House which has been restored by the Bermuda National Trust. Since most ships spend two or three days in Bermuda, you'll have time to enjoy the magnificent beaches, great restaurants (favorites are the Waterfront and the Lobster Pot, for lobster of course). If you find yourself with a free afternoon, take a glass-bottomed boat ride and see ancient ship wrecks, coral reefs and marine life, or take a ferry ride to one of the smaller islands and picnic in near seclusion.

TTT: Don't put cameras and/or other valuables (purses) in the basket attached to motor bikes (mopeds). Snatchings by fast riding motorcycle thieves are reported by ship passengers. Crime rate, otherwise, if very low.

THE CAYMAN ISLANDS

GRAND CAYMAN

(Population 12,000)

The lovely Cayman Islands were not as popular a hundred years ago as they are today. Because of the treacherous coral reefs that surround them, more than 300 ships have met their doom here and now provide a fascinating attraction for underwater divers. The Cayman Islands are also known as Las Tortugas ("the islands of the turtles"), and cuisine is appropriately noted for turtle soup and steaks. The islands are south of Cuba and northwest of Jamaica, and cruise ships have discovered the port. Grand Cayman, the largest of the three Caymans, is a low island of coral lime-stone. Its spectacular crescent beach of powder-fine white coral extends for six miles along the west end. Diving and swimming are popular, and the fishing is excellent. Unspoiled and under-populated, Grand Cayman is a friendly island with magnificent beaches. The Caymans were first sighted by Columbus back in 1503 on his last voyage to the New World. He tagged them Las Tortugas, or islands of the turtles because of all the tortoises he saw there. Although the name didn't last officially, turtle soup and turtle steaks are still the specialty of local chefs. The islands are surrounded by a ring of coral reefs, a graveyard for over 300 ships. These sunken vessels are an attraction for underwater divers. Tales of buried treasure and buccaneers adds romantic flavor to the history of the Cayman Islands.

Size: 22 miles long and 8 miles wide.
Climate: Same as Bahamas.
Currency: Cayman Island dollar (CI).
Language: English.
Shopping: British imports, china, wools, and Caribbean handicrafts are available at very good prices.
Time: One hour ahead of EST.
Tipping Ashore: Similar to the United States and Canada.
Transportation: Shore excursions (3 hours), $9, Taxis, cars, motor bicycles available for rental.
What to See: Pedro's Castle, Henry Morgan headquarters in pirate days; Turtle Crawls in North Sound; wild orchids and wild parrots on Rum Point; "Hell," the weird coral formation on the north end of

the island; and Georgetown, formerly a quiet capital city, now with international banks offering "numbered" and "secret" banking facilities.

What to Wear Ashore: Casual, lightweight summer clothing.

More Information: Cayman Islands Department of Tourism, 420 Lexington Avenue, New York, NY 10017.

TTT: Turtle products are a great attraction in the Caymans, but unless you want to donate the turtle shell to U.S. Customs Inspectors, don't buy them. Turtleshell products are sold throughout the island but they are not allowed in to the U.S. because the turtle is considered an endangered species even if it is a farmed turtle.

COLOMBIA   CARTAGENA

(Population 350,000)

Cartagena, one of the best-preserved walled cities in the world, recently emerged as a popular port of call for visiting cruise ships. This fortified city has withstood pirate, military, and naval attacks and is referred to as Ciudad Heroica. It was founded in 1533, but a fire wiped out much of the settlement. Cartagena's position on its landlocked harbor seemed impregnable, but it wasn't. Sir Francis Drake sacked the city before it was refortified in 1586. The city was never again conquered, and fortifications costing $70 million withstood attacks for the next 300 years.

Climate: Warm summer days, in the 80s; cooler in the winter.

Currency: Colombian Peso

Language: Spanish.

Shopping: Native ruana (woolen panchos in vivid colors), leather duffel bags, handbags, gloves, jewelry, and linen shirts for about $10 U.S.; emeralds, available in varying quality and size, are best purchased from reliable jewelers.

Time: Same as EST.

Tipping Ashore: It is not customary to tip taxi drivers, but 10 percent is added to bills in restaurants and hotels. Patrons are expected to tip an additional 5 percent.

Transportation: Shore excursions (3 hours), $15. Taxis are metered, car rentals are available.

What to See: The historic castles of San Felipe and San Fernando; the fortress of San Sebastian and Boca Chica; the vaults; the clock tower; the Inquisition Palace; the Gold Museum, and the walls and beaches surrounding the city. The Old City, admirably restored and maintained, is a huge, historical relic of a great past. Visitors can walk the walls as Spanish sentries once did, but to cover them all means a 7-mile hike. In places they are 50 feet thick, and automobiles can drive over them. Also well-preserved inside the walls is a magnificent array of balconied mansions and buildings remaining as they were more than 300 hundred years ago.

What to Wear Ashore: Comfortable shoes, casual clothes.

More Information: Colombian Government Tourist Office, 140 East 57th St. New York, NY 10022.

TTT: For a refreshing pause, try the native beer (Club Colombia) and the inexpensive local rums. Average price of a whiskey and soda or a bottle of wine is about $6.00 U.S., and coffee is no longer free at most places, but it is the best bargain in Colombia. Many shops sell coffee, pre-packaged for perc or drip in one pound boxes for about $1.00 per pound. A package of 12 pounds cost me U.S. $10 in the Greenfire Emerald Shop and they happily accepted greenbacks. No pressure to buy emeralds. They take their chances. If you succumb to emerald-temptation they want it to be in their store.

CURACAO

(Population 158,000)

A Spanish navigator, Alonso de Ojeda, serving under Christopher Columbus, discovered Curacao in 1499. The Spaniards settled on the island in the early 1500s, and in 1634 the Dutch captured the island and founded a settlement. Peter Stuyvesant became governor in 1643 (and three years later became the governor of Nieuw Netherlands, of which New Amsterdam, now New York City, was the capital). The English and French tried to take Curacao from 1666 through the early 19th century. In 1800 it came under a British protectorate, and it was finally returned to the Dutch in 1816 through the Treaty of Paris and the Treaty of London. Curacao is an autonomous part of the Kingdom of the Netherlands, and it is administered by a parliamentary government. Willemstad, the capital city, is best seen by walking across the Queen Emma Bridge (the largest pontoon bridge in the Western Hemisphere) and through its bustling streets. A canal-like inlet bisects the sparkling-clean city into what are called Punda and Otrabanda. Gabled houses in early Dutch Colonial style are painted pastel colors, and the bayfront area is characteristic. Willemstad is one of the world's largest bunkering stations and one of the most important financial and commercial centers in the Caribbean.

Willemstad, the island's capital city, is really a Dutch masterpiece with its waterfront lined 17th and 18th century buildings painted in shades of yellow, lime and blue. Architecture is strictly Dutch influenced. The entrance to the harbor has been renovated and is near the Governor's Palace, Dutch Reform Church (1769) and the Mikve Israel-Emanuel Synagogue, oldest in the Western Hemisphere is in continuous use. Curacao is the largest island in the Netherlands Antilles and probably the most sophisticated. In case you wonder, the Queen Emma Bridge opens about 20 times a day.

Size: 38 miles long; the width goes from 2.5 to 7 miles.

Climate: Temperatures average 81 degrees but reach a low of 75 during the winter months. Trade winds are constant, and evenings are cooler. Some rain in November and December.

Currency: Guilder (or florin)

Language: Dutch; Spanish and English spoken almost everywhere.

Shopping: Curacao of Curacao, of course, at $4.00 a fifth. Like Aruba, Curacao is a duty-free haven, and everything from all over the world is available at good prices: china, crystal, jewelry, watches, clothing, perfume, and so on.

Time: One hour-ahead of EST.

Tipping Ashore: Hotels add 15 percent, and restaurants add a 10 percent charge. Taxi drivers will be happy with 10 percent.

Transportation: Shore excursions (3 hours), $15.00. Metered taxis, buses, rental cars available. Two-hour countryside tour bought on shore, about $10.00 per person.

What to See: The oldest Protestant church (1759), on the square behind Governor House; the 1732 synagogue; the view from the top of Ararat Hill and the oldest Caucasian cemetery in the hemisphere; the coral caverns and the lighthouse. Visitors to this lovely island will want to spend at least some of their time at Willemstad, a tidy little town whose streets are lined with 17th century Dutch homes and stores. The island also has a floating marketplace, several fine hotels, and a friendly population that will make any tourist feel right at home.

What to Wear Ashore: Summer-weight clothing. Dressier in the evenings at hotels and casinos. Jacket and tie suggested for men (required in some restaurants).

More Information: Curacao Tourist Board, 400 Madison Ave. New York, NY 10017.

TTT: Do take the square nickels should a shopkeeper offer them in change. They make great souvenirs and are available from banks. Las Vegas-type gambling casinos operate in the large hotels. Usually open at 8 p.m., but some accommodate cruise passengers and start the action at 1 p.m. when ships are in port.

MORE TTT's: Don't leave Curacao without tasting some of the outstanding cuisine. Here you can dine on Indonesian rijstattafel, Chinese, French, Italian, German, and Swiss specialties, not to mention American fast foods and Curacao liquor known world wide. Samples of the latter are available at the 17th century distillery. Curacao is a pot pouri of everything nice about the Caribbean, blended with Dutch cleanliness, tradition, and reliability. It is one of my favorite islands. If unusual beaches turn you on, don't miss the beach at the Hilton Hotel or the Holiday Inn. I head for the cove at the Hilton as soon as my ship docks. You can make arrangements to use the changing facilities and locker rooms for a nominal charge (sometimes, no charge depending on how busy the hotel happens to be). Be sure to bring a head scarf if you are concerned with the way your hair looks. Those tropical trade winds work on a 24 hour basis and can ruin the most lacquered look within seconds. But, it's worth it!

THE DOMINICAN REPUBLIC

(Population 4 million)

The Dominican Republic's first tourist was Christopher Columbus in 1492. The country occupies the eastern two-thirds of the island of Hispaniola. The other one-third belongs to Haiti. In 1496, Columbus's brother Bartholome founded Santo Domingo de Guzman, capital of the Republic, making it the oldest European settlement in the New World. About 100 years later, Sir Francis Drake almost burned it to the ground, and Spanish rule was reasserted in 1809. The Dominicans declared the country independent of Spain 12 years later, but the Haitians invaded and occupied it for 22 years. Independence was finally established in 1944. The republic has a system of government similar to that of the United States. In the years following Columbus's discovery, the country was a favorite stopping-off place for Spanish Conquistadores as they pursued legendary treasures. Being "first" in development of the Western Hemisphere is commonplace in the Dominican Republic where visitors can see the first hospital, the first university, the oldest street, the oldest Cathedral. The Dominican Republic also claims a "last." Dominicans say the remains of that great explorer, Columbus, are entombed in the first Cathedral, although this claim is disputed by cities in Spain and Cuba. Restoration of historic sites is also a "first" for Caribbean islands. A zone has been restored to almost the way it was back in those colonial days.

Size: 200 miles wide and 150 miles long, the Dominican Republic covers 18,816 square miles.

Climate: Similar to Miami, with high humidity in August and September. Rainy season in May and September.

Currency: Dominican peso

Language: Spanish.

Time: One hour ahead of EST.

Transportation: Taxis and rental cars available in major cities.

What to See: In Santo Domingo—Shore excursions (3 hours), $12.00. The Basilica Santa Maria in Menor with its carvings, treasure rooms and Columbus's tomb; the restored Alcazar de Colon built by Don Diego, Columbus's son; the Viceregal Museum with its Spanish antiquities; the Tower of Homage, the oldest stone fortress in the Americas, now a prison; Santo Domingo University; the national capital; the famous Boca Chica beach; and a couple of the fabulous new hotel-resort complexes. In Puerto Plata—on the north coast, there are long stretches of beaches, an unspoiled-by-tourists community, the new Jack Tarr Village, a marvelous golf course, water sports, and a magnificent coastline. It is basically an agricultural countryside. For the best views and an exciting experience, try the cable car ride up the mountains behind Puerto Plata.

What to Wear Ashore: Lightweight summer clothes. No beach attire in cities or on tours. Some hotels require jacket and tie for dinner. Cruise ships call at two ports in the Dominican Republic: Santo Domingo, the capital city, which has developed a new harbor facility and terminal with duty free shops; and Puerta Plata on the north shore of the country. There is a city atmosphere in Santo Domingo; more rural around Puerto Plata.

More Information: Dominican Tourist Information Center, 485 Madison Avenue, New York, NY 10022.

TTT: Casino gambling in major hotels; action starts at 8 p.m. but casinos open at 2 p.m. when ships are in port.

GUADELOUPE

(Population 330,000)

Named by Columbus after a Spanish monastery, the two islands of Guadeloupe were settled by the Spanish but became a center of buccaneer activities. There were occupied by the French in 1635 but the English and French changed control four times before it settled down as a bit of France in the Caribbean. It became an Overseas Department of France in 1946 and a Region of France in 1974.

The island is shaped like a giant butterfly with the wings made by the two island, Grand-Terre on the east and Basse-Terre forming the mountainous area crowned by La Soufrier at 4,813 feet. Scenery is a mix of mountains, volcanic peaks, green forests, lakes, waterfalls and tropical flora. Pointe-a-Petre is the commercial port city. There are good beaches a 15-minute ride away and excellent hotels have been built. Basse-Terre is the capital.

Size: 687 square miles.

Climate: Tropical with rainy season August–November.

Currency: French franc

Language: French and Creole

Shopping: Shops are open same hours as Martinique and same 20 percent tax refund is available when payment is made in travelers checks or by credit card. (See Martinique TTT). Anything French is cheaper than back home but selection seems better in Martinique.

Tipping: 10–15 percent for all service. Usually added to check in restaurants.

Time: One hour ahead of EST.

Transportation: Shore excursions (4 hours) $20.00. Good public transportation is inexpensive and it's easy to get around on your own if you speak a little French. Taxis, rental cars available.

What to See: The Creole architecture that reminds you of New Orleans; three very interesting museums, 18th century fort, the sugar town of Sainte Anne and its beaches, Guadeloupe National Park with its tropical forest, Basse-Terre and if time permits, some of the neighboring small islands accessible by ferry.

More information: French West Indies Tourist Board, 610 Fifth Avenue, New York, NY 10020.

TTT: Do try the local beer; also Guadeloupe rum is inexpensive.

GRENADA

(Population 102,000)

Southernmost of the Windward Islands, Grenada lies 90 miles north of Trinidad. Discovered by Columbus in 1498, it is now independent. Known as the Spice Island because it grows one-third of the world's supply of nutmeg, Grenada is where you find famous black-and-white beaches. Only 50 yards separate the jet-black sand of the Atlantic from the pure white sand of the Caribbean. St. George's is the capital city.

Grenada is a mountainous island, laden with exotic plants and trees — cinnamon, cloves, cocoa, vanilla, ginger, nutmeg, avocado, papaya, mango, banana, breadfruit. No one goes hungry in Grenada. As rich as the foliage, so rich is Grenada's heritage. A visit to Carib's Leap at the north end of the island is a look at one chapter in the island's history. There, Indians chose suicide over slavery and leaped to their death after a battlestand against the French. If your ship is in port on a Saturday, visit the local market for a kaleidoscopic view of everything grown on the island. Locals come into town for chatter and communication with other locals. Bring your camera.

Size: 21 miles long and 12 miles wide.
Climate: Temperatures range between 70 and 85 degrees. Dry season is January through May, with rainy weather from June to December. Rain seldom lasts more than an hour.
Currency: Eastern Caribbean dollar (ECD)
Language: English.
Shopping: Some jewelry and art objects, native handicrafts from Trinidad, and spices of all kinds and hard to get in other parts of the world.
Time: One hour ahead of EST.
Tipping Ashore: Similar to the United States (10 to 15 percent).
Transportation: Shore excursions (4 hours), $10. Taxis are available at moderate rates. Rental cars also available.
What to See: Massive battlements of Fort George and Fort Frederick; Great Etang, a volcanic crater lake; black-and-white sand beaches

at Point Saline; Annandale Falls on the Beausejour River; nutmeg processing stations; Carriacon, a tiny island accessible by ferry. This island is famous for the abundance of spices it produces (its flag even shows the nutmeg). Its mountainous landscape is dotted with crater lakes and picturesque beaches.

What to Wear Ashore: Lightweight summer clothing or sportswear daytime; dressier casual evenings. Some hotels suggest cocktail-type clothes, jacket and tie after dark.

More Information: Grenada Tourist Information Office, 141 E. 44th St., New York, NY 10017.

TTT: U.S. Health Department permits importation of spices from Grenada. Spices are inexpensive and in many cases not available back home. Best place to shop for spices is in local supermarkets right off the shelf for 30 to 50 cents per container. Some examples of unusual condiments are: Trinidad mustard, tonic wine, Tulong, and English bitter chocolate.

TTT: Grenada has settled down in the aftermath of the American Marine landing in 1983 and the subsequent change in government. Whereas the natives were a lot less than friendly prior to 1983, there has been a complete reversal and Americans are now hailed as friends. Cruise ships are again including Grenada in Caribbean itineraries. The Medical School from which American students were evacuated is included in some shore excursions.

HAITI

(Population 15 million)

Haiti occupies the western third of the island of Hispaniola, and cruise passengers don't take long to discover it is different from any other port in the itinerary. Shaped like a horseshoe, the country sits on the coast encircling the Gulf of Gonave. Highest peaks rise to 10,000 feet, with numerous rivers and heavily wooded areas. Although most of the natives are black, there are many who are descendants of former French settlers. Established as a French colony on what was Columbus's first New World landfall, Haiti fought for and achieved independence in 1804 as the world's first black republic and the Americas' second republic. Since then it has experienced times of glory and disaster. The French influence remained in Haiti long after the French left

380

the island. It is interesting to note, that it never really displaced the African influence. This combination makes for an unusual blend and is obvious in the Haitian's native creativity. The period of most grandeur was probably during the time of King Christophe, whose fantastic monument is a prime attraction today. After Christophe proclaimed himself king, he fortified his entourage by building the Citadelle, considered the most awesome fortress in the Western Hemisphere. While he was protecting himself from the French, he could not help but admire many of their ways, so he built the palace of San Souci for himself; and, he imitated the style and scale of Versailles.

The Citadelle Laferriere perches on a hilltop a few miles from Cap Haitien. It is reached by a donkey ride that offers a dramatic introduction to the massive fortress built in the early 1800s as a defense against the French. Cruise ships visit two ports in Haiti—Cap Haitien and the capital city of Port-au-Prince.

Size: Covers almost 10,000 square miles, of which 75 percent is mountainous.

Climate: Humidity is high, especially in autumn. Temperatures average 80 degrees, with more rain in May and September.

Currency: Gourde

Language: Officially, French, but 80 percent of the population speaks Creole (a combination of French, English, and Spanish).

Shopping: Mahogany carved figures, Haitian art, tropical shirts and dresses, water colors and oils, and in-bond, duty-free shopping.

Time: EST.

Tipping Ashore: 10 percent is acceptable and usually added as a service charge. Taxi drivers are not tipped by locals but expect 10 percent from tourists.

Transportation: Taxis and rental cars available. Local buses not recommended for visitors. Taxi rates require bargaining.

What to Wear Ashore: Your most comfortable summer-weight clothing and shoes. No short shorts. It is never necessary to dress up in Haiti.

More Information: Haiti Government Tourist Bureau, 1270 Avenue of the Americas, New York, NY 10020.

CAP HAITIEN

What to See: Shore excursions (3 hours), $18. Citadelle tours (6 hours), $25.00. Cap Haitien is a mellow, tranquil city on the north coast, where ghosts of French colonial planters and their sullen slaves once walked the hills. In the nineteenth century, when its sugar and cacao plantations supplied half of Europe, Cap Haitien was the wealthiest French possession. Interesting sights are the San Souci in the village of Milot; the Citadelle on the peak of La Ferrier Mountain, reached only on horseback and considered one of the wonders of the world; the old fort of Cap Francais; the Caves of Le Dondon; the small village of Limondale, the first outpost of the Americas constructed from the remains of Columbus's ship, which ran aground nearby.

TTT: A fun shore excursion is the mule-back trip up to the Citadelle. Fully escorted (front and rear of the animal), it is safe and gets rave reviews. from cruise passengers. They also have small horses riding this trail and some passengers are more comfortable on them than on the donkeys.

PORT-AU-PRINCE

What to See: Shore excursions (3 hours) $10.00. As with most capital cities, there is a degree of sophistication, but here it is mixed with primitive atmosphere. You will want to see the Iron Market (crowded with stalls selling fruits, vegetables, and handicrafts); pseudo-chateaux on stilts, gingerbread houses; the National Museum; Barbancourt rum factory in Petionville (and taste the dozens of samples offered by the friendly host); the Cathedral Saint Trinite, where the walls are covered with primitive murals by Haitian artists (Jesus is black and Judas is white); the Roman Catholic cathedral; the palace.

TTT: Haitian art is a good buy if you like primitive works. Everyone buys something in Haiti, and this is the place to practice your bartering skills. Watch out for termites in the wood, and don't buy any drums. Goatskin products are not allowed into the United States. Cruise ship passengers do not need passports. All other arriving U.S. visitors need valid passports.

JAMAICA

(Population 2 million)

Columbus discovered Jamaica on his second voyage in 1494. Impressed by what he saw, the Discoverer called his landing place Santa Gloria, but Spaniards who came after him learned that the gentle Arawak Indians who lived on the island called it Xamaca, which meant "islands of springs". Diego Columbus decided to colonize Jamaica in 1509, and an expedition built the first settlement. For the next 150 years the Spanish ruled the island. When they found no gold and learned that crops of almost any kind would grow with little effort, they enslaved and gradually killed off the Arawaks. In 1655, England took over the island, and it remained British until independence a few years ago. Jamaica retains much British tradition and influence in day-to-day lifestyle, but continues to shed many of its colonial fringes. Smaller than some Caribbean islands, larger than others, Jamaica has had years of unrest. With the recent election, it is again emerging as a stable island nation with strong democratically-inclined leadership. The native Jamaican is a mixture of the millions of African slaves who were sold to plantation owners, European traders and Asians who arrived here in the late 1800s. What has emerged is a people with unique accomplishments in music, culture, art, and handicraft. It is an island of contrasts with mountains and beaches, rural and urban communities, resorts and small guest houses. A winding coastline surrounds the island and cruise ships which sought other ports during Jamaica's troubled period are again including Ocho Rios, Montego Bay and other ports in itineraries.

Size: Jamaica covers an area of 148 by 55 miles.

Climate: More than 300 days of sunshine a year, temperatures from 75 degrees in the winter to 81 in the summer. It can be as much as 15 degrees cooler in the mountain areas.

Currency: Jamaican dollar (see **TTT**)

Language: English.

Shopping: Visitors have opportunities to purchase duty-free merchandise all over the island. Duty-free purchases must be sent to your ship (or to the airport). Free port items include perfume, cashmeres, silks, Swiss watches, cameras, crystal, china, and photography equipment. Jamaican-made items are batik, carvings, ceramics, rum, straw work. Every port city has a native market, and shops have branches with similar merchandise in all port cities.

Time: EST and EDT.

Tipping Ashore: Similar to the United States (10 to 15 percent).

Transportation: Cars and limousines available for rental. Shore excursions in every port. Average 3 to 4-hour tours, $15.00.

What to Wear Ashore: Casual summer clothes, shorts, slacks, etc. for daytime. Dressier in the evening at some hotels and nightclubs. Informal at others.

More Information: Jamaica Tourist Board, 866 Second Ave., New York, NY 10017.

KINGSTON

Kingston, largest city and leading port of Jamaica, is also its capital. Its natural harbor, seventh largest in the world, plays host to a good number of ships each year. Founded in 1693, Kingston has been the capital since 1872. It is a flourishing port city with a busy dock area, manufacturing sector, and lovely residential suburbs stretching out to the foothills of the Blue Mountains. The city itself is located on a broad, sloping arm of the Port Royal peninsula. On the peninsula, past the busy modern airport, stands what is left of the buccaneer city of Port Royal, once known as the "richest and wickedest spot on earth."

What to See: Shore excursion (4 hours), $12.00. Worth a visit are the Royal Botanical Gardens at Hope; the Folk Museum; Spanish Town and Morgan's Harbor at Port Royal.

MONTEGO BAY

No one can doubt that the popularity of Montego Bay has stood the test of time. Long before Columbus and the Spaniards arrived, Arawak Indian tribes worked and played at this spot, which is situated captivatingly on the water's edge at the foot of a range of green hills. Many Spanish colonists of the early sixteenth century were quick to recognize the advantages of settling there, and the English, who took over in 1655, were just as enthusiastic. Present-day visitors are no less so. Montego Bay (the Spaniards called it Manteca Bahia, meaning "Lard Bay") is second only to Kingston in area and population. Built around a charming old town square, it has a number of churches (one dating from 1775), a town hall (1808), banks, many shops, movie houses, nightclubs, an art gallery or two, the usual civic amenities.

What to See: Rose Hall, Good Hope Plantation; Montego Bay Straw Market; Doctor's Cave (for swimming); banana, sugar cane, and coconut plantations. Time permitting, take a leisurely ride on the Governor's Diesel Coach, which takes visitors into the heart of Jamaica with stops at interesting points along the way.

TTT: From either Ocho Rios or Montego Bay, take the Dunn's River Falls rafting trip for a memorable experience.

OCHO RIOS

Along a stretch of coral on the north-central Jamaican coast is the popular resort of Ocho Rios. This area embraces a spectacular 42-mile expanse from Discovery Bay in the west to Port Maria in the east, with lovely holiday spots—Runaway Bay, Mammee Bay, Ocho Rios, and Oracabessa—in between. Over the past few years, the port of Ocho Rios, having enjoyed phenomenal development, now offers the facilities a modern deep water cruise ship pier within walking distance of the complex of convention hotels and resort facilities. Foremost among the area's attractions are Dunn's River Falls, which cascade down from the nearby hills, splashing into the blue Caribbean. To climb from sea level though the cascading torrents is a thrilling and memorable experience.

What to See: This is one of the more popular resort areas of Jamaica, 67 miles east of Montego Bay and 58 miles northwest of Kingston. Sightseeing is the same as for Montego because they are so close.

PORT ANTONIO

Embraced by the enchanting natural twin harbors, quaint, historical Port Antonio has preserved its marine and agro-industrial advantages in the development of this delightfully appealing resort. Although acknowledged to be the cradle of Jamaica's tourist industry, this picturesque town in the northeastern section of the island has advanced more slowly than its sister resorts. For many visitors, the leisurely pace is its greatest charm, and they return year after year to enjoy the delightful setting of one of the island's most beautiful regions. After Spanish Settlement as early as 1510, a notable event in the port's subsequent history was the arrival in 1793 of Captain Bligh, of *Bounty* fame, with breadfruit and other plants from the Pacific. The business of growing and exporting bananas is largely accountable for the region's prosperity.

What to See: Port Antonio has the island's heaviest rainfall and is probably the most photographed area. Rafting down the Rio Grande is the traditional excursion. There are restroom facilities at the Rafter's Rest, and it takes better than 2 hours to go down the river ($20.00).

TTT: It is recommended that this trip be taken in a bathing suit with a shirt over the shoulders. Also, do not choose a raftsman unless he is wearing a numbered badge and is licensed.

385

TTT: Jamaica is strict about enforcing currency exchange laws and it is illegal to bring Jamaican dollars into or out of the country. Money must be exchanged at official exchange points (banks, hotels, authorized exchange facilities at ports of entry, sea and air.) Resist money exchange offers on the street. Your voyage could be interrupted by imprisonment, fine and a lot of embarrassment. The country is trying to eliminate blackmarket activities. Also resist offers to sell you narcotics. Jamaican authorities also are cracking down on these sales and you are looking for trouble if you get involved.

MARTINIQUE

(Population 325,000)

Martinique, a French possession since the middle of the seventeenth century, became an Overseas Department of France in 1946 and a Region of France in 1974. It lies in the Windward group of the Lesser Antilles between Dominica and St. Lucia. After the abolition of slavery in 1848, the island was opened to immigration, and there was an influx of Hindus, Chinese, and Annamites from French Indochina. Martinique's famous Mount Pelee erupted in 1902 and in three minutes wiped out the entire population of the former capital city St. Pierre, whose ruins are called the "Pompeii of the New World." Martinique is also renowned as the birthplace of Napoleon's Empress Josephine, and for H.M.S. Diamond Rock, which was commissioned as a ship by the British Navy in the eighteenth century and which held out for 18 months against the French. This is also the location of one of the island's best beaches. Fort-de-France is the capital city.

Size: 50 miles long and 22 miles wide. Martinique covers an area of 425 square miles.

Climate: There are three distinct seasons, with an average of 79 degrees; very fresh from November to April; dry and warm from April to July; and rainy from September to November.

Currency: French franc

Language: French.

Shopping: Since the island is French, anything French is a good buy. Rue Victor Hugo is the main shopping street. Perfumes, crystal, china, Lalique, and rum.

TTT: Shops are normally closed between 12:30 and 2:30 P.M. and Saturday afternoons, except when a couple of small or a large cruise ship is in port. Some shops also stay open beyond the normal 6 P.M. closing and on Sunday morning when cruise ships are in port. There are a number of shops in Martinique, but I have dealt with Roger Albert for the last 20 years and do not hesitate to recommend it. Roger Albert has the largest selection of French and other imported merchandise of interest to travelers. The store is reliable and prices are highly competitive. You can take advantage of a 20 percent tax refund allowed if you pay for your purchases by traveler's checks or major credit cards. Clerks are courteous, and Roger Albert is an enthusiastic community leader who welcomes Americans. This tax refund amounts to a 20 percent reduction in prices on top of the already lower prices on items from France and makes Martinique the cheapest place to purchase your French fragrances. Inventory includes just about every French perfume and cosmetic available in France. If your ship is heading for Martinique and your shopping list includes French items, save some of your purchases for this island.

Time: One hour ahead of EST.

Tipping Ashore: 10 to 15 percent when not included as service charge. Most taxi drivers own their own cars so tipping is optional.

Transportation: No metered taxis but rental cars available. Plan on paying $2.50 per gallon for gas. Taxi for 3 hours, approximately $30.

What to See: Shore excursions (3 hours). $22. By taxi, $15 per person if two persons go together. It is possible to see the island by bus or car. The Volcanology Museum of St. Pierre is devoted to the 1902 eruption of Mount Pelee, now considered extinct. Also worth seeing are La Pagerie, the birthplace of Empress Josephine, and the countryside and downtown Fort-de-France. **TTT**Cock fights and snake and mongoose fights are legal, and inquiries to taxi drivers will lead you to the right place.

What to Wear Ashore: Summer clothes are suitable. Bring lightweight rainwear during September, November. Martinique, like other islands, has become more casual and it is not necessary to wear a jacket and tie at night except for very special occasions.

More Information: French West Indies Tourist Board, 610 Fifth Avenue, New York, NY 10020.

PANAMA AND THE PANAMA CANAL

(Population 418,000)

One of the most incredible journeys possible today is one our ancestors couldn't sail because the body of water just wasn't there: the

Panama Canal. For hundreds of years great explorers, from Christopher Columbus to Lewis and Clark, searched for an east-west passageway, a path of water through the American land mass. The dream was so great that what couldn't be found had to be engineered and created.

The Panama Canal today is a tranquil, 8-hour daylight journey between the Atlantic and the Pacific, less than 40 miles in all, but 40 miles of continuous excitement and astonishment.

Christopher Columbus would have envied us as our ships rise and fall in the mighty locks, sail through Gatun Lake, the largest man-made lake in the world; then into the Gaillard Cut, hewn through 8 miles of solid rock, past jungles that seem close enough to touch.

Although the Canal isn't making as many headlines as it did during the past couple of years and during the hot debates on the treaties, the Panama Canal is still one of the world's top tourist attractions, and transiting on a cruise ship is a very "in" experience.

The Canal is a shining example of American initiative, ingenuity, and know-how; the Big Ditch has been around for more than six decades, with its wonders practically ignored until recently by world travelers. Today the Canal is a popular route for cruise ships transporting passengers between east and west. Some ships highlight the Canal transit for the passage itself and do not dock on either side of the Republic of Panama. But most vessels combine the trans-Panama experience with stops in the Caribbean and Mexico and within the country of Panama itself.

Every cruise ship passing through the Canal boards a Canal guide before entering the first lock. The guide takes over the ship's loudspeaker and keeps up a running commentary on the history, construction, operation, and other interesting information about the Canal and the Canal Zone.

Some ships are taking advantage of the fact that Panama is a destination in itself and is more than just the Big Ditch. A popular diversion is a visit to the San Blas Islands. Ships anchor about a mile or so from one of the more inhabited San Blas, and passengers are taken ashore by ship tender for a tour of an Indian civilization that has changed very little during the past five or six decades. This is home of the mola (colorful pieces of cloth, sewn layer by layer into a fabric used by the Cuna Indians as blouses and by *Norte Americanos* as wall-hangings). Prices are rising, but a fairly nice San Blas mola is still available for about $25.

Other ships offer tours to Panama City and through the countryside. Figure on about $35 for a half-day ride through the Canal Zone. The narrow land that divides the Pacific and the Caribbean is a natural short cut from ocean to ocean and an interesting cruise route. The Spanish set out to explore South America from Panama and discovered the treasure of the Incas. Gold was shipped up to Panama City and carried across the isthmus on muleback to Portobelo. This traffic attracted roving buccaneers, and in 1671, Henry Morgan (later governor of Jamaica) sacked both cities. Panama again came into its own as an inter-ocean route when the Canal was completed in 1914. The country today is prosperous and relies heavily on the Big Ditch. Some ships stop on the Atlantic side, others on the Pacific, and some merely pass through the Canal. There's a lot more to this country than a canal, and if you want to see it, make sure your ship docks for a day.

TTT: The rings in the nose, hoops through the ears, and colorful garb are not tourist put-ons in the San Blas. The Indians dress that way even without visitors. True, some of the more savvy are "adjusting" to large numbers of tourists, and "authentic old molas" are being manufactured as quickly as they sell.

TTT: When I have a choice, I prefer the westbound Panama Canal itinerary. The most interesting locks are closer to the east and the ship passes through them during morning hours. Also, Panama City is closer to the west side and if the ship is going to dock, I would rather spend the evening in that city than in Cristobal. Much more going on.

Climate: Hot and very humid. Best months are January to April.

Currency: Interchangeable with the United States; Balboa equals U.S. $1. Panama doesn't bother printing paper money. The U.S. dollar is official currency.

Language: Spanish, English spoken almost everywhere.

Shopping: Panama is a free zone, and best buys are in English bone china, Irish crystal, perfume, Oriental jade, and precious stones. Molas are available for framing or for blouses and dresses.

Time: EST.

Tipping Ashore: Similar to the United States, except taxi drivers do not expect tips.

Transportation: Shore excursions vary with length of time in port. Cruise ships listing San Blas as a port of call do not charge for the shore excursion which is made by ship tender. Taxis, buses, cross-country, train, and rental cars available.

What to See: Each area of Panama is different. The Canal and its locks head every visitor's list, but if time permits, fly over and visit the San Blas Islands for a look at an unfamiliar culture. Panama City has old buildings museums, but the Canal Zone has developed into a bit of transplanted United States.

What to Wear Ashore: Comfortable, casual lightweight clothes; no beachwear, except to San Blas Islands or resort areas.

More Information: Panama Government Bureau, 630 Fifth Avenue,New York, NY 10020.

PUERTO RICO   SAN JUAN

(Population 500,000)

San Juan is one of the oldest cities in the Western Hemisphere. Columbus discovered Puerto Rico in 1493 and named it San Juan Bautista in honor of St. John the Baptist. During the Spanish-American War in 1898, American troops landed on the south coast, and Puerto Ricans refused to come to the aid of the Spanish. The Commonwealth of Puerto Rico was formed in 1952, and the U.S. flag flies alongside the Puerto Rican. The original section of San Juan (the Old City) is a tiny islet just off the northeast coast. It is connected to the mainland by three bridges over the San Antonio Channel between the Atlantic Ocean and San Juan Harbor. The Old City is being carefully restored, and the streets remain paved with the original blue-glazed blocks brought over as ballast in old Spanish sailing ships. Seventeenth-century Spanish homes are pastel colored, and iron grillwork is everywhere. In spite of its aggressive North American business atmosphere, San Juan is very Spanish in customs and flavor. The newer sections are residential, hotel, and shopping areas.

Although Puerto Ricans have been U.S. citizens since 1917, Spanish is spoken a lot more often than English and there is some difficulty outside of San Juan in being understood, but visitors should be able to get by. One day in San Juan is hardly enough. There is much to see and to do. Most ships dock within walking distance of the Old City and the best way to see this area is on foot. Vehicular traffic is bumper-to-bumper and it is faster and less frustrating to walk. An easy tour by foot takes you to the most important historic sites: La Fortaleza, official residence of the Governor (said to be the oldest executive mansion in continuous use in the Western Hemisphere); Casa Blanca, built as the home of Ponce de Leon and now a museum; San Jose Church, second oldest Roman Catholic church in the New World.

It is sometimes hard for visitors to remember that San Juan is not all of Puerto Rico. Time permitting, a rental car ride circling the island gives visitors an entirely different view of Puerto Rico, its variety of lifestyles, industry, coastal areas, topography.

Climate: Summer's 86-degree temperatures drop a few degrees during winter months; average is 77 degrees.

Currency: U. S. dollar.

Language: Spanish and English

Shopping: Everything you can buy in the United States or Canada is available in Puerto Rico at slightly higher prices. Although merchants claim prices to be lower than in St. Thomas, I have not found this to be the case. They say jewelry, gold, perfumes and liquor are priced competitively with the Virgin Islands but I found liquor and perfume to be 10 to 30 percent higher than in St. Thomas or St. Croix. I do not consider San Juan as one of the better shopping ports in the Caribbean, although some trendy jewelry and accessory boutiques have opened and are inviting cruise passengers to view their wares. Everything purchased in Puerto Rico enters the United States without duty.

Time: One hour ahead of EST, same as Daylight Saving Time.

Tipping Ashore: Same as in the United States.

Transportation: Shore excursions (3 hours), $12.00; nightclub tour, up to $35.00. Taxis are plentiful, but drivers are reluctant to use their meters although the law says they must. Taxis by the hour, about $15 but depends on how well you negotiate.

TTT: Expect an argument from the taxi driver if he does not use his meter and you have not agreed on the fare in advance. When the meter has not been turned on and you request he use the meter, expect the reply to be, "It is broken, but I charge you the same as meter." And, expect the fare to be higher. Bus and car rentals are available.

Another word about taxi meters—I have never had the good fortune to find a cab at the pier with a meter that isn't "broken." Also, a word of caution is in order. Every port area of the world qualifies as an area where "innocents" should not take a walking tour or stroll after dark. San Juan is no exception. While the Old City is bustling with people window shopping and patronizing the fine restaurants and cafes, if you walk in the opposite direction (right from the piers and away from the Old City), it's another story. My best advice is outside of the Old City and the hotel areas, walk during daylight hours, taxi at night. I have had a number of reports of muggings, etc. in the area, although there are lots of police around. There also are lots of honky-tonk bars, women of the streets, and hangers-around and that breeds crime. Leave your jewelry and money on board. Take only what you will need. Credit cards recommended.

What to See: Old San Juan; the Condado section; El Morro, the 16th century fortress; San Geronimo; La Fortaleza, built in 1533; the Cathedral of San Juan Bautista, built in 1527 and burial spot of Ponce de Leon; the Rain Forest (El Yunque); the hotels, nightclubs, and casinos.

What To Wear Ashore: Lightweight summer clothes with a sweater or wrap for evening; dressier at night for nightclubs and casinos. Tie and jacket sometimes required in hotels after 7 P.M.

TTT: Casinos in hotels are supervised by the Government and operate in all of the large hotels. Minimums are still $2 at the blackjack tables. Casinos open at 8 p.m. Jackets (no ties) required for men at most casinos.

TTT: Nightclub tours are expensive, and patrons are seated close together. Shows are fairly good to poor and are sometimes staged exclusively for the cruise ship crowd. If nightclubs are not your thing, opt for hotel-hopping and watch the casino action. If nightclubs turn you on, you should know the night tour sold on board ship may be expensive, but it's cheaper than doing it on your own.

More Information: Commonwealth of Puerto Rico, Tourism Commission, 1290 Avenue of the Americas, New York, NY 10019.

ST. LUCIA

(Population 110,000)

St. Lucia, second largest of the Windward Island chain, is French in heritage and British in character. A British colony from 1803 to 1967, when it became an associated state, St. Lucia is in the process of becoming a fully independent state. It is a popular port of call for cruise ships, and the number arriving increases annually. It is an island free of noise and pollution, and reputable girl-watchers claim it has the most beautiful women in the Antilles. Sugar-loaf peaks dot the island up to 3,000 feet high, and the southern approach through Soufriere lies in the shadow of two peaks, Gros Piton and Petit Piton. There is some mystery as to St. Lucia's discovery, but there is nothing mysterious about its democracy. The Castries City Council is the oldest elected ruling authority in the English West Indies. The island is fertile all year, and rivers run down from its mountainous backbone. The capital city is Castries, which is also the commercial heart of the island.

Size: 27 miles long and about 14 miles wide, with a 150 mile coastline

Climate: Temperatures range from 70 to 93 degrees, rain heaviest between June and December.

Currency: East Caribbean Dollar (ECD)

Language: English and Caribbean patois.

Shopping: Good buys are silk-screened fabrics and native handicraft.

Time: One hour ahead of EST.

Tipping Ashore: 15 percent where no service charge is added automatically.

Transportation: Shore excursions (3 hours), $15. Taxis and rental cars available. There is no bus or limousine service.

What to See: St. Lucia's 238 miles are crisscrossed with valleys of orchids, hibiscus, roses, bougainvillea, and tropical fruit. Visit Castries Harbor, Gros Island, Sulphur Springs, and the residential Cap; see Soufriere, with the world's only drive-in volcano.

What to Wear Ashore: Summer clothes, very casual.

More Information: St. Lucia Tourist Board, 41 E. 42 Street, New York, NY 10017.

TTT: St. Lucia is more of an island that offers sightseeing than it does shopping. Enjoy the unpolluted island and shop elsewhere.

ST. MARTIN (ST. MAARTEN)

(Population 24,000)

The island is shared by Holland and France and is called St. Maarten or St. Martin, depending on which side of the border you're on. Of its 37 square miles, Holland has 16 and France 21, with an international, unfortified boundary line dividing the two sections. Legend has it that the division of the island stems from a boundary dispute settled in 1648 by a walking match. The Frenchman walked faster, but the Dutch seem to have gotten the best of the bargain. Philipsburg's gingerbread houses with Dutch "tray" roofs are scrubbed and freshly painted, and many old buildings have been authentically restored. The tiny Dutch capital is made up of only two streets lined with shops and restaurants. In contrast, the French capital, Marigot, is very much like a small fishing village in the South of France. All ships dock at Philipsburg.

Size: The island's most distant points are only 8.5 miles apart.

Climate: Year-round average of 80 degrees. September is the hottest month; January, February are the coolest.

Currency: Netherland Antilles Florin and French francs, depending on which side you're on, but currency is interchangeable.

Language: Dutch on one side; French on the other; and almost everyone speaks English on both sides.

Shopping: This is a free-port shopping center; good buys in European imports — perfume, liquor, fabrics, crystal, china, watches, etc., especially Delft and other Dutch or French items. Shops close between noon and 2 P.M.

Time: One hour ahead of EST.

Tipping Ashore: Same as the United States.

Transportation: Shore excursions (3 hours), $15.00. Taxis and rental cars are available. No limousine service. Cassette tours on tape available from car rental agencies.

What to See: The ruins of Fort Amsterdam; Simson Bay; Mount William Hill, for a beautiful view; the Great Salt Pond; the border crossing; Marigot; the picturesque plantations, beautiful resort complexes with golf courses, and the casinos.

What to Wear Ashore: Summer clothes, with no special requirements for dressing, even in hotel casinos.

More Information: St. Maarten Tourist Information Office, 25 W. 39 Street, New York, NY 10018.

TTT: St. Maarten is a port favorite with travelers. I have never met a cruise passenger who didn't enjoy the day in St. Maarten/St. Martin. A number of cruise ships sailing out of Miami discontinued calls at St. Martin during the fuel and energy crisis of a few years ago because ships ran at full steam in order to include it in one week itineraries. With fuel costs leveling and more efficient engines on new vessels, St. Maarten is again being included in one week, and longer, sailings. One of my favorite ports. Easy to get around on your own.

TRINIDAD

(Population 942,000)

Trinidad is the southernmost island of the West Indies, but it wasn't always an island. Originally, it was part of the South American

394

mainland, and its flora and fauna are similar to Venezuela's. Columbus discovered the island on his third voyage in 1498 and named it the Trinity for the three hills around the harbor where he anchored. Hummingbirds still thrive there, but Trinidad today is better known as the birthplace of calypso, the steel band, and the limbo. Trinidad and neighboring Tobago became an independent territory within the British Commonwealth in 1962. The population is a mixture of races and nationalities from all over the world—Africans, Chinese, Dutch, East Indians, English, French, Near Easterners, Portuguese, and Spanish. The customs, costumes, and many languages they brought with them make Trinidad a colorful meeting place of east and west. San Fernando is Trinidad's second largest city. Port of Spain, the capital, is the largest.

Size: 50 miles long and 38 miles wide.

Climate: Best time to visit is late winter and early spring. Annual temperature is 84 degrees in the daytime and a comfortable 74 in the evening. June is the rainy month.

Currency: Trinidad-Tobago dollar

Language: English is the official language; Spanish, French, and Chinese are also heard frequently.

Shopping: French perfume, gloves, woolens, Swiss watches, German- and Japanese-made cameras, Japanese everything; native crafts, musical instruments, and recordings of steel bands and calypso music.

Time: One hour ahead of EST.

Transportation: Shore excursions (3 hours), $12.50. Taxis and local bus service available, also rental cars and motorcycles.

What to See: Walk over Pitch Lake, which is said to be 300 feet deep (it's asphalt); drive over the North Coast Road; swim at Maracas Bay; see the cove near the shore of the Gulf of Paria with its sugar factories, the magnificent small waterfalls in Diego Martin and Maracas Valleys; the governor's house; botanic gardens; Moslem mosques; Hindu temples; the Devil's Woodyard.

What to Wear Ashore: Lightweight summer clothing. It is never necessary to dress up. Rainwear in summer, but rain doesn't last long.

More Information: Trinidad and Tobago Tourist Board, 400 Madison Avenue, Suite 712–14, New York, NY 10017.

TTT: A new attraction was opened recently. Operated by the Tourist Board on the island of Gasparee, caves were opened to the public after preservation work and improvements were made. Visitors descend into the caves and guides are available to help show the way. Ferries take visitors to the island which also has picnic facilities and a beach. Roundtrip boat ride is about $13.

VENEZUELA

LA GUAIRA (CARACAS)

Venezuela is the third largest producer of oil in the world and probably the richest country in South America, although the economy here has sagged along with oil prices. As he was in many other Caribbean nations, Columbus was here first. He was followed by the Spaniards in 1499 and by Sir Walter .pa Raleigh a hundred years later. Raleigh begged Queen Elizabeth to place the country under her crown, but Venezuela remained firmly in Spanish hands until Simon Bolivar and his revolutionaries defeated them in 1821. Venezuela's miracle was the discovery of oil in 1917, resulting in the highest standard of living and the highest income per capita on the continent. The country has superb beaches backed by mountains and forests that hide gold, wild game, and the world's highest waterfall. Caracas, the capital, is a modern, cosmopolitan city with hotels, restaurants, and expensive shopping centers. The night life is lively and international.

TTT: Most cruise brochures list this port of call as "Caracas." Actually, the port is La Guaira, about one hour's ride (20 miles) from the city. Cruise schedules normally allow enough time to explore Caracas and for tours into the interior.

Climate: Caracas is 3,418 feet above sea level, so evenings are cool in spite of the 80-degree daytime summer climate. Winter temperatures can fall into the low 50s. Rainy months are from June through November.

Currency: Bolivar

Language: Spanish.

Shopping: Main shopping areas in Caracas are along the Avenida Lincoln and the Centro Comercial Beco. Shops are not outstanding. While prices are comparable to some islands along cruise ship routes, selection of merchandise is not as extensive. Handicraft items and souvenirs are plentiful—rugs, ceramics, Indian masks, bead necklaces. Chocano gold is used for charm bracelets. The Hand of Fatima in ebony, gold, or silver is a favorite souvenir. Best buys are probably pearls from Isla Margarita.

Time: One hour ahead of EST.

Tipping Ashore: 15 percent is added to bills in restaurants and hotels. Taxi drivers do not expect to be tipped.

Transportation: Shore excursions into Caracas (8 hours, including lunch), $35. Local bus service from La Guaira is reasonable and runs on a regular schedule. Taxis are plentiful and inexpensive, but be sure to agree on the price, because there are no meters. Rates go up after midnight. Rental cars are available and chauffeur-driven cars can be hired with no extra charge for English-speaking drivers, but most taxi drivers do not speak English (although they claim they do). Public bus transportation is available two blocks from the pier for the equivalent of 50 cents U.S. Buses can be very, very crowded, particularly during rush hours. If you plan to use the bus, plan on riding between 10 and 11 a.m., and between 2 and 4 p.m., or after 7 p.m.

What to See: The cathedral, built in 1595; Plaza Bolivar, where the stone walks are scrubbed daily; Iglesia de San Francisco, where Bolivar was given the title of Liberator in 1813; the Museo Bolivar with its fascinating relics of the revolution; the Museo del Arte Colonial, a replica of an 18th century villa; Museo de Ciencias Naturales with fine specimens of pre-Colombian ceramics; the cable-car ride to the top of Mount Avila; the residential area.

TTT: If your ship offers an excursion to Angel Falls and Canaima Lagoon, consider it seriously. This is an air flight over oil fields to the Bolivar Iron Mountain. Highlight is the view of Angel Falls and the mysterious mesas that were hidden from the world until an American pilot, Jimmy Angel, discovered them in 1937. The falls are 3,212 feet high, 15 times higher than Niagara Falls. Lunch is included, and the tour price runs around $125 for the 12-hour excursion.

What to Wear Ashore: If you are going into Caracas, do not wear shorts or beachwear. Summer-type clothing (darker colors during winter months) is suitable for city wear. Men wear jackets and ties in restaurants, hotels, and clubs after 7 P.M.

More Information: Venezuelan Government Tourist and Information Bureau, 7 East 51 Street, New York, NY 10022.

TTT: Siesta is noon to 2 P.M. when everything closes tight, so plan your day around those hours.

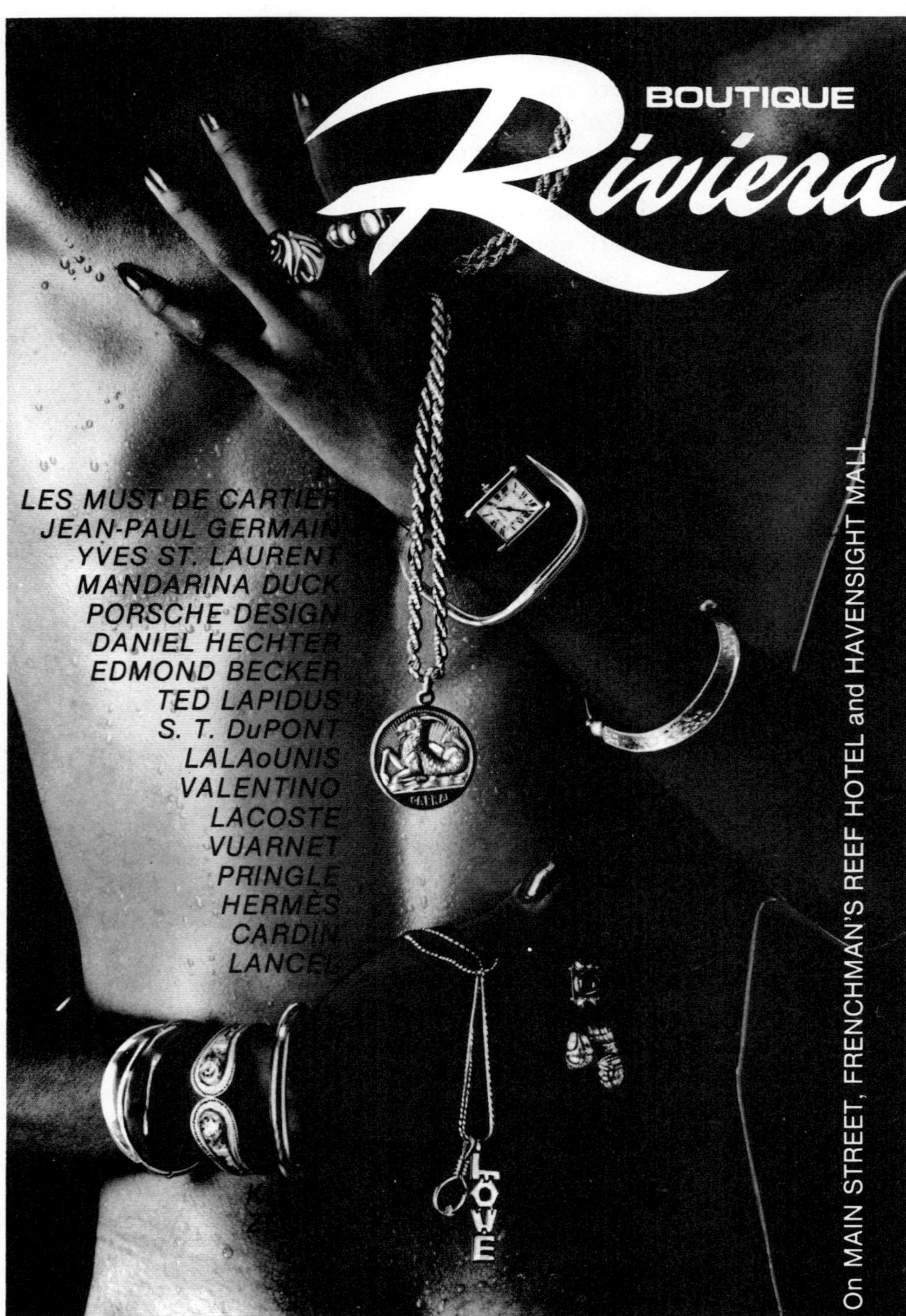
BOUTIQUE
Riviera
LES MUST DE CARTIER
JEAN-PAUL GERMAIN
YVES ST. LAURENT
MANDARINA DUCK
PORSCHE DESIGN
DANIEL HECHTER
EDMOND BECKER
TED LAPIDUS
S. T. DuPONT
LALAoUNIS
VALENTINO
LACOSTE
VUARNET
PRINGLE
HERMÈS
CARDIN
LANCEL
On MAIN STREET, FRENCHMAN'S REEF HOTEL and HAVENSIGHT MALL

THE U.S. VIRGIN ISLANDS

Christopher Columbus, the first tourist of record from the Old World was greeted with a hail of arrows when he landed on the north shore of the Virgins about five hundred years ago. Today's visitor to St. Croix is more likely to be hailed by golf-cart riders; by a shopping bag in St. Thomas; and by a bikini-clad scuba diver in St. John. The three American Virgins are the best known of the nearly one hundred in the Caribbean but they differ greatly in personality and terrain.

St. John is famous for its unspoiled tropical beauty, and cruise ships offer snorkeling excursions that take about four hours and allow time for exploring underwater coral trails. Some ships even provide box lunches for this expedition, which costs about $17.50.

St. Croix is again becoming a cruise ship port, and many St. Thomas shops have branch stores in St. Croix. The island is best known for its old world atmosphere, manicured golf courses, and fine resort complexes.

St. Thomas manages to combine qualities of the other two islands with a twentieth-century calypso lilt that classifies the Virgins as "foreign."

The discovery process initiated by Columbus is being repeated constantly by visitors from all over the world. THE TOTAL TRAVELER BY SHIP is devoting more than a proportionate share of pages to St. Thomas, because almost every cruise ship sailing the Caribbean stops there.

On Chris's second voyage in 1493, he sailed past the chain of islands, found them too numerous to name and beautiful beyond words. He tagged the group Las Once Mil Virgenes ("the 11,000 Virgins"), probably in honor of the army of maidens from Cornwall massacred by the Huns during the Middle Ages. Columbus inspected two of the islands, named them St. Thomas and St. John, then sailed away to discover Puerto Rico.

No one paid much attention to the lonely Virgin Islands for many years until pirates discovered the protected channels, bays, and coves and moved into them as sanctuaries for their ships. St. Thomas became a pirate base of some fame when buccaneers made their headquarters in Charlotte Amalie. The Dutch tried to take possession and finally sold out to the Danes, who took over in 1672 and operated the Virgins under the authority of the Danish West Indies Company. They were serious about their island colony and were successful. Under Danish rule, sugar plantations flourished on St. Croix and St. John.

Denmark offered to sell the Virgins to the United States in 1869, but negotiations were not completed until 1917. The strategic position of the Virgin Islands as an outpost for the protection of the Panama Canal persuaded the United States to pay $25 million to Denmark. The islands were first administered by the Navy, and in 1927, the islanders were made U.S. citizens. In 1931 the Virgins were put under Department of the Interior jurisdiction with an appointed governor. The first popular election for governor of the islands was held in 1972.

Three factors contribute to the popularity of the Virgins. The climate is almost perfect, with few days below 70 or above 85 degrees. Accessibility is also an important reason. They lie in the sea lanes and are reached quickly by plane or ship. Lastly, and probably most important, is the free-port status of the islands and the customs exceptions allowed by the United States for returning residents.

Contrary to the saying, the best things in life are not free. But they are reasonable in the Virgins, the only place in the Caribbean where visiting Americans can buy $800 worth of merchandise and bring it home without paying duty. It has been estimated that more liquor is sold in St. Thomas on any day to cruise ships that happen to be in port than in the average city of 100,000 in a month. Uncle Sam is responsible for this phenomenon by allowing five fifths of alcoholic beverages to be included in that $800 allowance.

But St. Thomas is more than shops, although no visitor has ever left the island without meeting temptation on Main Street. The more than a hundred shops are housed in nineteenth-century restored ware-

THE FINEST FRAGRANCES AND COSMETICS AT DUTY FREE PRICES

NINA RICCI

CLARINS

GUERLAIN

JEAN DESPREZ

Y̱VES ST. LAURENT

STENDHAL

OSCAR DE LA RENTA

LANCÔME

AMALIE

COSMETICS AND TREATMENTS

**CHANEL · CLARINS · STENDHAL
CLINIQUE · ESTEE LAUDER
ORLANE · LANCÔME · ULTIMA II
CHRISTIAN DIOR** in the largest
perfume department in St. Thomas

A.H. RIISE GIFT SHOPS

37 Main Street at A.H. Riise Gift Shops Alley, St. Thomas (809)776-2303
FOR MERCHANDISE INQUIRIES & MAIL ORDERS, CALL TOLL FREE 800-524-2037

The TRADITION of ELEGANCE CONTINUES
The ENGLISH Shop
BOSSON'S MASKS
PEN DELPHIN
...a world of fine tradenames at prices 30% to 50% less than Stateside!
CHINA
Bernardaud Limoges
Bing & Grondahl
Ceralene Limoges
Coalport
Gorham
Haviland Limoges
Minton
Noritake
Paragon
Richard Ginori
Royal Albert
Royal Doulton
Royal
Worcester
Spode
Villeroy & Boch
Wedgwood
CRYSTAL
Royal Brierly
St. Louis
Stuart
Swarovski
Val St. Lambert
Wittwer
FIGURINES
Anri
Bosson's Masks
Capodimonte
Irish Belleek
Nao by Lladro
Pen Delphin
...and many, many more.
ROYAL WORCESTER
BELLEEK
DOULTON
SPODE CHRISTMAS TREE
WEDGWOOD
Order by phone, toll-free
1- (800) 524-2013
The ENGLISH Shop
HAVENSIGHT MALL
and MAIN STREET at MARKET SQUARE
CHINA
DUTY FREE OUTLET
CRYSTAL

EXCLUSIVE DISTRIBUTORS FOR:

<u>China</u>: Spode • Royal Worcester • Royal Albert • Paragon • Bernardaud Limoges • Haviland Limoges • Herend (Hungary) • Noritake. <u>Crystal</u>: Stuart • St. Louis • Val St. Lambert • Spode • Royal Albert • Figurines. <u>Gift Items</u>: Náo by Lladró • Beswick • Hammersley • Bing & Grondahl • Capodimonte.

ALSO AVAILABLE:

<u>Cutlery</u>: Christofle. <u>Linens</u>: Exclusive selection. <u>Jewelry</u>: Selection in 14k and 18k gold. <u>Seiko watches</u>: Full range.

We also accept Direct Factory and Mail Orders on any of the above manufacturers at 30% to 50% below Stateside prices.

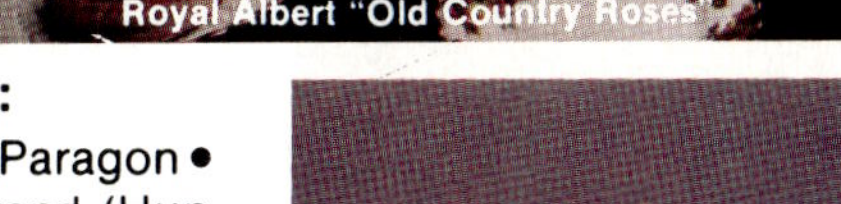

**THE ENGLISH SHOP
HAVENSIGHT MALL AND MAIN STREET AT MARKET SQUARE**

houses, and their shelves are stocked with merchandise from every corner of the world.

St. Thomas sits pertly on the edge of a landlocked harbor. Homes sprawl up the hillsides that rise sharply to a height of 1,500 feet. These hillsides are actually three volcanic spurs named Frenchman's Hill, Denmark Hill, and Government Hill, but they are better known as Foretop, Maintop, and Mizzentop.

The first view from the deck of an arriving cruise ship is of an irregular coast line with coves and deep bays, many fringed with white sand beaches. From the shore, the hills rise steeply to low peaks, excellent observation points for the pirates who policed nearby channels in the old days, and great picture-taking points today.

A good road leads around the island and to its main settlements and points of interest. Traffic patterns are a holdover from Danish times, and you're right if you drive on the left in the Virgins. Charlotte Amalie is the only city most visitors see, but its population is less than half the total of that of the island group. Originally called Taphus by the Danes, the city was renamed Charlotte Amalie by King Christian V (for his Queen) when he took possession of the islands in 1666. The Danish influence is evident in street names, and the architecture reflects influences of various occupants. There are Dutch doors, French grill-work, Spanish patios, Danish roof-lines, and modern, Miami-type hotel structures.

The town has a diverting European aspect — narrow streets lined with solid, high-walled houses. Charlotte Amalie has more 100-year-old buildings in use than any other community of its size in the United States. Several outstanding architectural structures have been selected by the Historical American Buildings Survey as worthy of note. Fort Christian, built in the mid-17th century, was the first building erected on St. Thomas by the Danes and served as the governor's residence, the courthouse, a parsonage and church, and a jail, all at one time. Today it serves only as the police station and jail. The courtyard is paved with slabs of gravestones, and its dungeons and torture chambers are open to visitors.

Bluebeard's Tower is three stories high with 5 1/2-foot-thick walls. In 1934 workmen found an ironbound chest with old papers relating the tale of Musa Ben Hasser (Bluebeard). This information and the seven grave markers on the terrace are convincing evidence that the famous pirate had his headquarters here. Later residents added buildings to the tower and used it as a private home. The buildings have been restored and expanded, and the complex is now a popular resort. Also selected by the Historical Survey were the Dutch Reformed

406

Church, one of the oldest on the islands, the Frederick Evangelical Lutheran Church, second oldest in the Western Hemisphere and with its original 17th century ecclesiastical silver still in use; and the Jewish synagogue, founded in 1796.

Jews have lived in St. Thomas since 1665, the year the island was first settled by pioneers. Gabriel Milan, a Jew, was the first governor of the islands, commissioned in 1684 by King Christian V. For almost three centuries, the St. Thomas synagogue has been a symbol of peace, blessing, and refuge to Jewish families. Danish archives for the 1697–98 period list Jacob and Diana Elias and their two children as taxpayers. The Eliases, Sephardic Jews, evidently were trying to eke out a living from the soil on the small plantation they owned.

A contemporary account of Jewish historical development in the Virgin Islands claims the growing community followed a wide variety of occupations. Eminent men who have emerged through the years have ranged from Emmanual Vass, who represented the Danish governor in negotiating the transfer of St. Croix from French to Danish sovereignty, to famous people like the artist Camille Pissarro and Judah P. Benjamin, who was attorney general and Secretary of War and State under Confederate President Jefferson Davis. Dozens of others became merchants, professional people, and politicians. In addition to the first governor, two others were Jewish. Morris Fidanque de Castro was appointed governor by President Dwight D. Eisenhower in 1950 and Ralph M. Paiewonsky was appointed governor by President John F. Kennedy in 1961 and reappointed by President Lyndon Johnson. The Paiewonsky family continues to reside in St. Thomas and are active business, community, and religious leaders.

The synagogue has been restored over the past hundred years but maintains Sephardic architecture and customs, which call for the Ark to be placed on the east wall. Sand-covered floors are in the same tradition, which, according to Isadore Paiewonsky, "reminds Jews of the exodus from Spain, like the historic Exodus over the desert to the Promised Land."

Even if you have been to St. Thomas a dozen times, there's always something new to discover on this island rated as the favorite port of call by cruise ship passengers. This probably explains why almost every ship cruising the Caribbean includes a call in the Virgin Islands.

In the "what's new" department, visitors need only opt for the ship tour to Coral World or hop a taxi for the 15-minute ride for assurance that there is indeed something new and exciting on the island. It's the chance to walk through a deep-sea diver's dream for a

We're holding a seat for you at Cable Beach Casino, the world's most exciting gambling resort. Come play our 57 gaming tables and 585 electronic slot machines with progressive jackpots up to $100,000. All under the grandeur of Bahamian skies. Enjoy our internationally acclaimed musical revue "Les Fantastiques." Reward yourself with a sure bet for culinary delight, Ristorante Sole Mare, featuring northern Italian cuisine. Or for a lighter bite, pass... to the Backstage Deli.

We've got your table, and the winning combination. Cable Beach Casino -- your first resort in the Bahamas.

Cable Beach Casino
NASSAU, BAHAMAS

closeup view of magnificent and mysterious marine life without ever getting your toes wet.

Coral World is a $2.5 million, 4-acre complex that opened about four years ago on the northeastern shore of St. Thomas. Billed as "the Caribbean's newest and most spectacular underwater experience," Coral World doesn't shortchange the visitor. It is an imaginative enterprise offering access to seascapes, an underwater encounter with live barracudas, sharks, and stingrays, not to mention the magnificent coral. The complex is the only one of its kind in the Western Hemisphere; the second to be found anywhere in the world outside of Eilat in Israel.

Coral World offers land-lovers the opportunity to understand what makes divers underwater addicts. The underwater observation tower rises from the sea just 100 feet offshore and takes the visitor down into a marine wonderland. Standing on the ocean floor, 14 feet beneath the surface, one is witness to a piscatorial pageant. Through twenty-four picture windows, visitors see rainbow-colored tropical fish and coral formations in their natural state. At mid-level in the tower, sharks, sting rays, and barracudas swim in an amazing circular reef tank that surrounds the visitor. Seawater constantly pumped into the reef tank enables the marine life, including the living coral reef backdrop, to exist in its own natural environment under normal conditions. This single factor distinguishes Coral World from nearly all other aquariums in the world.

Coral World ranks as a "must" for families, children of all ages, the curious and the interested. Every ship offers excursions that include Coral World tours and entrance fee (about $6.00). Coral World is a lot more than a sightseeing attraction. It's an experience. On my last visit, I spent about six hours there, and I didn't even get acquainted with half the species.

Other Facts About St. Thomas:

Size: island covers an area of 32 square miles.
Currency: U. S. dollar.
Language: English.
What to See: (and how to see it all) Your time in St. Thomas will be the most hectic of your entire cruise. There are so many tempting things to do, see and buy, you'll be hard pressed to fit it all in, especially if this is your first visit to the island. Shopping opportunities are so overwhelming, there is a lingering, nagging temptation to spend the whole day in port going shop-to-shop. But, if you give in to the

temptation you would miss really seeing the island. A variety of shore excursions are sold on board ships. If you are pressed for time and have a long shopping list, consider taking one of the excursions. That will still leave ample time for shopping. The city tour, for example, takes about two hours and includes a ride through the busy city of Charlotte Amalie, a stop at Bluebeard's Castle for a drink, general orientation and a look at some of the island's better known beaches (about $10.00). For visitors who know St. Thomas, there's a tour to St. John. It begins with a safari car ride to a ferry which takes you on a 20-minute ride to the neighboring island. After landing, another safari-type four wheeler takes you through the lush National Park, the famed Rockefeller resort, Caneel Bay, and to one of the most perfect snorkeling or swimming experiences anywhere in the world. This is for us snorkelers and swimmers considered less than expert. Actually our qualifications should be enough to just keep us above water. The guide supplies equipment and instruction and the adventure is enjoyed by first time underwater explorers from eight to 80. (About four hours, $17.50). For more expert scuba addicts, most ships offer special scuba tours into deeper waters (about five hours, $30). For folks who like to view underwater life in the comfort of a glass bottom boat, there is two to three-hour Kon Tiki cruise with stops for swimming and spirits from a "bottomless rum keg." ($15) The city tour takes in all of the historic sites and, on request, will leave passengers in town at the end of the route so they can shop before returning to the ship on their own. There are several good restaurants in town, but they are very crowded when ships are in port, so I usually hold out until I get back on board, or I settle for a fast food place along Main Street.

Shopping: Now we're down to the nitty-gritty of a cruise visit to the Virgin Islands. St. Thomas is probably the world's largest luxury-type shopping center, with merchandise from the four corners being sold usually at less than what it would cost in the country of origin. Number one on every American's shopping list is liquor. Before you do any serious alcohol buying, stop at one of the famous tasting bars that are common in several liquor selling stores and sample their fine selection of liquors from around the world. Be sure to have the store send the liquor back to the ship for you. There's no point in lugging the boxes around when most ships have arrangements with the better, and more reliable shops, so liquor delivery is guaranteed to arrive on board without leakage or breakage. In the rare instance when a problem does arise (breakage, delivery not complete), contact the purser's office immediately. Some of the more reliable stores have a special arrangement that allows the ship's purser to replace damaged or missing liquor on board the vessel. Should a problem be discovered after you get home, the best approach is to contact the merchant by mail with complete information. If you have been dealing with a reputable shop, there will be a refund but no liquor. It's not allowed through the mails.

TTT: There are some 80,000 different kinds of liquor sold on the island, so don't think decisions will be easy. In your haste to take advantage of $3.50 Scotch, don't overlook the possibility of poking around "sale bins" in some of the stores. Labels may be slightly damaged, but the contents haven't been touched.

TTT: If you want some spirits in your cabin and plan to drink them en route, hand-carry a bottle of your favorite brand back to the ship. Costs less than drinking in the bar and is a great contribution to "drinking-up parties" held in cabins the night before the end of the voyage, when shipboard friends bid each other tearful farewells.

MORE SHOPPING TTT: Other outstanding buys are in the crystal, china, camera, and perfume departments. Prices run from 20 to 50 percent below stateside.

Most taxis and buses from the pier stop right at what used to be the Continental Shop and is now owned by Little Switzerland. I can't comment on the merchandise because the store was being rebuilt when I last checked in November 1984.

Heading down the street, you'll pass shops showing a king's ransom in jewelry and watches, crystal, china, fine leather goods, cosmetics, and fragrances; not to mention fashions for men and women. You'll find names like Omega, Concord, Corum, Bulova, Citizen, Seiko, Gucci, Lamy Pens, Staffordshire, Orlane, and Lancome inside every door.

For boutique items, try Boutique Riviera which carries unusual jewelry and a collection of European designer separates at low prices. Trendy shoppersare in the right store if they are looking for Louis Vuitton, Emilio Pucci, Marimekko, Lalaounis, Givenchy, LaCoste, Balmain, Hermes, and dozens of other "name" designer fashions and accessories. The shop looks like an antique gallery, and the jewelry collection is spiced with unusual items and designs. Zodiac medallions by French artist Edmond Becker, for instance, and "les must de Cartier" are sold at affordable prices. Take a look at the Pringle cashmere sweaters, particularly if you hail from northern climates.

Shoppers who do not want to waste time should head directly for the A.H. Riise Gift Shop. It is the most complete on the island and has several locations with the headquarters store on Main Street. It is located in an historic renovated Danish Warehouse stretching from Main Street to the Waterfront and offers the largest selection of merchandise at competitive duty free prices. You'll find contemporary jewelry as well as a collection of antique and estate pieces from around the world. Fine china, crystal and hard to find items are everywhere. Newest designer fragrances and cosmetics, housewares featuring Wusthof-Trident knives and Italian acrylic-ware, lambswool and cashmere sweaters, plus a liquor department make it a recommended one-stop shop. Be sure to visit Crabtree & Evelyn Boutique in the A.H. Riise Gift Shop Balcony store. It's a replica of an "olde country general store" down to cookies, jams, jellies and herb vinegars.

Browse in the A.H. Riise Gift Shop Alley where aged stone walls set the mood for several outstanding shops. (Gucci, Lion in the Sun, Animal Crackers Fun Factory and Cafe Amici, a European-style outdoor cafe for lunch, and the Carib Shop). A.H. Riise Gift Shops has opened an Art Gallery in the Alley and it features a wide range of

original Caribbean art, including paintings, prints, ceramics and sculpture. The Alley is also a good place for a "clean" comfort stop. Facilities are available.

Don't end your walk down Main Street. You'll pass dozens of other shops. There's the Leather Shop for Bottega bags, Tropicana Perfume Shop with its extensive fragrance collection, Jolly Roger with a collection of pipes priced from $1.50 to $1,500., the Scandinavian Center with its Georg Jensen and David Anderson collection, Blue Carib Gems selling Caribbean amber, black coral and agates, the Cloth Horse with its Finnish Marimekko fabrics by the yard, and just about every European designer shop you'll find in Paris or Rome.

Just before you get to Market Square you'll find the English Shop and you'll know the walk was worthwhile. The English Shop features very fine china and crystal mostly imported from England (Royal Doulton, Wedgewood, Baccarat, Orrefors, Lauffer, Christofle). They are also the exclusive distributors for Limoges and Noritake. If you're into china and crystal, The English Shop is the place to find such distinguished patterns as Stuart, St. Louis, Val St. Lambert, Spode, and Royal Albert. The shop also carries a full range of Seiko and 14 and 18-carat jewelry and guarantees 35 to 50 percent savings on U.S. prices on all china and crystal.

Direct factory and mail orders are accepted by A.H. Riise Gift Shop and English Shop on all merchandise at the same savings percentage, so when you get back home and find you should have lengthened your shopping list in St. Thomas, write to A.H. Riise Gift Shop or the English Shop and your orders will be filled.

International jeweler H. Stern has a shop on Main Street and features Brazilian as well as stones from other parts of the world. Stern products carry a world-wide guarantee.

Shops mentioned are all members of the St. Thomas Chamber of Commerce and are very reliable. You can depend on them for prompt delivery of your purchases to ships and planes. There are other reputable shops, but space does not permit a complete listing. All shops mentioned in this section accept major credit cards; some will accept personal checks with proper identification. As for prices, how does $2.50 for a fifth of vodka or $3.25 for the same measure of Scotch sound. These prices were accurate at press time.

TTT: A new shopping area has been built at Havensight Mall at the West Indian Company Dock which is where most cruise ships dock if they don't tender their passengers to shore. It's a restored warehouse area and if you opted for scuba diving or snorkeling at St. John, you'll

413

still have time to shop at the same prices and in many of the same shops that line Main Street. Havensight Mall is practically at the foot of your gangway. Among other stores, you'll find the English Shop, Cavanagh's, Boolchand's, A.H. Riise Gift Shop, Arts & Jewels, and H. Stern.

Time: One hour ahead of EST.

Tipping Ashore: Same as in the United States.

Transportation: Shore excursions average $8.50 for four hours. Taxis are metered, but price was fixed at $1.50 per person from dockside to center to Charlotte Amalie but it will probably go to $2.00 before the end of 1985. Rental cars are available by the hour, day, and longer.

What to Wear Ashore: Your most comfortable clothing. Feet get mighty weary after hours of shopping, so wear sandals or whatever makes the walking easier.

More Information: United States Virgin Islands Government Tourist Office, 1270 Avenue of the Americas, New York, NY 10020.

TTT: You'll find the same prices and many of the same shops in St. Croix as you will in St. Thomas. Because the island doesn't have as many shops or as many visitors who come by cruise ship, the competition is not quite as keen. If you are a real bargain hunter and your ship stops in St. Thomas before going on to St. Croix, do your shopping when you find the item at the right price.

Speak Sea Language

ABOARD — Same as on board and used instead of "on" or "in" a boat or ship.

ABOUT — When the ship turns around.

ABOVE BOARD — Decks above the waterline.

AFT — Near, toward, or in the stern (rear of vessel).

ALL HANDS — Everyone working on the ship.

AWASH — At water level.

BACKWASH — The water thrown by propellers.

BARGE — A flat-bottomed craft.

BEACON — A light by which the ship steers.

BEAM — The breadth of the ship at its widest point.

BEARING — Ship's direction.

BERTH — A bunk in a cabin, or the ship's place at anchor or dock.

BOW — The front of the ship, or the sides of the forward part of a freighter.

CHART — A map of the sea bottom.

CHOW — food referred to by the crew.

COLORS — The flag flying from the mast.

DEBARK — Abbreviation of disembark.

DERELICT — A vessel abandoned on the high seas.

DISEMBARK — To land, to go ashore from a ship.

DRAFT (OR DRAUGHT) — The depth of water a ship draws.

EMBARK — To go aboard a ship.

FATHOM — A measure of length containing 6 feet used chiefly in measuring.

GALLEY — The kitchen on board ship.

GANGWAY — Portable stairway or ramp used for entering or leaving ship.

HEAD — Also known as facilities, it's the toilet.

HULL — The body or frame of a ship.

JACOB'S LADDER — The rope ladder often used by pilots.

KNOT — A speed unit equivalent to 1.15 land miles per hour.

LATITUDE — The distance north or south of the equator in degrees.

LEEWARD — The side facing away from the wind.

LOG — The official daily record of the ship's speed and progress.
LONGITUDE — The distance east or west expressed in degrees off the First Meridian.
MANIFEST — A list of the ship's passengers and cargo that must be supplied in every foreign port.
MUSTER — To assemble passengers and/or crew.
NAVIGABLE — Water that is deep enough for the ship's passage.
PORT — The left side of the ship when you are facing forward.
REGISTRY — The country in which the ship is registered.
SCREW — The propeller.
STARBOARD — The right side of the ship when you are facing forward.
STERN — The back of the ship.
STOWAWAY — An illegal passenger.
WAKE — The ship's sea tracks.
WINDWARD — Facing into the wind.

After Thoughts

Disagree with ship Ratings? Feel THE TOTAL TRAVELER BY SHIP should have recognized your favorite vessel, or awarded a rusty anchor to a ship that disappointed you? Want to comment on ships, ports of call, prices or other aspects of travel by sea?

Your comments will be counted and your evaluations considered in future ship ratings if you complete this form and send it to:

THE TOTAL TRAVELER
P.O. Box 41-4298
Miami Beach, FL   33141-0298

We'll send you an Evaluation Report which should be completed and returned to the same address. What you tell us about your cruise experiences will influence our opinions. While we may not always agree, we promise to check trends and tell the cruise lines what you think.

TO: TRAVEL PUBLICATIONS
P.O. Box 41-4298
Miami Beach, FL   33141-0298

Please send me your Ship Evaluation Report. I have sailed _______ ships during the past _______ years. I want my opinion of ships counted in future TOTAL TRAVEL SHIP ratings.

____ Please print name

____ Signature

____ City, State, Zip